Critical Human Geography

'Critical Human Geography' is an international series which provides a critical examination and extension of the concepts and consequences of work in human geography and the allied social sciences and humanities. The volumes are written by scholars currently engaged in substantive research, so that, wherever possible, the discussions are empirically grounded as well as theoretically informed. Existing studies and the traditions from which they derive are carefully described and located in their historically specific context, but the series at the same time introduces and explores new ideas and insights from the human sciences as a whole. The series is thus not intended as a collection of synthetic reviews, but rather as a cluster of considered arguments which are accessible enough to engage geographers at all levels in the development of geography. The series therefore reflects the continuing methodological and philosophical diversity of the subject, and its books are united only by their common commitment to the prosecution of a genuinely human geography.

Department of Geography
University of Cambridge
England

MARK BILLINGE
DEREK GREGORY
RON MARTIN

Critical Human Geography

The Geography of De-industrialisation

edited by

Ron Martin

Department of Geography
University of Cambridge

and

Bob Rowthorn

Faculty of Economics and Politics
University of Cambridge

M

MACMILLAN
EDUCATION

First published 1986
Reprinted 1988

Published by
MACMILLAN EDUCATION LTD
Houndmills, Basingstoke, Hampshire RG21 2XS
and London
Companies and representatives
throughout the world

Printed in Hong Kong

British Library Cataloguing in Publication Data
The Geography of de-industrialisation—
(Critical human geography)
1. Great Britain—Economic conditions—
1945–
I. Martin, Ron   II. Rowthorn, Bob
III. Series
330.941′085   HC256.6
ISBN 0–333–37124–0 (hardcover)
ISBN 0–333–37125–9 (paperback)

Contents

List of Figures

vii

List of Tables

Acknowledgements

The compilation of an edited book such as this clearly depends on the successful collaboration on the part of the various contributors. From the start, when we invited the authors to write original papers for the volume, each was eager to participate in the project, and we owe a debt of gratitude to them all for their constructive and sustained support. We also wish to thank Steve Kennedy of Macmillan who in his own inimitable style gave invaluable editorial advice and encouragement.

Where previously published work has been utilised or drawn upon, full acknowledgement has been made at the appropriate point in the text.

Ron Martin
Bob Rowthorn

List of Contributors

Peter Daniels   is Senior Lecturer in Geography at the University of Liverpool

Mick Dunford   is Lecturer in Human Geography in the School of European Studies at the University of Sussex

Steven Fothergill   is Senior Research Associate in the Department of Land Economy at the University of Cambridge

Graham Gudgin   is Director of the Northern Ireland Economic Research Centre at Belfast

Felicity Henwood   is Research Fellow in the Science Policy Research Unit at the University of Sussex

Ray Hudson   is Senior Lecturer in Geography at the University of Durham

Michael Kitson   is Research Officer in the Department of Applied Economics at the University of Cambridge

Ron Martin   is Lecturer in Economic Geography and Fellow of St Catharine's College at the University of Cambridge

Doreen Massey   is Professor of Geography at the Open University

Sarah Monk   is Research Associate in the Department of Land Economy at the University of Cambridge

Kevin Morgan   is Research Fellow in the School of Social Sciences at the University of Sussex

Diane Perrons   is Senior Lecturer in Social Economics at the City of London Polytechnic

John Rhodes   is Senior Research Officer in the Department of Applied Economics and Fellow of Wolfson College at the University of Cambridge

Bob Rowthorn   is Reader in Economics and Fellow of King's College at the University of Cambridge

Sally Wyatt   is Research Fellow in the Science Policy Research Unit at the University of Sussex

Editors' Preface

This volume of essays is concerned with the geography of industrial decline in post-war Britain, with the regional anatomy and implications of 'de-industrialisation'. Since it first 'gate-crashed' the economic literature at the end of the 1970s (Blackaby, 1981) the term 'de-industrialisation' has been used in various ways, both descriptively and analytically, to refer to the most dramatic indicator of Britain's ailing economic performance, the rapid decline in the country's manufacturing base. Whether this decline is measured in terms of the fall in industrial employment (Thirlwall, 1982), as the progressive deterioration in the balance of manufacturing trade (Singh, 1977) or as the chronic and cumulative elements of a relative and absolute decline in the contribution of manufacturing output, investment, exports and jobs to the national economy (Sheriff, 1979; Hughes, 1981), the conclusion is the same: that since the late 1960s, and especially since the early 1970s, British manufacturing has become caught in a process of progressive and accelerating contraction. Moreover, while there is evidence to suggest that the 'British disease' has recently spread to a number of other advanced industrial economies, such as the USA, Canada, France and Germany, in no other country has de-industrialisation been so intense. Why the process should have afflicted Britain so acutely is not altogether clear, although there is a growing body of opinion that it may be the manifestation of a longer-term, deep-seated systemic problem of structural weakness and relative economic decline that is rooted in the country's earlier industrial history and its traditional role in world capitalist development (Gamble, 1981; Smith, 1984). In the same way that Britain was the first country to industrialise, so it has been the first to de-industrialise.

Undoubtedly the most visible evidence of industrial decline in Britain has been the collapse of manufacturing employment. The number of workers engaged in manufacturing activity has fallen by more than 35 per cent since 1966. In that year employment in the manufacturing sector stood at its historical peak of 8.4 million; by the end of 1984 it had fallen to 5.4 million, and half of this drop occurred in the last five years of the period, between 1979 and 1984. The scale of this contraction is unparalleled anywhere else in the world. Of itself, a fall in manufacturing employment, even of this magnitude, need not be problematic. After all, according to 'post-industrial' theorists, a decline in the significance of manufacturing was to be expected as one of the long-term consequences of post-war socio-economic change in advanced industrial societies (Bell, 1974; for a review see Gershuny, 1978). Just as the industrial revolution involved a massive shift of workers out of the primary sector of the economy into a rapidly expanding industrial base, so in the second half of the twentieth century there would be a subsequent movement of labour out of industry into the new leading growth sectors of services and tertiary activity.

This predicted transformation from an industrial society to a service-based 'post-industrial' one is assumed to be an inevitable consequence of rising income levels which generate increasing demands for and consumption of services, and of rising productivity levels in industry itself, made possible by technological advance, which permit workers to be released into service jobs. While the affluent decades of the 1950s and 1960s may have provided some measure of empirical justification for this prognosis of a 'post-industrial' trajectory to economic development, the realities of the 1970s and 1980s have been quite different. The long economic boom of 1945–72 has since been replaced by an extended period of relative economic stagnation and recession in the major capitalist countries, and particularly in Britain. Under these conditions of slow economic growth the job losses in British manufacturing over the past two decades have been associated not so much with rising productivity due to technological progress as with fluctuating productivity growth and falling output in manufacturing. Nor has the labour expelled from industry been reabsorbed by the service sector; and this, in combination with the growth of the population of working age, has resulted in the emergence of record levels of mass unemployment. The shift in the employment structure towards services has, therefore, taken place in a somewhat different context: post-industrialisation has been overshadowed by de-industrialisation.

To date the analysis of Britain's industrial crisis has been dominated by aggregate economic inquiry. Yet the phenomenon of de-industrialisation manifestly has not occurred in a social or spatial vacuum. It is not a single or mono-causal economic mechanism with undifferentiated social and geographical consequences, but rather a diverse set of complex processes affecting different social groups and different localities in different ways. For example, in social terms the contraction of manufacturing has imposed a particularly severe burden on manual and unskilled workers, who have borne the brunt of the 3 million job losses and among whom there is now a serious problem of long-term structural unemployment; it has entailed a widening segmentation of the workforce between falling numbers of traditionally skilled production workers on the one hand and an increasingly important core of stably employed technical, supervisory and managerial staff on the other; and it has weakened the relative socio-economic status and comparative wage position of workers in what were, until the early 1970s, leading industries in the economy. The impact of these and similar aspects of industrial decline on the social class incidence of unemployment, de-skilling, living standards and poverty, has only just begun to be studied (e.g. Urry, 1983; Murgatroyd and Urry, 1984; Rose *et al.*, 1984). It is already clear, however, that de-industrialisation is restructuring the social fabric of Britain in significant and selective directions.

Likewise, as the contributions to this book demonstrate, while few major areas of the country have remained unscathed by industrial decline, none-the-less de-industrialisation has had a distinct and progressive geographical pattern. Over the past two decades three sorts of locality have fallen victim to the contraction and retrenchment of manufacturing industry and the loss of manufacturing employment. The problem first became evident in the old geographical bases of nineteenth-century industrialisation and labour organisation. It began in the 1960s (if not earlier) in the cities, especially London, but including all the major conurbations. The dramatic erosion of jobs in these centres is at the heart of present-day urban decline and the 'inner-city problem'. As the pace of de-industrialisation quickened in the 1970s, so industrial rationalisation and job loss spread more widely to affect most of the traditional industrial Development Areas, those districts which first experienced structural economic decline in the inter-war period and which have remained relatively depressed ever since. And then, more recently, from the late 1970s onwards, de-industrialisation has undermined the employment base of large parts of Britain's core manufacturing belt, notably the West Midlands and the North-West, areas with economies built around the growth industries (such as vehicles and engineering) of the 1950s and 1960s. Within the last fifteen years the West Midlands, Britain's 'workshop region', has fallen from being the country's leading manufacturing area, at the top of the industrial wage hierarchy, to a depressed region with a shattered economic base and the lowest manufacturing wages in the country. By contrast, the south and east of Britain, with the important exception of London, have experienced a much less intense and considerably less disruptive pace of industrial decline. Thus what two decades of accelerating de-industrialisation have done is to create a new map of unemployment. To the established post-war pattern of high unemployment in the industrial periphery of Britain, a geography inherited from the crisis of the 1920s and 1930s, have been added both the major cities and conurbations, and the previously prosperous manufacturing heartland of the nation. De-industrialisation has sharpened the socio-economic divides between the south and the rest of Britain, and between the heavily urbanised and more rural parts of the country.

It is only over the past few years that British economic geographers and regional analysts have seriously started to explore and explain post-war regional trends in employment change and industrial reorganisation (for example, Fothergill and Gudgin, 1982; Goddard and Champion, 1983; Massey and Meegan, 1982; Massey, 1984). It is fair to say, however, that none of these studies has been explicitly concerned with the geography of de-industrialisation. In fact, one may suggest that in general, regional and economic geographical research in Britain has been somewhat slow to react, in terms of theoretical and empirical work, to the condition of a shrinking manufacturing base in a slow-growing economy. As a result, industrial geographers have as yet contributed little to our understanding of de-industrialisation; instead the tendency has been to shift research effort, much of it conducted within a largely unaltered methodological orthodoxy, to the study of the 'locational behaviour' of small firms and high-technology business, the sectors believed to hold some prospect of growth and job generation. Important though these 'growth sectors' may be, the de-industrialisation issue remains of paramount significance: on account of the magnitude of the job losses involved, because these have far outweighed the impact of new small firms and high-technology activity, and crucially because de-industrialisation is central to understanding the current regional restructuring process. In Britain the spatial patterns of capital disinvestment, industrial reorganisation and job loss are not well synchronised with those of new investment and new jobs in the small firm and scientific, advanced technology sectors: the primary locations attracting the development of these new 'sunrise' industries are precisely those that have suffered least from de-industrialisation. This serves to point up the economic, social and political significance of the spatiality of de-industrialisation: it takes on meaning because of its differential impact on and consequences for the absorptive capacities of different regions. It is this dimension of the phenomenon, the problem of the re-absorption of unemployed economic resources, that has stimulated the strong spatial emphasis of recent American studies of de-industrialisation in the United States (Bluestone and Harrison, 1980, 1982; Bluestone, Harrison and Baker, 1981; Bluestone, 1984; Gordus, Jarley and Ferman, 1981; McKenzie, 1984). The aim of the present book is to introduce a similar geographical perspective into the discussion of British de-industrialisation.

The book begins with a paper by **Bob Rowthorn** which describes in some detail the extent of industrial decline in Britain in relation to the post-war experience of other capitalist nations, and suggests three broad hypotheses which in combination might help to account for the severity of the British case. This discussion provides a contextual background for the remaining chapters, which fall into three main groups. Chapters 2, 3 and 4 focus attention on the different ways in which de-industrialisation has restructured the social and spatial division of labour within Britain. In Chapter 2, **Doreen Massey** argues that a major factor shaping the internal geography of production and jobs has been – and continues to be – the UK's changing role in the international division of labour, in conjunction with the enduring international orientation of British industrial and finance capital. The successive changes in the spatial division of labour are examined in Chapter 3 by **Mick Dunford** and **Diane Perrons**, who use a mode of regulation/regimes of accumulation approach to highlight the regional consequences of the growing crisis of intensive and monopolistic production. Then, in Chapter 4, **Felicity Henwood** and **Sally Wyatt** reveal how the changing structure of industry and the impact of new technology have affected women's jobs within manufacturing and service industries across the regions of Britain.

The subsequent three essays report on some of the specific regional and urban features of the decline of manufacturing. **John Rhodes**, in Chapter 5, draws out the structural and policy bases of differential regional industrial decline over the period since the mid-1960s, while in the following chapter **Ray Hudson** demonstrates, in the context of the north-east region, how post-war state policies on nationalised industries have contributed to the de-industrialisation process. The pattern and problem of urban industrial decline make up the theme of Chapter 7, where **Steve Fothergill**, **Graham Gudgin and their co-workers** argue that the demise of the city as the centre of manufacturing production and employment is an almost inevitable consequence of the process of change under advanced capitalism, particularly as this has affected the nature of capital–employment–output relationships within the firm.

The final three contributions explore certain facets of the 'economic regeneration' issue. **Ron Martin** in Chapter 8 critically assesses the New Conservative response to and policy prescription for the de-industrialisation problem and argues that the Thatcher government's pursuance of monetarist-based neo-market policies aimed at 'recapitalising' Britain have in fact played a major part in accelerating the pace of industrial contraction since 1979. In his view the continuance of such policies is likely to exacerbate the growing economic gaps between the regions. As **Peter Daniels** and **Kevin Morgan** then show – in Chapters 9 and 10 – neither service industry nor high technology activity can be relied upon to generate compensating job growth or re-industrialisation in the country's depressed areas. According to Peter Daniels, producer and business services, the fastest-growing branches of the service sector, are concentrating increasingly in the more prosperous south of Britain, and are themselves beginning to experience their own 'de-industrialisation' because of the application of new technologies to labour-intensive functions. And as far as high technology and innovative industry is concerned, Kevin Morgan shows that not only is Britain's international performance weak in this sphere, but also that there are strong forces in operation, backed up by government policies, which imply that a major focus on the so-called 'sunrise' industries as a vehicle for economic regeneration is almost certain to have profound uneven social and spatial consequences.

In commissioning these contributions no attempt was made to force authors' views and approaches into a single, rigid methodological mould. Instead, the reader will be aware of significant differences in conceptual orientation. The content of individual chapters remains the personal responsibility of the author(s) concerned; but the collection in total is offered as a comprehensive commentary on the evolving geography of British de-industrialisation. We hope that the book will be of interest and value not only to geographers and economists, but to all those concerned with the industrial problems and policy issues of regional Britain.

RON MARTIN
BOB ROWTHORN

Bibliography for the Preface is overleaf

Bibliography

Bell, D. (1974) *The Coming of Post-Industrial Society* (London: Heinemann).

Blackaby, F. (ed.) (1981) *De-industrialisation* (London: Heinemann).

Bluestone, B. (1984) 'Is De-industrialisation a Myth? Capital Mobility versus Absorptive Capacity in the US Economy', in G. Summers (ed.) *De-industrialisation: Restructuring the Economy*, Annals of the American Academy of Political and Social Science, vol. 475 (Beverley Hills: Sage Publications) pp. 39–51.

Bluestone, B. and Harrison, B. (1980) *Capital and Communities: The Causes and Consequences of Private Disinvestment* (Washington: The Progressive Alliance).

Bluestone, B. and Harrison, B. (1982) *The De-industrialisation of America: Plant Closings, Community Abandonment and the Dismantling of Basic Industry* (New York: Basic Books).

Bluestone, B., Harrison, B., and Baker, L. (1981) *Corporate Flight: The Causes and Consequences of Economic Dislocation* (New York: The Progressive Alliance).

Fothergill, S. and Gudgin, G. (1982) *Unequal Growth: Urban and Regional Employment Change in the UK* (London: Heinemann).

Gamble, A. (1981) *Britain in Decline* (London: Macmillan).

Gershuny, J. (1978) *After Industrial Society* (London: Macmillan).

Goddard, J. B. and Champion, A. G. (1983) *The Urban and Regional Transformation of Britain* (London: Methuen).

Gordus, J. P., Jarley, P. and Ferman, L. A. (1981) *Plant Closings and Economic Dislocations* (Kalamazoo: W. E. Upjohn Institute for Employment Research).

Hughes, J. (1981) *Britain in Crisis: De-industrialisation and How to Fight It* (Nottingham: Spokesman).

McKenzie, R. B. (1984) *Fugitive Industry: The Economics and Politics of De-industrialisation* (San Francisco: Pacific Institute for Public Policy Research).

Massey, D. B. (1984) *Spatial Divisions of Labour: Social Structures and the Geography of Production* (London: Macmillan).

Massey, D. B. and Meegan, R. (1982) *The Anatomy of Job Loss* (London: Methuen).

Murgatroyd, L. and Urry, J. (1984) 'The Class and Gender Restructuring of the Lancaster Economy, 1950–80', in L. Murgatroyd *et al.* (eds) *Localities, Class and Gender* (London: Pion).

Rose, D., Vogler, C., Marshall, G. and Newby, H. (1984) 'Economic Restructuring: The British Experience', in G. Summers (ed.) *De-industrialisation: Restructuring the Economy*, Annals of the American Academy of Politics and Social Science, vol. 475 (Beverley Hills: Sage Publications) pp. 137–57.

Sheriff, T. (1979) *A De-industrialised Britain*. Fabian Research Series, no. 341 (London: Fabian Society).

Singh, A. (1977) UK Industry and the World Economy: A Case of De-industrialisation?', *Cambridge Journal of Economics*, **1**, **2**, pp. 113–36.

Smith, K. (1984) *The British Economic Crisis* (Harmondsworth: Penguin Books).

Thirlwall, A. P. (1982) 'De-industrialisation in the UK', *Lloyds Bank Review* (Apr) pp. 22–37.

Urry, J. (1983) 'De-industrialisation, Classes and Politics', in R. King (ed.) *Capital and Politics* (London: Routledge & Kegan Paul) pp. 28–48.

1
De-industrialisation in Britain

BOB ROWTHORN

1. Introduction

The aim of this chapter is to provide a general context for the more specialised chapters which follow. It is primarily concerned with manufacturing employment in Britain since the Second World War, although there is some discussion of industrial employment as a whole. We show how Britain has experienced an enormous reduction in manufacturing employment over the past thirty years – greater than in almost any other advanced capitalist country – and we consider various hypotheses which might explain this phenomenon. Three main hypotheses are identified which for convenience we label: the 'Maturity Thesis', the 'Trade Specialisation Thesis' and the 'Failure Thesis'. All three hypotheses, it turns out, have considerable evidence in their favour and all three help to explain what has happened to manufacturing employment in Britain.

The present chapter draws heavily upon material contained in a longer and more comprehensive study by Rowthorn and Wells (1987). Of necessity, many of the arguments are presented in a condensed form and many of the details have been left out. Anyone desiring a more comprehensive treatment should consult the longer study.

2. Britain's Post-war Record in an International Context

Figure 1.1 shows what has happened to employment in the major sectors of the British economy since the Second World War. There

1

has been an almost continuous fall in the number of people employed in agriculture, from around 1.8 million in 1946 to under 1 million in 1983. Over the same period employment in the service sector has risen dramatically, from just under 10 million to over 14 million. In the so-called 'production' industries – manufacturing, mining, construction and public utilities – the picture is more complex. In the immediate post-war years, under the impetus of reconstruction and a government-sponsored export drive, employment in these industries increased rapidly. Then, in the 1950s, the pace of expansion slackened. Employment continued to rise in manufacturing and construction, though at a slower pace than before; while coal mining began to shed labour as pits were closed because of competition from oil. For a time the new jobs created in manufacturing and construction more than offset those lost in mining, with the result that industrial employment, as a whole, carried on rising right through into the 1960s. However, this expansion came to a halt in 1966 when, following a major sterling crisis, the Labour government of the day imposed a deflationary budget on the economy. Since that time industrial employment of all kinds – mining, construction and manufacturing alike – has fallen dramatically. From an all-time peak of 11.5 million in 1966, the total number of people employed in industry had fallen to less than 7 million by 1984. Over the same period manufacturing employment alone fell from 8.7 million to 5.4 million. About half of this enormous decline took place before the present Thatcher government took office in 1979, while the rest has occurred since.

The picture is much the same if we look at relative shares rather than absolute numbers, although the timing is somewhat different (see Figure 1.2). After rising strongly immediately after the War, the share of industry in civil employment reached a peak in 1955 of around 48 per cent. In that year approximately one-third of the entire population between the ages of 15 and 64 were employed as industrial workers, while most of the rest were students, housewives and service workers. These figures for industrial employment have rarely been equalled and certainly never surpassed in the whole of British history. Moreover, they are almost without equal in the experience of other capitalist countries. This last point can be verified from Table 1.1 which compares Britain's employment structure in 1955 with that of other highly industrialised economies at an equivalent stage in their development. In the

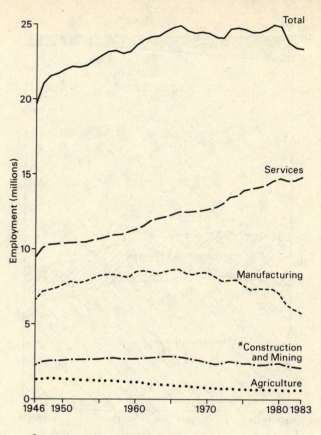

FIGURE 1.1   *Employment in the UK by Sector, 1946–83 (millions)*

SOURCE   Based on historical data from Ministry of Labour and Department of Employment.

entire history of world capitalism the all-time peak of industrialisation was probably achieved by Germany in 1970 and Switzerland
in 1963. In each case industry accounted for 47–48 per cent of civil
employment – which is virtually identical to the figure reached in
Britain in 1955. Thus, in employment terms, the British economy
in 1955 was one of the most highly industrialised economies the
capitalist world has ever seen. Never before, nor since, in any

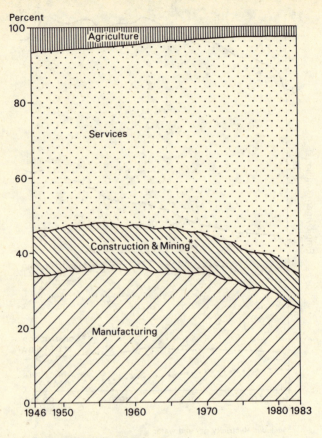

FIGURE 1.2   *Employment in the UK by Sector, 1946–83 (percentage shares)*

SOURCE   Based on historical data from Ministry of Labour and Department of Employment.

capitalist country, at any time, has industrial employment been significantly more important than it was in Britain in 1955. Yet no sooner had this pre-eminence been achieved than the process went into reverse. Industrial employment began declining in importance, at first slowly and then with gathering speed. By 1984 the share of industry in civil employment had fallen to 34 per cent, and

TABLE 1.1 *Comparative Employment Structure in the West's most Industrialised Economies*

| | Industrial employment as % of | | Manufacturing employment as % of | |
	Civil employment	*Population aged 15–64*	*Civil employment*	*Population aged 15–64*
Belgium (1957)	47.0	26.9	36.0	20.6
Germany (1970)	48.5	33.1	37.7	25.8
Luxemburg (1966)	46.9	28.8	35.8	22.0
Switzerland (1963)	47.6	n.a.	38.5	n.a.
UK (1955)	47.9	32.8	36.1	24.7

SOURCE OECD – The dates in parentheses refer to the year in which industrial employment reached its all-time peak as a share of civil employment in the country concerned.

that of manufacturing alone to 26 per cent. To illustrate the scale of the transformation which has occurred since 1955, consider the relationship between industry and the services which is implied by this transformation. In 1955 there were more workers employed in industry than in all of the services combined, both public and private. By 1983 there were almost two service workers for each industrial worker, and the public services alone employed about three-quarters as many people as the whole of manufacturing put together (4.3 million as compared to 5.8 million). Under ideal conditions of prosperity and full employment such a transformation over such a short period of time would have been disruptive. Under the actual conditions of stagnation and unemployment it has been traumatic.

Let us now consider the experience of other countries over the past thirty years. We shall concentrate on the manufacturing sector, but our remarks apply with only minor qualifications to the industrial sector as a whole, including mining and construction. Tables 1.2 and 1.3 show what has happened to manufacturing employment in the advanced capitalist countries over the past thirty years. Wherever possible the figures shown go back to 1955 or even before, although there are gaps caused by a lack of reliable information. Table 1.2 shows the average annual growth rate in manufacturing employment in three distinct periods: 1956–66, 1966–73 and 1973–83. Looking at these growth rates the following

TABLE 1.2   *Manufacturing Employment in the Advanced Capitalist Countries*

	Annual percentage change			Cumulative percentage change	
	1955–66	1966–73	1973–83	1955–66	1966–83
Italy	1.0	2.0	−0.9	10.3	5.3
Japan	3.9	2.9	−0.4	47.3	18.3
Finland	n.a.	1.6	0.5	n.a.	17.5
Austria	n.a.	n.a.	−0.6	n.a.	n.a.
Iceland[1] [2]	1.5[1]	2.1	2.8	15.6	52.1
France	0.8	0.6	−1.9	8.7	−14.0
Norway	n.a.	n.a.	−0.9	n.a.	n.a.
Denmark[2]	2.2	−1.2	−1.9	24.5	−24.4
Canada	2.4	1.4	−0.4	26.5	6.7
Luxemburg[1]	1.3[1]	0.9	−2.3	14.3	−15.5
Germany	1.2	0.2	−1.9	12.2	−16.2
Sweden[1]	1.0[1]	−1.3	−1.2	10.7	−18.8
Switzerland[1]	1.7[1]	−0.2	−2.0	18.5	−19.9
New Zealand[1]	n.a.	1.9	0.4	n.a.	18.9
Netherlands	1.0	−0.8	−2.4	11.0	−25.7
Australia	n.a.	1.7	−2.7	n.a.	−14.3
Belgium[2]	0.6	−0.3	−3.4	7.1	−30.8
USA	1.3	0.7	−0.4	13.5	0.6
UK	0.4	−1.2	−3.1	4.1	−33.2

Notes   [1] Initial date is 1957, estimate for cumulative change 1955–66 is based on annual growth rate 1957–66.
[2] Terminal date is 1981, estimate for cumulative change 1966–83 is based on annual growth rates for 1966–73 and 1973–81.

SOURCE   See notes to Table A1 of the Appendix to this chapter.

points stand out. In the first period manufacturing employment increased in every country shown, often at an extremely high rate. In the second period growth continued in most countries, although at a slower pace; moreover there were a few countries in which manufacturing employment began to fall. Finally, in the third period there was an almost universal decline in manufacturing employment with only three minor exceptions: Finland, Iceland and New Zealand. Thus, the first period is one of general expan-

TABLE 1.3 *Share of Manufacturing in Civil Employment 1950–81*

	1950	Percentage share 1955	1966	1973	1981	Change 1955–81
Italy	n.a.	20.0	25.8	28.5	26.1	+6.1
Japan	n.a.	18.4	24.4	27.4	24.8	+6.4
Finland[3]	n.a.	21.3	22.8	25.4	26.1	+4.8
Austria[1]	n.a.	29.8[1]	29.8	29.7	29.7	−0.1
Iceland[3]	21.5	23.7	25.5	25.2	26.3	+2.6
France	n.a.	26.9	28.7	28.3	25.1	−1.8
Norway	22.0	23.1	23.7	23.5	20.2	−2.9
Denmark	n.a.	27.5	29.0	24.7	21.3	−6.2
Canada	24.9	24.1	23.9	22.0	19.4	−4.7
Luxemburg[2]	n.a.	33.2	35.8	33.8	27.4	−5.8
Germany	n.a.	33.8	35.2	36.7	33.6	−0.2
Sweden[2]	n.a.	31.7	31.2	27.5	23.3	−8.4
Switzerland[3]	n.a.	36.1	37.8	35.0	32.0	−4.1
New Zealand[3]	n.a.	23.7	25.4	25.7	24.0	+0.3
Netherlands	29.3	29.3	28.9	25.7	21.1	−8.2
Australia[3]	n.a.	29.6	28.6	25.6	19.4	−10.2
Belgium	35.0	35.3	33.6	31.8	24.7	−10.6
USA	27.9	28.5	27.8	24.8	21.7	−6.8
UK	34.8	36.1	34.8	32.3	26.4	−9.7

SOURCE   Diverse OECD publications and Bairoch (1968).
[1] Initial date is 1956, figure in the final column refers to 1956–81.
[2] Figure in second column is for 1957, figure in the first column refers to 1957–81.
[3] Figure in second column is for 1959, figure in the final column refers to 1959–81.

sion in manufacturing employment, the second is a period of transition and the third is one of general contraction. Comparing Britain's performance with that of other countries, we find that between 1956 and 1966 manufacturing employment grew more slowly in Britain than in any other country shown in Table 1.2; between 1966 and 1973 it fell by more than in any other country with the exception of Sweden; and between 1973 and 1983 it fell by more than in any other country with the exception of Belgium. Taking the period 1955–83 as a whole, or even the subperiod

1966–83, we find that Britain has experienced the greatest percentage decline of manufacturing employment of any Western country.

Looking at relative shares the picture is not quite so clear as in the case of absolute numbers. Between 1955 and 1981 the share of manufacturing in civil employment in Britain fell by 9.7 percentage points, from 36.1 per cent to 26.4 per cent. This is certainly a much greater reduction than occurred in most of the countries shown in Table 1.3. However, enormous though it is, even greater reductions were recorded in Australia and Belgium where the share of manufacturing fell by 10.2 and 10.6 percentage points respectively. Thus, if we take as our index the share of manufacturing in civil employment, the extent of de-industrialisation over the thirty years has been much greater in Britain than in most other advanced capitalist countries, although slightly less than in Australia and Belgium.

3. **Towards an Explanation: Three Theses**

Whether we consider relative shares or absolute numbers the decline in manufacturing employment in Britain has been spectacular. What accounts for it? Why did this decline begin to much earlier in Britain than in most other countries and why has it been so great? In this chapter we shall examine three potential explanations for what has happened. For convenience we shall call these: the 'Maturity Thesis', the 'Specialisation Thesis', and the 'Failure Thesis'.

(i) *The Maturity Thesis*

The first thesis locates Britain's own historical experience within a more general theory of economic development and structural change. This theory asserts that, in any country which develops, the structure of employment undergoes the following sequence of transformations. When development first gets under way the share of industry in total employment rises rapidly. After a time this share stabilises. Then, at a certain point, it starts to fall. An economy which has reached this final stage is said to be 'mature'. The reason why the share of industry falls in the final stage of development can be readily appreciated by means of a diagram. Figure 1.3 shows in a stylised form what happens to the structure

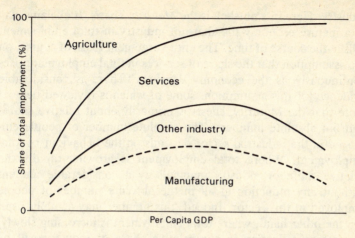

FIGURE 1.3 *Employment Structure and Economic Development*

of employment in the course of development. From the diagram we can see how development is accompanied by a continuous rise in the share of services in total employment. We can also see how the impact of this on the industrial sector depends on what stage of development the economy has reached. When development first gets under way, services grow at the expense of agriculture, and their share in total employment rises while that of agriculture falls. Meanwhile the share of industrial employment rises. Thus, in relative terms, both industry and the service sector increase their share at the expense of agriculture. In the intermediate stage of development the share of industry stabilises, while the share of services continues to rise at the expense of agriculture. Eventually, in the final stage of development, the share of industry starts to fall. The reason for this is obvious from Figure 1.3. In the final stage only a small fraction of the labour force is employed in agriculture and the vast majority work in industry or the services. Under these conditions any major rise in the share of services in total employment must be at the expense of industry. As a matter of arithmetic the share of industry must fall. There is simply no other way in which the service sector can continue to increase its share in total employment.

Thus, at first the service sector increases its share at the expense of agriculture. Later, as the potential for this kind of expansion is exhausted, the services increase their share at the expense of industry. Here in a nutshell is the *Maturity Thesis*. It explains why in a mature economy the share of industry in total employment falls in the course of time. The entire argument rests, of course, on the assumption that the share of services in total employment rises continuously as the economy develops. There is considerable evidence for this assumption, some of which is reviewed below.[1] Note that the Maturity Thesis is primarily about relative shares and not absolute numbers. The absolute number of people employed in the industrial sector depends on the behaviour of total employment. Where total employment is growing rapidly the relative share of industry may fall by a considerable amount without any reduction at all in the absolute number of people employed in this sector. Indeed, this number may actually rise.[2] On the other hand, where total employment is increasing slowly, any major reduction in the relative share of industry will be accompanied by an absolute fall in industrial employment.

One cannot lay down a mechanical rule to determine exactly when any particular economy will reach maturity as there are many different factors which can influence the turning-point. However, from evidence considered elsewhere, it seems that the typical capitalist economy reaches maturity when per capita GDP is in the region of 4000 US dollars (at 1975 prices).[3] At this stage agriculture normally accounts for between 5 and 10 per cent of total employment, although the figure may be higher, depending on the economy concerned and its pattern of specialisation.

The *Maturity Thesis* is of obvious relevance to Britain in the 1950s. At that time Britain was still one of the most advanced countries in the world and was just approaching maturity. Per capita income in 1955 was $3305 (at 1975 prices), which is not far short of the turning point at which the share of industry in total employment starts to fall. Moreover, agriculture accounted for only 5 per cent of total employment, so any substantial rise in the share of services, however caused, could only come at the expense of industry. The situation was very different in other Western countries. Some were still relatively poor and had enormous reserves of labour in agriculture. These countries were nowhere near mature, and there was ample room for services to increase their share of employment at the expense of agriculture without significantly affecting the share of industry. Others were more advanced, but even in these countries the share of agriculture in total employment was considerably higher than in the UK and in this respect their economies are less mature.

The contrast in experience between Britain and other countries can be seen from Table 1.4 which shows how the structure of employment has evolved since 1955, the year in which the share of manufacturing, and that of industry as a whole, reached a peak in Britain. Countries have been divided into three groups, depending on how agrarian they were in 1955. At one extreme are the 'immature' economies in group A, all of which were still agrarian in character in 1955, having more than 21 per cent of their employed labour force in agriculture. At the other extreme is the UK which forms a group of its own, being the least agrarian economy in the world in 1955 with just over 5 per cent of its labour force in agriculture. Between these two extremes lie the transitional economies of group B, all of which were still moderately agrarian in character in 1955, with agriculture accounting for between 9 and 18 per cent of total employment.

From Table 1.4 we can see how the share of services has risen dramatically in all of the countries shown since 1955.[4] In the immature economies of group A this increase has been matched by an almost equal reduction in the share of agriculture; as a result the share of industry has hardly altered. This can be seen from Table 1.5 which summarises some of the information given in Table 1.4. Between 1955 and 1981 the share of services in total employment rose from 36.0 per cent to 55.2 per cent in the immature economies of group A – a rise of 19.2 points. Over the same period the share of agriculture fell from 31.0 per cent to 9.9 per cent – a fall of 21.1 points. Meanwhile the share of industry rose very slightly, from 33.0 per cent in 1955 to 34.9 per cent in 1981. At the other extreme is the UK, where the relative expansion of services has been almost entirely at the expense of industry. Between 1955 and 1981 the share of services in total employment rose from 46.7 per cent to 61.7 per cent in the UK – an increase of 15.0 points. There was some decline in agriculture, whose share fell by 2.8 points, but the vast bulk of service expansion was at the expense of industry whose share fell by 12.2 points. This is hardly surprising. Given the small size of the agricultural sector at the beginning of the period (5.4 per cent) it was mathematically impossible for this sector to shrink sufficiently to offset a 15.0 per cent rise in the share of services. As a matter of arithmetic, such a

TABLE 1.4 Employment Structure and Stage of Development

	Percentage share of civil employment				change		
	1955	1966	1973	1981	1955–73	1973–81	1955–81
Agriculture							
Group A (immature)	31.0	20.6	14.1	9.9	−16.9	−4.2	−21.1
Group B (transitional)	14.6	9.3	7.0	5.8	−7.6	−1.2	−8.8
UK (mature)	5.4	3.6	2.9	2.6	−2.5	−0.3	−2.8
Manufacturing							
Group A (immature)	23.8	26.2	26.6	25.0	+2.8	−1.6	+1.2
Group B (transitional)	30.5	30.8	28.9	24.7	−1.6	−4.6	−5.8
UK (mature)	36.1	34.8	32.3	26.4	−3.8	−5.9	−9.7

Industry							
Group A (immature)	33.0	36.6	37.2	34.9	+4.2	−2.3	+1.9
Group B (transitional)	40.7	41.2	38.6	33.7	−2.1	−4.9	−7.0
UK (mature)	47.9	46.3	42.6	35.7	−5.3	−6.9	−12.2
Services							
Group A (immature)	36.0	42.8	48.7	55.2	−12.7	+6.5	+19.2
Group B (transitional)	44.7	49.5	54.4	60.5	+9.7	+6.1	+15.8
UK (mature)	46.7	50.1	54.5	61.7	+7.8	+7.2	+15.0

Note The group figures refer to an unweighted average of the countries concerned. Group A contains those advanced capitalist countries in which the share of agriculture in civil employment was greater than 21.0 per cent in 1955, viz. Italy, Japan, Finland, Austria, Iceland, France, Norway and Denmark. Group B contains those countries in which the agricultural share was between 9.7 and 18.0 per cent in 1955, viz. Canada, Luxemburg, Germany, Sweden, Switzerland, New Zealand, Netherlands, Australia, Belgium, and the USA. The UK, with an agricultural share of 5.4 per cent in 1955, is the only advanced capitalist country not in one of these groups.

SOURCE See Table A1 of the appendix to this chapter.

TABLE 1.5   *Summary of Employment Changes, 1955–81*
(change in percentage share)

	Group A (immature)	Group B (transitional)	UK (mature)
Agriculture	−21.1	−8.8	−2.8
Industry	+1.9	−7.0	−12.2
Services	+19.2	+15.8	+15.0
	0.0	0.0	0.0

SOURCE   last column of Table 1.3.

rise in the *share* of services could only be at the expense of industry whose *share* was bound to fall.

Thus, at one extreme are the immature economies of group A where, as a rule, services have increased their share at the expense of agriculture, leaving industry largely unaffected.[5] At the other extreme is the UK, which had virtually no agricultural employment in 1955, and where the relative expansion in services has been almost entirely at the expense of industry. Between these two extremes are the transitional economies of group B. These countries were moderately agrarian to start with and on average the increased share of services since 1955 has been at the expense of both agriculture and industry, almost equally (see Table 1.5).[6]

To explore this point a little further let us go back to Tables 1.2 and 1.3. The countries shown in these tables are arranged in a definite order, being ranked according to the share of agriculture in total employment in 1955. Thus, at the top of the list is Italy where the share of agriculture was 40.8 per cent in 1955; at the bottom is the UK where the share was only 5.4 per cent. Looking at the tables we find a clear pattern. The more agrarian economies, towards the top of the list, have normally experienced either faster growth, or a smaller fall, in manufacturing employment. Conversely the least agrarian economies towards the bottom of the list have experienced the greatest fall in manufacturing employment, either absolutely or as a share of total employment. This is exactly what we should expect from our discussion about maturity and structural change. In every economy service employment expands either absolutely or relatively in the course of development. In agrarian economies this expansion is at the expense of agriculture, while in mature, non-agrarian economies it is mainly at the expense of manufacturing and other industrial sectors. This explains why in agrarian economies, economic development will be accompanied by an increase in manufacturing employment, either absolutely or as a share of total employment; while in non-agrarian economies the opposite will normally be the case.

Quite apart from the light they throw on structural change in general, Tables 1.2 and 1.3 tell us something about the British economy. As the least agrarian economy Britain lies at the bottom in each table, and this in itself helps to explain why the fall in manufacturing employment, both absolutely and relatively, has been so great. Here, then, we have a possible explanation for the fall in industrial employment so early in Britain and why the decline has been so intense. By the mid-1950s the British economy was already close to maturity. The share of agriculture in total employment was already very small, and any major rise in the share of services – however caused – could only be at the expense of industry. The situation in most other capitalist countries was quite different. Many of them still had enormous reserves of labour in agriculture; they had not yet reached the stage of development in which economic growth involves an absolute or relative decline in industrial employment. Thus, from the evidence we have examined so far the maturity thesis looks quite convincing. It certainly helps to explain why the decline in industrial employment began earlier in Britain and has been more extensive than in most other countries. It is further supported by the fact that many other capitalist countries began to experience a similar decline in industrial employment in the 1960s and 1970s, as their reserves of agricultural labour were depleted and they reached the stage of maturity where the service sector increases its share of employment at the expense of industry.

(ii) *The Trade Specialisation Thesis*

A second potential explanation for the decline in manufacturing employment in Britain is concerned with foreign trade, with the huge changes which have occurred over the past thirty years in Britain's role in the international division of labour. These changes are described at length in a forthcoming book, so here we shall

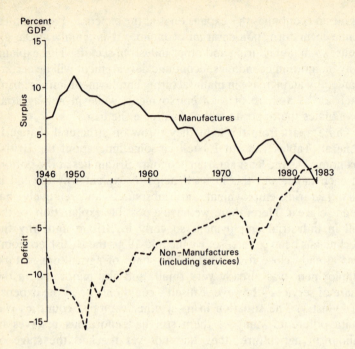

FIGURE 1.4   *UK Balance of Trade, 1946–83 (as per cent of GDP)*

SOURCE   Adopted from Rowthorn and Wells (1987).

only outline their main features.[7] By the time post-war recovery was complete in 1950 Britain had become a highly specialised 'workshop' economy, importing vast amounts of food and raw materials, and also oil, in return for manufactured exports. This can be seen from Figure 1.4, which shows what has happened to Britain's trade in manufactures and non-manufactures (including services) since 1950. In the years 1950–2 there was a surplus on manufacturing trade equal to some 10 per cent of GDP on average, while on non-manufacturing trade there was an even larger deficit. These are truly remarkable figures which have never been equalled, before or since, in British history and never surpassed elsewhere, not even in those archetypal 'workshops' economies of Germany and Japan. The reasons for such a remarkable situation are, briefly, as follows. On the non-manufacturing side global scarcities in the aftermath of the Second World War had forced up to unprecedented levels the cost of items which Britain had always imported in bulk, such as food and raw materials. Moreover Britain's previously massive income from service activities, such as shipping and the City of London, had fallen substantially, while receipts from her once considerable coal exports had almost vanished. This combination of inflated import prices and lost export earnings explains why the deficit on non-manufacturing trade was so large in the early 1950s. To cover this deficit Britain had no alternative but to export manufactured goods. Her profits from foreign investments had been greatly reduced by the enforced wartime sale of her overseas assets and her ability to borrow was limited. So, to finance the huge trade deficit in non-manufactures Britain required a surplus of roughly equal proportions in her manufacturing trade. This surplus she achieved through a vigorous combination of industrial protection and export promotion.

The early 1950s marked the high point of Britain's role as a workshop economy. Since then the picture has been transformed beyond recognition. In non-manufacturing trade the old deficit has disappeared completely to be replaced by a small surplus, of around 1 per cent of GDP in 1981–3; in manufacturing trade the opposite has occurred and the old surplus has been replaced by a small deficit (see Figure 1.4). This transformation is often cited as evidence of Britain's industrial decline, of the failure of her manufacturing industry to compete internationally. However, such an interpretation is largely unfounded. Certainly the performance of manufacturing industry has been very poor over the past thirty years, but this is not what explains the dramatic transformation which has occurred in the structure of trade. The origins of this transformation are to be found in events largely unrelated to the country's industrial performance. Since the early 1950s there has been a whole stream of autonomous developments on the non-manufacturing side whose cumulative impact on Britain's trade structure and pattern of specialisation has been enormous.

Imports of food and raw materials have become much cheaper in real terms; increased domestic food production has reduced the need for food imports; new methods of production and a changing composition of output has reduced the need for imported raw materials; service exports in such areas as civil aviation, construction and finance have risen; finally, the discovery of North Sea oil has turned Britain into a major oil-producer. Between them, these developments explain why the balance in non-manufacturing trade has improved so much over the past thirty years. They also explain why the balance of trade in manufactures has deteriorated so much over this period. In the early 1950s Britain was a 'workshop' economy because she had to be. To finance the huge deficit in non-manufacturing trade the country required a huge surplus on manufacturing trade. There was simply no other way to remain solvent. Nowadays, however, the situation is quite different. The deficit on non-manufacturing trade has disappeared and with it has gone the need for a huge surplus on manufacturing trade. Hence the deterioration in the manufacturing balance. Britain is no longer a massive net exporter of manufactures because she no longer needs to be, and industrial performance has only a marginal bearing on the matter. The marked decline in Britain's manufacturing surplus over the past thirty years is not a symptom of industrial failure, but is mainly a response to autonomous developments elsewhere in the economy. Autonomous developments in non-manufacturing trade have led to a new pattern of specialisation, a new role for Britain in the world economy, of which the loss of a formerly huge manufacturing surplus is but one expression.

Now, for obvious reasons, a country's internal pattern of employment depends on its pattern of specialisation, on its role in the international division of labour. *Ceteris paribus*, a 'workshop' economy such as that of Britain in the early 1950s, with her huge surplus of manufactured exports, will have a much larger manufacturing sector than a country such as the USA, whose trade structure is more balanced. Moreover, when an economy ceases to be a workshop economy and develops a new, less specialised pattern of trade its manufacturing sector is likely to contract, relatively, if not absolutely. Here then is a potential explanation for what has happened to manufacturing employment in Britain over the past thirty years. In the early 1950s, Britain was a highly specialised industrial producer, perhaps the most extreme example of a workshop economy the world has ever seen. This in itself helps to explain why such a large fraction of her labour force was employed in the manufacturing sector. Since those days, however, because of autonomous developments in non-manufacturing trade, the British economy has become much less specialised. Britain no longer requires a large surplus on her manufacturing trade and, as a result, no longer needs to employ anything like such a large fraction of her labour force in manufacturing. Moreover, no other country has experienced such a massive transformation in its pattern of trade over the past thirty years. No other country, not even Australia or Norway, has experienced such a vast improvement in its non-manufacturing balance over the period, nor such a deterioration in its manufacturing balance. This may help to explain why the decline in manufacturing employment has been so much greater in Britain than in most other countries.

(iii) *The Failure Thesis*

So far we have considered two explanations for the decline of manufacturing employment in Britain. There was the *Maturity Thesis* which located our industrial decline within the framework of a general theory of development and structural change. Britain, it argued, was the first country to reach the stage of development known as 'maturity', in which the share of manufacturing in total employment starts to fall. This in itself helps to explain why the decline in manufacturing employment began so much earlier in Britain than elsewhere and has been so much greater. A very different explanation was put forward by the *Trade Specialisation Thesis*. According to this thesis the decline in manufacturing employment is merely an internal consequence of Britain's changing external relations with other countries, of the huge improvements which have occurred in the realm of non-manufacturing trade since the early 1950s. Thus, one thesis argues that a fall in manufacturing employment was inevitable given the stage of development Britain had reached by the 1950s, while the other argues that improvements in non-manufacturing trade are responsible for this decline.

There is, however, a third possible explanation – the *Failure Thesis*. As its name suggests, this thesis sees the decline of manufacturing employment as a symptom of economic *failure*: of a growing failure on the part of manufacturing industry to compete internationally or to produce the output required for a prosperous and fully employed economy. The Failure Thesis can be summarised in the following propositions:

(1) Britain's economic record in the realm of incomes and employment has been poor;

(2) This is largely explained by the weak performance of manufacturing industry;

(3) If the manufacturing sector had been much stronger, output in the sector would have been much greater;

(4) This would have stimulated the non-manufacturing side of the economy and led to the creation of more employment in services and other non-manufacturing activities;

(5) Finally, if the manufacturing sector had been much stronger, neither the absolute number of people employed in manufacturing, nor the share of this sector in total employment, would have fallen anything like so fast as they have done.

Many of these propositions are uncontroversial and are universally accepted by economists of all persuasions. Even so, let us examine them briefly.[8]

Consider the question of Britain's economic record. Here the evidence is overwhelming. By international standards, real incomes have risen slowly in Britain. Moreover since 1973 the growth in GDP has been entirely the result of North Sea oil-production; indeed, between 1973 and 1983 non-oil GDP actually fell by 2 per cent (Figure 1.5). The cumulative effect of slow growth on Britain's position in the international hierarchy can be seen from Table 1.6. In 1953 she was among the half-dozen richest countries in the world. By 1983, of all the advanced capitalist countries, Britain was among the poorest. In the realm of employment the picture is much the same. In the 1950s there was almost full employment in Britain, and the bulk of her population had never enjoyed greater economic security. By 1983 well over 3 million people were out of work and, of all the advanced capitalist countries, only Belgium had a greater fraction of her labour force unemployed (see Table 1.7). Not since the 1930s have so many British people faced such a bleak and insecure future.

What about the role of manufacturing in all this? Here again the evidence is overwhelming. By international standards the performance of British manufacturing industry has been very poor, especially since the oil crisis of 1973, and even more so since the Thatcher government took office in 1979. Prior to 1973 both

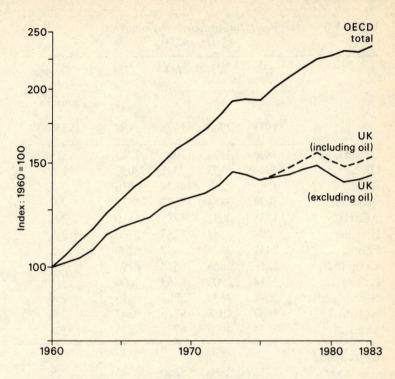

FIGURE 1.5   *GDP in the UK and OECD, 1960–83*

SOURCES   OECD and *Economic Trends*

output and productivity rose quite fast in Britain in comparison with past historical experiences, but they rose even faster in many other countries. As a result, despite moderately fast industrial growth, Britain was overtaken by many of her foreign rivals during this period, and by the time the world crisis broke at the end of 1973 she was no longer a first-rank industrial power. Thus, up to 1973, the decline of British manufacturing was relative rather than absolute. Since then, however, Britain's decline has become absolute. Manufacturing industry has experienced a large fall in output, most of which has occurred since 1979. Meanwhile output has continued to rise in other major OECD countries, albeit irregularly (see Figure 1.6). Between 1973 and 1982 manufacturing output in the major six fell by 18 per cent on average.[9] In the realm

TABLE 1.6   *GDP per Head in Selected Countries*
($ US 1975)[1]

	(1)	(2)	(3)	(4)	percentage growth per annum
	1953	1963	1973	1983	1953–83
Canada	3896	4688	7030	7701	2.3
USA	4946	5503	7371	8037	1.6
Japan	1054	2245	4974	6010	5.8
Australia	3074	3884	5337	5611	2.0
Austria	1735	3031	4785	5610	3.9
Belgium	2499	3384	5253	5860	2.8
France	2432	3476	5437	6280	3.2
Germany	2319	3866	5628	6291	3.3
Italy	1814	2903	4363	4600	3.1
Netherlands	2694	3639	5502	5815	2.6
Norway	3067	4058	5716	7347	2.9
Sweden	3536	4993	6769	7311	2.4
Unweighted average	2756	3806	5680	6373	2.8
UK	3125	3855	5097	5506	1.9

Note   [1] Exchange rates are based on purchasing-power parity.
SOURCE   OECD.

of labour productivity Britain's performance has also been poor by international standards since 1973. Despite a spectacular labour shake-out in vehicles, steel and certain other industries after 1979, output per person hour in British manufacturing rose by only 2.0 per cent per annum over the decade 1973–83, as compared with an average of 3.0 per cent per annum in the six major OECD countries. Although accurate comparisons in this field are notoriously difficult, available statistics establish beyond doubt that labour productivity in manufacturing industry is now much lower in Britain than elsewhere in the advanced capitalist world.

The weakness of manufacturing industry is certainly the main

TABLE 1.7   *Unemployment Rates in Selected OECD Countries*[1]
(Percentage of Total Labour Force)

	1964–73	*1974–9*	*1980*	*1981*	*1982*	*1983*	*1984*
US	4.4	6.6	7.0	7.5	9.5	9.5	7.4
Germany	0.8	3.2	3.0	4.4	6.1	8.0	8.6
France	2.2	4.5	6.3	7.3	8.1	8.3	9.7
Italy	5.5	6.6	7.4	8.3	9.0	9.8	10.2
Canada	4.7	7.2	7.5	7.5	10.9	11.8	11.2
Australia	1.9	5.0	6.0	5.7	7.1	9.9	8.9
Belgium	2.2	3.8	9.0	11.1	12.6	13.9	14.0
Netherlands	1.4	3.8	4.9	7.5	11.4	13.7	14.0
Japan	1.2	1.9	2.0	2.2	2.4	2.6	2.7
Norway	1.7	1.8	1.7	2.0	2.6	3.3	3.0
Sweden	2.0	1.9	2.0	2.5	3.1	3.5	3.1
Austria	1.5	1.6	1.9	2.5	3.5	4.1	4.0
Unweighted average	2.5	4.0	4.9	5.7	7.2	8.2	8.1
U.K.	3.1	5.0	6.9	11.0	12.3	13.1	13.2

Note [1] Standardised to accord with the ILO definition of unemployment.

SOURCE   OECD, *Economic Outlook* and *Main Economic Indicators*.

reason why Britain has become a relatively poor country, why per capita incomes in Britain are now the lowest in northern Europe. It also helps to explain why the unemployment rate is so high. Consider what it would mean if Britain's manufacturing industry were much stronger and more competitive than it is at present, having more equipment, using more advanced methods of production, and producing a wider range of higher quality of output. For a start, manufacturing output would obviously be much greater. Part of this additional output would go directly to meet domestic requirements, and part would be exported in payment for goods and services purchased from other countries. Some of these additional imports would be non-manufactures, such as raw materials or services; but there would also be a large increase in manufactured imports. Taking account of both the additional supplies from

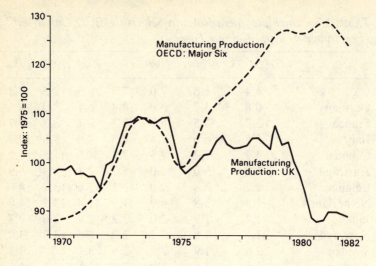

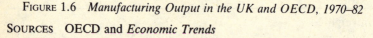

FIGURE 1.6   *Manufacturing Output in the UK and OECD, 1970–82*

SOURCES   OECD and *Economic Trends*

domestic industry and the additional imports from elsewhere, the total amount of manufactured goods available for home use would rise considerably. Since the production and distribution of manufactured goods involves a wide range of complementary activities, output would also rise in such areas as construction, mining, consulting, finance, transport and retail distribution. Moreover, real incomes would be higher and, consequently, consumers expenditure of almost every kind would be greater; as, indeed, would public expenditure on items such as health and education. Thus, with a stronger manufacturing sector, output would be greater in almost every sector of the economy.

What about employment? Would it also be greater? In considering this question we must distinguish between total employment in the economy as a whole and employment in particular industries or sectors. Taking the economy as a whole, there is no doubt that total employment would be greater than it is, if Britain's manufacturing industry had been stronger and had performed better over the past thirty years. The weakness of manufacturing industry has been responsible for the inflation and balance-of-payments crisis which have plagued the country over this period. In the face of these problems successive governments, Tory and Labour alike, have imposed deflationary measures which reduce employment in the short-term and inhibit its longer-term growth. With a stronger manufacturing industry, there would have been less need for such measures. Inflationary pressures would have been weaker, because more output would have been available to meet the competing claims of workers, employers and the state; and the balance of payments would have been stronger because British industry would have been more competitive in world markets. Thus, governments could have pursued more expansionary policies without jeopardising their targets for inflation and the balance of payments and, as a result, the overall level of employment would have been much higher.

How would this increase in total employment have been distributed between one sector of the economy and another? In particular, how would employment in the manufacturing sector itself have been affected, and what would have happened to the share of this sector in total employment? To answer these questions by means of *a priori* argument is not easy and specific numerical estimates are required if one is to go beyond the most general of observations. Such estimates are provided in the longer study mentioned at the beginning of this chapter, but here we must be content with a few general remarks.

If manufacturing industry had performed much better over the past thirty years we can assume that almost every major sector of the economy, including manufacturing itself, would have gained some of the extra jobs; either new jobs would have been created or old jobs saved. As a result more people would now be employed in construction, the services and, of course, in manufacturing itself.[10] Thus, employment would be greater than it now is in both manufacturing and non-manufacturing alike. However, this still leaves open several possibilities. Suppose the superior performance in manufacturing had been accompanied by an enormous rise in labour productivity. Then relatively few additional jobs would have been created in the manufacturing sector itself, despite a massive increase in the output of this sector; and most of the additional employment would have been in non-manufacturing, especially the services. In this case the *share* of manufacturing in total employment would have fallen as fast or even faster than it has actually done in reality. Conversely, suppose the superior performance in manufacturing industry had been accompanied by only a modest increase in labour productivity – an unlikely, but logically conceivable, combination. Then many of the additional jobs would have been in the manufacturing sector itself. As a result the *share* of manufacturing in total employment would by now be much larger than it is; and over the past thirty years this share would have fallen much less than it has done. Both these scenarios are logically conceivable and on *a priori* grounds alone there is no way of choosing between them. However, simulations by the author suggest that the former scenario is closer to the truth. According to these simulations industrial failure is of minor importance in explaining the fall in manufacturing employment. Had manufacturing industry been stronger, employment in this sector would still have fallen dramatically, and only a few hundred thousand jobs would have been saved. Moreover, the share of manufacturing in total employment would have fallen even more than it has done in reality. If these simulations are any guide the dramatic decline in manufacturing employment is not the result of poor industrial performance. It is almost entirely the result of other factors and would have occurred no matter how good the performance of British industry.

4. Concluding Remarks

The preceding discussion may be summarised as follows. Britain was the first country to reach the stage of 'maturity' at which services increase their share of employment at the expense of manufacturing and other 'production' industries. Moreover the country has experienced massive changes in her pattern of trade specialisation. Because of huge improvements in non-manufacturing trade she no longer needs such a large surplus on her manufacturing trade, and fewer people are now required to produce this surplus than was formerly the case. Between them these two factors – maturity and trade specialisation – account for virtually all of the decline in manufacturing employment. Poor industrial performance is of only minor importance in explaining this decline. Had manufacturing industry been stronger, manufacturing employment would still have fallen dramatically. For a more detailed assessment of the quantitative influence of the various factors considered in this chapter the reader is referred to Rowthorn and Wells (1986).

Notes

1. For a more extensive treatment of this subject see Rowthorn and Wells (1987) ch.1.
2. For example, in the USA, the number of people employed in manufacturing rose by 5.2 per cent between 1970 and 1981. However, total employment rose by 27.6 per cent over the same period, so the share of manufacturing fell considerably, despite an increase in the absolute number employed in this sector. The USA is unusual in this respect. In most other countries a falling share of manufacturing in total employment has been accompanied by a decline in its absolute number of people working in this sector.
3. See Rowthorn and Wells (op. cit.) ch. 1.
4. For more details see the Appendix to this chapter.
5. An exception to this rule is Denmark, which belongs to group A, but has also experienced a big fall in the share of industry in total employment (see Table A1 of the Appendix).
6. The principal exception here is Germany, where the share of industry hardly changed at all between 1955 and 1981.
7. See Rowthorn and Wells (op. cit.) chs 5 and 6.
8. For a clear statement of the Failure Thesis see Singh (1977) or Thirlwall (1982).
9. The six major OECD countries referred to here are: the USA, Canada, Japan, France, Germany and Italy.
10. See Rowthorn and Wells (op. cit.).

Bibliography

Bairoch, P., *et al.*, (1968) *The Working Population and its Structure* (Université Libre de Brussel, Institute de Sociologie).

Kravis, I. B., Meston, A. W., and Summers, R. (1978) 'Real GDP Per Capita for More than One Hundred Countries', *Economic Journal*, **88**, pp. 215–42.

Rowthorn, R. E., and Wells, J. R. (1987) *De-industrialisation and Foreign Trade: Britain's Decline in a Global Perspective* (Cambridge: Cambridge University Press).

Singh, A. (1977) 'UK Industry and the World Economy: A Case of De-industrialization?', *Cambridge Journal of Economics*, **1, 2**, pp. 113–36.

Thirlwall, A. P. (1982) 'De-industrialization in the United Kingdom', *Lloyds Bank Review* (April) pp. 22–37.

APPENDIX

The following table shows the pattern of employment in the advanced capitalist countries over the period 1950–81.

TABLE A1   *Percentage Shares in Civilian Employment, 1950–81*

	1950	1955	1966	1973	1979	1981
(a) *Agriculture*						
Italy	–	40.8	25.2	18.3	14.9	13.4
Japan	45.2	37.9	22.2	13.4	11.2	10.0
Finland[4]	–	38.3	29.0	17.1	11.8	11.1
Austria[1,2]	39.7	30.6	21.4	16.2	9.2	8.8
Iceland[3]	37.7	27.8	18.6	15.7	12.1	11.7
France	–	26.7	17.3	11.4	8.9	8.6
Norway	28.2	24.2	16.7	11.4	8.6	8.5
Denmark	–	21.8	14.2	9.5	7.2	7.3
Canada	23.2	18.0	9.0	6.6	5.7	5.5
Luxemburg[3]	–	17.9	11.5	7.9	5.9	5.6
Germany	23.8	17.8	10.6	7.5	5.8	5.5
Sweden[3]	20.4	16.3	10.0	7.1	5.8	5.6
Switzerland[4]	–	15.3	10.3	7.7	7.4	7.0
New Zealand[4]	–	15.0	12.7	11.2	11.1	11.2
Netherlands	16.0	14.0	8.6	6.8	5.3	5.0
Australia[4]	–	11.3	8.9	7.4	6.5	6.5
Belgium	12.2	10.4	5.9	3.8	3.2	3.0
USA	12.1	9.7	5.6	4.2	3.6	3.5
UK	6.1	5.4	3.6	2.9	2.6	2.6

	1950	1955	1966	1973	1979	1981
(b) *Industry*						
Italy	–	29.2	36.9	39.2	37.7	37.5
Japan	23.2	24.8	32.7	37.2	34.9	35.3
Finland[4]	–	31.7	33.8	35.7	34.4	34.8
Austria[1,2]	36.3	40.0	40.1	40.6	40.1	39.5
Iceland[3]	32.1	34.3	38.2	37.6	38.0	37.4
France	–	36.2	39.9	39.7	36.3	35.3
Norway	31.2	33.0	33.7	33.9	30.1	29.3
Iceland	–	34.9	37.2	33.8	32.5	29.3
Canada	33.9	34.0	33.6	30.6	28.9	28.3
Luxemburg	–	43.4	46.9	44.3	38.8	38.1
Germany	41.7	45.5	48.2	47.5	44.4	43.5
Sweden[3]	38.4	41.9	41.6	36.8	32.5	31.3
Switzerland[4]	–	44.8	46.9	44.1	39.3	39.3

New Zealand[4]	–	35.3	36.4	36.1	33.6	32.6
Netherlands	39.5	40.1	40.5	36.5	32.5	30.2
Australia[4]	–	37.9	37.0	35.5	31.3	30.6
Belgium	45.6	46.1	44.8	41.5	35.5	33.4
USA	36.7	37.6	36.3	33.2	31.3	30.1
UK	46.6	47.9	46.3	42.6	38.8	35.7

(c) *Manufacturing*

	1950	1955	1966	1973	1979	1981
Italy	–	20.0	25.8	28.5	26.7	26.1
Japan	–	18.4	24.4	27.4	24.3	24.8
Finland[4]	–	21.3	22.8	25.4	25.8	26.1
Austria[2]	–	29.8	29.8	29.7	29.5	29.7
Iceland[3]	21.5	23.7	25.5	25.2	26.9	26.3
France	–	26.9	28.7	28.3	26.1	25.1
Norway	22.0	23.1	23.7	23.5	20.5	20.2
Denmark	–	27.5	29.0	24.7	23.3	21.3
Canada	24.9	24.1	23.9	22.0	20.0	19.4
Luxemburg[3]	–	33.2	35.8	33.8	28.3	27.4
Germany	–	33.8	35.2	36.7	34.5	33.6
Sweden[3]	–	31.7	31.2	27.5	24.5	23.3
Switzerland[4]	–	36.1	37.8	35.0	32.3	32.0
New Zealand[4]	–	23.7	25.4	25.7	24.2	24.0
Netherlands	29.3	29.3	28.9	25.7	22.3	21.1
Australia[4]	–	29.6	28.6	25.6	20.2	19.4
Belgium	35.0	35.3	33.6	31.8	25.9	24.7
USA	27.9	28.5	27.8	24.8	22.7	21.7
UK	34.8	36.1	34.8	32.3	29.5	26.4

(d) *Services*

	1950	1955	1966	1973	1979	1981
Italy	–	30.0	37.9	42.5	47.4	49.1
Japan	31.4	37.3	45.1	49.4	53.9	54.7
Finland[4]	–	30.1	37.2	47.2	53.8	54.1
Austria[1,2]	29.0	29.4	38.5	43.2	50.6	51.7
Iceland[3]	30.2	37.9	43.3	46.7	49.9	50.9
France	–	37.1	42.8	48.9	54.7	56.2
Norway	40.6	42.8	49.6	54.7	61.3	61.7
Denmark	–	43.3	48.6	56.7	60.3	63.3
Canada	42.9	48.0	57.4	62.8	65.4	66.2
Luxemburg[3]	–	38.7	41.6	47.8	55.3	56.3
Germany	34.5	36.7	41.2	45.0	49.8	51.0

Sweden[3]	41.2	41.8	48.4	56.1	61.7	63.1
Switzerland[4]	–	39.9	42.8	48.1	53.2	53.6
New Zealand[4]	–	49.7	50.9	52.8	55.4	56.1
Netherlands	44.5	45.9	50.9	56.7	62.2	64.8
Australia[4]	–	50.8	54.1	57.1	62.2	62.8
Belgium	42.2	43.5	49.3	54.7	61.3	63.6
USA	51.2	52.7	58.1	62.6	65.2	66.4
UK	47.3	46.7	50.1	54.5	58.6	61.7

Notes
[1] Initial year is 1951.
[2] Figure in second column refers to 1956.
[3] Figure in second column refers to 1957.
[4] Figure in second column refers to 1959.

Definitions
Agriculture – agriculture, forestry and fishing,
Industry – mining and quarrying, manufacturing, construction, gas,
electricity and water.
Services – all other civil activities.

SOURCE   OECD Labour Statistics (various) and Bairoch (1968). The
statistics used in these publications have been used to construct consistent series.

2
The Legacy Lingers On: The Impact of Britain's International Role on its Internal Geography

DOREEN MASSEY

1. The Argument

The 'British regional problem' has changed, almost beyond recognition, a number of times in the last two centuries or so. The general story is well known. For much of the nineteenth century the dynamic areas of the country were in the north and west. Many of the areas which we now think of as prosperous were in the depths of agricultural depression. By the 1920s and 1930s this picture was changing fast. It was the industrial regions of north and west where were to be found the highest rates of unemployment and some of the worst levels of poverty. The newer industries, this time around, were clustered more in the south and east of the country, and in the Midlands. In terms of many of the basic measures of social inequality the geography of the country had to a large extent been reversed. It is one of my contentions in this paper that we are at such a turning-point now, that the changes in the national economic geography which have, in different ways and at varying paces, been under way since the mid-1960s, mark just such another structural shift. What we are experiencing at the moment is a change of a magnitude not dissimilar to that of half a century ago.

There are new areas now with disastrous levels of unemployment – the inner cities and the West Midlands above all – to add to the old. There are new structures and patterns of inequality. The concentration of high-status and high-paid jobs in what has come to be called the British Sunbelt, while the rest of the country gets – if it gets jobs at all – relatively de-skilled and low-paid jobs in production, is the most obvious and celebrated feature of the new geography of the British economy.

The purpose of this chapter is to set these changes in a wider context. There are obviously many causes, at many different levels of explanation, which lie behind these geographical shifts. What I want to emphasise and explore is one particular aspect, one particular thread of that explanation, that of *the continuing influence of Britain's historical international position*. A focus at this level is by no means meant to provide a complete explanation for what is happening to the internal geography of the country. It clearly does not, and other papers in this collection will explore different aspects of that causal structure. But this, none-the-less, is an element of the explanation which it is particularly important to highlight, for it forces us into consideration of the broader perspective and the longer view.

We are used to pointing to the countries of Africa, or of South America, and explaining how their internal spatial structures (or at least that part of those structures which is marked on our maps) reflect clearly the international role and position of those countries – in other words, their previous colonised status. The dominant ports, the focused transport systems, the superimposition of external orientation of one sort or another on a previously-existing form of indigenous economy and society, are all a clear reflection of a country drained for export by those we now call the First World.

It is perhaps less often recognised that much the same kind of framework of analysis applies also to the UK – that understanding the internal organisation of the British economy, its regional differences, the rise and fall of its cities, cannot be done by focusing only on the internal organisation of Britain. It is necessary, in parallel fashion, to place the UK economy also in its international context, to understand its changing international role. The difference, of course, is that the British economy – or British capital, anyway – has for long been on the dominating end of international economic relations.

2. The Inheritance

In the nineteenth century, in so far as levels of unemployment and wages were concerned, some of the most serious social distress was in the agricultural south and east of England. In terms of industrial jobs the focus of the dynamic of growth was in the regions of the west and north. It was coal, ships, cotton, iron and steel which led the way. Even migration was in the opposite direction from that of a century later, with Poor-Law women and children being shipped north as cheap labour for the factories there. Internal geography reflected international role. The very dominance in the economy of this range of industries, and their dominance therefore in the spatial economy too, was a result of Britain's superordinate world position. The story is often told of this country's early start in modern industry, its commitment to free trade (the competition it could win) and to its manufacturing role within that. In some cases, such as coal-mining and shipbuilding, the growth of an industry in Britain simply reflected this dominant role. In others the expansion of British industry clearly entailed decline elsewhere. The rise of the cotton industry in Lancashire and the west of Scotland necessitated the destruction, among others, of flourishing textile industries in Egypt and India. Nor, it should be remembered, was it just, or always, a matter of free and fair competition. India's textile industry was undermined by monopoly and trade barriers. The British East India Company gained a virtual monopoly over the purchase of India's exports and forced down prices to the point of bringing ruin. Meanwhile, back home, the British government levied massive duties on Indian imports while British goods entered the Indian market at will. 'Had this not been the case', wrote Horace Wilson, 'the mills of Paisley and Manchester would have been stopped in their outset, and could scarcely have been again set in motion, even by the power of steam. They were created by the sacrifice of Indian manufacturers' (quoted in Clairmonte, 1960: 87) (Buchanan, 1982, p. 29). Britain's domination, its international role, was more than in terms of the economics of the market.

More generally the spatial division of labour being established in the UK in that period was the result of the other end of those international relations which were at the same time building the port-focused urban and transport infrastructure of 'the colonies', and of much of what was to become the Third World. From the UK point of view, we look back now with the wisdom of hindsight and point to the problems of the heavy-industry Development Areas as a result of their domination by these one or two major sectors of production. But it didn't look like that in the nineteenth century. The early British Empire, and British dominance of world trade, was built on the backs of these areas, and on the labour of the people of these regions.

Nor was that growth, even in these regions, entirely unproblematic. Apart from the appalling conditions suffered by a massively expanding working class newly crowding into towns, the international strategy adopted – the form of the growth – produced its own problems, even for the regions where growth was concentrated. For they suffered from the chronic instability of the trade cycle, an instability which was 'part of the price Britain paid for an apparently prosperous industrial system based on exports rather than indigenous demand, and it seems clear that the burden fell most heavily . . . on those regions which created [that] prosperity' (Southall, 1983). Instability was an effect, not of growth itself, but of the nature of that growth – of British capital's particular place in the world economy.

And just as it was the growth of Empire and international dominance which created the spatial structures of a century ago so it was the decline of that dominance which was at the heart of the regional problem which has preoccupied us for most of this century.

Again the story is well known; of how changes in international production and trading patterns, the economic decline of British Empire and of wider British dominance, the reorganisation of the international division of labour, brought with it the collapse of the economies of South Wales, the north-east of England, central Scotland and Lancashire. Those who had worked in the basic industries of these regions now began paying the price for British capital's nineteenth-century international role.

But this emergence of the British regional problem of the 1920s and 1930s was not a result *only* of the decline of Britain's international role and certainly not only of forces external to the country. The devastation which was wrought on many of the peripheral regions of the country through this period was also in part a result of the attempt by the British state to *maintain* an international position which seemed to be slipping away. The victory of the banking establishment in getting a return to the gold standard had major geographical effects. Industries working for export markets – engineering, coalmining, heavy industry more generally – were hit hard; wages fell further and unemployment rose higher. And the impact, necessarily, was felt hardest in 'the continued depression of the old high-wage areas of the north and west' (Foster, 1976, p. 16). The subsequent attempts to maintain the value of sterling only reinforced the effect. Even revenge against a potential international rival took precedence over the economic health of regions of Britain already suffering greatly: 'At the beginning of the slump in the mining industry only particular coalfields chiefly dependent on the export trade were seriously affected. The conditions for reparations imposed upon Germany under the Versailles Treaty played no small part in this. France, Italy and Belgium, which formerly were customers of the coalfields of South Wales, Durham and Scotland, no longer needed to import the same amount of British coal because of the large supplies of reparation coal which they were receiving from Germany' (Hannington, 1976, p. 32). In other parts of the country the effect was very different. The war itself had created protected conditions for the rise of a new range of industries, this time serving the domestic market. These new elements of the industrial structure were mainly located in the South-East and Midlands of England and with the end of the war and the return to the gold standard tariffs were in many cases retained (for instance on cars and electrical goods). Service trades, too, again largely based in the south and east, continued to flourish. For all these sectors of the economy wages rose, a fact which could only further have added to the market-pull of the South-East and Midlands as a location for the consumer-goods industries which expanded in the interwar years. It was not just changing international economic position, but British economic and political international *strategy* which lay behind the gross inequality of the country's internal geography during the interwar period.

Sometimes that age is now looked back upon as though from another planet. But many of the themes of that period are still with us today. First, and most generally, Britain's international position, and changes in its position, are still fundamental to its internal economic geography. Second, that international position stems both from economic forces and from political strategy, a strategy of a particular form of international orientation which has been as contradictory for the internal geography of the UK as it has been for its national economy. And third, and most problematical politically, many of the waves of decline that have hit the British economy, and reduced the former prosperity of its regions, are the result of the decline of an international dominance which it would be extremely difficult on a wider political canvass to defend.

3. The Issues Today

As was argued in the beginning of this chapter, the last twenty years have seen another major shift in the economic and social geography of Britain. And once again this major structural reorientation in internal geographical patterns and relations can only be understood in the context of shifts in the UK's international position. Once again, changes in internal geography are in an important part a reflection of international changes. There is a whole series of ways in which this influence of shifting international relations on internal geography could be traced. The following sections focus on five aspects of present changes, all of them related to the central fact of de-industrialisation, and all associated with the changing international position of British economy.

Decentralisation of Production

In 1959 the geography of British manufacturing employment was dominated by the big cities and by the central regions of the West Midlands and the South-East. It was, in other words, a very different geography, almost the mirror-image, of that of the old coal–steel–shipbuilding complexes in the 'problem regions of the periphery'. The main concentrations of manufacturing employment, which together accounted for over half the national total, were: Greater London 18 per cent, West Midlands 8 per cent, Greater Manchester 7 per cent, the Outer Metropolitan Area 7 per cent, West Yorkshire 6 per cent and Clydeside 6 per cent (Keeble, 1976). In most of these areas the composition of these jobs was very mixed. The West Midlands, in Birmingham, still had a notable presence of those metal-bashing, small-capital industries which made that city for a while the centre of the workshop of the world. But by now there were other layers of manufacturing too, most notably in this region the multinationally organised car and associated industries. In all these regions, by the 1960s labour had become, in economic terms, quite strong. And it was in the 1960s that began the now famous relative decentralisation of manufacturing, from conurbations to less urban areas and from central regions to peripheral. The impact over a decade and a half was a quite considerable shift in the geographical balance of manufacturing industry in Britain.

One of the most crucial causes of this decentralisation of production was the pressure on British capital to cut costs. Urban labour, and labour in the old centres of manufacturing production, was better organised and commanded higher wages than some of the reserves of labour in less urban areas and in the periphery. The precise circumstances of decentralisation varied from industry to industry. In some engineering sectors it was importantly connected to technological change; in other industries it was much more simply a move in search of cheaper conditions of production. But whatever the individual particularities, one thing is clear: the decentralisation of production jobs which took place in the 1960s and the first half of the 1970s was in part a response to the pressures of increasing international competition – the threat of, and increasingly actual, decline of an old role. Previously 'guaranteed' markets were no longer guaranteed, new markets were more competitive, and increasing numbers of countries were engaged in the competition. The geographical reorganisation of British capital within Britain (as well as externally) was an important element in its early response to impending crisis.

De-industrialisation

It was on this already changing pattern that de-industrialisation made itself felt. The decentralisation had anyway itself been relative (the result of a net balance between growth and decline) and by no means always the result of actual locational change. The massive loss of manufacturing jobs has, in a sense, been clear evidence that the strategy of spatial restructuring did not work.

Since the mid-1960s the world economy has been undergoing

another reorganisation of its internal structure. It is slow and halting in its progress, but its effects on metropolitan capitalist countries are already considerable. In Britain these effects, reinforced by long-term structural weaknesses and monetarist economic policies, have been dominated by de-industrialisation. While all metropolitan capitalist economies have lost manufacturing employment, the decline in Britain has been particularly marked. Britain's international role as a manufacturing economy is under threat.

The geography of this decline is different from that of the 1920s and 1930s. This time it is not a few major sectors but virtually the whole span of manufacturing industry which is at stake. It is, in consequence, a much more general geography of decline. Not just a few regions, but almost all parts of the country seem to some degree or another to have been affected.

De-industrialisation hit the cities first, especially London. Indeed London had already been losing manufacturing jobs in the 1950s. The numbers are so spectacular they are difficult to comprehend. Between 1962 and 1982 London lost 60 per cent of its manufacturing jobs. And of course it has not just been London; city after city has seen its manufacturing base collapse. And the reason the cities have been hit so badly is not, to repeat, on the whole that firms have actually moved out to other locations; those jobs lost in the cities have been lost from the economy as a whole. Nor have the cities been hit hardest because their industrial structures were dominated by the most vulnerable sectors, those declining most at national level. Rather it has been that within each industrial sector the cities lost jobs earlier and faster than elsewhere. The reasons are complex and vary by industry, but if two elements were to be picked out as crucial to the broad explanation they would be the vintage of capital and the strength of labour. In the cities industry had the oldest plant and machinery and faced, very often, the best-organised labour. And in a sense the story of the geography of subsequent de-industrialisation is that of the loss of manufacturing jobs chasing both of those variables. After the cities, whole regions were affected, above all the former engineering regions of the country – the West Midlands and the North-West – as the wave of decline spread out from the major urban areas. Today few places seem safe. Manufacturing industry is closing down in non-central regions to which it decentralised in the 1960s (the 'women's jobs' in the Development Areas are now being lost, for instance). And jobs are being lost, too, in those smaller urban areas and free-standing towns only so recently thought to be immune. If 'the upturn' ever comes it is unlikely – without radical policy-intervention – to bring back many manufacturing jobs to major cities or to those regions where manufacturing industry once formed the economic core. In a sense, a major clear-out is under way, spatially as well as industrially, and the new industrial geography will look very different from the one we used to know.

This is important to recognise – that any new geography of private-sector manufacturing industry will look very different from the old. For what has been lost for good is an earlier generation and an earlier geographical pattern. And much of that decline, again, especially in the cities and the old engineering regions, is the decline of industry which could not ever have been there had it not been for a previous era of UK international economic dominance.

The Labour Movement

Decentralisation and de-industrialisation are both, then, responses to and results of, Britain's declining international role as a manufacturing economy. Together, they are having a major impact on the social and political geography of the country. For each wave of decline has taken with it, or has substantially altered, an era in the geography of the labour movement, too. The 1920s/1930s decline of the old basic industries of the peripheral regions, a decline still going on, has taken with it the unions and the geographical bases of traditional labourism. Today the wider collapse of manufacturing, in the cities and central regions, is taking with it other, very different heartlands: the rich diversity of the industrial mixtures of the cities, with their networks of trades councils, the newer brasher forms of militancy in some of later generations of big industry – the car workers of the Midlands being the most obvious example. Each of these has a very different political and organisational history, both from each other and from the big unions of the periphery. In both, history has been stronger on economic militancy than on wider political issues. In both there has been a far shakier attachment to Labour as a party. Just as the older industries in these regions were based in British international supremacy so that history is often claimed as the root of the conservatism of the unions that developed within them:

> working-class conservatism . . . its roots are much deeper and probably more profound in Britain than elsewhere in Europe. These relate to the impact of colonialism and imperialism on the formation of working-class consciousness. . . . The skilled craft unions of the last century benefited enormously from Britain's imperial role. Joseph Chamberlain had a massive base in the working class of the Midlands. This . . . still colours the modern labour movement. If you look at the divisions in the TUC you find that the skilled craft unions that grew out of the Empire are the extreme right of the movement. The engineers backed Healey in the struggle for Deputy Leadership – the electricians are virtually in the arms of the SDP. (Livingstone, 1983, p. 27.)

What is being built is very different. The newly tapped reserves of the peripheral regions and the less-urban areas still have to muster their strength. The new greenfield peripheral locations of the most recent years are not just different locationally – in the geographical conditions for organisation – and different in the kinds of workers they employ, they have also been established under very different economic conditions – those of general de-industrialisation. They are also being established in a period when, compared with the older layers of manufacturing investment, industry's locational flexibility both within the country and inter-nationally is far greater. All this together means that new invest-ment now in manufacturing industry takes place in the context of a desperate competition between workers and between regions. In that context management has been able to enforce conditions of trades union organisation (such as single-union plants) which are very different from those which have characterised British manu-facturing industry in its history so far.

Meanwhile in some of the cities a new kind of radicalism is springing up, formed in conditions very different from those of any of the older arms of the labour movement. It has little connection at all, very often, with organised manufacturing industry; indeed much of it brings together groups left behind by the tide of de-industrialisation, and those, for instance in the public sector, who are struggling to deal with its effects.

The City

But there is one part of the economy, and one geographical place, which has remained unscathed through both these major periods of flux when other sectors and other areas were in steep decline – the City. Its political and social importance must be evident to all, but the City is also important spatially. Most evident is its own geographical concentration, at least of its upper-echelon functions. Its very name is inextricably entangled with its location – 'The City'. And its dominant position has been an important element both in the size of the subsequent growth of the financial services sector in this country (outbidding for instance that of Paris) and in its location within the country. For while some aspects of Empire and international dominance may have waned, others have continued to prosper. While the price of a declining Empire was paid heavily in 'the regions', the City carried cheerfully on. There was, nor is there, little unemployment in Lombard Street and thereabouts. In an analysis of investment in offices, and the demand for office space, in London in the 1980s, Barras (1981) writes: 'Continued expansion can, however, be expected in financial services and associated professional services such as law and accountancy. This reflects the dramatic growth of the financial sector, compared to the industrial and commercial sectors of the British economy. Much of the growth in the City can be attributed to its development as an international financial centre over the past twenty years, with the establishment of the Eurodollar market and the inflow of foreign banks (there was a fivefold increase in their number between 1963 and 1979)' (p. 15). Even in the recent years of most rapid de-industrialisation the City has continued to expand. And it has continued to focus on central London. While insurance employment began to decentralise in the 1970s, employment in banking rose by about a quarter: 86 per cent of office employment in financial services is in London.

Individual Industries

The impact of the changing international division of labour and the mechanics of de-industrialisation can be picked up more precisely by examining the international organisation of individual industries, and Britain's place within them. Both are reflected in the changing geography of British manufacturing. In a range of sectors such as *clothing and some textiles*, with fairly straightforward international structures, the UK is quite simply and over the long term losing out. The problem is primarily one of costs, and the effects have taken a very definite geographical form. To some extent the pressure on costs has itself been spatially differentiated. For instance in London the clothing industry found itself caught between two elements of the changing international division of labour. On the one hand challenged by lower-cost producers elsewhere in the world it was also facing rising costs and increased competition for its own labour as London's pre-eminence grew as a world financial and service centre. Big capital in the industry shut up shop in London and went off in search of cheaper labour elsewhere. Sometimes it went abroad, to become itself part of the problem and to contribute to the relative de-industrialisation of Britain. Sometimes it sought out cheaper labour in the peripheral regions of Britain. At the other end of the sector small capital, unable simply to change location, had either gone to the wall or implemented a variety of cost-cutting practices which have, over the last decade, significantly worsened conditions in the city (Massey, 1984; Harrison, 1983). In *electronics*, where hierarchical divisions within production straddle the world, the UK's place is not on the 'top rung'. Certainly both R and D and all stages of production are present in the economy (unlike for instance, in the case of Third World countries), but it is an intra-national spatial structure weighted more towards production and development than it is towards research. And this is not only because we have incoming production investment from foreign capital (from Germany, Japan, the US), but also because some British facilities are 'headless' too. A noticeable amount of 'British' investment in advanced R and D in this industry has been and still is, in the US – from British capital's early involvement in Silicon Valley to the present-day INMOS facilities in Colorado. It is the same again with *the car industry*, another in which fragmented production structures are increasingly organised internationally. The recent struggles in Vauxhall over the production of the S-car were in fact about the place of British production facilities within an international structure. And the changing international organisation of an industry such as cars has other effects, too, on their supplier-sectors. A good example is the *iron-castings industry*, often owned by small capital, not internationalised, and until recently apparently invulnerable to imports. Today it is reeling. This is in part because, as an industry producing intermediate goods and means of production, it suffers heavily as a result of the changing international organisation of other parts of capital. The castings industry is now subject to competition from imports – but as a result of indirect, embodied imports, castings in imported cars and imported car-components. So the global reorganisation of big internationalised capital, and the UK's changing place within it, brings major problems in its wake for small national capital too. The economic base of the West Midlands suffers a further blow, and the geography of British industry undergoes a further change.

None of this is meant in any way to be a call for a 'nationalist' politics towards industry. It is an argument for setting the changing geography of the country in an international context, and therefore for understanding it in terms wider than a series of 'location factors'. There are other ways, too, in which the changing international context has had an impact – entry into the EEC being one of the more obvious. But it is possible to detect already from these changes some of the elements of the 'new regional problem' – the new declining areas on the one hand, and decentralisation of some of the more thankless tasks of production on the other.

4. The Character of British Capital

That, then, is something of the spatial form of de-industrialisation in the UK. But there are other ways, too, in which the international position of the British economy, and the international role of British capital, have an impact on the internal geographical structure of the country. One of the most significant of these concerns the social structure of British industry. The character of British capital is deeply marked by its history, and in particular by its long history of internationalisation. In that sense the impact of Empire is still very much with us; the legacy lingers on.

There are a number of ways in which that is so, and each has its geographical implication.

The Financial Sector

Most obvious is the dominance of 'the City'. We have already noted its geographical importance in terms simply of its own employment distribution. But the City is important spatially in other ways than that. This is a financial sector with a very particular character. It is well known for its speculative nature, its 'money' as opposed to production, orientation, its great reluctance to invest long term in industry. These are characteristics derived from an internationalised past. They have, as is well-recognised, wide-reaching effects on the evolution of the British economy. The strategies of the City and the merchants have always been more effective in advancing their interests in trade and overseas investment than in strengthening and expanding domestic production. Home-based manufacturing industry has over and over again seen its interests subordinated to those of the City.

The City's financial strategies also have more immediate impacts. The deep association between a speculative financial sector and the property sector has led to London site-costs which are the highest in the world. In part these high site-costs are due to the importance of London as an international financial centre (i.e. they are a result of demand for *use* by the City). But there are at least two other reasons which it is important to note.

First, there is the nature of the City's own investment strategies, for long with a deep inclination towards property. The boom in office development in London in the 1960s was intially led by independent entrepreneurs. But seeing the gains to be made, the larger financial institutions moved in more directly, in search of prime property investments. The nature of this demand – for long-term capital assets – restricted it spatially to prime sites, and in the City excess demand built up for offices, not for use but as investments. Such a structure led to values shooting up and yields consequently sinking, a situation which in turn led to rents rising through the mechanism of diminishing rent-review periods (Barras, 1981). In other words the nature of the financial sector's holdings in property – one aspect of its wider, historical, 'money'-orientation – has itself pushed rents up, and thereby produced a steeper slope than there might otherwise have been, within the London land market.

This geographical concentration within London is mirrored in the spatial distribution of development profits, and the decline is not just from central London to outer London, but also from London as a whole to provincial cities (Barras, 1981, pp. 35–6).

But there is another reason, too, why rents are so high, not only in the City but in much of central London.

A more fundamental explanation lies in the fact that office labour costs are much lower in London than in other European or American cities. Since labour costs represent the major component of office operating costs, higher rents can be extracted in London while still maintaining its overall cost advantage for multinational companies and financial institutions choosing between locations in different national centres. A study commissioned by the Location of Office Bureau (Economist's Advisory Group, 1979) has calculated these labour and rental cost differentials for six European cities using 1977 data. For secretarial, clerical and managerial grades, salary costs in London were between one-half and one-third of those in the other European cities; for the top executive grades relative salaries were even lower, at between one-third and one-quarter of European levels. In contrast, prime rental costs in the City were between two and three times those in Amsterdam, Brussels and Geneva, and one-third to one-half higher than those in Düsseldorf and Paris. As a result of these contrasting differentials, estimates of combined labour and space costs for the six cities, under various assumptions about the mix of employment and floorspace standards, show that central London location costs were only around half of those in Paris, Düsseldorf and Geneva, and at least 50 per cent cheaper than those in Amsterdam and Brussels. Furthermore, space costs amounted to nearly 50 per cent of total costs in the City of London, compared to 10–20 per cent in the other cities. For London's cost advantage to disappear, the use of floorspace would have to increase from the assumed 160 ft per secretarial worker to approaching 400 ft per worker, or average salaries in London would have to double relative to those in the other European cities (Barras, 1981, pp. 24–6).

There are a number of ironies here. A non-industrially-oriented financial sector finds its dreams come true in its own home-base where rents, asset-value-prospects and development profits are all extremely attractive. Yet it can benefit from that situation at the same time as remaining competitive internationally as a location –

it can see itself grow as a user too – as a financial centre. Within the international structure of the finance industry London has low local labour costs and high site-costs, and British banking capital benefits from both, as employer and investor.

But within London all this has a major effect on other industries. A number of big firms which owned their sites have simply taken advantage of the situation, sold up, and decentralised. But much of London's industry, particularly around the central areas, has for long consisted of small firms, often in the sweated trades, and working close to the financial margins. They are caught on both sides. To the extent that high rentals in the office sector wash over through the land market to site-costs more generally, location costs go up. And while London office wages may be low by international standards they are highly competitive for such industries, particularly at a time when they are themselves under pressure from lower-cost imports. While, as was pointed out in the case of clothing, many of the big companies have got out to find cheaper labour elsewhere, a lot of the smaller firms simply collapsed.

So while the financial sector continues to flourish, and to consolidate British banking capital's position within the shifting international division of labour, intranationally such a structure can only have hastened the precipitate decline of smaller and manufacturing industry within London. The double inheritance of London, as a centre of banking capital on the one hand and of small manufacturing capital on the other, is an extremely uneasy one.

Manufacturing

British manufacturing capital also has a particular structure, and again it reflects its particular historical inheritance. For in many ways British manufacturing industry is split in two. On the one hand there is a highly international and dynamic sector; on the other there is a small domestic industry turning over quietly when it can and not wishing to be disturbed (Gamble, 1981; Massey, 1984). It is not simply a split between big and little capital. For there is much relatively small capital which is highly international in its orientation. And there is a good number of medium-sized and even larger firms which wish for nothing more than to survive within their chosen line of production. More than anything else it is a question of international capital and domestic capital. It is a division known in most other metropolitan capitalist countries, but in Britain the initiative is with international capital (both financial and industrial) to an extent seen nowhere else. In no other metropolitan country is international capital so overwhelmingly *politically* powerful. In no other country, perhaps, is non-internationalised domestic industrial capital so backward and undynamic (compare it, for instance, with that of Italy). Yet at the same time British capital is still the second biggest agent of external direct investment in the world. In few countries of the First World are national capital and national economy so lacking in equivalence, and so un-consonant in their interests. While the British economy sinks, British capital continues to invest abroad. Andrew Gamble has spoken of 'one of the great paradoxes of British decline – why an economy performing so poorly should nevertheless have produced more multinational companies than any country apart from the United States' (1981, p. 113). It is not a paradox, of course, as he makes clear. The two things are part and parcel of each other.

And together they have a major impact on the British space-economy.

The social character of British industry is part of what lies behind the structural weakness of the economy, its high degree of vulnerability to de-industrialisation, the geographical results of which have already been mentioned. It lies behind the ease with which even 'our' industry may choose to put its pioneering R and D elsewhere.

The split within manufacturing capital can be seen clearly in industries such as textiles. On the one hand internationalised firms such as Courtaulds, with the world as their oyster, their degree of international mobility astonishingly high; on the other hand a host of medium and small domestic producers with backward technologies and somnolent managements. It is a split which was accentuated in the 1950s, the last clear decade before de-industrialisation set in. It was a decade when British capital's mode of expansion stored up still further trouble for the British economy. While little was done to modernise the physical base of British industry at home, British capital invested massively abroad. There was an equivalent inaction on the spatial front. Today the argument is often advanced that little can be done about geographical inequalities because of the situation of overall employment decline. The irony of such an argument is that during the post-war period of uninterrupted growth in manufacturing jobs in the 1950s in Britain almost nothing was done to redress spatial imbalances.

Today this character of British manufacturing capital poses serious problems for the different regional economies of the country. In the old Development Areas it is the branch plants of multinational capital, much of it British multinational capital, which are seen as the most likely source of new jobs. But their very multinationality makes them insecure bases on which to try to reconstruct a regional economy. All too often and all too soon they are closing down and moving on elsewhere. They are part of the branch-plant instability so afflicting peripheral regions. Just as such elements of 'British capital' are part of the problem for the economy as a whole, so too they are part of the problem for the regions.

Yet what is there, in the present structure of British industry, as an alternative? Boswell has aptly characterised much of the rest of the cotton-textile industry as "a story of smaller firms: of their obsolescence and decay, their dogged resistance to outside pressures, their persistent refusal either to adapt or go under" (1973, p. 114). This kind of capital, broadly speaking, is the most important element of what remains today of regional control in British industry. It does not offer much prospect of future growth.

And ironically of course those companies which are still based in the regions and which do show signs of dynamism, when they do grow now frequently internationalise their production. It is a story which can be told in particular for the economies of the North-West and the West Midlands. Such regions are particularly acute microcosms of the economy as a whole. Their de-industrialisation has been part and parcel of the internationalisation of 'their own' home-based capital. Success for local capital has not at all been the same thing as success for the local economy – or decent standards of living for local people.

So the different regions of the country are left with a range of unpalatable options, within the present spectrum of policy. They can become even more what many of them are anyway fast becoming: the often temporary branch-plant outposts of multinational capital. Or they can cling on to jobs in older, smaller firms whose survival until now has been a result rather more of inertia than of competitiveness; a refusal to die rather than a will to live. Or if they do see 'their companies' grow, they are all too likely also to have to watch them leave. Such are the implications today of the internationalised economy (and of British capital in particular) and of Britain's changing national place within it.

And it is this dominant multinational element in the economy (both international manufacturing industry and the City) which, above all, is structuring the new spatial division of labour, the emerging form of geographical inequality in the UK today. It is its spatial form above all which structures the emerging dichotomisation between the Sunbelt and the rest of the country. Its headquarters are separated from production and are overwhelmingly concentrated in London – and when it does decentralise it is rarely beyond the Outer Metropolitan Area. It is its research and development facilities which have provided the intial base of activity for that crescent of high-technology which curves round from the Severn to Cambridge. And it is its production-only branch-plants, with their routinised and low-paid jobs, which have led the decentralisation to smaller towns, less urban areas and peripheral regions.

So now we are faced with new kinds of regional problems: those resulting from external control and from the more general separation of functions between regions. No longer are the prime bases of regional inequality founded in differences in industrial structure. As that lesson has been learned it has also become largely irrelevant. Now it is the internal geography of multinational capital which is at issue.

5. Political Strategy

Much, therefore, of what has happened and is still happening to the geography of the British economy can be traced to deeper causes in the UK's changing position within the international capitalist division of labour. But the successive changes in that position have not been given by economic, still less by 'market', forces alone. It has also, fundamentally, been a question of politics. Past and present strategies of the British state have entirely failed to confront the fact that there is a contradiction between the health of the British economy and the particular form of the internationalised perspective and interests of the dominant elements of British capital. There is also a contradiction between the perspective and the geography of the British economy.

It is a contradiction which the British state has never faced up to, and the British Left now faces the results of it. For the Left the contradiction is that, while de-industrialisation is clearly producing untold hardship for many sections of the working class, devastating the economies of cities and regions, and undermining many of the organisational bases of the labour movement . . . while it is doing all of these things, it also has to be faced that the growth of the economies of regions whose collapse we now mourn was, after all, in different ways, built on British international and Imperial dominance. It would be a peculiar kind of internationalism on the Left which would seek to reassert that position. What is required is a strategy for the British economy which dares to question the nature of recovery, what it would mean and what it would be for, and which is clearly related to a strategy about Britain's role in the international economy and its international political position.

It is an element of policy where there is plenty of room for initiative. For a century of history of the British state shows it to be transfixed by a political and economic role once briefly held in the nineteenth century and no longer tenable. It was in 1903 that Joseph Chamberlain, Social Imperialist, argued from his Birmingham base that the free-market internationalism of the British state could bring only the ruin of de-industrialisation: 'sugar has gone; silk has gone; iron is threatened; wool is threatened; cotton will go! How long are you going to stand it?' (quoted in Gamble, 1981, p. xx). As one surveys today the wreckage of the Birmingham economy, the evidence is clear.

And the contradiction continues. In the twenty years since manufacturing employment began to fall in absolute terms, each dominant economic and political strategy has, in the end, and under one pressure or another, sacrificed the interests of the home-based British economy to those of banking capital and the internationalised sections of manufacturing industry.

I was looking again the other day at a study I did in the 1970s with Richard Meegan (Massey and Meegan, 1979). It was a study of the geographical impact, within the UK, of the intervention of the Industrial Reorganisation Corporation. And it was all there. The increase in production in the periphery, both non-central regions and smaller towns. The collapse of the cities as the problems of 'overcapacity' were dealt with – in these cases indeed problems which resulted from the build-up of home production in once-safe markets of the Empire/Commonwealth. The concentration of headquarters in London. The hierarchies of research and development and their focus on the south and east. The IRC was an attempt to drag the economy out of the doldrums. It did so by spawning and by reinforcing yet more big industry. In the process it actively reinforced the tendencies towards a new spatial division of labour, a new form of geographical inequality, of 'regional problem' in this country. What we did not focus on in our write-up of the IRC project, though we had much of the information, and indeed it is confirmed by others (Singh, 1975) was the other contradiction in the process. For not only did the attempt to 'modernise' the British economy reinforce new patterns of internal inequality it also had extremely ambiguous results even in relation to its main aim of national economic recovery. For the larger companies which were created were also more internationalised. The enhanced international competitiveness was marked not so much, or not only, by increased exports, but by investment abroad. Perhaps it is not only if the problems of the British economy are to be solved, but also if the glaring inequalities which at present exist between different parts of the country are to be attacked, that it will be necessary to challenge the political and economic position of British multinational capital, and the particular commitment to it and its international role so long maintained by the British state.

Bibliography

Barras, R. (1981) 'The Causes of the London Office Boom', in Barras, R. (ed.) *The Office Boom in London: Proceedings of the First CES London Conference* (London: CES Ltd).

Boswell, J. (1973) *The Rise and Decline of Small Firms* (London: George Allen & Unwin).

Buchanan, A. (1982) *Food, Povery and Power* (Nottingham: Spokesman).

Clairmonte, F. (1960) *Economic Liberalism and Underdevelopment* (Bombay: Asia Publishing House).

Economist's Advisory Group (1979) 'Factors Influencing the Location of Offices of Multinational Enterprises' (London: EAG Ltd).

Foster, J. (1976) 'British Imperialism and the Labour Aristocracy', in Skelley, J. (ed.) *The General Strike: 1926* (London: Lawrence & Wishart), pp. 3–57.

Gamble, A. (1981) *Britain in Decline: Economic Policy, Political Strategy and the British State* (London: Macmillan).

Hannington, W. (1976) *The Problem of the Distressed Areas* (Wakefield: E. P. Publishing Ltd).

Harrison, P. (1983) *Inside the Inner City* (Harmondsworth: Penguin Books).

Keeble, D. (1976) *Industrial Location and Planning in the United Kingdom* (London: Methuen).

Livingstone, K. (1983) 'Why Labour Lost', *New Left Review* **140**, pp. 23–39.

Massey, D. B. and Meegan, R. A. (1979) 'The Geography of Industrial Re-organisation: the spatial effects of the restructuring of the electrical engineering sector under the Industrial Re-organisation Corporation', *Progress in Planning*, vol x, part 3.

Massey, D. B. (1984) *Spatial Divisions of Labour: Social Structures and the Geography of Production* (London: Macmillan).

Singh, A. (1975) 'Take-overs, economic natural selection and the theory, of the firm: evidence from the post-war UK experience', *Economic Journal*, **85**, pp. 497–515.

Southall, H. (1983) 'Regional Unemployment Patterns in Britain, 1851–1914', unpublished Ph.D. Department of Geography, University of Cambridge.

3

The Restructuring of the Post-war British Space Economy

MICK DUNFORD AND DIANE PERRONS

1. Introduction

Our aim is to outline some of the principal changes in the regional geography of the UK since 1945. At the root of the restructuring of its geography is a continuously changing functional and spatial differentiation of the process of social reproduction. In complex societies the process of social reproduction is split up into a large number of functionally differentiated activities. At the same time a territorial division of labour is established in which (1) different branches of production or particular phases in the production of a single commodity, good or service are confined to particular districts of a country, and (2) a variety of aggregated regional complexes of intra- and interregionally interdependent functions of production, distribution, circulation and consumption are established (see Läpple and van Hoogstraaten, 1980, pp. 117–32; Dunford and Perrons, 1983, pp. 352–7; and Marx, *Capital*, vol. 1, pp. 470–80).

In this study most attention will be paid to the way in which the structure of the UK space economy has been reshaped by the changing social division of labour within the formal sector of the economy. Of course processes of employment change are simultaneously processes of occupational and social change and are closely bound up with changes in other aspects of the reproduction of the means of human existence and of human life. But only occasionally shall we be able to integrate these other dimensions of the changing regional geography of the UK into the argument.

By the end of the Second World War the UK economy had an industrial history that extended back well over 250 years. In 1948 manufacturing accounted for nearly 34 per cent of output and employment and industry for nearly 53 per cent, while agriculture, forestry and fishing were unusually small, accounting for 6.2 per cent of output and 5.2 per cent of employment (see Feinstein, 1972, pp. T129–30).

Within industry and manufacturing, sectors which were now old, including coal-mining, textiles, clothing, textile machinery, iron and steel, railway equipment and shipbuilding, still accounted for a high proportion of output and employment. In the years up to 1974 many of these sectors were to grow only slowly or to contract. In shipbuilding and mining, for example, output declined after the mid-1950s, while in textiles output growth was very low in spite of the expansion of synthetic materials production in 1964–9 (see Figure 3.1 and Table 3.1).

Yet new manufacturing industries had been developing, and in 1952–74 were to spearhead a process of unprecedentedly rapid growth in which an expansion of investment led to increases in productivity, increasing incomes, widening markets and, until the late 1960s, comparatively high profitability. Most growth in output occurred in (1) electrical engineering, with the spread of electrical consumer goods, the expansion of the telecommunications network, the electrification of the railways and the development of new weapons systems, and (2) chemicals, coal and petroleum products and rubber and plastics production included under other manufacturing (see Figure 3.1). At the same time consumer spending shifted away from food and clothing and footwear and towards vehicles, electrical household goods, and housing.

Inequalities in the levels of capital investment and in the rates of productivity growth in different sectors meant that changes in employment did not, as we shall see, mirror changes in output. In so far, in particular, as changes in the actual numbers of jobs were concerned, most of the largest minimum list heading level increases up to 1974 were recorded in motor-vehicle manufacturing and in the production of radios, computers, and so on (see Wragg and Robertson, 1978, p. 89).

In our view an explanation of the way in which the social division of labour in the manufacturing and industrial sectors evolved rests as two sets of considerations. One concerns the way

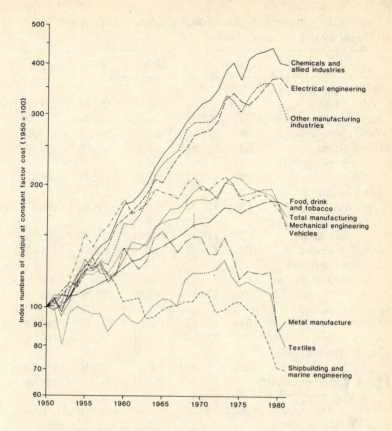

FIGURE 3.1 *Output at Constant-factor Cost by UK Sector, 1950–80 (index numbers, 1950 = 100)*

SOURCE GB: Central Statistical Office, *National Income and Expenditure*, various years

in which internal processes of development in the UK were shaped by the dynamic interaction of existing conditions on the one hand and a diffusion from the USA of processes of intensive accumulation and of monopolistic regulation on the other. The second concerns the particular way in which the UK economy was inserted in a new international division of labour and a new system of international economic organisation dominated economically and politically by the US (see Aglietta, 1982).

TABLE 3.1   *Output at Constant-factor Cost by UK Sector, 1950–81 (index number, 1950 = 100)*

	1950	1958	1966	1974	1981
Agriculture, forestry and fishing	100	116.07	146.70	182.03	203.80
Mining and quarrying	100	99.81	86.51	58.04	215.09
Total manufacturing	100	121.96	165.10	201.37	169.26
Construction	100	116.64	165.69	163.67	131.59
Gas, electricity and water	100	149.02	228.08	322.79	369.98
Total industrial production	100	120.94	161.85	188.80	180.71
Transport and communication	100	113.16	146.84	194.57	206.74
Distributive trades	100	116.44	148.29	174.27	175.62
Insurance, banking, finance and business services	100	123.81	163.79	275.69	331.38
Professional and scientific services	100	126.47	162.66	211.63	240.64
Miscellaneous services	100	107.60	135.41	150.13	160.44
Public administration and defence	100	98.05	100.43	109.36	113.83
Gross domestic product	100	116.71	152.01	182.41	186.88

SOURCE   GB, Central Statistical Office, *National Income and Expenditure*, various years

One of the most important concepts is that of an intensive regime of accumulation (see Aglietta, 1979, Boyer, 1978, and Lipietz, 1979). In the second and third quarters of the twentieth century the application of Taylor's principles of work-study and scientific management and of the assembly-line system, along with an emphasis on the production of goods capable of being produced in long runs and of yielding considerable scale economies, prepared the ground for a sustained rise in labour productivity in the equipment goods sectors. As a result one of the conditions which led to a steady expansion of the circuit of industrial capital was established.

At the same time the spheres of consumption and reproduction were transformed. On the one hand the wage relation was generalised with the result that increasingly large sections of the population had to satisfy the majority of their needs through the market. On the other hand a reduction in the cost of food and of other subsistence goods and an increase in real wages was associated with an enormous socially determined extension of human needs. And as wages came to be linked, via a complex of social and political processes, with productivity and the cost of living, mass consumption emerged as a corollary of mass production. But the spheres of consumption and distribution were radically changed not simply in order to supply outlets for new types of consumer goods and to harmonise the development of the two departments of production. They were also transformed in a way that enabled workers suited to the new kinds of production to reconstitute the energies expended at work and to preserve and reproduce the skills and attitudes they required (see Dunford and Perrons, 1983, ch. 12), while in this sphere capitalistically produced commodities were supplemented and complemented by services often provided by the state. In the fields of education, health and social security the state assumed a major role in the reproduction of individuals isolated from wider networks of support.

It was the consequent renewal of opportunities for investment that led, in many countries after the Second World War, to a spectacular development of (1) industries linked to the enlargement of the sphere of consumption producing housing, cars and durable household equipment, (2) industries connected with the transformation of the conditions of production, manufacturing machinery and durable producers' goods, and (3) process industries connected with the supply of energy and intermediate goods including electricity, oil and chemical and rubber products. In each case complex input–output relations existed. The increasing consumption of electricity led, for example, to a rapid expansion of industries producing generating, switching and transmission equipment and insulated wire and cables for national electricity–producing concerns.

But all nations did not develop in the same way. The process of development was differentiated according to the specific ways in which production and reproduction were organised and reflected the different economic, social and political complexions of each country. Moreover not only were there contrasting but often complementary patterns of international specialisation (see Aglietta, 1982), but also different economies grew at different speeds (see Figure 3.2).

Throughout the years of expansion of the capitalist world what differentiated the development of the UK economy was in part its specialisation in sectors that were contracting, its lack of competitiveness and its comparatively slow growth. Accordingly our account of the evolution of the economy of the country will also involve consideration of those factors which retarded its development and of the reactions of different social classes and the state.

In the early 1970s the questions of the direction of capitalist development and of slow growth acquired a new sense of urgency. A series of changes in industry and society in conjunction with a sequence of international events brought the wave of intensive accumulation to an end (see Aglietta, 1982). At that point the de-industrialisation of the UK economy was accelerated, with some of the growth sectors of the 1950s and 1960s joining the list of declining industries, the rate of inflation surged upwards and unemployment rose sharply. What expanded was the tertiary sector.

An expanding service sector had, in fact, played a major role in the post-war development of the economy. Output, which is difficult to quantify, increased in all service sectors except public administration and defence (see Table 3.1). But within the various groups some services declined, as in the case of private domestic service included under miscellaneous services, some followed the overall trend, many were transformed, as in distribution with the development of self-service and large chain stores to serve an increasingly motorised and suburbanised society, and some grew explosively. The most rapidly expanding tertiary activities included services to firms, functions connected with financial circulation, and health and education included under the professional and scientific category. And as productivity increased comparatively slowly, employment in these sectors increased particularly rapidly.

Occupational shifts supply a second way of considering the expansion of service work. What they highlight is an extremely sharp increase in white-collar employment from 30.9 per cent of

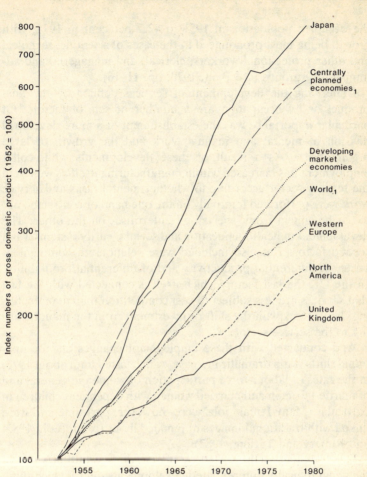

FIGURE 3.2 *Gross Domestic Product in the UK and the Rest of the World (index numbers 1952 = 100)*

[1] The country indices used for market economies were derived from official estimates of Gross Domestic Product at constant prices, while those for the centrally planned economies were obtained from data on gross output or net material product at constant prices. In calculating the world index use was made, in the case of market economies, of a series of indices relating to gross domestic product excluding services.

SOURCE   UN: 1969, vol. 2, pp. 157–86, and 1980, vol. 2, pp. 400–22.

the occupied population in 1951 to 42.7 per cent in 1971, with growth being most pronounced in the cases of scientific, technical and other professional workers, clerical, and managerial and administrative groups (see Bain, 1970, pp. 11–16).

Underlying the development of services defined by the final product or by occupation are a number of sets of factors. Of particular importance was the establishment of a more developed division of mental and manual work and the growth of large organisations. As a result of these developments white-collar employment has increased within manufacturing itself as well as in the tertiary sector according to whether mental tasks and service work were performed internally on the one hand or contracted out to, or bought in from, specialised enterprises on the other. The development of health, education and social security systems was a second factor. But also included were relations of complementarity, of differential productivity and of differential profitability. In the UK the last factor, which itself is connected with the fact that services are less subject to cost competition than manufacturing, helps to explain the shift of investment from the manufacturing to the service sector.

And connected with these employment changes and occupational shifts was a dramatic increase, which lasted until about 1977, in the rates of labour-force participation of women in general and of married women and married women with dependent children in particular. Many female jobs were, however, part-time and were linked with traditional images of female labour (see Joseph, 1983; and Rubery and Tarling, 1982).

In subsequent sections what we plan to do is to outline some of the geographically differentiated developments out of which these processes of expansion and contraction emerged.[1] The account itself will be developed chronologically with most emphasis on the period up to 1974. And into it we shall try to weave an interpretation of the way in which the macroeconomic developments to which they added up and actions of the state aimed at restructuring the economy and its constituent sectors, firms and regions interacted with and shaped changes occurring in particular localities and sectors.

2. The Years of Reconstruction 1945–52

In spite of a run-down stock of equipment and shortages of raw materials and fuel, a high and increasing level of output and a high level of employment were maintained in a context of 'suppressed inflation' (Pollard, 1969, pp. 364–76). It was manufacturing industry which expanded fastest and within manufacturing expansion was greatest in the metal manufacturing, engineering, chemicals and related sectors. As a result the composition of output was altered in favour of the new growth industries in the equipment and intermediate goods sectors.

The changing composition of output was a reflection not merely of the pattern of domestic demand, but also of exports. What was more, the war-related disruption of mainland Europe, and the general shortage of dollars, which acted as a constraint on trading with the technologically advanced US economy, enabled British industry to do well at first in European markets. In general, however, the economy was mainly geared to supplying markets in underdeveloped parts of the world and in the Commonwealth.

This particular pattern of trading was in part a consequence of a history of Imperial expansion. Yet it was also connected with a strategic outlook shared by virtually the whole of the political class. On this account Britain was situated at the centre of three overlapping circles of interest: the English-speaking North American community, the Empire and Commonwealth, and Europe and the Mediterranean, in that order (Barnett, 1983, p. 9). And in the field of international relations and international politics it was consequently intended that it should continue to play a major role, in spite of the underlying weakness of the national economy.

In the years of reconstruction output also increased in many of the branches that had led Britain's nineteenth-century industrialisation, as did employment, since attempts were made to meet the growth in demand by maximising the use of existing capacity and by investing only in a piecemeal fashion in new plant and equipment. In the coal industry, for example, output increased from a nadir of 175 million tons in 1945 to 204 million tons in 1950, while productivity only reached its pre-war level in 1950, in part because of the lack of investment in capital equipment in the years preceding nationalisation, but also because of the strategy of keeping open uneconomic pits in order to cope with the pressure for increased production from other sectors of the economy (Pollard, 1969, pp. 376–91).

Until the first of the balance-of-payments crises of 1947, 1949 and 1952 industrial expansion and factory building were particularly marked in the depressed regions. The construction of advance factories and the conversion of some 13 million square feet of surplus munitions factory space into plants for civilian production, along with the availability of labour, attracted industry to the Development Areas, while shortages of space and the use by the government at first of discretionary controls over the allocation of scarce building materials and, subsequently, of the Industrial Development Certificate system to ration and control the use of the limited resources available in the more prosperous regions, restricted expansion in the Midlands and the South-East.[2] As a result over 50 per cent of the new industrial building in the country occurred in the Development Areas in 1945–7, even though they contained less than one-fifth of the total population. And of the moves by manufacturing firms in the years 1945–50 almost exactly two-thirds of the employment provided in 1966 by those that had survived until then was in the peripheral parts of the UK (Brown, 1972, pp. 286–8).

The 1947 balance-of-payments crisis and the conditions attached to foreign loans led to cuts in expenditure on regional policy, to a relaxation of constraints on the location of export industries in the more prosperous regions and to a diversion of resources from capital formation to exports. In the years following the relaxation of controls on the location of industry increases in manufacturing employment in the growth sectors were concentrated in the Midlands and in the South-East. Whereas 51.3 per cent of approved new industrial floorspace had been located in the Development Areas in 1945–7, only 19.4 and 17.4 per cent were located in them in 1948–51 and in 1952–5 respectively (McCallum, 1979, pp. 8–9).

At the same time a striking growth in exports occurred. But the resulting improvement in the current balance-of-payments plus the proceeds from loans and from Marshall Aid were dissipated not in strengthening the precarious reserves, but in making foreign investments, in undetected exports of capital and in paying off some of the sterling balances. In the six years between 1945 and 1951 £1650 million were invested abroad, of which £350 million were invested by the public sector, while substantial amounts of money were spent on the maintenance of troops stationed in foreign countries (Pollard, 1969, pp. 356–64).

3. The Early Years of Expansion

The situation in the early 1950s is depicted in Figure 3.3. On the horizontal axis is recorded employment in each region, while the width of each column is proportional to the number of employees that would have been employed in the sector concerned if the structure of industry had been the same locally as nationally. The height of each column is proportional to the location quotient. If a column cuts the horizontal line drawn on the graph the location quotient exceeds one, and the sector concerned accounts for a higher percentage of employment in the region than in the country. The area of a column is proportional to total employment in the sector and region concerned. (The regional divisions are those that existed prior to the reform of local government in 1974.)

What it highlights is first the concentration of employment in London and the South-East. Within manufacturing, historically acquired regional sectoral specialisations were still very pronounced, with chemicals and textiles strongly represented in the North-West, mining and shipbuilding in the North, mining and metal manufacturing in Wales and shipbuilding, textiles and clothing in Northern Ireland. In the East Midlands high location quotients were recorded in mining, textiles and clothing and footwear, and in the West Midlands the manufacturing of metal goods and vehicles and modern engineering had high location quotients as did the production of non-metalic mineral products. But it should also be noted that 44 per cent of employees worked in the service sector. In general the service branches were over-represented in the south and east and under-represented in the old industrial regions of England and Wales.

In the years between 1951 and 1958 employers in many of the industrial sectors that had caused such problems in the Assisted Areas in the 1930s enjoyed protected markets or faced only limited competition, were making full use of existing capacity and carrying out some modernising investment, and seemed to be doing well. In 1951–2 the brief post-war boom in traditional branches of the textile industry came to an end, and employment declined, with the result that some of the areas in the North-West and in the West

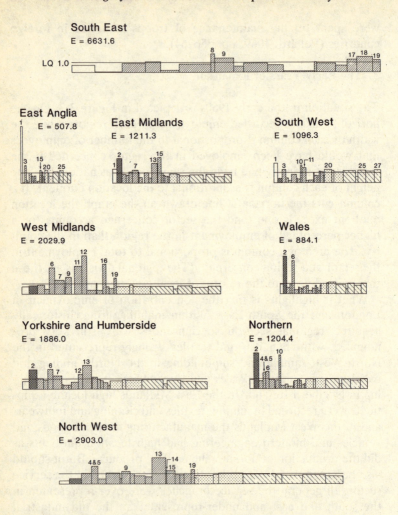

FIGURE 3.3   *Regional Specialisation in the UK: Employees in Employment by 1968 SIC Order and Region in 1952*

SOURCE   Based on statistics in S. Fothergill and G. Gudgin, 'Regional Employment Statistics on a Comparable Basis 1952–75', *Centre for Environmental Studies Occasional Paper No. 5* (Aug 1978) pp. 1–72.

Riding, where the losses in employment were concentrated, were given Development Area status in 1953. (The rates of growth and the actual changes in employment in the years 1952–73 are displayed in Figure 3.4). In the coal industry employment started to

South East (cont.)

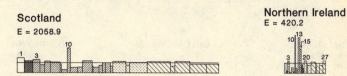

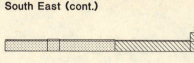

E = Employees in employment in 1952 (in thousands)

Number of jobs		Sectors
☐	5,000	☐ Agriculture (1)
☐	10,000	▨ Mining (2)
☐	15,000	▨ Manufacturing industry (3–19)
☐	20,000	▨ Non–manufacturing industry (20–22)
		▨ Services (23–27)

Standard Industrial Classification 1968

1. Agriculture, forestry, fishing	15. Clothing and footwear
2. Mining and quarrying	16. Bricks, pottery, glass, cement, etc.
3. Food, drink and tobacco	17. Timber, furniture, etc.
4. Coal and petroleum products	18. Paper, printing and publishing
5. Chemicals and allied products	19. Other manufacturing industries
6. Metal manufacture	20. Construction
7. Mechanical engineering	21. Gas, electricity and water
8. Instrument engineering	22. Transport and communication
9. Electrical engineering	23. Distributive trades
10. Shipbuilding and marine engineering	24. Insurance, banking, finance and business services
11. Vehicles	
12. Other metal goods	25. Professional and scientific services
13. Textiles	26. Miscellaneous services
14. Leather, leather goods and fur	27. Public administration and defence

fall in 1953, but did so only slowly and posed few problems of adjustment at first. On the other hand plans for the reorganisation of the coal industry were beginning to have important implications for the distribution of population in coal-producing regions. In Durham, for example, in which a high proportion of the pit closures were to be concentrated, the County Development Plan of 1951 included proposals for a key village policy aimed at channelling much of the area's employment and population, and a major part of the capital investment undertaken by the county and local authorities, into 70 of the county's 357 settlements, and at

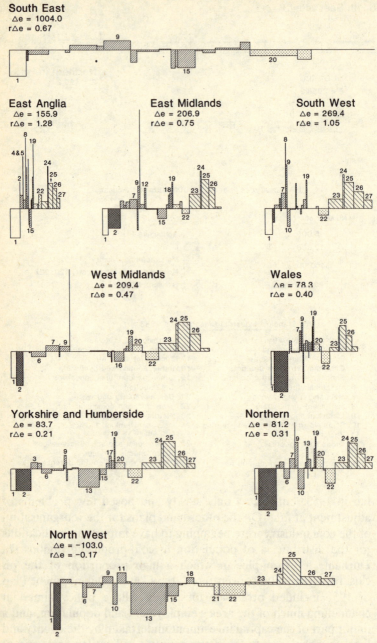

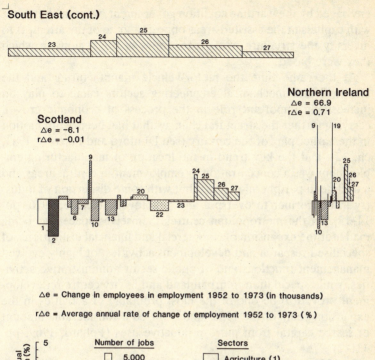

South East (cont.)

Scotland
Δe = -6.1
rΔe = -0.01

Northern Ireland
Δe = 66.9
rΔe = 0.71

Δe = Change in employees in employment 1952 to 1973 (in thousands)

rΔe = Average annual rate of change of employment 1952 to 1973 (%)

Average annual rate of growth (%)

Number of jobs
☐ 5,000
☐ 10,000
☐ 15,000
☐ 20,000

Sectors
☐ Agriculture (1)
■ Mining (2)
▨ Manufacturing industry (3–19)
▦ Non-manufacturing industry (20–22)
▧ Services (23–27)

FIGURE 3.4 *Growth and Change in UK Regional Employment: The Rate of Growth of, and Changes in, Employees in Employment by 1968 SIC Order and Region, 1952–73*

SOURCE Based on statistics in S. Fothergill and G. Gudgin, *op. cit.* pp. 1–72.

reducing considerably the population at first of 114, and subsequently of 121, settlements (Barr, 1969, pp. 523–5). But in the shipbuilding industry employment remained relatively stable, and in the steel and chemical sectors it increased.

As a result unemployment was at a low level in the depressed areas and in the country as a whole, and the regional policies, introduced in the 1940s as part of the programme of reforms envisaged by the wartime coalition government, were in abeyance, with capitals in the assisted areas opposing some of the attempts to diversify the structure of the economies of the regions in which they were based.

At the same time the motor-vehicle manufacturing and the electrical and mechanical engineering sectors came to play an increasingly important role in the process of economic growth carrying further the structural changes that had been set in motion in the earlier part of the century (see Dunford and Perrons, 1983, ch. 12), and the key trend in the location of manufacturing employment was a concentration of employment in central areas and a decline in peripheral regions, but with some dispersion of industry in the former to overspill and new towns (Keeble, 1976, pp. 14–15). In the metropolitan centres themselves space was being made for the expansion of commercial and financial institutions, of specialised research and development activities, of highly evolved management functions and of public sector administrative activities, while speculation in urban land and in city centre redevelopment proved to be one of the most profitable of activities in the expansion years of the 1950s and diverted a considerable amount of scarce capital from more productive uses (Pollard, 1969, pp. 431–2).

In 1958 a new recession coincided with an abrupt fall in the demand for the products of some of the traditional industries and an increase in competition on international markets, and led to massive reductions in capacity and in employment especially in the coal and shipbuilding sectors. In the case of coal-mining a major switch to oil as a source of energy coincided with a long-term fall in demand, caused by the adoption of increasingly successful techniques of fuel-saving, and with the beginnings of a switch to nuclear energy. The scaling-down of demand forecasts to a target of 206 million tons in 1967 allowed the closing of high-cost pits to proceed even faster than had been intended by earlier plans for the reorganisation of the industry. The number of National Coal Board mines in production fell from 901 at the beginning of 1951 to 438 in March 1967. A high proportion of the closures occurred in Scotland, the North-East, and South Wales, and production was concentrated on the fields in Yorkshire and the East Midlands (see also Figure 3.4). In the late 1950s the level of capital investment was raised as well. As a result productivity increased sharply, and the fall in employment was accelerated, with employment declining over the period as a whole from 711 000 jobs in 1952 to 419 000 in 1967. At this stage the reduction in employment occurred with a minimum of dismissals and redundancies and without arousing major opposition from the miners themselves. By contrast the announcement in a new White Paper in November 1967 of continuing contraction and of a reduction of employment to a mere 65 000 jobs in the seven main regions by 1980 was bitterly opposed in mining areas (Pollard, 1969, pp. 412–15, and Hobsbawm, 1976, pp. 253–4).

In the shipbuilding sector the industry in Britain was increasingly unable to compete with those in other countries in which more emphasis was placed on the construction of standardised vessels, or on the use of standardised components, and on the application of mass-production techniques and of a highly efficient technology. At the same time the number of ships afloat came to exceed the requirements of the shipping industry (Pollard, 1969, pp. 422–3). As a result output and employment fell.

The ending of the boom in coal and shipbuilding and in other traditional sectors, and the effects of a trough in the trade cycle on the steel industry, led to a sharp rise in unemployment in the depressed areas in particular.

In line with its role as a means of coping with localised unemployment, of maintaining social control and of reproducing the relations of capitalist production, regional policy was amended and intensified in two acts passed in 1958 and 1960 respectively, and regional policy expenditure increased from £3.6 million in 1958–9 to £8.6 million in 1959–60, to £11.8 million in 1960–1, and to £24.0 million in 1961–2 (McCallum, 1979, pp. 10–12).[3]

In 1958 it was also announced that Industrial Development Certificate policy was to be applied more rigorously, and pressures on firms to locate in the assisted areas were increased. One of the most famous examples was the government decision embodied in Macmillan's self-styled judgement of Solomon. In 1958 the government was faced with a choice between two strip mills, of which one was to be located at Ravenscraig in the Central Belt of Scotland, and one was to be located at Llanwern in South Wales. In the end the government succeeded in reducing the initial capacity of one of the projects and in having both of them constructed, meeting the steel companies' investment shortfall itself. As a result two suboptimal plants were simultaneously provided, of which neither could operate at full capacity, and of which at least one was badly sited (Cockerill and Silbertson, 1974, p. 54).

But the most striking movements of industry to the depressed areas at this time occurred in the motor-vehicle manufacturing sector. In the years of reconstruction the expansion of this sector and of other new consumption good industries was restricted by shortages of fuel and raw materials and by the priority given to arms expenditure and to the heavy industrial sectors (Aaronovitch, 1981, pp. 69–70). The level of output was nevertheless raised by a substantial amount, and the degree of concentration in the industry increased with six firms producing 85 per cent of the cars and commercial vehicles by volume and 60 per cent by value in 1948. In the 1950s output continued to expand rapidly, and the industry was modernised, in particular by the introduction of automatic transfer machines, but its competitiveness fell well behind that of the industries in other developed capitalist countries. Yet in the years between 1948 and 1959 investment and speed-ups were such as to enable the output of cars to be increased by 180 per cent with only an 18 per cent increase in employment (Pollard, 1969, p. 381), while employment itself was subject to marked oscillations, especially after the fall in home demand and the intensification of international competition after 1956, because of the hire-and-fire strategy of the employers in this sector and the stop–go cycles of the national economy.

By the late 1950s the expansion of the motor-vehicle industry in areas in the Midlands and the South-East, where land costs were high, and where shortages of workers were experienced, with the result that increases in productivity could only be achieved by giving way to wage demands, was posing difficulties for the employers, while speed-ups were generating resistance in the forms of strikes, stoppages, and absenteeism which were extremely costly. It was precisely at this time that many of the companies expanded by establishing new plants of which most, but not all, were located in the depressed regions. In March 1961 truck assembly started at the Ford Motor Company's new plant at Langley in Buckinghamshire. In 1963 the three Halewood plants on Merseyside, where construction had started as early as 1958, were completed. At the end of August 1964 an administrative headquarters was completed at Warley in Essex, and in September tractor operations were transferred from the Dagenham Estate to Basildon in Essex. In 1965 a new plant at Swansea extended the company's machining and sub-assembly capacity. At about the same time Rootes opened a new plant at Linwood in Scotland for the production of the Imp model, Vauxhall developed a unit at Ellesmere Port and Standard–Triumph one at Speke on Merseyside, and the British Motor Corporation opened a new works at Llanelli in South Wales and a commercial vehicle and tractor plant at Bathgate in Scotland (Friedman, 1977, p. 211, and Beynon, 1973, pp. 45–6).

The movement of some major new developments in this sector to the assisted areas was obviously in part a consequence of government pressure and the provision of grants and loans, but the state of the labour market was also of considerable importance. The existence of high levels of unemployment in the depressed areas chosen for new vehicle manufacturing plants enabled the firms moving to them to pay low wages and to impose conditions of employment on locally recruited workers that were worse than those prevailing in existing plants. In addition production could be organised in a way that was free from the job control that had been built up in long-established works (Beynon, 1973, pp. 64–6).

But whatever the reasons for these moves a significant growth of employment occurred in the assisted areas. In 1959 72 per cent of UK employment in the motor-vehicle manufacturing sector was concentrated in the West Midlands conurbation, the Coventry area, Greater London, the Outer Metropolitan Area of South-East England, and the Oxfordshire subregion. Only 11.8 per cent of the industry's workers were employed in Scotland, Wales, the North, and the North-West. But by 1968 22.4 per cent were working in these depressed areas. By 1971 employment in the five central subregions had increased by nearly 30 000 jobs, but it had nevertheless fallen to only 58 per cent of the total. On Merseyside employment increased from 1500 jobs in 1959 to 33 000 in 1971 (Friedman, 1977, p. 243, and Keeble, 1976, pp. 181–6. See also Figure 3.4).

In the end the recruitment strategy of the companies often foundered, in part because the new centres of production were also old centres of working-class militancy. But the main reasons for the problems faced by vehicle manufacturers in the 1960s lay in the industry's loss of the protection it had enjoyed and of international competitiveness, and also in the more general crisis of Fordism and of its characteristic mode of surplus-value production.

In the view of Aglietta (1979) the origins of this more general crisis lie in part in the fact that successive intensifications of the output norm are increasingly costly in terms of the means of production because of the technical rigidity of the machine system. As a result 'this method of raising labour productivity . . . makes investment propel investment on an ever more colossal scale, while markets must be expanded at whatever cost, with increasing risks of devalorisation of the fixed capital thus immobilised'. In addition limits are set 'by barriers internal to the labour process itself and by the class struggles that occur within it'. As the fragmentation of tasks is pushed to an extreme limit, at least three elements combine to prevent a further reduction in the amount of wasted time and even to reverse its direction. One is the increase in the balance delay time caused by imbalances on the assembly line itself. In the words of Aglietta 'this phenomenon derives from the fact that the spatial configuration of the assembly line imposes certain constraints on the disposition of the series of partial tasks, the result of which is that not all workers have a cycle of movements of the same duration'. The impossibility of distributing time equally leads to a total time lost equal to the sum of those periods spent waiting by the workers with shorter cycles. The amount of time lost in this way increases with the further fragmentation of tasks. The second is the contradiction between the subjection of the workers to a uniform but ever-increasing pace of work and the maintenance of the mental and physical equilibrium of the workers themselves and its consequences in the forms of high levels of nervous exhaustion, of accidents, and of absenteeism. The third is the erosion of individual accountability for the work performed and the growing problems of quality control in increasingly collectivised flowline systems (Aglietta, 1979, pp. 119–22). The responses of capital to these problems were new forms of internationalisation and neo-Fordism.

In spite of the intensification of regional policy and the diversion of new investments in the motor-vehicle manufacturing industry to the north and west of the country the problems of the depressed areas worsened especially in the years following the 1962 recession. The response of the government was to equip Hailsham with a cloth cap, in order that he could act in a suitably patronising manner, and to give him special responsibility for the North-East, which, with Scotland, was most hard-hit. At the end of 1963 White

Papers for central Scotland and for north-east England were issued in which growth zones or growth areas were defined and infrastructural investment programmes were proposed as parts of strategies for modernising and diversifying the structure of the economies of the two regions.

4. Slow Growth and Unequal Development: The Decline of the UK Economy

The construction of modernising blocs and the formulation of plans for modernising the economies of Scotland and of the north-east were part of a broader stategy of industrial modernisation. In the late 1950s increasing attention was being paid to the fact that the rate of investment and the rate of economic growth were much lower in the UK than in other advanced countries, with the result that the UK economy was being caught up and overtaken in *per capita* output by those countries which for centuries had had much lower incomes and products *per capita* than Britain (Figure 3.2 and Table 3.2) (Pollard, 1969, pp. 434–60, and Hobsbawm, 1976, pp. 256–62).

In all the main branches of industry the economy of the UK was behind its competitors in output and productivity growth owing to the low rate of return on capital, and to low investment and the low efficiency of capital. As a result profitability continued its downward path, and the competitivity of the economy was undermined. The methods of scientific management and Fordism on which, in those years, high productivity depended had in fact been less fully applied than in other developed countries, the structure of the industrial system had not been changed sufficiently radically, and modern consumption norms had been far from fully developed.

The gap that was emerging was of course the outcome of a long historical process. But its roots lay in a number of interrelated factors. Within the ranks of the industrial bourgeoisie the absence of a culture of growth, in conjunction with managerial and political weakness, were important factors in shaping the development of industry and its environment. Among other things they help explain why the education system and government policy were not harnessed to the achievement of industrial growth. What was more

TABLE 3.2 *Some Indicators of the Average Annual Long-run Rate of Growth of the Economies of France, the FRG and the UK (in percentages)*

Indices	1950–60			1960–70			1970–75		
	France	FRG	UK	France	FRG	UK	France	FRG	UK
Gross national or domestic product[1,2]	4.6	7.8	2.7	5.6	4.6	2.8	5.1	3.9	2.5
Exports[1]	6.4	16.9	2.4	8.9	8.1	4.9	9.0	7.6	4.8
Imports[2]	5.9	17.2	4.3	11.0	9.2	4.1	10.4	8.0	4.1
Implicit price of gross national product	6.5	3.0	4.0	4.4	3.5	4.2	6.0	4.5	7.6
Corrected implicit price of changes in the country's exchange rate	3.4	3.5	4.5	3.1	4.9	2.6	5.2	7.2	3.7

Notes [1] The rate of growth of Gross National Product in the period 1950–60 and of Gross Domestic Product in subsequent periods.
[2] In 1963 prices in the period 1950–60 and in 1970 prices in subsequent periods.

SOURCE Y. Barou, M. Dolle, C. Gabet and E. Wartenberg, 'Les Performances Comparées de l'Économie en France, en R.F.A. et au Royaume-Uni', *Les Collections de l'Insee*, series E, no. 69 (Nov 1979) p. 12.

the pattern of specialisation inherited from the past was such that capitals in coal, cotton, railways and heavy engineering were comparatively strong especially in the years when the foundations of the new regime of accumulation were being laid. In the new growth sectors of cars, chemicals and light engineering the international leaders were US firms. In Britain only second-league firms were to be found along with foreign multinationals, while some of the large national manufacturing firms that emerged after the Second World War were international financial groups more than manufacturing concerns.

British society was also characterised by the existence of a large, strong, well-organised and economically class conscious working class itself divided for historical reasons along craft lines. With the recognition as part of the post-war settlement of the right of workers to join independent trade unions, and in a context of full employment, the working class made some striking gains. On the one hand it secured a high degree of job control and was able to impede the introduction of new technology, changes in the technical division of labour and attempts by employers to increase the intensity of work: demarcation, apprenticeship, manning level, rate of work and overtime arrangements were all manifestations of this strength. On the other hand wages came to form a high share of the value added, and the welfare system was financed at least in part out of profits.

In the third place the separation of industrial and financial interests was linked with problems of financing industrial investment, while the strength and political ascendancy of the financial sector were connected with the priority given to a reserve function for sterling and high rates of interest and exchange and with the consequent harm done to the competitiveness of domestic manufacturing industry.

A fourth set of factors was related to the actions of a political class under whose leadership priority was given to an international financial function, an imperial role and substantial military spending that the economy could ill afford, and that diverted resources from the reconstruction of domestic civilian production.

In this situation a modernising bloc was unable to achieve hegemony. But until the early 1960s the retreat into protected Empire and Commonwealth markets, along with the development of the economy in an environment not subject to intense competition, hid underlying weaknesses: with low investment costs production could often proceed even with old and nearly exhausted machinery, the need to raise productivity was postponed, and conflict over an accelerated remoulding of the structure of industry was avoided. And what was observed in the early 1960s was mainly the severity of the external constraint. Structural weaknesses were not highlighted at first.

In fact the slowness of the growth process had led to a steady deterioration in the competitiveness of the economy and was itself reinforced by the stop–go policies to which the lack of competitiveness contributed. In the 1950s and early 1960s, in particular, the normal response of the government to an adverse balance-of-payments position was to slow down the growth process, mainly by blocking investment at home. As a result productivity increased even more slowly, and costs were increased by below-capacity working. Yet the exchange rate of sterling was maintained, and devaluation, which could have been used to lower export prices to the extent that firms selling abroad chose to adjust external prices downwards and did not merely use it as an opportunity for increasing their profits, was precluded largely because of opposition from financial interests and from the City of London in particular. In the absence of a fall in the value of sterling the lack of efficiency caused by slow growth was translated not only into a fall in the quality, but also into an increase in the relative prices of exports from the UK. As a result the share of UK exports in world trade declined very rapidly, and the country's underlying balance-of-payments position deteriorated.

In addition the lowering of import restrictions, and the transmission of the effects of slow growth and of the loss of export competitiveness to capitals serving the domestic market, led to the provision of insufficient capacity in many key branches of production, to high costs and to growing import penetration in the durable consumption and industrial equipment good sectors.

The unfavourable movements of commodity exports and imports which resulted, and the weakening of the country's trading position to which they contributed, ensured that any new wave of growth would unfold in even less favourable conditions than the one preceding it, and that it would lead even more quickly to balance-of-payments problems. In short an external constraint reinforced the problems posed by the structure of the industrial system and by the internal conditions of surplus production on which its growing backwardness as a capitalist system lay.

Yet in absolute terms exports had increased substantially in the years of reconstruction and in the period up to the middle of the 1960s, and the commodity trade balance of the UK had improved slightly, in part because of improvements in the terms of trade in the 1950s and early 1960s, while invisible and other private net earnings from abroad, which had languished, were nevertheless sufficiently large to more than offset the trade deficit in most years. What turned a strong positive balance on the current private account into an overall deficit was net government expenditure abroad, of which a high and increasing proportion was composed of military expenditures, net capital investment abroad by the government and net foreign investment abroad by the private sector, whose aim was usually one of opening out and developing markets and supply areas in foreign countries, and on which some of the country's invisible earnings depended. It was in fact in this context that the dependence of the economy on the attraction of short-term capital from abroad, which itself involved keeping up interest rates and the exchange value of sterling, and on loans from international agencies assumed considerable importance.

5. Towards a Strategy of Industrial and Regional Modernisation

In the late 1950s and in the early 1960s an important turning-point in the development of the state occurred. The nationalisation of some branches of production and the loss of colonial and Commonwealth markets either had weakened or were in the course of weakening the position of some sections of the dominant classes and were enabling modernising factions to gain a certain degree of hegemony within the ranks of industrial capital. At the same time the need to reorganise the international trading relations of the UK economy, to increase the competitiveness of its manufacturing base, and to surmount the obstacles to growth posed by the external constraint and by stop–go policies led to considerable pressure for a state strategy aimed at achieving a more rapid rate of economic growth. What emerged was the setting up of an indicative planning system on the French model and a reorganisation of the state apparatus along with the development of a corporatist tripartite framework of state, industry and trade unions to deal with questions of planning, resource allocation and growth. One of its corollaries was a reconceptualisation of the regional problem and of regional policy by the state and by industrial capital.

At the end of 1961 the National Economic Development Council (NEDC) was set up with a view to clearing a path for a 4 per cent rate of growth, and the squeezes were designed so as to have as small an impact as possible on investment and production, while a variety of measures aimed at ensuring that resources were used more productively were introduced. It was at this stage that leading sections of industrial capital started arguing for a more active regional policy as part of a state strategy for growth.

In 1963 a pamphlet published by the Federation of British Industries accordingly included arguments in favour of higher financial incentives, a more rigorous application of Industrial Development Certificate policy, the designation of growth areas, an increase and acceleration of public investment programmes aimed at improving economic and social infrastructures in the assisted areas to which expanding industries were to be diverted, and the establishment of autonomous regional planning agencies with industrial representation (Federation of British Industries, 1963).

In the same year the National Economic Development Office published two major reports. The report on the *Growth of the United Kingdom Economy to 1966* was a study of the implications of an annual growth rate of 4 per cent for the period 1961–6, while the one entitled *Conditions Favourable to Faster Growth* was a policy-oriented document suggesting some of the ways in which the public and private sectors would have to act in order to achieve the prescribed rate of growth. The second of these two reports included a long discussion of the regional question in which it was pointed out that a policy of making full use of the country's resources of labour and of drawing on the labour reserves to be found in areas with high unemployment and with low activity rates would make a substantial contribution to national economic expansion, especially in view of the expected emergence of acute labour shortages in the near future. In particular a strategy of moving work to the workers was thought to be the only satisfactory way of tapping the reserves of female labour available in the old industrial regions and in the South-West: women whose husbands were working were not geographically mobile. In addition the authors of this report pointed to the fact that a growing concentration of employment and population in congested areas in the Midlands and in the South-East was creating serious problems in the form of high costs of public service provision, inflationary pressures on land prices and wages, and increased traffic congestion, while social capital in the depressed areas was being under-utilised. It was this type of argument which led to the advocacy of an extension of controls over the location of industry to the office sector. At the same time it was being argued that a reduction in regional inequalities in the distribution of unemployment would make it possible for higher levels of aggregate employment to be attained without generating wage inflation which, at that time, was being transmitted by national wage-bargaining procedures to all regions as soon as unemployment fell to low levels and wages increased in the Midlands and in the South-East. What was more, it was maintained that the tendency of the market to concentrate economic activity in existing centres is not a good indication of the disadvantages of remoter locations, not only because of the social costs of congestion, but also because of the importance of externalities and of the inability of the market to co-ordinate the decisions of individual firms. In effect what was being claimed was that situations often arose in which each of a group of firms whose activities were complementary would have chosen to locate in a new area if the others were already present, but in which none of them would have chosen to set the process in motion in the absence of knowledge about the intentions of the others. Only through some form of planning could such a problem of co-ordination be solved (McCallum, 1979, pp. 13–4, and Hardie, 1972, pp. 218–22).

In 1963 the incentives available for firms locating and expanding in the assisted areas were extended and strengthened in the Local Employment and Finance Acts passed by the Conservative government,[4] and in the same year the Location of Offices Bureau was set up to advise on and to promote the decentralisation of office-building and office employment from London (McCallum, 1979, p. 14).

In 1964 the Labour Party won the General Election. Soon after its election the new government established the Department of

Economic Affairs with the intention that it should assume a leading role in the fields of overall economic management and economic planning. In each of eleven Economic Planning regions a Regional Economic Planning Council composed of local business-people, trade unionists and local notables was appointed to advise on the elaboration of a broad strategy for regional development and on the formulation of regional plans, and a Regional Economic Planning Board composed of civil servants was set up to co-ordinate the activities of different departments at a regional level and to act as the nucleus of an integrated regional branch of the administration.

At first the government worked within the framework of the 1960 and 1963 Local Employment Acts, but it increased expenditure on regional policy, added 16 more areas to the list of Development Districts, and tightened Industrial Development Certificate control, and at the beginning of 1965 it introduced the Office Development Permit system. In the same year *The National Plan* was published. In it a major emphasis was placed on the role of regional policy as an instrument of national economic planning, as had been done by the National Economic Development Council in the early 1960s. At the end of the year the Highlands and Islands Development Board was set up with very wide powers 'for the purpose of assisting the people of the Highlands and Islands to improve their economic and social conditions and of enabling the Highlands and Islands to play a more effective part in the economic and social development of the nation, (Carter, 1974, pp. 279–311), and in 1966 a plan for Scotland was published.

In August the government passed the Industrial Development Act of 1966. It contained two important measures. One was the replacement of the 165 Development Districts by 5 broad Development Areas, in which firms could locate in centres with real growth potential and were not confined to districts with exceptionally high levels of unemployment and limited prospects of development. In addition the system of incentives was radically altered to fit with a new investment grant system.[5] In particular the 10 per cent grant for investment in plant and machinery and the free depreciation provisions of 1963 were replaced by a 20 per cent grant for investment in plant and machinery in the manufacturing, extractive and construction sectors anywhere in the country and a 40 per cent grant in the Development Areas and in Northern

Ireland. In 1967 and 1968 these grants were raised as a temporary measure to 25 and 45 per cent respectively. But at that time the part of a firm's investment that had been financed by a grant could not be included in the sum that it could deduct from its tax liability as depreciation, and so the real value of the grants was less than it appeared to be at first sight. Similarly the margin of advantage enjoyed by a firm locating in a Development Area as compared with one carrying out the same investment elsewhere in the country was less than the difference in the rate of grant.[6] But in contrast to earlier provisions the new grants were in no way conditional upon the creation of extra employment. As a result they could be used to help finance replacement investment which created no new jobs and which even involved a reduction in employment.

The aim of the grants was in fact one of increasing the rate of investment nationally, of restructuring and increasing the efficiency of industrial capital, and of increasing the international competitiveness of the national economy. Indeed the White Paper in which the proposals of the government were originally set out was presented to the House of Commons for approval with the White Paper on the Industrial Reorganisation Corporation as complementary parts of a programme of industrial modernisation in which questions of equity were to play a part. The main function of the Industrial Reorganisation Corporation was to accelerate the pace of rationalisation of industry by encouraging mergers and regroupings with a view to increasing the efficiency and competitiveness of the national economy. But it was also given the right to advance funds to help finance projects of special importance for the national economy, of which the pulp and paper mill which had been built at Fort William and the strip mills constructed at Ravenscraig and Llanwern were cited as examples. The main aim in giving grants was also, however, one of concentrating assistance on, and stimulating investment in, those sectors of the economy capable of making a major contribution to the task of maintaining and increasing the economy's share of world trade or of enabling firms based in this country to compete more effectively on the home market and of reducing the dependence of the national economy on imported goods (Great Britain: Parliamentary Debates (Hansard), 1966, cols 1119–29 and 1247–48). In September 1967 the Regional Employment Premium was introduced. It was a subsidy paid in respect of all manufacturing employees in the

Development Areas, and was administered through the Selective Employment Tax system, which had been set up to tax service employment and to subsidise employment in the manufacturing sector. In the view of Kaldor it was equivalent to a 5 or 6 per cent reduction in the efficiency wage in the depressed areas, and it was intended to have the effect of a regional devaluation, as a fall in the efficiency wage was expected to increase the competitiveness of manufacturing industry in the Development Areas and to stimulate a cumulative spiral of export-led growth (Kaldor, 1970, pp. 337–48, and 1972, pp. 1237–55).

In November 1967 the government announced the designation of a number of Special Development Areas in which additional rates of benefit were to be enjoyed. At first they were almost exclusively small coal-mining districts hard-hit by the accelerating rate of colliery closure of that time. In 1970 a number of small Intermediate Areas were designated in which some of the benefits available under the Local Employment Acts were to be provided, while in 1968 a new system of town and country planning had been introduced.

A process of industrial modernisation will only succeed if an ambitious programme of research and technological innovation is accompanied by a corresponding transformation of social and political relations and supporting macroeconomic policies. Neither of the last two necessary conditions was present. In particular in the years between 1964 and 1968 a succession of balance-of-payments crises led, as a result of a characteristic bending of the Labour Party in power to pressure from 'an all-powerful Treasury that was totally subservient to the doctrines and appraisals of the City transmitted by the Bank of England', to a long squeeze, and the plans for long-term modernisation were abandoned (Pollard, 1969, pp. 481 and 483).

The rate of investment increased very slowly and remained well below the rates recorded in other developed market economies, and the long-term decline in the rate of profit, whose roots lay in the stability of the share of wages in value added, in the relatively inefficient way in which capital was being used and in the increases in the costs of new plant and equipment and the relative prices of investment goods, was not stemmed (Barou, 1977, pp. 75–91, and Dunford, Geddes and Perrons, 1981, pp. 387–96).

What did occur was a great merger movement. In 1968 the

intensity of mergers was such that spending on acquisitions exceeded gross domestic fixed capital formation and was nearly double net capital formation. By implication more than one-quarter of the capital stock of the companies sector of the entire economy was subject to takeovers. By 1970 the top one hundred firms accounted for 40 per cent of net manufacturing output compared with 20 per cent in 1949 (Cowling, 1982, pp. 72–3 and 76).

As a result large industrial groups were formed. But manufacturing concerns often remained small in size, geographically dispersed or insufficiently specialised, were short of internally generated funds and were deficient organisationally and technologically.

Overall the attempt to promote growth via an indicative planning system failed, and the mechanism of capital accumulation was not re-established, with capitals in Britain continuing not to invest and with what investment that did occur not contributing adequately to output.

At the level of the state increasing priority was given to attempts to contain the growth of real wages, to transfer the burden of taxation on to wage-earners and to curb trade-union rights. But at the same time the new instruments and agencies of urban and regional planning survived, as did the involvement of the state in highly selective industrial intervention and assistance aimed at reorganising and rationalising individual branches of production. In other words what occurred was a financial restructuring and rationalisation of industry without significant growth (see Figure 3.6 below).

6. Industrial Change in the Periphery in the 1960s

In the 1960s the economies of the old industrial regions were nevertheless transformed by the continuing decline of employment in many of the traditional industries, by the implantation of new manufacturing firms in sectors varying from branches of modern engineering to textiles and clothing and by the growth of the service sector.

Some of the main changes can be identified in Figure 3.4 (p. 66) in spite of the fact that it covers a longer period. In this figure total employment in each region is recorded along the horizontal axis, and the width of each column is proportional to employment in the SIC order concerned in the base year. On the vertical axis is recorded the average annual rate of growth in the number of employees in employment in the sector and region concerned. Thus the area of each column is proportional to the number of jobs lost or gained.

In the case of the county of Durham, for example, employment in the coal-mining industry fell from 98 000 jobs in 1951 to 83 000 in 1961 and to 33 000 in 1971. Some 99 collieries were closed in the years between 1958 and 1970, of which 42 were closed in 1964–8, and deep mining was moved from the west to the east of the county (Austrin and Beynon, 1980, pp. 1–5 and 10–11). At the same time employment declined in other traditional sectors in the region such as the metal manufacturing, shipbuilding and rail transport industries, but it remained more or less stable in the chemical industry.

The new establishments in the manufacturing sector implanted in the old industrial regions were in a high proportion of cases branch plants of multinational firms. At this time many of them were expanding by setting up new plants in the UK or outside of the congested metropolitan centres in the Midlands and in the South-East in particular, and were attracted to the Assisted Areas by the availability of workers, by the quantity and quality of the infrastructural facilities provided by the state and by the availability of grants. But what were decentralised were, in most cases, production operations and assembly work requiring unskilled or semi-skilled workers and routine managerial jobs. The research and development and the decision-making functions of such firms were located or remained outside of the region. At the same time the plants themselves were integrated into the operations of the companies to which they belonged and established few links with other parts of the economies of the regions in which they were located. As a result the decisions to buy up, to expand, to run down or to close a plant, on which the livelihoods of the people in an area depended, were increasingly determined in board rooms located outside of the region, where the only criterion was the ranking of the plant in the light of the return on the investment incurred by the company, with the help of the state, and of the company's overall production and marketing strategy (Austrin and Beynon, 1980, pp. 27–35). (Indeed the subsidisation of investment by the state reduced the value losses incurred by the firm if a plant proved unsuccessful or if it were run down or closed and, in a way, reduced its commitment to the sites at which it was located).

At the same time the type of employment provided was radically different from the kind of work provided by the traditional sectors. In the case of the North-East the work in the traditional sectors was in general skilled or heavy manual work done entirely by men and often organised on a shift system, whereas the new light manufacturing firms attracted to the area tended to employ semi-skilled and unskilled workers often to carry out routine assembly work, and gave employment for the first time to large numbers of married women, partly by organising production in such a way as to enable them to combine part-time work or twilight or night shifts with domestic work. One of the consequences of this pattern of industrialisation was an increase in the importance of the mass worker not divided into occupational groups but graded bureau-cratically within each of the corporations. A second, which was reinforced by the growth of the service sector and by the transfer of central government offices to the periphery, was an increase in female activity rates. At the same time the whole pattern of social life in the old industrial region was transformed (Austrin and Beynon, 1980, pp. 16–17).

The new firms attracted to the area were not normally located in all of the places in which employment in the coal industry or in other traditional sectors was contracting. Instead they moved to the areas where pools of labour, unused for the most part to the conditions of factory life, had been assembled and organised by the area's local authorities whose investments in economic and social infrastructural facilities were concentrated in certain growth-points. In the case of Durham, employment and popula-tion were allowed to fall in the west. On the east coast where the pits remained open a New Town had been built at Peterlee. But the firms attracted to it were mainly employers of women workers who, because of the constraints on their mobility posed by the continuing need to perform domestic tasks and by the pattern of public transport provision, formed a captive labour market (see Lewis, 1982, pp. 13–15). A number of other New Towns were built in a central corridor of growth extending from the estuary of the Tees in the south to those of the Tyne and Wear in the north where the chemicals, steel and shipbuilding sectors were concentrated;

while the old coal and steel town of Spennymoor slightly to the west of this central belt, which was designed as a Special Development Area, was converted, in the words of Beynon and Austrin, into a 'global outpost' of Thorn Electrical Industries, which expanded as the pits in and around the town were closed, and of Courtaulds and the Black & Decker Manufacturing Company, which moved to the area in the middle of the 1960s. In the 1970s, however, the worsted spinning plant which had been set up in the town by Courtaulds was to be closed, as were many of the branch plants which had been located in the Development Areas in the preceding decade (Austrin and Beynon, 1980, pp. 51–60 and 42–50).

Investments in the textile and garments sectors and in particular by Courtaulds were another characteristic of the industrial transformation of some of the old industrial regions. After 1962 Courtaulds developed a strategy of vertical integration entailing the acquisition of a large amount of capacity in fibre-using sectors as well as internal expansion in fibre-making and using. Its movement downstream on a broad front was motivated by several considerations. One was the wish to be able to exert some leverage over the government especially over tariff policy. In particular Courtaulds wanted to stop the duty-free entry of Commonwealth cottons into the UK. A second aspect of its strategy was the intention of developing a series of ultra-modern plants of high capital intensity and high value added per worker. A corollary of this element of its strategy was a combination of rationalisation of existing and acquired capacity, a re-equipping of some plants to raise productivity and construction of entirely new units on greenfield sites usually in the Assisted Areas. In the case of the Lancashire industry, for example Courtaulds acquired a large amount of spinning capacity, reduced the number of mills, but re-equipped those that survived, and raised overall capacity. In weaving it built and equipped new plants outside of the traditional weaving area at Carlisle, Lillyhall and in the new town of Skelmersdale, inhabited largely by people from the dockland districts of Liverpool, using Development Area grants and other financial help. As a result existing weaving capacity was squeezed.

The new worsted spinning mill at Spennymoor where capital and training grants were obtained was a product of the development of a similar strategy in the acrylic-fibre strand. Other plants were built in Northern Ireland where substantial financial aid was a major factor in attracting investment, not only by Courtaulds, but also by other fibre-producing firms including Monsanto and Du Pont. In the case of Courtaulds the suitability of local workers played an important part in the decision to build a plant at Carrickfergus in the late 1940s. But after 1962 the availability of grants was a second major factor and contributed to the development of Courtaulds as the second main employer, after Harland & Wolff, in the region. Of £182 million invested by the Courtaulds Group in the five years up to March 1970 £40 million came from government aid, of which the major part was made up of the additional aid provided in the Assisted Areas (see Knight, 1974, pp. 37–45 and 173–8). The resulting pattern of investment and disinvestment was a major factor in reshaping the map of textile production. In 1952–73 employment fell in the UK by 374 000 and in the North-West by 209 000 jobs. But in the Northern region it increased by 10 700 and in Wales by 4200 jobs (see Figure 3.4, p. 66).

The strategy adopted by Courtaulds was, however, quite different from that of German and Italian textile concerns. Instead of attempting to compete frontally with the standardised products of producers in low-wage economies the Italian strategy was, for example, one which gave emphasis to considerations of quality, design and flexibility in responding to changing fashions. In the face of competition from producers in newly industrialising countries, and, more importantly, in other developed market economies in the 1970s it was Courtaulds' strategy which proved to be least successful (Shepherd, 1983, pp. 57–60). What was more, major cuts occurred in the man-made fibres industry in which production fell from a peak of 731 000 tonnes in 1973 to 578 000 in 1979 and 364 000 in 1982. In 1980 capacity was reduced by 26 per cent via closings. Of seven units closed four were in Northern Ireland where capacity fell by 73 per cent. With rationalisation occurring simultaneously, average production employment fell from 37 000 in 1975 to 28 500 in 1979, and by the third quarter of 1982 employment stood at just over 11 000 persons (National Economic Development Council, 1982, pp. 1–2, and 1983, p. 38).

In the 1960s important changes also occurred in some of the marginal rural areas of Britain. In the Scottish Highlands the farming and fishing sectors were rationalised, while some development occurred in the forestry, hydro-electric energy supply and tourism sectors. But one of the most striking developments was the implantation of large-scale industries exploiting local resources and which, in many cases, were of necessity located away from centres of population due to the dangerousness of some of the processes involved and the environmental problems with which they were associated. In the case of the remoter parts of Scotland several experimental investments occurred in the nuclear-power- supply industry, a pulp and paper mill was built at Fort William with the government providing one-half of the £20 million investment and substantial sums of money for improved infrastructural facilities, and a new aluminium smelting plant was constructed at Invergordon by British Aluminium, which already owned three smaller installations in the region.

The aluminium smelter was one of three investments in this sector which were supported by government grants and by the provision of subsidised electricity after the government had decided in 1967 to develop a large-scale primary aluminium industry in this country in order to reduce the dependence of the economy upon imports from Canada and Norway and to lower the country's import bill. The others were the plants to be built by the Rio Tinto Zinc Corporation and Kaiser at Holyhead in North Wales and by Alcan at Lynemouth in Northumberland. In addition plans for the development in Scotland of an oil-refining and petrochemical complex were formulated, and in the early 1980s were revived with the growth of oil exploration and production in the North Sea (Warren, 1980, pp. 402–8).

7.   Urban and Regional Development in an Age of Impending Crisis

The restructuring and redeployment of capital, with which the diversion of employment in some of the more modern manufacturing sectors to the periphery was associated, and the slackening of growth at a national level, had important implications for the development of the economies of the more prosperous regions and of the country's metropolitan areas in particular. In the case of the South-East, employment in manufacturing and in the service sector expanded rapidly in the 1950s, and attempts were made to channel growth, whose scale had been underestimated, into the New and Expanded Towns. In the 1960s similar plans continued to be formulated, and only in the 1970s was concern about the loss of population and employment from the capital and the social polarisation with which it was associated given any emphasis in planning documents (Keeble, 1980a, pp. 155–70 and 142–50, and Eversley, 1972, pp. 347–68).

In the years up to 1966 employment in the region continued to increase, but growth was most marked in areas outside of Greater London. In the capital the growth that did occur can be largely attributed to the expansion of service employment in the country's public administration, in the commercial and financial services sector, and in the headquarters and research departments of large manufacturing firms in the private and public sectors. In the manufacturing sector itself employment declined. What remained were increasingly the white-collar jobs, which had increased in importance ever since the introduction of the methods of scientific management, and which were given a continuing impetus by the increasing scale of operation and the growing complexity of organisation of large firms (Hymer, 1975, pp. 43–8).

In the late 1960s employment in the basic service sector increased more slowly in Greater London, while the number of jobs in those service activities whose location was more dependent upon the distribution of the population they served fell, along with the size of the capital's population. At the same time a process of polarisation was occurring with a relative and even an absolute decline in unskilled clerical jobs and an increase in the relative importance of administrative, managerial, and professional office jobs in the capital itself; and a decentralisation of routine work in particular to offices in areas away from central London, but also of some offices with concentrations of higher staff, in which case movement was mainly to the west of London. In the service sector relatively unskilled work was in the course of being mechanised, albeit slowly, in many offices, while quite a lot of routine work was being decentralised to small and medium-sized towns and to office centres in the suburbs of large cities especially as the use of automated office and telecommunications equipment increased, as the distribution and costs of labour and of infrastructural facilities changed, and as the costs of land in the central areas of large cities increased (Rhodes and Kan, 1971, part 1 and ch. 7).

In central London office employment actually declined in the 1960s, while corporate control functions and other high-level activities were increasingly concentrated in the central part of the capital. The processes of decentralisation and of recentralisation which lay behind these trends in the location of office employment were in part a result of the operation of market mechanisms. But the sifting process was reinforced by government controls over the location of offices whose effect was one of encouraging the 'dispersal of routine office functions from Central London and their replacement by more specialised national and international functions', and whose primary aim was the 'promotion of Central London as an international level centre for prestige corporate headquarters, banking and financial institutions, and political representation' (Pickvance, 1981, pp. 247–58).

At the same time manufacturing employment declined sharply, more than offsetting the increases recorded in some of the remoter parts of the South-East. In some cases firms were moving to the Assisted Areas or, more frequently, to other regions or to other parts of the South-East. But of most importance was the loss of jobs caused by the closure of factories in the capital or by reductions in employment in the plants that remained. In the years between 1966 and 1974 only about 9 per cent of the job loss in manufacturing industry in Greater London stemmed from the transfer of firms or the movement of branch plants to the Assisted Areas. And only 18 per cent was a result of moves and in particular of transfers to new and overspill towns and other locations outside of the capital, of which most were in the South-East and East Anglia. The remaining 73 per cent of the fall in manufacturing employment was a result of closures and of *in situ* reductions in employment in plants in Greater London itself (Dennis, 1978, pp. 63–73).

The fall in manufacturing employment in Greater London was part of a more general collapse of the manufacturing base of large cities and of their inner-city areas in particular, not only in the more prosperous regions, but also in the Assisted Areas. In every case the problem was mainly one of a restructuring and rationalisation of production aimed at increasing the rate of profit in a context of low investment and low output growth. In a study of the impact of the financial restructuring stimulated by the Industrial Reorganisation Corporation on the operations of twenty-five firms in the electrical engineering, electronics and aerospace equipment restructuring of production, whose aim was to increase productivity or to reduce capacity, led to a net loss of 36 016 jobs at a national level. Of this total, 84 per cent were losses to the cities of Greater London, Liverpool, Manchester and Birmingham. A high proportion of these losses stemmed from closures or from reductions in the numbers employed in plants with low levels of labour productivity which were themselves concentrated in the industrial areas of major cities. The rest resulted from net transfers of employment, in which large numbers of jobs were lost in transit, to existing plants or to new greenfield developments in areas outside of the cities. Almost two-thirds of the net locational gains accrued to the Assisted Areas (Massey and Meegan, 1978, pp. 273–88).

The trends we have outlined were associated with marked changes in the pattern of regional development in Britain. In the years between 1958 and 1966 a significant part of the national increase in manufacturing employment occurred in the Outer Metropolitan Area of the South-East, in the West Midlands conurbation and its surrounding subregion and in the area centred on Nottingham and Derby. Increases were also recorded in almost all of the less-industrialised subregions, and only in the industrial conurbations of Greater London, the North-West, West Yorkshire, Teeside and Clydeside did manufacturing employment fall. But in the period 1966–71 employment in the manufacturing sector declined in the country as a whole, and major reductions occurred in almost all of the large industrial cities, with very pronounced falls occurring in the most important conurbations of Greater London, the West Midlands, the North-West, West Yorkshire and Clydeside. What was more, major declines in manufacturing employment occurred around the axial belt extending from the capital to the North-West and to the West Riding. At the same time above-average increases in unemployment were recorded in the more prosperous areas and in the conurbations, while the rate of immigration fell off, resulting in the cases of the South-East and West Midlands in net migration losses. By contrast employment in manufacturing industry increased in almost all of the peripheral subregions and especially in hitherto unindustrialised rural areas and in the rural parts of the Assisted Areas (Keeble, 1976, pp. 15–21).

In the decade as a whole, increases in manufacturing employment were most pronounced in small towns and in rural districts, with the rate of growth increasing as the size of centre fell and as the degree of rurality increased. In the service sector increases in employment were concentrated in the South-East, in East Anglia, and in parts of the Midlands, while increases in non-production employment in manufacturing were heavily concentrated in the South-East (Gudgin, Crum and Bailey, 1979, ch. 5).

The changes in the geography of the UK in the late 1960s and early 1970s were part of a more general turning-point in the development of its economy and society. In particular the opening of a crisis at an international level of the regime of accumulation based on the introduction and generalisation of the methods of scientific management and of Fordism and the declining competitiveness of the national economy, which was increasingly exposed to international competition, were leading to an accelerated rationalisation and restructuring of many of the sectors that had played a leading role in the preceding wave of expansion, while the slackening of the process of growth and of increases in real incomes eventually led to reductions in orders for many branches of production and to the appearance of substantial amounts of excess capacity in many sectors.

In the West Midlands in particular, output and employment were stagnating from the middle of the 1960s onwards with the weakening of motor-vehicle manufacturing, of metal working and of related sectors. At the same time metropolitan economies were being tertiarised, and manufacturing and assembly operations in the manufacturing sector were being decentralised to small and medium-sized towns and to rural regions or to the less-industrialised parts of old industrial regions where inexpensive and less-militant workers could be recruited, where improved infrastructural facilities had been provided by the state, where grants were sometimes available, where space for expansion existed and land costs were lower; and where, as a result, firms transferring from congested urban areas could take advantage of the general increase in land values caused by urban land and property speculation by realising the value of the sites they owned. But what was perhaps most important was the way in which the transfer or the development of production in new less-congested areas was related to the development of new technology, of new processes and products, of new principles of work organisation and of new ways of structuring economic life.

The changes that have occurred in the material and social

conditions by which manufacturing firms are attracted and the dispersed pattern of industrialisation which was emerging, as well as changes in production and employment at existing sites, can be explained in part by the development of functionally fragmented units of production sometimes without, but perhaps increasingly with, market mediation units of production incorporated with wider circuits of valorisation of capital which, with the development of improved methods of communication and transport and of more efficient methods for the long-distance transmission of information, can be dispersed geographically (Perrons, 1981, pp. 81–100). In turn many of these changes in the structure of manufacturing enterprises are largely a product of changes in the strategy of capital and of the experimentation by capital with neo-Fordist techniques whose purpose is to overcome some of the obstacles to increases in the productivity of labour and in the rate of surplus-value which have arisen in particular on the semi-automatic assembly line. In some cases firms have simply sought out new sources of labour and have made greater use of female workers especially in areas where costs are lower. But of more importance is the way in which advances in the development of electronic information systems and in computer technology and the development of new instruments of measurement and control have made it possible to construct machines that control their own operations. As a result of the introduction of automatic production control, which has been made possible by these developments in the forces of production, and of the new principles of work organisation now in embryo known as the recomposition of tasks 'a far more advanced centralisation of production becomes compatible with a geographical decentralisation of the operative units' in which manufacturing and assembly work is carried on. In addition it holds out the possibility of a substantial increase in the rate of surplus-value, if only the increase itself can be realised, and of a reduction in the value of constant capital capable of counteracting the rise in the organic composition of capital (Aglietta, 1979, pp. 122–30, and Table 3.3).

The new geographical division of labour connected with the development of new management strategies and of neo-Fordist techniques and with the emergence of new growth sectors is superimposed upon and articulated with preceding ones. In the late 1960s and early 1970s it led to a convergence in some of the

TABLE 3.3   *A Decomposition of Trends in the Profitability of Manufacturing Industry*

Country	Period	Profit-ability of capital	Effect of the efficiency of capital	Effect of the real wage cost	Effect of relative prices
USA	1960–66	+5.6	+3.9	+6.2	−4.5
	1966–74	−6.4	−0.9	+1.4	−6.9
	1974–77	+6.4	−0.6	+1.0	+6.0
	1977–80	−8.3	−2.8	−1.5	−4.0
France	1963–70	+0.8	−0.6	+4.8	−3.4
	1970–5	−8.8	−2.9	−3.7	−2.2
	1975–80	−2.8	−2.0	+4.3	−5.1
Federal	1960–4	−5.1	−2.3	−1.0	−2.1
Republic	1964–9	+0.1	−0.1	+1.9	−1.7
of	1969–73	−5.2	−2.1	−5.4	+2.3
Germany	1973–8	−0.7	−1.1	−1.6	+2.0
UK	1963–70	−3.6	0.0	+2.1	−5.7
	1970–5	−8.7	−2.5	−6.3	+0.1
	1975–80	−5.8	−3.2	−1.2	−2.4
Japan	1960–5	−6.5	−3.3	+1.5	−4.8
	1965–70	+4.3	+1.6	+2.8	−0.1
	1970–5	−15.0	−5.0	−1.6	−0.4
	1975–80	+1.1	+4.6	+14.1	−17.6

SOURCE   CEPll, cited in M. Aglietta and R. Boyer, *Pôles de Compétivi-té, Stratégie industrielle, et Politique macroéconomique* (Paris: Cepre-map, 1983) p. 44.

conventional indicators of regional inequality. But it also resulted in the development of new types of regional problem and of new types of regional inequality. One of these was the growing gap between centres of management and control and areas in which externally controlled industrial development was occurring and a high proportion of jobs were relatively unskilled and low-paid (Hymer, 1975, pp. 48–56; Hymer and Semonin, 1979, pp. 154–60;

Lipietz, 1977, pp. 82–92, Lipietz, 1980, pp. 3–17; and Massey, 1979, pp. 236–9). A second related problem was that the types of diversification of regional industrial structures associated with the implantation of firms which produce only parts of products and establish few linkages with other parts of the regional economy was resulting in a reduction in the coherence of regional productive systems and in the establishment of a new hierarchy of regional and national economies headed by those areas in which modern investment-goods sectors and knowledge-intensive industries were concentrated (Palloix, 1975, pp. 173–9).

8. The Collapse of the UK Manufacturing Sector

After the first and second oil crises and, in particular, after the election of a Conservative government and the implementation of a monetarist economic strategy a number of sharp and very deep recessions occurred.

Some of the changes in the structure and location of industry mentioned in the last section continued. In some sectors production and employment continued to be decentralised to small and medium-sized towns as a result of movement, new investment or a differential expansion of existing concerns. Often these developments were connected with the growth of new sectors and the production of new products, and with changes in work organisation and a physical fragmentation of production facilitated by automation and information technology. In the service sector many routine jobs were similarly decentralised to areas outside of the cores of large cities and some government functions were transferred to Assisted Area locations, while the distribution of non-basic service employment changed with the changing distribution of the population they served.

In addition the research and development functions of many large firms, independent business service concerns and hi-tech firms employing a high proportion of high-status professional, scientific and managerial staff, developed in an arc extending from Sussex and Bristol through Oxford and Berkshire to Cambridge.

But what assumed overwhelming importance was the pronounced relative contraction of the UK manufacturing sector and

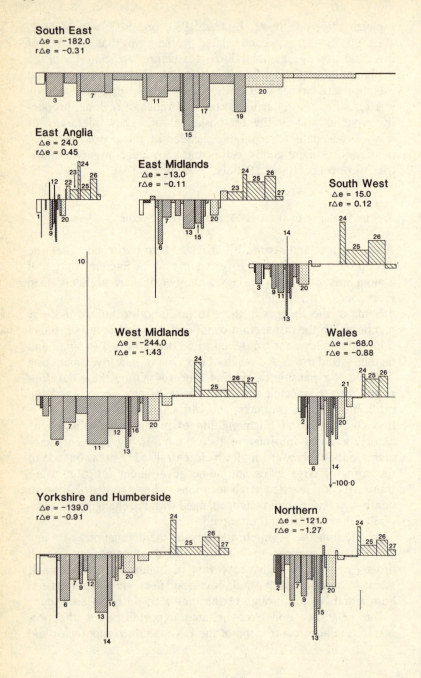

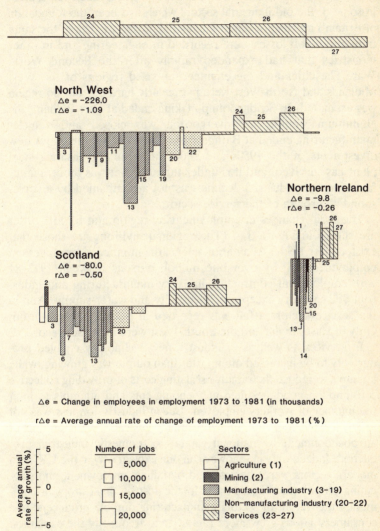

South East (cont.)

North West
Δe = −226.0
rΔe = −1.09

Scotland
Δe = −80.0
rΔe = −0.50

Northern Ireland
Δe = −9.8
rΔe = −0.26

Δe = Change in employees in employment 1973 to 1981 (in thousands)

rΔe = Average annual rate of change of employment 1973 to 1981 (%)

Average annual rate of growth (%)

Number of jobs	Sectors
5,000	Agriculture (1)
10,000	Mining (2)
15,000	Manufacturing industry (3–19)
20,000	Non-manufacturing industry (20–22)
	Services (23–27)

FIGURE 3.5 *The Geography of De-industrialisation: The Rate of Growth of, and Changes in, Employees in Employment by 1968 SIC Order and Region, 1973–81*

SOURCE Based on Census of Employment statistics published in *Department of Employment Gazette* (various years).

of manufacturing employment. After 1974 employment fell sharply in some of the old industrial sectors which had been the foundation of Britain's nineteenth-century industrial prosperity. But at the same time major job losses were recorded in engineering and in other industries that had expanded rapidly after the Second World War. The cities and the engineering-based regions of the West Midlands and North-West were particularly hard-hit, but no region was exempted. In Scotland pulp-making ended at Fort William, the aluminium smelter at Invergordon was closed and vehicle-manufacturing ended at Bathgate and Linwood. Of the major new investments of the 1950s and 1960s only the Ravenscraig steel plant has survived, and it is under threat. What was more, manufacturing and industrial decline was not accompanied by a corresponding growth of the service sector.

The main changes in employment by region and by SIC order are shown in Figure 3.5. (The regional divisions are those that existed after 1974.) At a national level the number of employees in employment fell by over one million persons between 1973–81 with employment contracting in every manufacturing and industrial SIC category except gas, electricity and water-supply. And in the service sectors a fall was recorded in public administration. Only in East Anglia and the South-West were increases recorded.

In services as well as in industry new technology enabled productivity to be increased often faster than output was growing, while attempts to reduce the rapidly escalating costs of providing collective consumption goods resulted in spending cuts and attempts to limit the number of workers employed. But in industry job loss was not simply a product of structural adjustment. Instead it was a product of an abandonment by national capitals of domestic industrial production. Indeed only in that way can one explain why in the UK even modern sectors were characterised by falling employment and stagnating output (see Figure 3.6). In the rest of the European community the output of sectors manufacturing durable producers' and consumers' goods grew more rapidly, and frequently the expansion of output more than counteracted the downward effect on employment of productivity growth.

The events of the 1970s and early 1980s were the most recent steps in a process whose roots go back a long way and whose unfolding since 1945 we have outlined. Underlying them are a low rate and a low level of efficiency of investment and a lack of competitiveness of the manufacturing sectors with their origins in the weight of the past and the strategies and actions of the major social actors. In particular only slowly was the rate of investment increased by the policy of raising profitability and of modernising the economy of some sections of the political class and some corporatist state institutions.

But also the years of rapid post-war growth had given way to a new crisis of capitalism. In that situation demand was changing, and new competition was emerging. Sectors in which modernisation had been slow were unable to compete, while many new investments did not secure the level of social validation on which profitability depended and were devalorised.

Yet the path of de-industrialisation and tertiarisation of the economy and the corresponding social and spatial polarisation of employment and unemployment and of wealth and poverty are not necessary implications of the crisis even for an advanced capitalist economy. Indeed they are very damaging.

On the one hand the demand for services is not increasing dramatically outside of the field of health, and many services can be supplied through the provision of durable goods. Many services are protected from foreign competition and are associated with high costs, while in so far as methods of work-study and automation are introduced the possibility of solving the central problem of employment is limited. On the other hand manufacturing industry is a source of a large range of very important material goods, of which many are used in the service sector. It is a major source of dynamically increasing returns. And without it the possibility of paying for net imports, including imports of necessary manufactured goods, and of financing a service sector will be limited.

At present regional inequality is widening, while almost the whole of the UK economy is being transformed into a problem region of Europe at a pace that is currently concealed by the yield of the oil wells in the North Sea. In our view such a process can only be reversed by two developments. One is a process of reindustrialisation of Britain within Europe capable of reversing the historic decline of the UK economy. The other is the overturning of those mechanisms which in a capitalist society result in a polarisation of wealth and poverty.

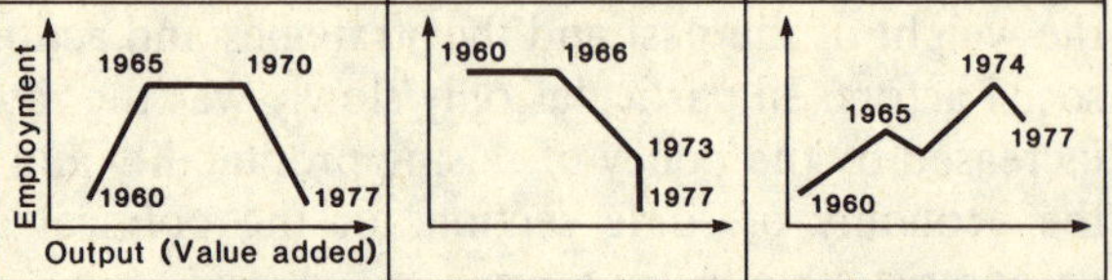

SECTOR	TYPE I	TYPE II	TYPE III
	Employment ↑ 1965—1970; 1960, 1977 — Output (Value added)	1960—1966; 1973; 1977	1974; 1965, 1977; 1960
Equipment goods		UK	EEC, FRG, The Netherlands, France, Belgium, Italy(1)
Intermediate goods	EEC, The Netherlands, Belgium	UK, FRG,	France, Italy
Consumption goods	FRG, The Netherlands, Belgium	UK, France	Italy
Food processing		EEC, FRG, France, Italy The Netherlands, Belgium, UK	
All Industry	EEC, FRG, The Netherlands, Belgium	UK	France, Italy(1)

FIGURE 3.6　*The Major Patterns of Change in Value Added and Employment by Manufacturing Sector and Country in the EEC, 1960–77*

Note　(1). In Italy in these sectors employment did not fall after 1974.
SOURCE　R. Boyer and P. Petit, 'Emploi et Productivité dans la CEE', *Economie et Statistique*, no. 121 (Apr–May 1980) pp. 35–59, p. 50.

Notes

1. The task we have set ourselves is complicated by several factors. One is the fact that all processes of change operate at a local as well, perhaps, as at other levels. A concept of branch-plant industrialisation, for example, subsumes not only a wide variety of manufacturing investments that differ from case to case, but also developments that occur in a different way in, say, a rural district in East Anglia from in, say, a New Town in the North-East. In this study, however, we shall have to give most emphasis to aggregate trends, and we shall often abstract from particular forms and local detail, identifying instead only general processes: rural depopulation, city and metropolitan growth, suburbanisation, residential and employment decentralisa-

tion, city-centre redevelopment, reindustrialisation of nineteenth-century industrial areas, inner-city decay, de-industrialisation of the industrial regions of the first and second industrial revolutions and counter-urbanisation. A second problem is related to the fact that the regional divisions used in the presentation of published official statistics, on which we shall draw, do not stem from a grouping of areas exhibiting similar trends. Added emphasis must consequently be given to the caveat that the geographical subdivisions of any region do not all exhibit variants of the aggregate trends or the more abstractly identified processes which are statistically dominant within the larger territorial unit.

2. In the years of reconstruction after the Second World War new regional and urban planning policies were introduced in Britain as part of a programme of reforms envisaged by the war-time coalition government. Under the 1945 Distribution of Industry Act a number of Development Areas were established in the depressed industrial regions and, in 1948, in a part of the Highlands of Scotland, and the Board of Trade was given powers to build advance factories and to make loans to industrial estate companies, to reclaim derelict land and to offer grants and loans to firms locating in the Development Areas. Under the 1947 Town and Country Planning Acts a system of Industrial Development Certificates which enabled the state to restrict the building of new factories and the extension of existing ones in specified regions was introduced, as was a system of development control and development planning by counties and county boroughs, and development rights and development values were nationalised. In order to end the unco-ordinated urban sprawl of the inter-war years fourteen new towns were designated, of which eight were to be located in the vicinity of London, and steps were taken to protect the countryside.

3. In 1958 the Distribution of Industry (Industrial Finance) Act was passed, and in 1960 the Distribution of Industry Acts were repealed and replaced by the new Local Employment Act, as a result of which regional policy was recast. The Development Areas were abolished and Development Districts composed of Local Employment Exchange Areas were to be scheduled by the Board of Trade on the basis of an unemployment criterion. In practice areas with unemployment rates of at least 4.5 per cent were designated as Development Districts. The main incentives provided for by the 1945 Act were retained, but the conditions under which grants and loans were conceded in the scheduled areas were eased, the decision to make them available to non-manufacturing firms, which had been taken in 1958, was reaffirmed, and building grants were introduced for firms which chose to build their own factories in the Development Districts.

4. In these Acts standard 10 per cent grants for plant and machinery were introduced, the building grant introduced in 1960 was set at 25 per cent and firms in the Development Districts were entitled to depreciate investment in plant and machinery at any rate.

5. In the view of the government the old investment and depreciation provisions (1) did not possess the necessary qualities of simplicity, certainty and speed of payment, and (2) only helped firms that were making profits in the early years after investing and did not assist new firms or firms not declaring profits in the UK, even if the projects were commercially sound, while (3) the value of the aid given had been reduced by a fall in the rate of company taxation and by the introduction of the new Corporation Tax in particular.

6. It has been estimated by Wilson that the effect of the 1966 measures was to reduce the present value of the gross cost of an investment in plant and machinery by an extra 12.7 per cent and of an investment in buildings by an extra 18.8 per cent in the Development Areas. In the case of the earlier position under the Local Employment Acts the corresponding figures for the differences in the discounted gross cost of an investment in the Development Areas as compared with one in the rest of the country were 10.3 and 14.4 per cent respectively. T. Wilson, 'Finance for Regional Industrial Development', *The Three Banks Review*, no. 75 (Sep 1967) pp. 3–23, pp. 13–16.

Bibliography

Aaronovitch, S. (1981) 'The Relative Decline of the UK', in S. Aaronovitch and R. Smith with J. Gardiner and R. Moore, *The Political Economy of British Capitalism: A Marxist Analysis* (Maidenhead: McGraw-Hill).

Aglietta, M. (1979) *A Theory of Capitalist Regulation* (London: New Left Books).

Aglietta, M. (1982) 'World Capitalism in the Eighties', *New Left Review*, no. 136 (Nov–Dec), pp. 5–41.

Aglietta, M. and Boyer, R. (1983) *Pôles de Compétivité, Stratégie industrielle, et Politique macroéconomique* (Paris: Cepremap).

Austrin, T. and Beynon, H. (1980) *Global Outpost: The Working Class Experience of Big Business in the North-East of England, 1964–1979*, mimeo.

Bain, G. S. (1970) *The Growth of White-Collar Unionism* (Oxford: Clarendon Press)

Barnett, A. (1983) 'The Dangerous Dream', *New Statesman*, 17 June, pp. 9–11.

Barou, Y. (1977) 'Contrainte exterieure et Declin industriel au Royaume-Uni', *Economie et Statistique*, **97** (Feb) pp. 75–91.

Barr, J. (1969) 'Durham's Murdered Villages', *New Society*, **13**, no. 340 (3 Apr) pp. 523–5.

Beynon, H. (1973) *Working for Ford* (Wakefield: EP Publishing).

Boyer, R. (1978) 'Les Salaires en Longue Periode', *Économie et Statistique*, **103** (Sep) pp. 27–57.

Boyer, R. and Petit, P. (1980) 'Emploi et Productivité dans le CEE',

Économie et Statistique, **121** (Apr–May) pp. 35–59.

Brown, A. J. (1972) *The Framework of Regional Economics in the United Kingdom* (Cambridge: Cambridge University Press).

Carter, I. (1974) 'The Highlands of Scotland as an Underdeveloped Region', in E. de Kadt and G. Williams (eds), *Sociology and Development* (London: Tavistock Publications) part 4.

Cockerill, A. and Silberston, A. (1974) *The Steel Industry. International Comparisons of Industrial Structure and Performance*, University of Cambridge Department of Applied Economics Occasional Paper, no. 42 (London: Cambridge University Press).

Cowling, K. (1982) *Monopoly Capitalism* (London: Macmillan).

Dennis, R. (1978) 'The Decline of Manufacturing Employment in Greater London: 1966–74', *Urban Studies*, **15**, 1 (Feb) pp. 63–73.

Dunford, M., Geddes, M. and Perrons, D. (1981) 'Regional Policy and the Crisis in the UK: A Long-Run Perspective', *International Journal of Urban and Regional Research*, vol. 5, no. 3, pp. 377–410.

Dunford, M. and Perrons, D. (1983) *The Arena of Capital* (London: Macmillan).

Eversley, D. E. C. (1972) 'Rising Costs and Static Incomes: Some Economic Consequences of Regional Planning in London', *Urban Studies*, **9**, 3 (Oct 1972) pp. 347–68.

Federation of British Industries (1963) *The Regional Problem* (London: Federation of British Industries).

Feinstein, C. H. (1972) *National Income, Expenditure and Output of the UK, 1855–1965* (Cambridge, Cambridge University Press).

Foot, P. (1975) 'Anglesey: Aluminium and Oil', in P. J. Smith (ed.), *The Politics of Physical Resources* (Harmondsworth: Penguin Books) ch. 6.

Friedman, A. (1977) *Industry and Labour: Class Struggle at Work and Monopoly Capitalism* (London: Macmillan).

Great Britain: Parliamentary Debates (Hansard) (1966) *House of Commons, Official Report*, Fifth Series, vol. 724 Session 1965–66, 15 Feb 1966 (London: HMSO) cols 1119–29 and 1247–48.

Gudgin, G., Crum, R. and Bailey, S. (1979) 'White-Collar Employment in UK Manufacturing Industry', in P. W. Daniels (ed.) *Spatial Patterns of Office Growth and Location* (Chichester: Wiley) ch. 5.

Hardie, J. (1972) 'Regional Policy', in W. Beckerman (ed.), *The Labour Government's Economic Record: 1964–1970* (London: Duckworth) ch. 6.

Hobsbawm, E. (1976) *Industry and Empire* (Harmondsworth: Penguin).

Hymer, S. (1975) 'The Multinational Corporation and the Law of Uneven Development', in H. Rodice (ed.) *International Firms and Modern Imperialism* (Harmondsworth: Penguin) ch. 2.

Hymer, S. and Semonin, P. (1979) 'The Multinational Corporation and the International Division of Labour', in R. B. Cohen *et al.*, *The Multinational Corporation: A Radical Approach. Papers by Stephen Herbert Hymer* (Cambridge: Cambridge University Press) pp. 140–64.

Joseph, G. (1983) *Women at Work* (Oxford: Philip Allen).

Kaldor, N. (1970) 'The Case for Regional Policies', *Scottish Journal of Political Economy*, **17** (Nov) pp. 337–48.

Kaldor, N. (1972) 'The Irrelevance of Equilibrium Economics', *The Economic Journal*, **82**, **328**, (Dec) pp. 1237–55.

Keeble, D. (1976) *Industrial Location and Planning in the United Kingdom* (London: Methuen).

Keeble, D. (1977) 'Spatial Policy in Britain: Regional or Urban', *Area*, **9**, **1**, pp. 3–8.

Keeble, D. (1980) 'The South East II. Greater London' and 'The South East III. Outside London', in G. Manners, D. Keeble, B. Rodgers and K. Warren (eds) chs 5 and 6.

Keeble, D. (1980) 'Industrial Decline, Regional Policy, and the Urban–Rural Manufacturing Shift in the United Kingdom', *Environment and Planning A*, **12**, pp. 945–62.

Knight, Sir A. (1974) *Private Enterprise and Public Intervention*, (London: Allen & Unwin).

Läpple, D. and van Hoogstraaten, P. (1980) 'Remarks on the Spatial Structure of Capitalist Development: the Case of the Netherlands', in J. Carney, R. Hudson and J. Lewis (eds) *Regions in Crisis: New Perspectives in European Regional Theory* (London: Croom Helm) pp. 117–66.

Lewis, J. (1982) 'Changing Patterns of Gender Differentiation in Peterlee New Town 1948–1982', *Queen Mary College Working Papers in Geography*, no. 2.

Lipietz, A. (1977) *Le Capital et Son Éspace* (Paris: François Maspero).

Lipietz, A. (1979) *Inflation et Crises: Pourquoi?* (Paris: François Maspero).

Lipietz, A. (1980) 'Interregional Polarisation and the Tertiarisation of Society', *Papers of the Regional Science Association*, **44**, pp. 3–17.

McCallum, D. (1979) 'The Development of British Regional Policy', in D. Maclennan and J. B. Parr (eds) *Regional Policy. Past Experience and New Directions* (Oxford: Martin Robertson).

Marx, K. (1976) *Capital. A Critique of Political Economy*, vol. 1 (Harmondsworth: Penguin Books).

Massey, D. (1979) 'In What Sense a Regional Problem?' *Regional Studies*, **13**, pp. 233–43.

Massey, D. and Meegan, R. (1978) 'Industrial Restructuring Versus the Cities', *Urban Studies*, **15**, **3** (Oct) pp. 273–88.

National Economic Development Council. (1981) 'Man-Made Fibre Production SWP', *Progress Report* (Nov) (London: NEDO, 1982).

National Economic Development Council. (1983) *Annual Report 1982–83* (London: NEDO).

National Economic Development Office (1963a) *Conditions Favourable to Faster Growth* (London: HMSO).

National Economic Development Office (1963b) *Growth of the United Kingdom Economy to 1966* (London. HMSO).

Palloix, C. (1975) *L'Internationalisation du Capital. Elements critiques* (Paris: François Maspero).

Perrons, D. (1981) 'The Role of Ireland in the New International Division of Labour: A Proposed Framework for Regional Analysis', *Regional Studies*, **15**, **2** (Apr) pp. 81–100.

Pickvance, C. (1981) 'Policies as Chameleons: An Interpretation of Regional Policy and Office Policy in Britain', in M. Dear and A. J. Scott (eds) *Urbanisation and Urban Planning in Capitalist Society* (London and New York: Methuen) ch. 10.

Pollard, S. (1969) *The Development of the British Economy, 1914–67*, 2nd ed. (London: Arnold).

Rhodes, J. and Kan, A. (1971) *Office Dispersal and Regional Policy* (Cambridge: Cambridge University Press).

Rubery, J. and Tarling, R. (1982) 'Women in the recession', *Socialist Economic Review 1982* (London, Merlin Press).

Shepherd, G. (1983) 'British Manufacturing Industry and the EEC', in C. D. Cohen (ed.), *The Common Market: 10 Years After. An Economic Review of British Membership of the EEC 1973–1983* (Deddington, Oxon. Philip Allan) ch. 3.

Warren, K. (1980) 'Scotland', in G. Manners, D. Keeble, B. Rodgers and K. Warren, *Regional Development in Britain*, 2nd ed. (Chichester: John Wiley) ch. 14.

4
Women's Work, Technological Change and Shifts in the Employment Structure

FELICITY HENWOOD AND SALLY WYATT

1. Introduction

During this century the proportion of women in the labour force has risen from 29 per cent in 1901 to 30 per cent in 1951 to 40 per cent in 1983. Over this period there have been substantial changes in both the availability and the structure of employment for women. Despite the increased availability of waged work, women's status in the labour market has remained consistently lower than men's. In this chapter we discuss the implications for women's waged labour of post-war changes in the structure of employment nationally and regionally, in terms of industries and occupations. We also look at the effects and implications of new information technology for employed women. First, however, we examine briefly the origins, causes and consequences of women's status in the labour market.

2. Women's Status in the Labour Market: The Interaction of Patriarchy and Capitalism

To explain women's present status in the labour market it is necessary to examine the transition from feudalism to capitalism, associated with the 'Industrial Revolution'. Two consequences of

106

this transition were the division between domestic and wage labour and also divisions within the labour market itself.[1]

For the feudal family the consequences of the growth of capitalism were related to the separation of labour involved in the production of goods from the labour involved in the reproduction and maintenance of the family. At the beginning of this process the family was not recognised as an economic unit. Wages were low, women and children as well as men became wage labourers. Thus, the role of the family in maintaining the labour force was threatened. Capitalists recognised that women working outside the home undermined the work capacity of both the present and future labour force. This recognition, combined with the labour-saving potential of various technical innovations, led to pressures on women to give priority to their domestic obligations – including legislation prohibiting women's paid work opportunities. Parallel with this, as a result of the increasing strength of the organised working class, men successfully demanded wages that would cover the costs of providing for himself and his family.

Before the Industrial Revolution women worked in many types of trade, industry and agriculture. (Until the Colliery Act of 1842 women worked in the coal mines.) With industrialisation women had less opportunity to learn new skills, now associated with factory work. The replacement of rules of custom by rules of capitalist production excluded women from skilled areas of work. This was related also to the organisation of skilled craftsmen who used the guild organisations to restrict numbers and force up wages. The elimination of women as skilled workers provided the basis for women to become a flexible, reserve labour force. These divisions between work and home, and within the labour market, arose not from some Utopian past but from a system in which patriarchy was already deeply entrenched. In feudal society the subordination of women was characterised by authority relations, enshrined by the Church and the legal system. Women were involved at all levels of production, often on the basis of their marital relations. The new economic relations of capitalism undermined the productive relevance of this relationship, but not the way in which it tied women to domestic labour.

Feminists have often argued that the present status of women in the labour market and the current arrangement of sex-segregated work is the result of a long process of interaction between two social and economic systems: patriarchy and capitalism. Hartmann, for example, argues that job segregation by sex is the primary mechanism in capitalist societies that maintains the superiority of men over women: it operates by enforcing lower wages for women than for men. Lower wages for women keep women economically dependent on men. In the home women perform domestic service tasks for their husbands and children for no financial reward (Hartmann, 1976). This analysis stresses the way in which men benefit from the operation of this system. Men benefit both from higher wages and from the domestic division of labour. We cannot ignore the part played by male workers in constructing the present situation. While it remains true that capitalists have used women as unskilled, underpaid labour to undercut male workers, this has only been possible because of patriarchal social relations operating in the first place. Hartmann has called this undercutting of the make workers wage a case of 'men's cooptation by and support for a patriarchal society with its hierarchy among men, being turned back on themselves with a vengeance' (ibid. p. 168).

The status of women's work, whether in the home or the labour market, continues to be consistently lower than men's. The low value accorded to women's work is reflected in the terms used in discussions of employment and unemployment. For example, far fewer women than men are defined as 'economically active' (a category which includes employed plus registered unemployed people) largely because the various types of domestic work which women do lead to women's exclusion from the formal economy. Of the 16 million women of working age (16 to 60 years) 37 per cent were defined as 'economically inactive' in 1983, as compared with 4.6 per cent for men (Central Statistical Office, 1983). This category includes the unregistered unemployed, women performing either domestic outwork (who are employed but not registered) as well as women engaged in unwaged household work. The way in which the formal economy is defined reflects and reinforces the consequences of the interaction between capitalism and patriarchy, particularly the assignment of the tasks of reproducing and maintaining the labour force to women in the private or informal sphere.

When in waged work women are far more likely than men to be employed part-time. In June 1980 there were 4.4 million part-time workers, of whom 3.8 million were women. Married women and women with children are especially likely to be employed part-time. While the percentage of married women in the labour force has increased dramatically over the last fifty years, most of these women have been employed part-time. Married women's participation increased from 3.8 per cent of the labour force in 1921 to 25.9 per cent in 1981. (Equal Opportunities Commission, 1983). Whereas only 5 per cent of single employed women were employed part-time in 1981, 32 per cent of married women were. The figures for women with children show a similar pattern. In 1980 61 per cent of all women with children were in waged work. However, only 30 per cent of women with children in the 0–4 age group were. While the figure for women with children in the 5–9 age group had risen to 62 per cent, 42 per cent of these women were employed part-time (Office of Population Censuses and Surveys, 1981). These shorter amounts of time spent in 'formal' employment allow women to fulfil the domestic responsibilities seen to be theirs; but part-time employment has severe disadvantages compared with full-time employment. While the occupations of those in part-time employment parallel the occupations of the majority of those in full-time employment, there is a greater tendency among those employed part-time to be on the lowest grade of work.[2]

Another disadvantage experienced by those in part-time employment concerns earnings. Recent industrial tribunal cases have shown that not only are part-time workers more likely to be discriminated against over redundancy payments, but they are paid less per hour for the same job because they *are* part-time (TUC, 1983). Those in part-time employment are also less likely to be in a union than those in full-time employment and, therefore, have less bargaining strength.

Between 1971 and 1981 the number of full-time jobs, largely done by men, fell by 1.7 million. Over the same period the number of part-time jobs, largely done by women, increased by more than 1 million. In the present economic climate the needs of capitalists can be met by employing women part-time at a less than *pro rata* rate of pay. However, in this situation of high *male*-unemployment, the increasing participation of women in the labour market, if only on a part-time basis – threatens patriarchal structures and it is by no means clear how this conflict between capitalism and patriarchy will be resolved.

Recent legislation concerning equal pay for women highlights a potential conflict between capitalism and patriarchy. Earnings constitute one of the most important differences between women's and men's position in the labour market. Taking into consideration only those in full-time employment, in 1981 women in manual occupations earned only 62.6 per cent of male and manual earnings and women in non-manual occupations earned only 60.7 per cent of male non-manual earnings. There are several explanations for this differential in earnings. First, women are concentrated in the low-paid sectors of the economy (e.g. textiles). Second, women are concentrated in jobs defined as low in skill and at the lower levels of the job hierarchy. Third, women's and men's pay are constituted differently – men's pay often includes greater amounts of overtime pay, night-shift premiums, etc. Fourth, a far smaller proportion of women than men are in trades unions. In 1981 64 per cent of men and 38 per cent of women were members of trades unions. Lastly, protective legislation prevents women from gaining access to certain well-paid jobs.[3]

The concept of equal pay is inconsistent with the concept of the 'family wage', which has been fought for and protected by trades unions since industrialisation. The family wage is based on the premiss that one man financially supports various dependants, including a woman. Equal pay is based on a premiss of independent people working for a particular wage for a particular job. Rather than campaigning for equal status for women in the labour market and, necessarily, in society as a whole, men have continued to defend their superior position by such tactics as negotiating with employers to maintain the 'family wage' and to keep certain skilled areas of work for themselves and keep women out.[4] As a result of men's determination to maintain superiority over women in the labour force and in the home, they have allowed women to be segregated in the low-paid sectors of the economy and in the lowest-paid, lowest-skilled jobs within all sectors. It has been possible for employers to exploit this situation and use the cheaper form of women's labour when necessary. This illustrates how the interests of patriarchy and capitalism have coincided. However, if in the current economic recession the struggle for equal pay results in the lowering of the average wage for everybody, patriarchy and capitalism may come into conflict. Capitalists would benefit through the lowering of their labour costs, but men would be threatened by women's increased economic independence.

Before discussing the details of women's position in the post-war UK labour market, we shall briefly examine the relationship between technological change, industrial structure and levels of employment.

3. Technological Change, Industrial Structure and the Level of Employment

The complex set of relationships between technical change, economic growth and employment cannot be understood simply by reference to case studies. Appeals to case studies alone are unlikely to provide any broad understanding of the issues because it will always be possible to find examples of firms and/or sectors which support competing theories. Case-study work is much more likely to yield interesting and important information about the micro-level effects of technical change for employment and about the qualitative ways in which work organisation and working conditions are being affected. For an understanding of the macro-level factors affecting the relationship between technical change and employment, it is necessary to examine the historical process of innovation and its relationship to employment. We need to be able to explain, for instance, why for decades there could be rapid technical change plus a high demand for labour (i.e. near full employment) and then, a similar technical change *rate*, in the late 1970s and 1980s, accompanied by a fall in employment.

Long-wave theorists,[5] especially those who have given great attention to the role of technical innovation, have added much to our understanding of the historical process of economic development. Technical innovations are seen as being one important factor affecting the growth of new industries and hence, of growth in the economy as a whole. They are also seen as playing an important role in generating new employment opportunities in the 'upswing' period of a long wave. Less frequently mentioned is the potential for changes in gender relations, both in the home and in paid work, as a result of the new employment opportunities. Freeman (1982) argues that new industries initially use labour intensive methods of production. This generates a strong demand for labour which is reinforced by multiplier effects through the expansion of the economy as whole. The delayed response of the capital goods sector to the expansion of demand in the new industries often has the effect of drawing out the diffusion process and lengthening the period of upswing and growth. At the peak of a long wave the demand for certain types of labour, particularly 'unskilled' labour can become so strong as to stimulate major flows of immigration (as in the pre-First World War period and in the 1950s and 1960s in the UK) and to facilitate entry into waged labour of new groups of workers (women in the 1960s). Eventually, changes in the relative costs of labour and other inputs leads to an erosion of profit margins; thus the emphasis of investment shifts from simple capacity extension to 'rationalisation' and cost-saving investment, with an eventual decrease in the demand for labour.

In all OECD countries in the 1960s there was a marked shift from new capacity to 'rationalisation' – that is – the *share* of plants and machinery in total investment increases and the share of new buildings associated with new factories, decreased. This shift of emphasis in investment from capacity extension to 'rationalisation' has serious implications for employment. During this same period there was a marked change in the rate of employment growth in manufacturing. As the investment pattern changed so employment growth levelled off (see Table 4.1). Freeman, Clark and Soete (1982) have argued that, 'the forces of increased competition, greater concentration, economies of scale and other factors associated with the "maturing" of industries of the 1950s and early 1960s contributed significantly to the onset of "rationalisation" which began before the onset of the 1974–5 recession'. In the years following the mid-1960s the annual change in labour input is negative and towards the end of the decade declines at an accelerating rate, despite continued high investment. This is in clear contrast to the 1957–62 period where rather slower rates of investment growth are accompanied by overall positive and generally increasing increments in employment. The implication here is that the onset of employment decline was not initiated by a reduction in the rate of growth of investment (although the latter has declined during the 1970s with further reductions in the labour force) but by a change in the nature of that investment. This change in the pattern of investment and the consequent effect on employment is linked closely to the level of profitability. When expected profits are high, at the early stages of the upswing, many

TABLE 4.1   *Investment and Employment Growth Rates, Manufacturing Industry 1960–1975 (employment in brackets)*

Country	1960–5	1965–70	1970–5
France	6.9	9.6	3.5
	(1.1)	(0.5)	(0.4)
West Germany	3.2	5.2	–7.3
	(1.4)	(0.4)	(–1.9)
Italy	–3.3	11.3	–0.4
	(0.4)	(1.5)	(0.9)
Japan	6.0	21.5	–4.7
	(3.9)	(3.6)	(–0.5)
UK	3.7	4.2	–4.6
	(0.3)	(–0.5)	(–2.1)
USA	8.0	2.4	–2.2
	(1.1)	(1.7)	(–0.7)

SOURCE   C. Freeman, J. Clark, and L. Soete, *Unemployment and Technical Innovation: A Study of Long Waves and Economic Development* (London: Frances Pinter, 1982) p. 158.

firms invest in the new technologies and the swarming process 'takes off'. At the upper turning-point, when expected profits are lower, the search for labour- and cost-saving innovations begins. The time-lags involved mean that it can take between five and twenty years for the full effects of such technological changes to work through the system. It could well be argued that the energy and cost-saving innovations of the late 1960s and 1970s are being felt now, in the 1980s.

Following on from such theories about cycles of economic growth and the role of technological innovation in them, it seems reasonable to assume, as many have done (e.g. Rothwell, 1981) that innovation in new products and the growth of new industries would provide the impetus for a new spurt of growth in the economy. However, it seems that there are at least two main problems with such an over-simplified approach to understanding the current economic crisis. Most importantly, investment in new technology, leading to a new boom period, does not necessarily provide any long-term solutions: indeed, long-wave theory itself suggests that boom will be followed by recession. Second, the nature of current technological advances point towards a very different future of work. It is to this latter point that we shall now turn.

The development of technological systems as opposed to single discrete innovations is making possible the automation of a wide range of tasks that were previously separated from one another. Information technology can be seen as the convergence of three technologies – microelectronics, telecommunications and computing technology. In manufacturing industry the automation of complete production processes through the use of CAD/CAM (Computer Aided Design and Manufacturing) systems means that productivity and output remain high while far fewer workers are required. However, to date, perhaps the most significant effects of information technology, as least in terms of employment, are being felt in the service industries or in service occupations within manufacturing industry – areas previously relatively unchanged by technology, and, as we shall see in the next section, a major source of employment for women. This is not to underestimate the effects of the introduction of new technology into manufacturing. Indeed, as shown in our discussion below, when exploring the implications of new information technology for women's jobs, it is important to examine both the manufacturing and the service sectors. Before turning to this discussion, however, we shall first examine how the industrial/occupational structure of employment, both nationally and regionally, has changed in the post-war period and how far this change has resulted in genuine new employment opportunities for women.

4. The Changing Industrial/Occupational Structure of Employment and Women's Waged Work

(i) *Aggregate Trends*

Using data on the changing structure of industry and on the distribution of women's and men's employment across industrial sectors, some commentators have argued that women's employment opportunities have increased as men's have decreased. Broadly speaking, over the last 30–40 years at least, there has been a shedding of labour in mining and quarrying and in the older, heavy industries such as ship-building and steel-making – industries employing large numbers of men – and at the same time a growth in both the service sector and the consumer-based light industries employing large numbers of women. While there is clearly some truth in this argument, the picture is more complex. First, as Table 4.2 shows, there have been some significant shifts in the distribution of women's employment between industries over the last 30–40 years; but the origins of these shifts are discernible as early as 1841. Between 1841 and 1971 traditional employers of female labour such as the clothing and textile industries (which together accounted for 30 per cent of the total female waged labour force in 1841) were gradually replaced by the distributive trades and professional and scientific services whose share of total women's waged labour rose to about 40 per cent in 1971. The declining importance of 'miscellaneous services' which includes private domestic service as a source of employment is reflected in the fall in the relative numbers in this group, from 55 per cent in 1841 to 15 per cent in 1971.

Another interesting feature discernible in Table 4.2 is the differences in the growth of women's share of total employment between the various industries. Women's share rose in all groups over this period; however, the increases were most marked in those groups in which women had an important stake initially. For example, women's share of employment in the clothing and footwear industries rose from 36 per cent in 1841 to 73 per cent in 1971. On the other hand, the share of women in heavy industries (i.e. group 3), construction, public utilities (group 9) and transport and communications (group 10) – which together accounted for about half the total of male waged labour force in 1971 – increased from about 1 per cent in 1841 to only 17 per cent in 1971.

In order to make meaningful and accurate statements about people's jobs, it is necessary to know not only in which industry they work, but also their *occupation* in that industry. Thus, while Table 4.2 shows, for both men's and women's employment, the declining importance of agriculture and related activities and the growing importance of the service sector between 1841 and 1971, it does not tell us anything about the *type of jobs* being done by women and men over the period. An understanding of the occupational structure of employment is, in many senses, more important

TABLE 4.2 Percentage Distribution of Male and Female Workers in Britain by Industrial Groups, 1841–1971

Industrial groups	1841			1901			1931			1951			1961			1971		
	Female	Male	% Female workers	Female	Male	% Female workers	Female	Male	% Female workers	Female	Male	% Female workers	Female	Male	% Female workers	Female	Male	% Female workers
1. Agriculture, mining, etc.	4.9	33.0	5.1	1.6	19.5	3.2	1.4	16.7	3.6	1.9	12.0	6.5	1.5	9.3	7.3	1.5	6.0	12.4
2. Food, drinks, tobacco	1.6	4.3	11.5	4.6	6.2	23.2	4.2	3.1	37.7	4.0	3.0	37.1	3.6	2.7	38.7	3.3	3.0	39.3
3. Chemicals, metal manufacturing, engineering, etc.	0.8	7.3	3.7	2.2	13.9	6.1	6.0	15.0	4.7	12.1	21.5	20.1	13.3	23.8	21.2	12.0	24.4	22.1
4. Textiles	19.1	10.3	39.8	16.8	4.8	58.8	11.3	3.5	58.8	8.0	2.9	55.6	5.6	2.6	53.9	3.2	2.1	46.5
5. Leather, leather products, etc.	0.2	0.9	6.5	0.6	0.7	23.6	0.4	0.4	31.6	0.4	0.3	35.4	0.3	0.2	41.1	0.3	0.2	42.3
6. Clothing and footwear	10.9	7.0	35.8	16.6	3.6	65.1	8.9	2.4	62.6	7.0	1.3	70.5	5.2	1.0	72.3	4.0	0.8	73.3
7. Other manufacturing industries	1.2	4.1	9.7	4.1	5.8	22.5	5.2	6.4	26.4	6.0	6.5	28.9	5.7	6.9	28.6	5.0	7.4	28.3
8. Construction	0.1	7.3	0.4	0.1	10.9	0.2	0.2	7.1	1.4	0.6	8.8	2.9	0.9	9.7	4.3	1.1	10.9	5.8
9. Gas, electricity and water	0.0	0.0	2.0	0.0	0.7	0.2	0.1	1.7	3.3	0.4	2.1	8.8	0.5	2.1	11.0	0.7	2.0	16.9

10. Transport and communications	0.2	3.3	1.7	0.6	11.3	2.0	1.8	10.8	7.0	3.1	9.7	12.6	3.0	9.2	13.5	3.0	8.6	17.0
11. Distributive trades	0.9	0.7	32.1	1.2	0.8	37.4	15.2	14.2	32.1	16.9	9.9	43.1	19.9	10.7	47.2	18.0	9.7	51.8
12. Banking and other financial services	0.0	0.1	0.7	0.0	1.0	1.6	1.5	2.3	22.7	2.2	1.9	34.4	3.1	2.1	41.2	5.3	3.2	50.1
13. Professional and scientific services	2.6	2.1	30.0	6.7	2.7	50.2	8.5	3.1	54.6	13.1	4.1	58.6	16.9	5.3	60.5	21.4	6.9	64.1
14. Miscellaneous services	55.2	6.6	74.8	42.5	5.1	77.4	32.1	6.3	69.3	20.1	6.3	58.5	16.3	6.9	53.4	14.8	7.1	54.7
15. Public administration	0.1	1.7	1.2	0.6	3.2	7.2	2.7	6.7	15.2	4.0	9.4	15.9	3.7	7.2	19.8	5.2	7.4	28.8
16. Not classified	2.2	11.2	6.7	1.9	9.7	7.4	0.3	0.4	2.6	0.1	0.1	34.0	0.5	0.3	36.1	1.1	0.6	52.8
Total	100.0	100.0	100.0	–	100.0	100.0	100.0	–	100.0	100.0	100.0	–	100.0	100.0	100.0	–	100.0	–

Note To allow for higher degree of comparability between groups, Lee split up the data series into Series A 1841–1901 and Series B 1901–1971. Hence the figures for 1841 and subsequent years are not strictly comparable.

SOURCE   G. Joseph, *Women at Work* (Oxford: Philip Allen, 1983) pp. 136–7.
C. H. Lee, *British Regional Employment Statistics* (Cambridge: Cambridge University Press, 1979).

than an understanding of the industrial structure. 'People become qualified to do particular sorts of jobs rather than work for particular sorts of firms. And when the needs of the economy change, people become unemployed because they cannot find new employment which demands their particular skills.' (Gershuny, 1983.) However, while data on the industrial distribution of employment are relatively easy to obtain,[6] precise and reliable data on the occupational distribution of employment are more difficult to find.

In an attempt to arrive at a more accurate picture of the occupational structure both in specific industries and in the economy as a whole and to examine the way this has changed over time, Gershuny has compiled industrial/occupational employment matrices. These combine information on the occupational distribution of employment within industries (from the New Earnings Survey) with the annual Census of Employment. Estimates were arrived at by comparing five-year averages (which has the effect of smoothing sampling fluctuations). Data for the matrices were available only for the late 1960s and 1970s. Table 4.3 is a summary of the industrial/occupational distribution of employment in the UK over the years 1968–78. This table confirms that employment in the primary, manufacturing and utilities sectors has fallen as a proportion of total employment while the proportion of the service sector has grown. More important, however, this table illustrates changes in the *occupational* distribution of employment. While the proportion of total employment in manual occupations has fallen quite considerably over time it appears that this fall has not been to the benefit of all categories of service workers. The increase is concentrated in the first of these categories: the professional, technical, administrative and clerical workers with the remaining service categories (including sales, catering, cleaning, security and transport workers) showing no proportional increase.

Table 4.4, a slightly more disaggregated form of Table 4.3, expresses employment in each industrial/occupational category as a proportion of the total in the particular industrial sector. This table is particularly interesting when considering the causes and implications of changes in the employment structure for women's waged work. Although it is always difficult to identify the precise effect of technical change on the industrial/occupational structure of employment Gershuny has argued that Table 4.4 shows 'two relatively straightforward consequences of process innovation;

TABLE 4.3 *Broad Occupational – Industrial Distribution of Employment, UK*

Per cent of total employment

Occupations

Average 1968–73

Industries	Administrative, Professional, Technical, Clerical	Other White Collar	Manual	All
Primary	0.4	0.1	3.4	3.9
Manufacturing	8.1	2.1	25.7	35.9
Utilities	1.6	0.3	5.8	7.7
Services	24.4	15.9	12.2	52.5
All Sectors	34.5	18.4	47.1	100.0

Average 1974–8

	Administrative, Professional, Technical, Clerical	Other White Collar	Manual	All
Primary	0.5	0.1	2.7	3.3
Manufacturing	8.2	1.9	22.5	32.6
Utilities	2.1	0.2	4.9	7.2
Services	31.1	16.2	9.6	56.9
All Sectors	41.9	18.3	39.8	100.0

Change 1968–73 to 1974–8

	Administrative, Professional, Technical, Clerical	Other White Collar	Manual	All
Primary	0.1	0.0	-0.6	-0.6
Manufacturing	0.2	-0.2	-3.3	-3.3
Utilities	0.4	0.0	-0.9	-0.5
Services	6.7	0.3	-2.6	4.4
All Sectors	7.4	0.1	-7.4	

SOURCE Gershuny, J., *Social Innovation and the Division of Labour* (Oxford: Oxford University Press, 1983), p. 95.

TABLE 4.4 Occupational Distributions within Industrial Sectors, UK

Per cent of Employment in Industry

Occupations → / Industries ↓	Administrative and Technical	Educational Medical Professions	Clerical	Sales Workers	Security Workers	Catering and Cleaning	Farming Gardening	Transport and Communications Workers	Other Manual	All
Industries, 1968–73										
Primary	4.9	0.1	5.4	0.9	0.1	1.7	37.2	4.9	44.4	100.0
Manufacturing	10.8	0.3	11.4	2.9	0.4	3.5	0.1	3.0	68.4	100.0
Utilities	11.3	0.1	9.8	1.3	0.3	1.8	0.2	3.9	71.5	100.0
All Services	11.3	12.5	22.6	11.4	1.8	17.1	1.0	7.1	15.2	100.0
Trans/Telecoms	8.4	0.2	20.5	0.8	0.7	3.8	0.1	35.6	20.9	100.0
Distribution	11.3	0.2	16.6	41.9	0.2	4.9	0.3	5.5	19.9	100.0
Ins/Banking	16.1	0.2	60.5	9.0	0.7	7.1	0.9	0.5	5.0	100.0
Prof/Ed. Servs.	9.9	45.0	12.3	0.2	0.9	25.9	0.9	0.5	4.5	100.0
Misc. Serv.	10.0	3.3	15.9	6.3	0.6	38.3	1.1	2.4	22.0	100.0
Pub. Admin.	15.4	3.0	31.2	0.0	10.2	13.5	3.0	3.6	20.0	100.0
All Sectors	10.8	6.7	16.9	7.1	1.2	10.1	2.0	5.3	39.8	100.0
1974–8										
Primary	8.2	0.3	6.2	0.7	0.2	1.4	37.9	8.5	36.5	100.0
Manufacturing	13.0	0.4	11.9	2.4	0.5	2.8	0.1	7.2	61.7	100.0

Utilities	16.4	0.3	11.9	1.2	0.4	1.4	0.2	7.1	61.2	100.0
All Services	14.4	15.5	24.9	9.4	2.1	16.9	0.9	7.1	8.9	100.0
Trans/Telecoms	13.0	0.4	30.7	0.8	0.9	6.7	0.0	28.9	18.5	100.0
Distribution	16.3	0.7	20.2	36.1	0.3	3.6	0.2	10.3	12.2	100.0
Ins/Banking	21.8	0.5	60.6	7.6	1.5	4.0	0.4	1.0	2.6	100.0
Prof/Ed. Servs.	9.6	48.4	13.8	0.1	0.3	23.8	0.7	0.6	2.7	100.0
Misc. Servs.	12.5	8.1	15.5	4.6	0.6	40.2	1.2	3.5	13.6	100.0
Pub. Admin.	20.2	2.5	40.0	0.0	13.5	9.8	2.9	5.6	6.0	100.0
All Sectors	13.8	9.0	19.1	6.2	1.4	10.7	1.8	7.2	30.8	100.0

CHANGE, 1968–73 to 1974–8

Primary	3.3	0.1	0.8	−0.2	0.1	−0.3	0.7	3.6	−8.3	0.0
Manufacturing	2.2	0.2	0.4	−0.5	0.1	0.3	0.0	4.2	−6.7	0.0
Utilities	5.1	0.2	2.2	−0.1	0.0	−0.2	0.0	3.2	−10.3	0.0
All Services	3.1	2.9	2.2	−2.0	0.3	−0.2	−0.1	0.1	−6.3	0.0
Trans/Telecoms	4.6	0.2	1.2	0.0	0.2	2.9	0.0	−6.7	−2.3	0.0
Distribution	5.0	0.5	3.6	−4.9	0.1	−1.4	−0.1	4.8	−7.7	0.0
Ins/Banking	5.7	0.3	0.0	−1.3	0.8	−3.1	−0.5	0.5	−2.4	0.0
Prof/Ed. Servs.	−0.3	3.4	1.5	−0.1	−0.6	−2.1	−0.2	0.2	−1.8	0.0
Misc. Serv.	2.6	4.8	−0.4	−1.6	0.0	1.9	0.2	1.1	−8.4	0.0
Pub. Admin.	4.8	−0.6	8.8	0.0	3.1	−3.7	−0.1	1.9	−14.1	0.0
All Sectors	3.0	2.3	2.1	−0.9	0.3	0.6	−0.2	1.9	−9.0	0.0

SOURCE Gershuny, J., *Social Innovation and the Division of Labour* (Oxford: Oxford University Press, 1983) pp. 98–9.

that is, the proportion of manual workers declining relative to the Professional, Administrative and Technical workers and the clerical workers and, within these latter categories, the clerical workers' proportions declining relative to the others' (Gershuny, op. cit.). We know (see Table 4.5) that women are the majority of clerical workers (71 per cent in 1971) and therefore are most likely to be affected by any further introduction of new technology into this area of work. Table 4.4 also shows a marked decline in the proportion of sales and catering and cleaning workers in almost all industries over the two periods. Again, we know from other sources that the vast majority of workers in these occupational groups are women. (Women were 60 per cent of all shop owners, managers and assistants and 86 per cent of all charworkers in 1971, see Table 4.5.)

The changing industrial/occupational structure of employment over the last 40–50 years has increased the availability of waged work for women. However, the concentration of women into a few occupations defined as 'women's work' has largely continued. Table 4.5 shows the percentage distribution of women waged workers in England and Wales in thirteen occupations during the period 1911–71. These occupations between them contained about 80 per cent of all women in employment over the whole period, although the relative number of women employed in the different categories has changed. This occupational structure reflects and reinforces the generally subordinate position of women. While the jobs which women do in the formal labour market parallel the tasks they perform in the household, i.e. caring, cooking and cleaning, the sexual division of labour within both the home and the labour market continues to benefit both men and capitalists.

(ii) *Regional Trends*

As Figure 4.1 shows, there have been great regional variations in the proportion of employees who are women. Since the 1950s there has been a marked convergence between the different regions, with the rate of change in those with a low percentage of women in the workplace increasing sharply after 1961. For the period between 1951 and 1971, this rise in the proportion of women paid workers does not appear to be a result of an absolute decline in the number of men in paid work. Women's employment

TABLE 4.5 *Principal Occupations of the Female Work Force In England and Wales 1911–71*

Occupational groups	Percentage of total employment					Percentage of women workers in each group for 1971
	1911	1931	1951	1961	1971	
Private domestic servants	26.1	20.7	5.7	3.8	2.2	83.8
Clothing workers	14.0	9.4	7.2	5.5	3.6	80.0
Textile workers	13.5	11.1	6.5	4.0	1.9	53.8
Laundry workers	3.5	2.0	1.5	1.0	0.7	77.4
Clerks, typists	3.0	10.2	20.3	25.4	27.3	71.1
Shop owners, managers and assistants	9.3	10.9	12.0	13.3	10.8	60.0
Waitresses, cooks and kitchen hands; maids and domestic staff in hotels and schools	3.2	4.5	7.8	7.1	7.0	82.9
Metal workers, (including electrical and electronic)	2.2	3.2	6.0	5.5	4.4	11.0
Charworkers, etc.	2.6	2.5	3.4	4.4	4.5	86.0
Nurses	1.7	2.5	3.3	3.7	4.3	91.4
Teachers (school)	3.8	3.2	2.9	3.7	4.1	63.6
Packers and bottlers	–	1.8	2.1	2.2	2.4	72.9
Hairdressers	0.1	0.6	0.7	1.4	1.4	78.3
Total for above occupations	82.9	82.6	79.4	81.0	74.6	53.7 (68.5)*

Note * excluding metal workers

SOURCE G. Joseph, *Women at Work* (Oxford: Philip Allen, 1983) p. 143

in Great Britain increased by nearly 2 million between 1951 and 1971. During the same period men's employment declined by less than 300 000. However, between 1971 and 1981, women's employment increased by 300 000 whereas men's employment decreased by 3.1 million. We shall examine these two periods separately.

Those regions which initially had a low percentage of women paid workers were characterised either by the predominance of

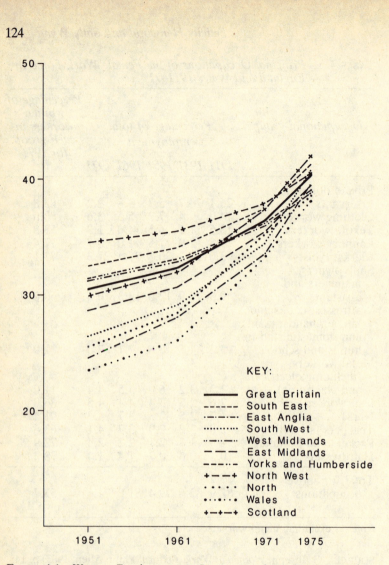

FIGURE 4.1 *Women Employees as a Percentage of Total Employees, by Region, 1951–75*

SOURCE   C. H. Lee, *British Regional Employment Statistics 1841–71* (Cambridge: Cambridge University Press, 1979). (1951, 1961, 1971 data).

British Labour Statistics Year Book 1975 (London: HMSO, (1975 data).

heavy industry (East Midlands) or agriculture (South-West and East Anglia). Some regions (Wales and the North) were dominated by a combination of heavy industry and agriculture. The sharp increase in the proportion of women paid workers in these regions which occurred after 1961 is largely a result of an increase in the opportunities for work in the services. For example, in 'insurance, banking, finance and business services', in 1951, of all regions, Wales had the lowest proportion of women (24.3 per cent); but by 1971, although Wales still had the lowest proportion of women, the proportion had doubled (48.4 per cent). As Figure 4.2 shows, the difference in the proportion of women workers in this sector across regions has converged. The regions in which the increase in the proportion of women paid workers was relatively small between 1951 and 1971 were the South-East, which has a traditionally high demand for women's labour, especially in the services; the West Midlands, which has a large light engineering industry; and Yorkshire, Humberside, the North-West and Scotland, which have large textile industries. The potential for increased participation of women in these regions was, therefore, smaller.

In the second period, between 1971 and 1981, the rise in the proportion of women in the workforce is more likely to reflect the absolute decline in the number of men in paid work. For example, the relatively large increase in the proportion of women paid workers in Scotland (see Figure 4.1) probably reflects the decline of shipping and heavy industrial activity in Scotland during that period. While it is useful to examine the changes in the participation rates of women in different regions it is also important to be aware of regional differences in industrial structure. Table 4.6 lists the industries which accounted for 85 per cent of women's employment, nationally and for each region in 1951 and in 1975. This table illustrates how service industries have become major sources of employment for women in all regions since 1951. In 1951 there was great diversity of the industrial composition of regions. By 1975 there was greater uniformity across regions in the relative importance of different industries, but there continued to be important disparities between regions. Such disparities suggest that the introduction of new technology will have different effects in different regions.

Electrical engineering; food, drink and tobacco; and clothing and footwear are important sources of employment for women in all

126

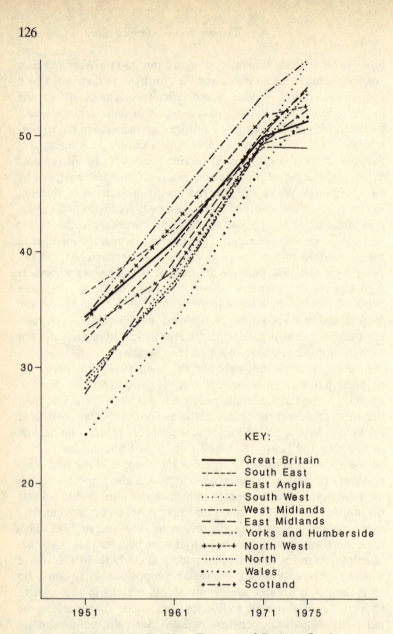

FIGURE 4.2 *Insurance, Banking, Finance and Business Services: Women Employees as a Percentage of Total Employees, by Region, 1951–75*

SOURCE   See Figure 4.1.

TABLE 4.6 *Industrial Composition of Women's Employment by Region, 1951 and 1975*

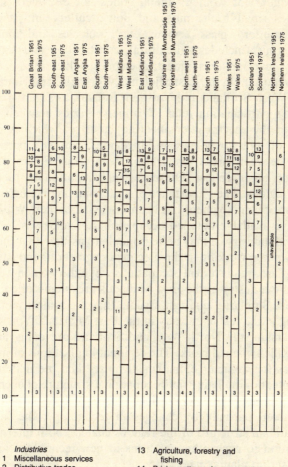

	Industries		
1	Miscellaneous services	13	Agriculture, forestry and fishing
2	Distributive trades	14	Bricks, pottery, glass, cement
3	Professional and scientific services	15	Vehicles
4	Textiles	16	Metal manufacture
5	Clothing and footwear	17	Mechanical engineering
6	Food, drink and tobacco	18	Other manufacturing industries
7	Public administration and defence		
8	Transport and communication		
9	Electrical engineering		
10	Paper, printing and publishing		
11	Metal goods, not elsewhere specified		
12	Insurance, banking, finance and business services		

SOURCES C. M. Lee, *British Regional Employment Statistics 1841–1971* (Cambridge: Cambridge University Press 1979). *British Labour Statistics Year Book 1975* (London: HMSO, 1975).

Note Industries which together account for 85 per cent of women's employment regions, except the West Midlands. The West Midlands is exceptional in the importance of the following industries as sources of employment for women: 'metal goods not elsewhere specified' (includes small tools, nuts and bolts, cutlery and jewellery), 'bricks, pottery, glass, cement, etc.', 'vehicles' and 'mechanical engineering' (includes agricultural, construction and textile machinery, machine tools, industrial engines, valves, etc.). Textiles is more important in the East Midlands, Yorkshire and Humberside, North-West, Scotland and Northern Ireland: as Figure 4.3 shows, women's participation relative to men's varies between regions. Even in the electrical engineering industry, which is a major source of jobs for women in all regions, women's participation varies between areas, as can be seen from Figure 4.4. This variation might reflect differences in occupational structure between regions. The importance of understanding the occupational structure of employment has been discussed earlier. While we do not have available detailed occupational breakdowns by sex, region and industry, it may be reasonable to assume that the majority of women working in the electrical engineering industry in the South-East are in clerical occupations while the women working in the same industry in the East Midlands are 'semi-skilled manual' workers. Similarly, one can assume that the majority of women working in the textile industry in the East Midlands, Yorkshire and Humberside, the North-West and Scotland are doing low paid, semi-skilled manual work. The regional implications of new technologies for women's employment must, then, be understood in the context of the industrial/occupational structure of each region, bearing in mind the ways in which these structures are themselves determined partially by changes in technology; the industrial/occupational structure of the regions change, both internally and in relation to each other, as firms in new technology industries either set up plants or relocate.

(iii) *New Information Technology and Women's Jobs*

Whenever new information technology is introduced women's jobs are affected, either by direct application to the tasks being performed by women, or indirectly when production lines are automated and the plant requires less support staff. A substantial proportion of the women employed in each sector of the economy,

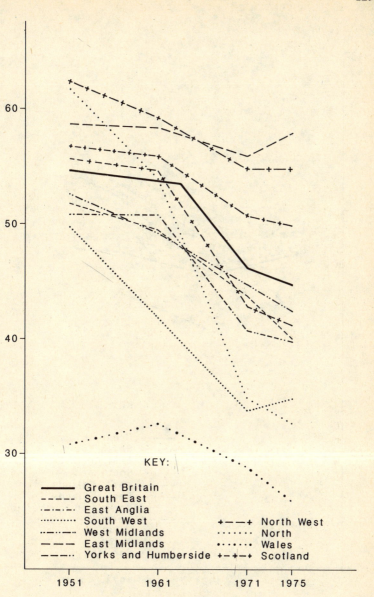

FIGURE 4.3 *Textiles: Women Employees as a Percentage of Total Employees, by Region, 1951–75*

SOURCE See Figure 4.1.

130

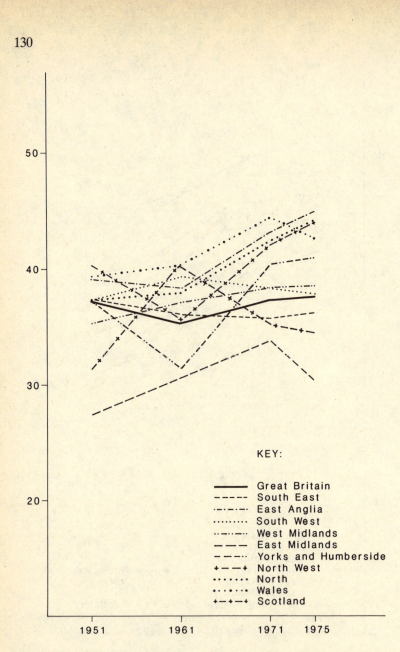

FIGURE 4.4 *Electrical Engineering: Women Employees as a Percentage of Total Employees, by Region, 1951–75*

SOURCE See Figure 4.1.

across the country, though perhaps to a greater extent in the South-East, do clerical work. There are many examples of jobs loss which have occurred when clerical work has been computerised – for example, a mail order firm in West Yorkshire has reduced its full-time clerical staff from 1000 to 550 and its part-timers from 100 to 50 (Huws, 1982). Not all job loss is directly attributable to the introduction of new technology, but it is a major contributing factor. The increased productivity made possible by new technology reduces the need to hire more staff in many cases, even if no jobs are actually lost.

The introduction of new technology in offices has undoubtedly brought some benefits for some clerical workers. There are opportunities to learn new skills. For example, for typists boring and repetitive tasks such as retyping and correcting are made easier and quicker; in theory, giving women more time to become involved in more interesting tasks. However, the use of word processors brings its own set of disadvantages. Many women sit in front of word processors and VDUs for long periods of time. Machine pacing, monitoring (resulting in further deskilling of workers, as well as providing capitalists with the opportunity to increase control over the labour force) and health hazards such as eyestrain, headaches, backaches and stress have all been cited as examples of the ways in which word processors have led to a deterioration in the quality of work (SPRU Women and Technology Studies, 1982).

Another example of an area of women's work being dramatically affected by new technology is in selling. Several social and technological innovations of the last decade have combined to effect major changes in the organisation and structure of selling. For example, there has been a trend away from the 'corner shop' and towards larger, self-service stores where the use of computerised equipment for stock control, reordering and pricing is resulting in a reduction in the demand for workers in these areas. It has been suggested that the potential for job reduction in these superstores is huge, especially in areas such as checkouts, stocktaking, pricing and consumer assistance – all jobs where large numbers of women are employed. This trend has implications for the intra-regional distribution of women's work. For example, as large self-service shops open up in the centre of towns, smaller corner shops have been forced to close. This has resulted not only in a loss of waged work for women living on the outskirts of towns and cities who had been employed in these small shops, but an increase in the amount of unwaged work these women are expected to undertake. Travelling to and from the town centre to shop can be extremely costly and time-consuming.

Both intra- and inter-regional shifts in employment may occur as a result of changes being brought about by the introduction of new technologies in banking, insurance and other financial institutions. A study by Moore and Levie (1981) concluded that new technology will bring about a reorganisation of the banking system into a three-tiered operation (centre, area office and service branch). Gershuny and Miles (1983) suggest that this reorganisation will have important consequences for the structure of employment. More specialised staff will be employed at the centre and area offices, located in urban areas, and service branches will be increasingly automated. In these service branches, in particular, the demand for clerical workers, cashiers and tellers seems likely to decrease. These jobs are most often held by women. In manufacturing industries, women's employment opportunities have also been affected in various ways. Many of the routine assembly, sorting, catering and packaging (jobs women do) are affected when production lines are automated. The use of microelectronics to control production lines in many industries where women work – textiles, food, drink and tobacco, electrical engineering, clothing – has resulted in an overall reduction in the number of workers needed to produce the same or greater output. Cadbury's plans to reduce its workforce from 6000 to 1000 over the next ten years, by using robots to select, sort, grade and package chocolates (Huws, op. cit. p. 48). Many women's jobs have been deskilled with the introduction of new technology, and workers who previously had skilled or semi-skilled work have been reduced to machine operators or minders in some cases.

Another effect of automating production processes is that employers, in order to maximise profits, want to run their new machines almost constantly. This results in an increase in shift work. For women, shift-working, especially the night shift (which tends to be the best paid) is difficult; both because women with children have to ensure that they are available when their children are home and because, in law, women are prohibited from working at night in some industries. Again, the loss of jobs which results directly from increased automation of the production process might lead indirectly to a loss of support jobs. Fewer workers 'on the line' means fewer workers are needed in service-type jobs such as clerical work, cleaning and catering, which are traditionally women's jobs. Women living in the Midlands, Yorkshire and Humberside, the North-West and Scotland are most likely to be directly affected by any technological changes in these manufacturing industries. It is often argued that compensation for jobs lost will be provided in the form of jobs producing new consumer products and the new machines themselves. While employment has increased since 1970 in the computer and electronic capital goods sectors, men's employment has increased three times faster than women's employment in these areas. Furthermore, women's employment in these sectors continues to be concentrated in the lower-paid clerical and operator grades (Electronics EDC, 1983).

As discussed earlier, when examining the effect of technological change on employment it is important to distinguish between process innovations – which often result in loss of jobs, particularly when demand is stagnant, and product innovations which might secure or even create jobs. Some recent case-study work by Goddard and Thwaites (1983) has explored the regional employment effects of product and process innovations. Their research was undertaken in an effort to explain the higher rate of job loss than is observed in the North as compared to the South-East. Analysing surveys of the introduction of new products and processes into manufacturing plants in different regions of the UK, they find that the rate of introduction of new and improved products is significantly higher in the South-East. The rate of adoption of new manufacturing processes was not significantly different between regions – but process innovations appeared to displace jobs at a higher rate in the North than in the South-East. They also found changes in the structure of employment, specifically 'any increases in employment tended to be biased in favour of scientists, technologists and administrative staff and decreases in employment biased towards operators, craftsmen (*sic*), clerks and draughtsmen (*sic*)'. (ibid.). They point out that it is the South-East which has the strongest representation of the professional occupations. They fail to point out that it is also men who continue to be most strongly represented in the professional occupations. New technology does not appear to be opening up many new opportunities for women.

One further issue concerning the implications of new technology for women's jobs deserves mention. New technologies have opened up the possibility of working from home with the use of a computer. Women's employment is the focus of attention here, both because the types of work women do (for example, clerical work) are more adaptable to 'work at a distance' and because of the association of women with the household. It is, therefore, argued that women could combine waged work and domestic responsibilities by working from home. The potential for increased home-working through use of new technology could well appear advantageous to women, especially if other forms of paid work are not available. However, women's past experience of home-working in traditional industries, i.e. textiles and garment-making, have taught us to be wary of optimistic claims for this new form of home-work. Traditional home-workers, almost all of whom are women, are among the most exploited of all workers: women working alone from home have little opportunity for social contact or organisation with other workers which could lead to better pay and conditions. Women in these circumstances may find it difficult to resist unrealistic demands on their time, not only from their employers, but also from their family.

5. **Conclusions**

Over the past century there has been a dramatic increase in women's participation in paid work across all regions of the UK. We have witnessed a convergence of industrial structures of the different regions largely due to the growth of the service sector, which has brought increased employment opportunities for women. However, women's experience of paid work is still very different from that of men. Women remain concentrated in a few occupations defined as 'women's work', they are more likely to work part-time and they still bear most of the responsibility for child-care and domestic work.

It is clear that the new microelectronics-based technologies are going to have wide-reaching implications for both the quality and quantity of women's work. It is very difficult to move beyond broad generalisations based either on aggregate data or on isolated case studies. In order to assess better the implications of new technology there is a need for more reliable data on the industry/ occupation structure of employment by region and sex, and a more

dynamic theoretical framework which incorporates both technological change and the specific characteristics of women's work. In
this chapter we hope to have moved some way towards establishing such a framework.

On the basis of the earlier sections regarding the interaction of
capitalism and patriarchy and on the relationship between technology and employment, various scenarios for the future of women's
work emerge. If present levels of unemployment continue or
increase, there may be renewed efforts by both government and
trades unions to preserve the remaining jobs for men and to force
women more firmly back into the household. Alternatively the
new technologies, though making it technically possible for
women to enter areas of the formal economy previously closed to
them, will allow capitalists to take advantage of women's generally
lower rates of pay. There exists a potential conflict between
capitalism and patriarchy as a result of new information technology and it is not at all clear how this conflict will be resolved.

Notes

1. This discussion draws heavily on Hilary Wainwright (1978) 'Women
   and the Division of Labour', in Philip Abrams (ed.) *Work, Urbanism
   and Inequality* (London: Weidenfeld & Nicolson).
2. A recent study by P. Elias and B. Main (1982) indicates that part-time
   work often means a drop in employment status for women. The study
   found that one in twenty-five women working part-time in low-skilled
   catering and cleaning occupations had teaching qualifications; one in
   twelve had nursing qualifications and one in six had clerical and
   commercial qualifications.
3. Protective legislation does not appear to adequately 'protect' women
   from night work (the supposed objective) when this work is considered women's work, i.e., nursing or cleaning.
4. Cynthia Cockburn (1983) has documented how men fought to keep
   women out of the printing industry, for example.
5. It was the Russian economist, Kondratiev, who, in the early part of
   this century, did most to propagate the idea of 'long cycles of economic development'. It was Schumpeter who, in the 1930s, took up
   these ideas and introduced technology and development into them.
   Schumpeter ascribed a central role to technological innovation in his
   interpretation of long waves, arguing that new technologies caused
   the expansion of the economy and that once such innovations had run
   their course, the economy went into a period of depression. It is on
   Schumpeter's work that much of the current literature on long waves
   is based.

6. J. Gershuny, (1983) *Social Innovation and the Division of Labour* (Oxford: Oxford University Press).

Bibliography

Abrams, P. (ed.) (1978) *Work, Urbanism and Inequality, UK Society Today* (London: Weidenfeld & Nicolson).

Bowlby, S., Foord, J., Lewis, J. and McDowell, L. (1982) *Urban Austerity – The Impact on Women*, mimeo. (Institute of British Geographers, Women and Geography Study Group).

Central Statistical Office (1983) *Social Trends* (London: HMSO).

Cockburn, C. (1983) *Brothers: Male Dominance and Technological Change* (London: Pluto Press).

Electronics EDC (1983) 'Employment and Technology Task Force' (London, NEDO) unpublished mimeo.

Elias, P. and Main, B. (1982) *Women's Working Lives: Evidence from the National Training Survey* (University of Warwick, Institute of Employment Research).

Equal Opportunities Commission (1983) *The Fact About Women Is* (Manchester: EOC).

Freeman, C. (1982) 'Science, Technology, and Unemployment', *Papers in Science, Technology and Public Policy* (London: SPRU/Imperial College Joint Publication).

Freeman, C., Clark, J. and Soete, L. (1982) *Unemployment and Technical Innovation: A Study of Long Waves and Economic Development* (London: Frances Pinter).

Gershuny, J. (1983) *Social Innovation and the Division of Labour* (Oxford: Oxford University Press).

Gershuny, J. and Miles, I. D. (1983) *The New Service Economy* (London: Frances Pinter).

Goddard, J. B. and Thwaites, A. T. (1983) Unemployment in the North; Jobs in the South – The Regional Dimension to the Introduction of New Technologies. Centre for Urban and Regional Development Studies, *Discussion Paper no. 54* (Nov).

Hartmann, H. (1976) 'Capitalism, Patriarchy and Job Segregation by Sex?', in Blaxall, M. and Peagan, B. (eds) *Women and the Workplace: The Implications of Occupational Segregation* (Chicago: University of Chicago Press).

Huws, U. (1982) *Your Job in the Eighties: A Woman's Guide to New Technology* (London: Pluto Press).

Joseph, G. (1983) *Women at Work* (Oxford: Phillip Allan).

Kondratiev, N. (1925) 'The Major Economic Cycles'. English translation reprint in *Lloyds Bank Review* (1978) no. 129.

Moore, R. and Levie, H. (1981) *The Impact of New Technology on Trade Union Organisation* (Oxford: Ruskin College). (Report to European Commission.)

Office of Population Censuses and Surveys (1981) *General Household Survey* (London: HMSO).

Rothwell, R. (1981) 'Technology, Structural Change and Employment', *Omega*, **9**, **3**, pp. 229–45.

Schumpeter, J. A. (1939) *Business Cycles; A Theoretical, Historical, and Statistical Analysis of the Capitalist Process*, 2 vols (New York: McGraw-Hill).

SPRU Women and Technology Series (1982) *Microelectronics and Women's Employment in Britain* (University of Sussex: SPRU Occasional Paper no. 17 SPRU).

TUC (1983) *Women in the Labour Market: A TUC Report* (London: TUC).

Wainwright, H. (1978) 'Women and the Division of Labour', in Abrams, P. (ed.) *Work, Urbanism and Inequality* (London: Weidenfeld & Nicolson).

Acknowledgement

We would like to thank Ian Miles, Luc Soete and Christine Zmroczek for comments on an earlier draft. Responsibility for the views contained herein remains, of course, our own.

5
Regional Dimensions of Industrial Decline

JOHN RHODES

1. Introduction

The objective of this chapter is to outline the regional dimensions of de-industrialisation in the UK, concentrating on the period from 1966 to 1982, when manufacturing employment has been on a falling trend. De-industrialisation is defined as the failure of a country or region to secure a rate of growth of output and net exports of all kinds sufficient to achieve full employment. In order to secure or maintain full employment a country or a region needs to secure a rate of growth of output in all sectors taken together, gross domestic product (GDP), sufficient to match the growth in labour productivity plus any increase in the labour force, after allowing for net migration. In Section 2 the growth of GDP in the UK regions is examined. It is shown that, at the national level, the main sectors of economic activity gave grown at different rates, so that the composition of these sectors in the regions has an important influence on the growth of GDP in the various regions.

Leaving the activities of government on one side a region is likely to experience a relatively rapid growth in GDP if its traded goods sectors perform well. If the region is very competitive in selling goods or services to other regions and abroad, its GDP will grow relatively quickly and/or its underlying balance-of-payments position will grow stronger. There are no balance-of-trade data for the UK regions. However, Section 3 attempts to estimate changes in the balance of trade of UK regions indirectly, using the CSO regional accounts data.

In considering the process of de-industrialisation prominence is given to manufacturing only because Britain, as most other advanced countries, has relied heavily on manufacturing activities as a source of net exports and employment. If Britain had alternative sources of net exports which were growing rapidly, then the relative decline of manufacturing industry would not matter. But with North Sea oil predicted to reach its peak in the mid-1980s, the growth in net exports for services and food cannot be relied on to replace the loss of manufacturing and oil net exports and secure further growth sufficient to achieve full employment. The same applies to the UK regions. All have historically relied to a greater or lesser extent on manufacturing industry as a source of output and employment.

There are good reasons for thinking that individual regions will not be able to escape the consequences of national de-industrialisation. Many of the pressures facing manufacturing firms are national or international in character and will therefore exert the same kind of influence on manufacturing firms in all regions. The forces of international competition, the exchange rate, the growth of demand and interest rates will be important in setting the business prospects for all firms irrespective of their regional location. But there are also good reasons for expecting the pace of de-industrialisation and its consequences to differ between regions. Regions have inherited manufacturing sectors of different sizes and different industrial compositions, and the characteristics of that inheritance will be important in determining the current performance of manufacturing industry. The average age and size of firms, the proportion of plants which are foreign-owned and branch plants of multiregional firms, the proportions located in densely urban areas, the location of the region and the quality of its labour force are just some of the inherited characteristics which may result in a variable regional outcome to any national trend towards de-industrialisation.

The *interaction* between a set of inherited regional characteristics and the government's response to de-industrialisation can also have important differential consequences for regions. For example, if central government's response to a substantial improvement in net exports from North Sea oil was to expand home demand via fiscal or monetary expansion the effect on regions would be different from an alternative response of restricting home demand and allowing the exchange rate to rise. Regions with large manufacturing sectors, such as the West Midlands, would suffer disproportionately from the latter type of response involving exchange-rate appreciation and high interest rates compared with a policy of allowing domestic demand to rise. Since 1979 domestic demand has been cut by restrictive fiscal and monetary policies and the West Midlands has shown an acceleration in its rate of de-industrialisation compared with the period before 1979. By contrast, regions which already had a proportionately small manufacturing sector, such as the South-East could be expected to fare relatively better under these nationally restrictive conditions.

Section 4, therefore, is concerned with the important question of how well the manufacturing sector has fared in the UK regions. Changes in manufacturing output in the regions are briefly examined and compared with changes in manufacturing employment. The regions which have fared worst in recent years are the central regions of Britain such as the North-West of England, Yorkshire and Humberside and the West Midlands, which traditionally constituted the industrial heartland of the nation. Consideration is also given in this section to a brief analysis of some of the factors which explain differential growth in manufacturing industry between the regions.

Before going on to consider issues relating to regional policy Section 5 breaks off to post the question whether a national economic policy of restructuring is likely to bring about meaningful economic recovery and regeneration. There is not scope here to answer the question comprehensively but the suggestion is made that de-industrialisation occurs in Britain because it secures only half the restructuring process. Old labour-intensive activities are rationalised and closed down, but insufficient new industries and activities are generated to take their place. Evidence is presented to illustrate this one-sided restructuring process taking place in UK manufacturing industries in the recent recession. There are few, if any, signs that a rapid recovery in manufacturing output, sufficient to move the economy and its regions back towards full employment, is likely to be achieved in the late 1980s. It is more likely that the process of de-industrialisation will continue with unemployment levels remaining high and rising further.

Section 5 then considers some implications of de-industrialisation for regional policy. There can be no doubt that de-industrialisation raises new dilemmas for regional policy-makers which are not going to be easily resolved.

There is, of course, no inevitable requirement for regions to have a large manufacturing sector. Provided there is sufficient activity in other sectors such as agriculture, mining and services to maintain full employment at average levels of income, there is no need for every region to have manufacturing industry. This is also true of small nations. However, the problem for British regions is that they support large populations, they have traditionally been centres for manufacturing activity and in general the prospects of having sufficient activity in non-manufacturing sectors, which have potential for growth, are severely limited. Most British regions still rely too heavily on manufacturing industry for output and employment to think in terms of abandoning it without a struggle.

Yet regions in general neither have the institutional framework nor the policy instruments with which to fight a war against de-industrialisation. While central government has policy instruments at its disposal such as the exchange rate, interest rates, tariffs and subsidies, the individual region has no such policy-setting autonomy. At best it can hope that central government will carry out a regionally differentiated policy of subsidisation in its favour. If this does not occur, or such a policy is ineffective, then the labour market consequences for the regions of de-industrialisation will be high levels of unemployment, poverty and outward migration on a large scale.

2. Regional Differences in the Growth of Output, 1966–81

The growth in GDP is a good indicator of the overall economic health of a region. If a region can secure a rate of growth of GDP sufficient to exceed any natural increase in the labour supply and the growth in labour productivity then employment will grow faster than labour supply and unemployment and net outward migration will fall. Traditionally in the UK the underlying rate of productivity growth, generated by such developments as new investment, innovation, reduced restrictive practices, improved skills and organisation, has been running at an average of between 2 per cent and 3 per cent per annum. To have maintained full employment therefore would have required a GDP growth rate of

TABLE 5.1 *Annual Growth Rates in GDP, by Region, 1966–81 (percentages)*

	1966–70	1970–4	1974–8	1978–81	1966–81
UK	3.1	2.3	1.7	−2.2	1.4
Assisted Area regions	3.2	2.8	2.1	−2.3	1.7
Central regions	2.6	1.5	1.7	−3.9	0.8
South/east regions	3.4	2.2	1.8	−1.3	1.1
North	1.9	2.4	2.5	−2.6	1.3
Wales	2.7	2.9	2.3	−1.9	1.6
Scotland	4.6	3.3	1.0	−2.7	1.7
Northern Ireland	3.1	2.3	1.7	−2.2	1.8
Yorkshire and Humberside	1.5	2.4	1.9	−3.1	0.9
West Midlands	2.3	0.9	1.1	−4.6	0.8
East Anglia	4.6	2.4	3.9	−1.0	2.7
East Midlands	1.0	4.3	2.7	−1.0	1.9
South-East	3.2	1.2	1.3	−1.5	1.2
South-West	2.4	5.3	2.3	−0.9	2.5

Note Regional groupings defined as in Table 5.2.

SOURCE Central Statistical Office Regional Accounts in *Economic Trends* (annually).

at least 3 per cent per annum, since there have also been significant increases in labour supply through increased population and increased activity rates among women.

Table 5.1 shows that both the UK and almost all of the regions have failed to secure this 'required' growth rate in GDP of 3 per cent per annum. Indeed between 1978 and 1981 the GDP growth rates were substantially negative. Growth in output in the UK as a whole has been slowing down persistently since 1966 from a figure in excess of 3 per cent per annum between 1966 and 1970 to one of −2.2 per cent per annum in the recession of 1978 to 1981. While all regions reflect this general pattern there are also some important differences. The Assisted Area regions taken together experienced a growth rate in GDP slightly better than the national average until 1978, after which it became slightly worse. The same is generally true for the south-east regions except, that they have declined relatively little in the recent recession. The central regions, by contrast, have grown at a rate less than the national average for much of the period, and in the downturn of 1978 to 1981 output in these central regions fell at almost twice the rate occurring in the nation as a whole.

Taking the period 1966 to 1981 as a whole, the individual regions which grew most slowly were the West Midlands (0.2 per cent), the North-West (0.8 per cent), Yorkshire and Humberside (0.8 per cent) and the South-East (1.2 per cent). The fastest-growing regions were East Anglia (2.7 per cent), the South-West (2.5 per cent) and the East Midlands (1.9 per cent).

One major cause of differences in regional growth rates is the sectoral composition of output. Table 5.2 shows the sectoral composition of output for 1981 in the Assisted Areas, central regions, the south-east and the UK as a whole. The volume growth of each sector nationally between 1974 and 1981 is also shown. The sectors in which the volume of output *declined* are construction (−20 per cent), manufacturing (−17 per cent) and mining, excluding North Sea oil, (−3 per cent). The south-east group of regions had only 26 per cent of their activity in these sectors compared with 34 per cent in the Assisted Areas and almost 38 per cent in central regions. The volume of output *increased* most in insurance, banking and finance, public utilities and ownership of dwellings. Again this favoured the overall growth rate in the south-east regions relative to central regions and Assisted Areas.

The extent to which these variations in sectoral composition have affected the growth of GDP in the regions is shown in Table 5.3.

For the UK as a whole *real* GDP in 1981 was similar to what it had been in 1974. But within this, central regions declined by about 5 per cent, the Assisted Areas grew by 1.7 per cent and south-east regions by over 3 per cent. Table 5.3 shows that the sectoral composition of output accounted for about half of these regional growth differences in the case of central and south-east regions. The other half was accounted for by differential growth performance of the sectors. The Assisted Areas shared an adverse sectoral composition effect of −1.2 per cent but a favourable differential growth effect of 2.9 per cent, the highest of the three regional groupings.

TABLE 5.2   *Sectoral Composition of Output in the UK and the Regions, 1981*

	UK		% of GDP in each area, 1981		
	% share 1981	*% volume change 1974–81*	*Traditional assisted Area regions[1]*	*Central regions[2]*	*South-east regions[3]*
Agriculture	2.3	+12	3.6	1.8	2.0
Mining (exc. North Sea oil)	1.8	− 3	3.2	2.2	1.0
Manufacturing	23.4	−17	23.3	29.2	20.1
Construction	6.4	−20	7.6	6.3	5.0
Gas, electricity, water	3.1	+15	3.9	3.2	2.8
Transport and comm.	7.9	+ 6	7.3	7.1	8.5
Distribution	9.4	+1	8.6	9.4	9.7
Insurance, banking and finance	9.0	+20	5.8	6.7	11.5
Ownership of dwellings	6.5	+14	4.8	6.3	7.3
Professional, scientific and miscellaneous services	22.8	+11	24.2	21.8	22.7
Public Admin. and defence	7.5	+ 4	7.8	6.1	8.1

Notes [1] Assisted Area regions are Scotland, Wales, Northern Ireland and the Northern region of England.
[2] Central regions are the North-West, Yorkshire and Humberside and the West Midlands.
[3] South-East regions are the South-West, the South-East, East Anglia and the East Midlands.

3. Regional Balance of Payments

Regions which have suffered most from de-industrialisation have experienced a disproportionate fall in manufacturing output. As

TABLE 5.3   *The Impact of Sectoral Composition on Regional Growth in GDP, 1974–81*

	Actual percentage 1974 to 1981	*Contribution[1] of sectoral composition*	*Differential[1] growth of sectors*
UK	−0.5		
Traditional Assisted Areas	+1.7	−1.2	+2.9
Central regions	−4.9	−2.2	−2.9
South-east regions	+3.1	+1.2	+1.9

[1] These are derived from a simple shift-share analysis. The sectoral composition column shows the effect of a region having a disproportionate share of sectors which are everywhere growing rapidly or slowly. The differential growth column measures how well individual sectors have grown in the region relative to their national counterparts.

Note   Regional groupings defined as in Table 5.2.

most manufactured products are sold predominantly on a national and international market, such regions are likely to register a relatively larger fall in exports (from the region) and consequently a deterioration in their balance-of-payments position or a fall in income.

The balance of payments of the UK regions has never been measured and indeed is never likely to be. Data for the very complex variety and large volume of interregional transactions would be very costly to collect. But it is possible to estimate the trade deficit/surplus of each region by taking the difference between income generated by production in each region and total expenditure in the region.

Such an estimation is made possible through the regional accounts produced by the Central Statistical Office.[1] These accounts are reasonably complete on the income side, but only cover part of expenditure, namely consumers' expenditure and a major part of gross fixed capital formation. This leaves some capital formation and the whole of public consumption to be allocated across the regions in order to complete the expenditure side of the regional accounts. Fortunately public consumption is largely made up of wages in the public sector and, since data on public sector employment are available by region, the allocation is likely to be reasonably accurate. Nevertheless it should be emphasised that this indirect method of estimating regional trade balances will be subject to a margin of error.

Regional balances of trade are not normally identified or measured and regions do not need special policy action in order to secure balance-of-payments equilibrium. Differences between income generated by production in each region and total regional expenditure are financed by a variety of transfers. On the government account, expenditure on public services, subsidies, grants and social security benefits is offset to a greater or lesser degree by indirect taxes and income taxes levied in each region. The business sector contributes some investment spending in each region offset by retained profits. In addition the personal sector may borrow to finance investment (mainly house purchase), offset to a greater or lesser extent by savings deposited in the banking and insurance system. Thus the balance-of-payments position of a region, within the full economic and monetary union which forms the UK, depends not only on what the region produces and how competitive it is, but also on the differential incidence of government tax and expenditure decisions between the regions and on the location of housing and other investment which in turn may reflect, *inter alia*, residential preferences.

Table 5.4 shows regional balance-of-payments estimates for each region for selected years between 1971 and 1981, expressed as £s per head relative to the UK average and measured at 1980 prices. The regions show wide differences both in terms of deficits and surpluses at any one point in time and also in terms of changes through time.

Two regions, Yorkshire & Humberside and the East Midlands, show a stable balance-of-payments position in surplus; while the Northern region has moved from deficit in 1971 to a small surplus by 1981. Production in these regions exceeds expenditure, and they can therefore be regarded as 'net exporters'.

Two regions, namely East Anglia and the South-West, showed a substantial deficit until 1978, followed by a rapid improvement between 1978 and 1981. The large deficits were caused by a high level of expenditure on defence in these regions and by an above-average rate of private house-building as more people moved out

TABLE 5.4   *Regional Balances of Payments Relative to UK Average (per capita £s 1980 prices)*

	1971	1976	1978	1981
North	−137	17	2	44
Yorkshire and Humberside	27	108	108	21
East Midlands	83	119	148	96
East Anglia	−348	−205	−249	117
South-East	188	−2	−307	−126
West Midlands	392	343	361	−81
North-West	78	323	337	−21
Wales	−225	−173	−118	−422
Scotland	−152	−109	−198	−108
Northern Ireland	−657	−863	−967	−907

SOURCE   Derived from regional accounts data published annually in CSO, *Economic Trends* and *Regional Trends*.

of London and registered their preferences to live in more rural regions. The improvement in their balance of payments position in the national recession after 1978 was partly caused by reduced public and housebuilding expenditure, but also by a relatively good performance in terms of manufacturing production. These regions did not have very traditional heavy and older industries which suffered disproportionately in the recession, but did receive a disproportionate share of the newer higher technology and service industries.

This point also applies to the South-East region, which showed a surplus in 1971, followed by a deterioration to a broadly neutral position in the mid-1970s, with a return to surplus by 1981.

Two major traditional manufacturing regions, the North-West and the West Midlands showed a very healthy balance-of-payments surplus up to 1978, reflecting the importance to these regions of manufactured exports. After 1978, however, both regions moved very sharply into deficit as a consequence of the ravages of recession on their manufacturing industries.

Wales and Scotland are countries of traditional deficit, following the earlier decline of basic industries, and high levels of unemployment. Both countries have Secretaries of State of Cabinet rank which helps to ensure high levels of government expenditure, which in turn 'finance' their deficits. After 1978 there was a large deterioration in the Welsh balance of payments partly as a consequence of the collapse of the steel industry. The deficit in 1981 amounted to about £400 per head at 1980 prices.

This, however, is less than half the deficit recorded in Northern Ireland, which had already reached the alarming figure of £967 per capita by 1978. The rising deficit here was caused in part by public expenditure associated with the political troubles, but also by the sustained and rapid decline of manufacturing industry and the growth of public sector employment in health and education. The deficit did not rise further after 1978 mainly because the growth of public expenditure was checked. Nevertheless, it remains true that at 1984 prices the average family in Northern Ireland (of two adults and two children) is substantially better off as part of the UK than it would be if Northern Ireland were independent. This is a very powerful economic influence supporting the objectives of 'no change' on the part of the Protestant majority.

The outcome of this brief examination of regional trends in GDP and the balance of payments is that the regional economic divergence, which threatened to create 'two Britains' in the inter-war years and which was to some extent reversed in the 1950s and 1960s, is beginning to reassert itself again. This time, however, that part of Britain which has severe economic problems is much larger and encompasses the industrial heartland of the West Midlands, Yorkshire & Humberside and the North-West. This has implications for regional policy which are taken up in Section 5 below. Before that, however, the analysis concentrates attention more closely on the performance of manufacturing industry in the regions.

4. Manufacturing Industry: Regional Output and Employment

It will be shown that the regions which have experienced a slow rate of growth of GDP and a deterioration in the balance of payments are precisely those which have large manufacturing sectors which have been in great difficulty both before and during the recent recession. Table 5.5 shows changes, from 1974 to 1981, in manufacturing output as a share of GDP.

The regions which have suffered above average rates of de-

TABLE 5.5 *Manufacturing Output Expressed as a Percentage of GDP, by Region, 1974–81*

	Manufacturing share (%)		Percentage change in manufacturing share 1974 to 1981
	1974	*1981*	
North	33.6	27.7	−17.6
Yorkshire and Humberside	32.3	25.7	−20.4
East Midlands	33.3	28.4	−14.7
East Anglia	24.9	22.4	−10.0
South-East	22.0	18.9	−14.1
South-West	23.5	20.4	−13.2
West Midlands	41.4	31.6	−23.7
North-West	34.8	30.0	−13.8
Wales	29.5	23.2	−21.4
Scotland	27.5	21.9	−20.4
Northern Ireland	27.5	18.7	−32.0
UK	28.5	23.4	−17.9

Note Manufacturing output figures are not yet available for years after 1981.

SOURCE Central Statistical Office, Regional Accounts annually in *Economic Trends*.

industrialisation are Northern Ireland, the West Midlands, Wales, Yorkshire & Humberside and Scotland. The regions which experienced below average rates of de-industrialisation are East Anglia, the South-West, the North-West, the South-East and the East Midlands.

(a) *Trends in Manufacturing Employment*

In the UK as a whole, manufacturing employment increased steadily from the end of the Second World War until a maximum was reached in about 1966. In the seventeen years since 1966 the upward trend has been reversed with a national decline of manufacturing employment of about 35 per cent between 1966 and

TABLE 5.6   *Changes in Manufacturing Employment, by Regional Groupings, 1966–83 (percentage change in each period).*

	Traditional Assisted Area regions[1]	Central regions[2]	South-east regions	UK
1966–74	−1.7	−11.2	−8.0	−8.0
1974–8	−10.3	−8.1	−6.0	−7.7
1978–83	−23.2	−27.4	−18.6	−23.8
1966–83	−36.8	−40.7	−29.6	−35.3

Note   Regional groupings defined as in Table 5.2

1983. All regions have been seriously and adversely affected by this decline, but again regions have been affected differentially.

Table 5.6 shows that in the period as a whole the central regions of the West Midlands, the North-West and Yorkshire & Humberside experienced a decline of 40.7 per cent in manufacturing employment. The traditional assisted area regions of Northern Ireland, Scotland, Wales and the Northern region also suffered an above-average decline of 36.8 per cent, although this would have been greater had regional policy not been pursued. The south-east regions experienced a below-average decline in manufacturing employment of 29.6 per cent between 1966 and 1983. These differential impacts reflect closely the output changes of the manufacturing sector across the regions.

However, the pace of employment decline in the recession of 1978 to 1983 has accelerated to a disturbing degree. In the earlier period, from 1966 to 1978, slow rates of growth in output gave rise to relatively small employment falls of 1 per cent to 2 per cent per annum. In the recent recession a fall in manufacturing output of about 15 per cent has resulted in a fall in employment of about 24 per cent in the space of five years. There has been a change in the output/employment relationship as industry has been forced to declare redundancies, close plants, and raise productivity in order to survive. The government has argued that such retrenchment was not only inevitable but also necessary if deindustrialisation was going to be halted and reversed by a process of industrial restructuring. This theme is taken up in Section 5 below. Before that, however, the analysis turns to the question of why manufacturing industry performs better in some regions than in others.

(b) *The Determinants of Regional Manufacturing Performance*

Recent research has shown that there are a set of regional structural characteristics which act as filters which influence the way in which the forces of international competition, technology and innovation, etc., impact differentially on the regions. These structural characteristics are the geographical and industrial legacy from the past. The main structural factors are:

(i) the region's industrial composition
(ii) the urban/rural mix of the region
(iii) the age and size distribution of firms and factories in the region
(iv) the propensity for new-firm formation
(v) occupational disparities and residential preferences.

A sixth factor of a different kind is whether the region has benefited from government regional economic policy or urban dispersal policy.

Regions which have deindustrialised most rapidly are those with a large share of declining industries, with large conurbations, with old firms in large factories, with a very low propensity to generate new-firm start-ups, and with the additional burden of being discriminated against by government spatial policy. The central regions of the North-West, Yorkshire & Humberside and the West Midlands fall largely into this category. So too does Scotland, except that regional policy does appear to have operated in its favour (Moore and Rhodes, 1976). The regions deindustrialising least rapidly have been those with a large proportion of new growth industries, with no major conurbations in the region and with a preponderance of smaller, new enterprises. The East Midlands, East Anglia, the South-West and Wales come into this category. Various government policies have also generally reinforced the growth process; either through New Town and overspill policies or via traditional regional policy in the case of Wales. The impact of each of these factors is now briefly examined.

(i) *The Effects of Industrial Composition*

In general, industries are now less concentrated in particular regions than they used to be and there is therefore less regional sectoral specialisation. Regions have a more even mix of growing and declining industries and consequently the impact of this structural factor has declined. Nevertheless, the old textile regions of Northern Ireland, the North-West and Yorkshire & Humberside continue to be adversely affected by between 0.5 and 1 per cent per annum in terms of manufacturing employment growth. The regions with the most favourable industry mix are East Anglia, the South-West, the South-East and the Northern region. In recent years these areas have typically *gained* manufacturing jobs at the rate of about 0.5 per annum above average as a consequence of an industrial structure favourable to growth. These calculations are based on the shift-share method of accounting for the impact of industrial composition.

(ii) *Age of Firm and Size of Plant*

Table 5.7 shows that in the East Midlands older firms and larger plants have declined most rapidly or grown most slowly. These results from Fothergill and Gudgin (1982) showed that founder-managed small firms grew faster than those run by professional managers, and very much faster than those run by the second generation of the owning family. This suggests that firms follow a distinct long-term profile of growth and decline.

TABLE 5.7   *Manufacturing Employment Change 1968–75 in the East Midlands by Size of Plant and Age of Firm (per cent)*

Size of plant (employment in 1968)	Firms founded 1947–68	Pre-1947 firms
1–125	+40.3	−4.1
26–100	+22.0	−12.8
101–500	+3.8	−18.6
500+	0.0	−19.0

SOURCE   Fothergill and Gudgin, 1982.

If these results for the East Midlands. region were a reliable indicator of the pattern more generally, then regional differences in the age of firms and size of plants would have a significant influence on manufacturing employment growth. For example, a region with an above-average proportion of manufacturing jobs in pre-war firms to the extent of one quarter would suffer an adverse impact on employment growth of the order of 1 per cent per annum.

(iii) *New Firm Formation*

Another structural factor accounting for changes in the distribution of manufacturing employment across regions is variability in the rate at which new manufacturing companies are formed. Areas dominated by large companies have lower rates of formation of new manufacturing companies. According to Fothergill and Gudgin (1982) the *long-term* effect on employment growth may be to create a difference of about 0.5 per cent per annum between manufacturing employment growth in areas dominated by large companies and in those with much less large-firm dominance. These results are supported by the work of Storey (1982). The reasons for the contrast may lie in the supply of entrepreneurs. Existing small companies produce more founders of new firms than do existing large companies, probably because of the relevance and directness of the experience gained in working for small companies. Heavy industrial regions such as the North or Wales, which have a preponderance of large plants are likely to generate few new firms, whereas much of the East Midlands and East Anglia are likely to gain from this process because of their low average plant size, and the existing predominance of smaller firms.

(iv) *Urban Rural Shift*

An important feature of post-war manufacturing industry is a clear trend towards increasing capital and land intensity of manufacturing plants. The number of workers typically employed in a given factory floorspace has been gradually falling. Firms located in densely populated urban areas, whose sites may be physically constrained, have therefore not been able to expand their premises on site (except at very high cost) and have tended to reduce their employment. By contrast firms located in more rural areas have access to sources of cheaper land and lower costs and are able to expand premises and employment more easily. This process of differential growth between urban and rural areas was first observed by Fothergill and Gudgin (1982) and termed 'urban/rural shift'. In Britain the process of urban/rural shift was significantly encouraged by restrictive IDC policies in urban areas in the period 1945 to 1975 and by New Town and overspill policies which sought to disperse population and economic activity away from the conurbations to their rural hinterlands. Such dispersal policies were gradually reversed in the second half of the 1970s and the urban/rural shift slowed down as a consequence. Nevertheless the same process of urban/rural shift was also found in the USA where such dispersal policies had not been pursued.

Table 5.8 shows that regions which are dominated by a large conurbation, such as the South-East, the West Midlands, the North-West and Scotland have tended to grow more slowly than regions composed largely of smaller towns, villages and rural areas such as East Anglia, the South-West, the East Midlands and Wales. In the period of relatively full employment up to 1974 manufacturing employment in the mainly rural regions, was growing 1 per cent per annum more rapidly than in the heavily urbanised regions. Under conditions of slow or stagnant national growth since the mid-1970s regions with larger urban areas have not been at such a disadvantage in terms of manufacturing employment change.

(v) *Regional Policy*

Recent work (Moore, Rhodes and Tyler (1983)) on evaluating the effects of regional policy has led to a revision of the estimated impact in an upward direction. Between 1961 and 1981 regional policy *diverted* some 500 000 manufacturing jobs to the Assisted Areas. These should be referred to as *gross* jobs, however, because some of them did not survive the twenty-year period. If those jobs which were destroyed during the period are discounted, a *net* number of 365 000 jobs are estimated to have been created over the twenty years up to 1981 in the main assisted areas of Scotland, Wales, Northern Ireland, the Northern region, Merseyside and the South-West. This represents almost a quarter of the total manufacturing jobs surviving in these areas in 1981. Regional

TABLE 5.8 *Manufacturing Employment Change in Groups of Regions Categorised by Urban/Rural Structure, 1966–83 (Index 1966 = 100, relative to UK)*

	1966	1974	1978	1981	1983
Regions with large urban area[1]	100	95.9	95.2	95.2	95.5
Regions with medium-sized urban area[2]	100	102.2	100.5	98.3	96.6
Regions with small urban area[3]	100	115.0	119.7	121.4	121.8

Notes [1] The South-East, West Midlands, North-West, Scotland.
[2] Northern Ireland, Yorkshire and Humberside, Northern region.
[3] East Anglia, South-West, East Midlands, Wales.

SOURCE Analysis based on Department of Employment *Gazette* data.

policy has thus had a substantial positive impact on manufacturing employment change in these particular regions, of the order of 1 per cent per annum.

The impact of policy in the two decades separately is worthy of note. Taking total gross jobs first, policy created about 307 000 jobs in the 1960s and around 199 000 in the 1970s. The impact of policy in the 1970s was thus one-third less than in the 1960s On the basis of net jobs, policy effectiveness declined by about two-thirds in the 1970s.

Distinguishing now between the impact of policy on immigrant and indigenous firms, almost two-thirds (64 per cent) of regional policy-induced jobs accrued in the immigrant (mobile) sector up to 1971. By contrast, in the 1970s mobile firms accounted for only about 20 per cent of the estimated total policy effect. While the policy impact arising from mobile firms collapsed in the 1970s, the contribution of indigenous firms to the total policy effect held up well and even increased in absolute terms compared with the 1960s.

While it is useful to know something of the historical record of the effectiveness of regional policy since 1960, it is of particular importance for policy-makers to know something about the effects of policy in recent years under conditions of worsening national and world recession. The estimated total *gross* policy effect for the period 1976–81 was 94 000 manufacturing jobs, compared with a figure of 105 000 jobs for the earlier period 1971–6. This means that regional policy was creating some 18 800 jobs per annum in the years of emerging recession 1976–81. This compares with an annual figures of 30 700 manufacturing jobs for the decade of the 1960s.

(vi) *Occupational Disparities*

So far the discussion of the employment implications of de-industrialisation has concentrated on regional disparities in the number of jobs in the regions. Perhaps of more significance in the longer run are disparities in the *types* of employment opportunities available in the regions. Table 5.9 compares the occupational structure of the male labour force in the southern regions of Britain with those in the Assisted Areas and central areas combined. For every 100 men in the labour force in 1981, the southern regions had about thirteen more in non-manual occupations and thirteen fewer in manual occupations than did the Assisted and central regions. This is a very significant structural difference because these occupational groups are growing at different rates (Table 5.10). For Great Britain as a whole, while the total labour force fell by 1 per cent between 1971 and 1981 manual occupations declined by 7 per cent whilst non-manual occupations increased by 9 per cent. There were larger differences within the manual and non-manual sub-groups. While employers, managers and professional workers increased by 17 per cent, skilled and unskilled manual workers fell by 12 per cent and 25 per cent respectively.

These national averages disguise substantial regional variation. The Assisted and central regions (broadly the north-western half of the country) showed an overall decline in the labour force of 4 per cent, compared with an increase of 3 per cent in the southern regions. Both halves of the nation registered an increase in non-manual occupations and a fall in manual occupations, but the southern regions experienced a faster growth in non-manual occupations and a slower decline in manual occupations. Thus occupational disparities between the north and south of Britain have been widening quite quickly in the last decade.

TABLE 5.9 *Proportion of the Male Labour Force in Selected Occupational Groups, 1981*

	Percentages		
	Assisted regions and central regions	Southern regions	GB
Employers, managers and professional	16.8	22.0	19.4
Workers on own account	4.3	6.3	5.3
Other non-manual	16.0	21.4	18.7
Total non-manual	37.1	49.7	43.4
Skilled manual	33.5	25.7	29.6
Semi-skilled manual	15.2	11.8	13.5
Unskilled manual	6.9	4.9	5.8
Others[1]	7.4	7.9	7.7
Total manual + non-manual	100	100	100

Note [1] A miscellaneous group which includes farmers, farm workers, armed forces and those whose occupation could not be allocated – including those with no previous occupations who were unemployed.

SOURCE *Census of Population*, 1981.

Within the southern regions a number of small areas have been particularly dynamic. The final column of Table 5.10 shows the position for Cambridgeshire, Berkshire and Oxfordshire, three counties which are reputed to have been successful in attracting high technology industries. The overall growth rate of 16 per cent is made up of a particularly impressive increase in non-manual occupations of 31 per cent (with an even larger increase for employers, managers and professional workers (+46 per cent)) coupled with a better than average growth in manual occupations (+6 per cent). These small economies can claim to be 'restructuring' in a dynamic way, but they represent small oases in what looks increasingly like an industrial desert, with the northern half of the country particularly hard hit.

One important feature of these widening disparities in the

TABLE 5.10   *Percentage Change in Male Labour Force by Occupational Group 1971–81*

	Great Britain	Assisted regions & central regions	Southern regions	Cambridgeshire, Berkshire, Oxfordshire
Non-manual				
Employers, managers and professionals	+17	+13	+19	+46
Workers on own account	+18	+12	+22	+35
Other non-manual	0	−6	+6	+14
Total non-manual	+9	+4	+14	+31
Manual				
Skilled manual	−12	+14	−11	+6
Semi-skilled manual	+5	+4	+6	+23
Unskilled manual	−25	−28	−21	−22
Other[1]	+20	+26	+15	+2
Total manual	−7	−9	−5	+6
Total manual and non-manual	−1	−4	+3	+16

Note [1] A miscellaneous group which includes farmers, farm workers, the armed forces and those whose occupation could not be allocated – including those with no previous occupation who were unemployed.

SOURCE   *Census of Population* 1971 and 1981.

occupational structure of the north and south is the structural problem of manual employment on unemployment rates. It is well established that the occupational hierarchy is associated with a gradation of unemployment rates. Employers, managers and professional workers everywhere have a lower unemployment rate than do skilled manual workers, who in turn have a lower unemployment rate than unskilled manual workers. The fact that northern Britain has a labour force biased towards manual occupations, and that the bias is increasing, helps to explain the high and increasing disparities in unemployment rates between northern and southern regions.

5. Policy Responses to De-industrialisation

In turning to the policy implications of de-industrialisation it should be emphasised that regional policies cannot by their very nature reverse what is a national phenomena of de-industrialisation. Reversing de-industrialisation is a task for national or macroeconomic policy and only when it is successful will it be possible to bring about any kind of complete solutions to regional problems with the help of regional policies.

(a) *Restructuring the National Economy*

The issue of whether and how to attempt to reverse the now well established trends towards de-industrialisation in Britain lies at the heart of the main central economic political debate. The debate is muddled, clouded and unsatisfactory for at least three reasons. First, economic and political objectives are inextricably interwoven so that, on both sides, the economic policy instruments brought to bear on the problem must first and foremost be acceptable politically. Second, there is considerable technical ignorance as to what package of policy measures could best halt or reverse the process of de-industrialisation. Third, there is even confusion about the meaning of terms used in the economic debate. Nowhere is this confusion more prominent than in the use of the term 'restructuring' itself. It has different meaning for different people.

At the national and international level calls for restructuring often imply a change from traditional slow-growing or declining industries towards more rapidly growing modern industries based on the more sophisticated technologies. It is frequently argued, for example in OECD 1982, that the industrial countries of Europe should move out of traditional industries such as textiles, footwear and shipbuilding in favour of producers in developing countries and move instead into industries requiring higher skills and technologies such as machine tools, electronic and instrument engineering and pharmaceuticals. A variant of this kind of restructuring is that advanced economies will gradually become more service-oriented because of the relatively high income elasticity of many services. Thus, as Rowthorn and Wells (1986) show, countries with strong and dynamic manufacturing sectors may well display a tendency for manufacturing output to fall as a proportion of GDP and for manufacturing employment to fall in absolute terms. Another interpretation of the process of restructuring emphasises the fact that in a world of free trade an economy will be restructured towards products and industries in which it has comparative advantage and away from products and industries in which other countries have comparative advantage. Each country will have some 'winners' and it will increasingly specialise and trade in those products – and others should be allowed to decline.

Running through all these interpretations is the idea of market forces automatically bringing about a restructuring of economic activity. Attempts to halt the decline of industries would not only be futile, but would actually be counter-productive and inhibit the growth of new industries. Providing governments leave well alone, the argument goes, restructuring will take place of its own accord, without any need for intervention: a sort of benign neglect.

As far as Britain is concerned this kind of restructuring of the national economy has taken on a distinctly unbalanced appearance. Rapid decline takes place in the older and weaker industrial sectors, with consequential plant closures and redundancies (Martin, 1982), but the new sectors do not grow fast enough to offset the decline. Table 5.11 shows that the current recession was no exception to this general rule in that, in spite of a reduction in imports of manufactured goods as a consequence of recession most sectors of industry suffered a weakening of their position in both home and overseas markets between 1978 and 1982. Of the thirty-five industrial sectors only five managed to hold or improve their performance. These five were other transport equipment (mainly aircraft and engines), non-ferrous metals, organic chemicals, metal-working machinery and chemical materials not elsewhere specified. Britain's performance also deteriorated in many of the sectors containing so called 'high-tech' industries, notably in tele-communications, office machinery and data processing and electrical machinery.

This continued failure of the British economy to secure both halves of the restructuring process is reflected in attitudes towards restructuring at a more micro-level among individual industries and firms. There is much discussion and activity of defensive rationalisation in which low-productivity plants are closed and run down rather than regenerated, as a means of securing the survival of the more efficient plants and restoring overall profitability. Merger and takeover activity goes largely unchecked so that strong management eliminates weaker management, strong companies can take over companies threatening potential competition and city financial institutions and large British firms invest heavily abroad to secure the highest short-term rate of return while some successful large British companies hoard cash because of a lack of profitable investment opportunities at home. These are signs of an industrial sector planning for further relative decline.

The Conservative administration came to power in 1979 claiming to have a policy prescription more effective than the Keynesian consensus which had previously produced thirty years of unprecedented growth in world production and trade along with virtually full employment (see Chapter 8). It argued that policies of monetary and fiscal restriction would sharply reduce inflation and thereby allow industry to secure lower costs and generate full economic recovery. Five years into this experiment and inflation has been substantially reduced, but the process of de-industrialisation which began to manifest itself after 1966 shows no sign yet of coming to an end. Indeed, the world recession combined with monetarist policies appear to have hastened the process considerably, but have so far failed to accelerate the growth of newer industries on a scale which is necessary to complete a meaningful restructuring of the economy. The balance-of-manufacturing trade has deteriorated by £8 billion per annum since 1979, an amount roughly equivalent to the net contribution of North Sea oil to the balance of payments. This contribution will now stabilise and will begin to decline in the late 1980s. Under these conditions the economy is unlikely to be able to sustain an average GDP growth rate in excess of 2 per cent per annum in the next decade without running into serious balance-of-payments deficits.

The manufacturing sector may be 'leaner' than it has been before, but it is very questionable as to whether it is fitter. At today's exchange rates *relative* unit labour costs, although falling, remain 20 per cent above their 1976 level. Profitability and investment in much the greater part of British manufacturing industry

TABLE 5.11   *Changes in Competitive Performance of British Industry in Home and Overseas Markets, 1978–82*

SITC classification	Exports minus imports expressed as a percentage of exports $\frac{X-M}{X}$%		
	1978	1982	Change 1978–82
51 Organic chemicals	13	26	+13
52 Inorganic chemicals	23	22	−1
53 Dyeing, tanning and colouring materials	58	57	−1
54 Pharmaceutical products	69	62	−8
55 Toilet, cleaning polishing materials	63	54	−9
56 Fertilisers	−31	−159	−128
57 Explosives and pyrotechnic products	81	70	−11
58 Resins and plastic materials	3	−16	−19
59 Chemical materials n.e.s.	45	45	0
61 Leather, furs and skins	29	23	−6
62 Rubber manufactures	37	22	−15
63 Cork and wood manufactures	−397	−427	−30
64 Paper and paperboard	−170	−234	−64
65 Yarns fabrics and made-up articles	−18	−62	−44
66 Non metallic mineral manufactures	−12	−6	−6
67 Iron and steel	5	−6	−11
68 Non-ferrous metals	−37	−20	+17
69 Manufactures of metal n.e.s.	45	32	−12
71 Power-generating machinery	54	47	−7
72 Machinery for specific industries	50	43	−7
73 Metal-working machinery	17	27	+10
74 General industrial machinery	36	32	−4
75 Office machines and data processing	−20	−33	−13
76 Telecommunications	17	−77	−94
77 Electrical machinery	13	−3	−16
78 Road vehicles	9	−45	−54

TABLE 5.11   *continued*

	Exports minus imports expressed as a percentage of exports $\frac{X-M}{X}$%		
SITC classification	1978	1982	Change 1978–82
79 Other transport equipment	−5	+51	+54
81 Sanitary plumbing and heating products	42	3	−39
82 Furniture	17	−66	−83
83 Travel goods	−364	−474	−110
84 Clothing and accessories	−38	−79	−41
85 Footwear	−159	−308	−149
87 Scientific instruments	20	16	−4
88 Photographic optical equipment	−32	−37	−5
89 Miscellaneous manufactures n.e.s.	10	−13	−23

SOURCE   *British Overseas Trade Statistics.*

Note to Table 5.11: The measure of competitive performance used in this table $\frac{X-M}{X}$% can be expected to be negative in conditions where an new income-earning resource such as North Sea oil permits rapid increases in imports of manufactured goods. Nevertheless the analysis is useful in showing just how few industries are showing dynamic export growth and meeting the overseas competition.

remains historically low. It may be some years before manufacturing output recovers to the level achieved in the late 1970s. Employment in manufacturing industry is expected to continue to fall.

(b) *Regional Policy Implications*

The prospects for those regions which have traditionally relied heavily on manufacturing industry are therefore far from good. The West Midlands, the North-West, Yorkshire & Humberside, the Northern region, Wales, Scotland and Northern Ireland come to this category. Half the population of the UK live in these regions and unemployment rates in all of them already exceed 15 per cent. It is the economic restructuring of these regions which constitutes the biggest economic challenge to British governments in the remainder of this century and the first quarter of the next.

Part of the south and east regions, with natural advantages of climate, communications and environment, have shown signs of an ability to restructure their economies towards business services and newer types of manufacturing and service activity. They now enjoy an occupational structure increasingly biased towards high skills of a managerial, professional and technical nature. This is enhanced by public finance of all kinds associated with a large capital city and by government expenditure in the fields particularly of defence and research and development. This so-called 'sun belt', which comprises counties such as Sussex, Hampshire, Avon, Berkshire, Oxfordshire and Cambridgeshire, by no means covers the whole of the southern regions. Relative success on this small scale cannot raise by very much the otherwise lack-lustre national industrial performance. Nevertheless, these activities have generated jobs elsewhere in the economy. To take one example: home computers which are designed and developed in Cambridge are assembled in Scotland and Wales – but also worryingly in Malaysia. American investment in Scotland and Japanese investment in Wales provide other examples of regional policy contributing towards a modernisation of the industrial composition of depressed regions. But how long will it be before these mainly assembly jobs disappear or are switched elsewhere?

How should regional policy respond to continued de-industrialisation in the northern half of Britain? The first essential prerequisite is a recognition in central government of the seriousness of the long-term nature of the problem, and the fact that market forces cannot be relied on to provide the solution. One of the outcomes of the competitive model in economics is that weak firms, weak regions and weak countries go out of business. Net migration flows from the weaker region cannot be relied upon to solve the problem either, as the Republic of Ireland has learned over the centuries. Migration flows are biased towards the higher-skilled, higher-income and more mobile groups in the population. When a region loses these kinds of people, dynamism and enterprise decline further, investors are more inclined to stay away, and left behind are increasing concentrations of lower-skilled, lower-income groups who are relatively disadvantaged and immobile.

The problems with adopting a strategy of cutting wages in backward regions in order to enhance their competitiveness are substantial. Such a cut could not take place in the private sector unless it also took place in the public sector, if private firms were to continue to hold on to their more skilled and productive employees. Moreover, to be effective the wage cut has to be very large. For example, in the 1950s and 1960s, wage and salary levels in manufacturing industries in Northern Ireland were about 25 per cent below those in the UK as a whole and yet the Province remained the region of highest unemployment by far, notwithstanding the inward movement of some firms in response to the most generous package of financial inducements available anywhere in the UK or Europe. Even if such a wage cut could be brought about again and the resulting poverty could be accepted, firms would quickly lose their most skilled employees who would be keen to migrate to the higher-wage regions. Net outward migration of skilled people would not be a recipe for industrial dynamism and success.

Third, it should be recognised that the only way to improve competitiveness of the backward regions is by manufacturing companies and their employees responding quickly and continuously to change in their home and overseas market. They have to be technologically advanced both in terms of their production processes and their product development in order to compete effectively with the world at large. Regional policy should therefore be concerned with making it easier for companies to make such responses, not only in one or two so-called high-technology industries in which Japan or the USA probably has a dominant position – but across the whole range of manufactured products for which there is going to be a demand in the 1980s and 1990s.

There can be little doubt that existing regional policy does make it easier for firms to adapt and adjust to technological and demand changes. In recent years the three main policy instruments have been regional development grants (RDGs), selective financial assistance (SFA) and the government's advanced factory building programme. A recent study by Thwaites, Edwards and Gibbs (1982) of the adoption of new process technologies in different parts of the country showed that about 50 per cent of respondents said that the availability of regional aid had brought forward the date of technical change, and in around 15 per cent of cases RDGs had been crucial to the adoption of new technology. Other surveys, notably by Herron (1981), Hood and Young (1984), and Begg and McDowall (1981), have reached the conclusion that

RDGs play an integral part in the investment decision of manufacturing firms in the Assisted Areas with about half the companies describing their role in the investment decision as either 'crucial' or 'considerable'.

This is not to say, however, that regional policy could not be improved. There is a strong case for limiting the automatic payments of RDGs to highly capital intensive projects such as the Sullom Voe Terminal which create few jobs after the construction phase. There is also a case for introducing a grant scheme to cover a (high) proportion of any increase in manufacturing firm's expenditure on new-product development in the Assisted Areas. Funds for this could be transferred from other research and development expenditures which have been too concentrated in aircraft and defence. More of the detailed administration of schemes could be devolved to the Scottish and Welsh Development Agencies. Such Agencies could be introduced for English regions such as the West Midlands, the North-West, Yorkshire & Humberside and the Northern region, and could be charged with co-ordinating the implementation of existing regional policy instruments with enterprise schemes for new small business and assistance with developments in the service sector.

6. Conclusions

De-industrialisation in Britain is a national phenomena which has seriously affected all regions. The problem is not so much that there is a deficit on manufactured trade: indeed this might be expected after a period in which net exports of oil, food and services had shown substantial growth. The problem is more that the UK manufacturing sector has fallen in size, in terms of both output and employment, compared with that of other countries. Given that net exports in oil, food and services, are unlikely to expand as rapidly in future, and might well decline, the manufacturing sector is potentially a major alternative source of income and jobs. If these are not forthcoming, and de-industrialisation continues, then the UK faces a sustained period of increasing unemployment and falling standards of living. There are few if any signs that de-industrialisation is being halted and reversed by the economic policies of the Thatcher administration – indeed the evidence so far points rather in the opposite direction of an acceleration in de-industrialisation (see Chapter 8). Plant closures and redundancies have occurred on a huge scale and are not being matched by the growth of new industries. Changes in macroeconomic and industrial policy are urgently required to ensure that the more creative and regenerative part of the restructuring process occurs on a substantially larger scale than hitherto. This requires much tougher government action on behalf of manufacturing industry in several policy areas including the exchange rate, tariffs, interest rates, taxation and subsidies for modernisation, expansion, and product and process innovation.

Although no region can escape the consequences of almost twenty years of de-industrialisation, it nevertheless has some quite serious regional dimensions. Most of the industrial decline has been concentrated in the traditionally industrial heartland of Britain in regions to the north and west including the West Midlands. Moreover to the extent that new industries have been established these are concentrated in the so called 'sun belt' which stretches from East Anglia and parts of the East Midlands, through the South-East to parts of the South-West region.

There are increasingly two Britains separated by widening economic and social disparities. The northern and western regions have suffered disproportionately from de-industrialisation with consequent adverse effects on output, incomes, the regional balance of payments and jobs. There is, moreover, a steady flow of net migration of technical, professional and skilled people to the southern and eastern regions where these groups are becoming concentrated, partly as a consequence of residential preference. A regional policy of wage reductions for the poorer half of Britain would not be an appropriate policy, even though it might generate some lower-paid manual jobs in the short term. The longer-term consequences of a policy of wage reductions would be to set in motion processes of relative and cumulative decline supplemented by accelerated rates of outward migration of qualified people to the south and east and increasing concentrations of disadvantaged groups in northern and western regions. Economic and social disparities would widen further and public expenditures would have to rise to provide infrastructure for migrants and support for the disadvantaged groups.

The appropriate regional policy is to encourage the modernisation and expansion of manufacturing industry in the Assisted Areas. This means devoting more resources to regional policy rather than less and broadening the scope of regional policy to encompass not only the traditional policy instruments of regional development grants and selective financial assistance, but also the expenditure of other government departments and the public sector as a whole.

Notes

1. These are published once a year in *Economic Trends* and in *Regional Trends*.

Bibliography

Begg, H. M. and McDowall, S. (1981) 'Industrial Performance and Prospects in Areas Affected by Oil Development', *ESU Research Papers*, no. 3.

Fothergill, S. and Gudgin G. (1982) *Unequal Growth: Urban and Regional Employment Change in the UK* (London: Heinemann).

Herron, F. (1981) 'Post Industry Act (1972) – Industrial Movement into and Expansion in, the Assisted Areas of Great Britain: Some Survey Findings', *Government Economic Service Working Paper*, no. 46 (London: Department of Industry).

Hood, N. and Young, S. (1984) *Multi-national Investment Strategies in the British Isles* (London: HMSO).

Martin, R. L. (1982) 'Job Loss and Regional Incidence of Redundancies in the Current Recession', *Cambridge Journal of Economics*, **6**, **4** pp. 375–95

Moore, B. C. and Rhodes, J. (1976) 'Regional economic policy and the movement of manufacturing firms', *Economica*, vol. 43, pp. 17–31.

Moore, B. C., Rhodes, J. and Tyler, P. (1986) *The Effects of Government Regional Economic Policy* (London: HMSO).

OECD (1982) *Economic Outlook*, 31 July 1982 (Paris: OECD).

Rowthorn, R. E. and Wells, J. R. (1986) *De-industrialisation and Foreign Trade: Britain's Decline in a Global Perspective* (Cambridge: Cambridge University Press).

Storey, D. (1982) *Entrepreneurship and the New Firm* (London: Croom Helm).

Thwaites, A. T., Edwards, A. and Gibbs, D. (1982) *The Inter Regional Diffusion of Product Innovations in Great Britain* (University of Newcastle upon Tyne: CURDS).

6

Producing an Industrial Wasteland: Capital, Labour and the State in North-East England

RAY HUDSON

We hev done wor very best as honest workin' men,
To let the pits commence again we've offered to them ten.
The offer they will not accept, they firmly do demand,
Thirteen and a half per cent or let the collieries stand.

Whey let them stand or let them lie; do with them what they choose,
Te give them thirteen and a half we ever shall refuse.
They're always willin' to receive but not inclined to give,
And very soon they won't allow a workin' man to live.

With tyranny and capital they nivor seem content,
Unless they are endeavourin' tek from us per cent,
If it was what they request we willingly would grant,
We knaa it's not, therefore we cannot give them what they want.

Extract (verses 6–8) from *The Durham Lock-out* (1898).

1. Introduction

The north-east of England (Figure 6.1) currently is, and for the foreseeable future will remain, an industrial wasteland (see also Cambridge Economic Policy Group, 1980; for a rather contrary

169

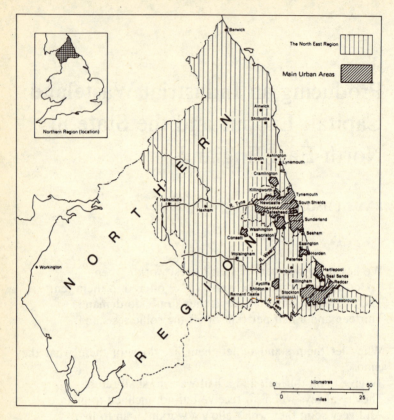

FIGURE 6.1 *The North-East Region*

view see Manpower Research Group, 1981) transformed over a long period from a region that occupied a pivotal position in the global capitalist accumulation process to one that increasingly has become marginal to its main currents (see Carney *et al.*, 1976; 1977). This increasing marginalisation has posed acute problems for that part of the working-class resident within it and, to a lesser degree, problems for the UK state in legitimising this changed position and coping with its worst impacts on those same residents. Even a cursory examination of Tables 6.1–6.3 reveals the depth of the crisis now facing the working class in the region as capitals and the UK state have responded to their various crises by cutting industrial capacity, investment and employment in recent years and unemployment within it has consequently risen further from already high levels (though to some extent this reflects the *generalised* character of employment decline and unemployment increase over much of the UK national space, severely restricting the scope for increased net out-migration from the north-east as one mechanism for coping with the rapidly expanding surplus population reproduced within it: see Table 6.4).

While the pace of de-industrialisation has recently accelerated sharply, it is important to stress that it is *not* a new process within the north-east, although precisely when it began depends upon how one defines de-industrialisation (on this point see Blackaby, 1979). For example, from having risen to a major role in the international capitalist economy as a producer of commodities such as coal, ships and steel, de-industrialisation in the sense of falling shares of global production and world markets has been in progress for many decades; the most striking example, in this sense, is that of shipbuilding, for in the first decade of the twentieth century north-east yards produced over 25 per cent of global output (McCord, 1979, p. 121), but by 1974 their share had fallen to 0.37 per cent (Thompson, 1975, p. 1). This relative decline has been accompanied by wide fluctuations in absolute output and employment in these industries, with production and employment often having reached their peak levels many years ago: the most striking example in this sense is coal-mining, output in County Durham having reached a peak level in 1913 (Reid, 1970, p. 302) while employment reached its maximum of over 170 000 in 1923 (Bulmer, 1978, p. 150).

It is against this background of wild cyclical fluctuation around a trend of absolute and/or relative long-period secular decline in such industries that this chapter will focus upon the more recent accelerated decline in industrial capacity and employment in the region.[1] This can be traced to 1958, initially confined to two of the 'traditional' industrial branches, coal-mining and shipbuilding, but since increasingly generalised over a wide spectrum of 'traditional' and 'modern' branches. This recent acceleration in the process of the de-industrialisation of the north-east, then, began in the midst of the post-war expansionary long-wave in the capitalist world economy and was intensified by the transition from this to the contractionary long-wave (see Mandel, 1975, pp. 108–46), to the 'Second Slump' (Mandel, 1978), a switch associated with but not

TABLE 6.1 Unemployment (Annual Averages), 1951–83

	(a) Numbers unemployed, Northern Region (000s)			(b) Total unemployment rate		
	Male	Female	Total	North	South–East	West Midlands
1951	18.2	9.3	27.5	2.2	0.9	0.4
1952	18.8	13.8	32.6	2.6	1.3	0.9
1953	18.0	11.4	29.4	2.4	1.2	1.1
1954	17.4	10.9	38.3	2.3	1.0	0.6
1955	13.8	8.5	22.3	1.8	0.7	0.5
1956	12.9	6.8	19.7	1.5	0.8	1.1
1957	15.1	6.5	21.6	1.7	1.1	1.3
1958	22.5	8.7	31.1	2.4	1.4	1.6
1959	32.4	10.7	43.1	3.3	1.3	1.5
1960	27.9	9.4	37.2	2.9	1.0	1.0
1961	24.4	8.0	32.4	2.5	1.0	1.4
1962	38.5	10.8	49.3	3.7	1.3	1.8
1963	51.5	13.9	65.4	5.0	1.6	2.0
1964	33.8	10.2	44.0	3.3	1.0	0.9
1965	26.7	7.5	34.3	2.6	0.9	0.9
1966	28.3	6.8	35.1	2.6	1.0	1.3
1967	43.7	9.5	53.1	4.0	1.7	2.5

Year						
1968	52.5	8.9	61.4	4.7	1.6	2.2
1969	53.5	8.4	61.9	4.7	1.5	1.7
1970	52.4	8.8	61.2	4.6	1.6	1.9
1971	62.4	11.4	73.8	5.7	2.0	2.9
1972	68.2	13.7	81.9	6.3	2.2	3.6
1973	50.5	10.2	60.7	4.7	1.5	2.2
1974	49.8	10.0	59.9	4.6	1.5	n.a.
1975	63.2	16.7	78.9	5.9	2.8	4.1
1976	74.1	26.7	100.8	7.5	4.2	5.9
1977	80.2	34.0	114.2	8.3	4.5	5.8
1978	84.7	36.9	121.6	8.8	4.2	5.6
1979	82.1	36.9	119.0	8.6	3.7	5.5
1980	101.5	45.9	147.9	10.4	4.2	7.3
1981	145.2	58.2	203.4	14.6	7.0	12.5
1982	158.8	88.8	214.6	16.6	8.5	14.7
1983	164.7	61.0	225.7	17.9	9.3	15.7
1984	165.9	64.6	230.5	18.3	9.5	15.3

Note From 1951 to 1964 (inclusive) the data for the South–East include those for East Anglia.

SOURCES Department of Employment and Productivity, *British Labour Statistics, Historical Abstract, 1886–1968*, table 168 (London: HMSO, 1971); Central Statistical Office, *Regional Statistics*, vols 11 and 16 (London: HMSO, 1975 & 1981); Eurostat, *Yearbook of Regional Statistics* (Luxemburg, 1983); *Employment Gazette*.

TABLE 6.2 *Employees in Employment (000s) in the Northern Region, 1956–82*

	1956	1960	1965	1966a	1966b	1967	1968	1969	1970	1971	1972	1973	1974	1975	1976	1977	1978	1981	1982
ALL INDUSTRIES	1257	1279	1270	1308	1277	1248	1221	1220	1233	1207	1205	1248	1245	1266	1255	1256	1242	1127	1079
of which																			
PRIMARY SECTOR	212	190	143	130	130	121	103	89	83	83	79	74	69	67	66	65	66	56	52
of which																			
Coal-mining	169	150	n.a.	100	n.a.	n.a.	n.a.	n.a.	n.a.	61	58	53	49	47	46	45	45	51	51
MANUFACTURING	437	454	459	463	461	452	444	456	478	461	444	462	467	454	438	434	418	339	309
of which																			
Food, drink and tobacco	35	34	30	34	31	31	32	33	34	34	33	33	34	33	32	30	30	30	28
Chemicals and allied indus.	50	60	59	57	60	59	54	59	62	61	56	56	54	53	54	55	55	50	
Metal manufacture	60	62	66	58	62	58	58	56	60	51	47	49	49	49	47	47	41	30	
of which																			
Iron and steel	56	57	n.a.	54	n.a.	n.a.	n.a.	n.a.	n.a.	48	43	45	44	45	42	42	37	25	
Mechanical engineering	56	58	61	67	61	61	59	60	66	65	60	63	65	67	66	63	58	47	
Instrument engineering	1	1	3	2	3	3	3	4	5	5	5	5	5	5	5	5	5	4	
Electrical engineering	36	40	45	53	49	48	50	51	52	51	52	56	56	51	46	46	45	36	
Shipbuilding and marine eng.	64	60	60	42	50	57	52	52	54	51	49	49	48	48	48	48	48	38	
Vehicles	17	15	11	12	10	10	11	11	12	12	12	12	12	12	11	12	12	10	
Other metal goods	14	12	13	14	13	13	13	14	14	13	13	15	16	15	15	15	14	12	
Textiles	16	19	21	21	21	20	20	23	23	22	22	24	26	23	21	20	19	10	
Leather, leather goods and fur	3	2	2	2	2	2	2	2	2	2	2	2	2	2	2	2	2	1	
Clothing and footwear	30	32	32	35	33	33	33	34	33	34	33	34	34	33	31	31	29	19	

Bricks, pottery glass and cement	19	19	17	19	16	15	16	16	17	16	15	15	15	14	15	14	14	13	10
Timber, furniture, etc.	14	13	13	15	13	13	13	13	13	13	12	13	12	12	11	12	11	10	9
Paper printing and publishing	13	14	15	17	16	16	16	17	18	18	19	19	23	22	21	21	21	22	21
Other manufacturing	9	12	12	15	14	14	13	12	14	15	16	16	14	15	15	15	15	14	14
CONSTRUCTION	85	87	94	109	105	90	101	97	88	84	89	98	96	96	95	96	89	70	63
GAS, WATER AND ELECTRICITY	19	19	23	23	24	24	23	23	22	21	19	19	20	20	20	20	20	20	19
SERVICES	503	528	550	524	558	554	551	555	562	559	575	595	596	629	634	642	649	643	636
of which																			
Transport and communications	98	92	87	86	85	83	78	73	73	70	69	67	66	68	68	65	67		64
of which																			
Railways	30	26	n.a.	19	n.a.	n.a.	n.a.	n.a.	n.a.	13	13	12	12	11	11	11	11		10
Distributive trades	145	159	152	166	152	145	142	137	137	133	136	141	141	144	144	145	142		139
Insurance, banking, finance	15	17	22	20	23	22	23	24	26	27	28	29	31	31	31	32	34		39
Professional services	91	104	125	133	130	134	135	141	148	150	155	162	163	179	180	179	184		180
Misc. services	85	87	95	103	97	95	96	101	100	102	108	115	109	116	123	130	132		135
Public admin. and defence	68	68	74	74	71	74	77	79	78	77	80	81	82	92	91	91	89		86

Notes The table is constructed from two sources; the data for 1956, 1960 and 1966a are from Fothergill and Gudgin; 1965, 1966b to 1982 from the Department of Employment. The two series are *not* strictly comparable but the general tendencies are broadly similar. The 1982 data are estimates for December

SOURCES   Department of Employment, *1971–8 Annual Censuses of Employment* and *Employment Gazette* (various issues); Fothergill, S. and Gudgin, G., 1978. *Occasional Paper*, no. 5 (London: Centre for Environmental Studies); Remit (1983) no. 15.

TABLE 6.3 *Notified Redundancies, Northern Region, 1978–83*

	Total in thousands									Redundancies as a % of employees in employment								
	1975	1976	1977	1978	1979	1980	1981	1982	1983*	1975	1976	1977	1978	1979	1980	1981	1982	1983*
ALL INDUSTRIES	21.0	21.0	22.0	19.7	14.6	36.0	40.1	31.8	6.9	1.7	1.7	1.8	1.6	1.2	3.0	3.6	2.9	0.6
of which																		
PRIMARY SECTOR	1.2	1.2	0.5	0.2	0	1.0	2.0	3.1	0.3	1.8	1.8	0.8	0.3	0	1.6	3.4	5.6	0.6
of which																		
Mining and quarrying	1.2	1.2	0.5	0.2	0	1.0	2.0	3.1	0.3	2.4	2.4	1.0	0.4	0	2.1	4.5	7.5	0.8
MANUFACTURING	17.7	14.7	13.3	13.7	11.0	29.3	28.9	23.1	5.7	4.0	3.4	3.0	3.3	2.7	7.5	8.5	7.1	1.8
of which																		
Other	4.1	2.0	2.2	3.9	1.6	4.5	5.6	6.6	1.3	3.4	1.6	1.8	3.3	1.4	3.9	5.4	6.6	1.3
Engineering	5.7	6.7	6.0	3.7	2.7	8.3	9.7	6.0	1.5	4.7	5.7	5.1	3.4	2.5	8.0	11.0	7.2	1.9
Chemicals	1.1	0.5	0.4	0.3	0.2	1.5	2.2	1.1	0.1	2.2	1.0	0.8	0.5	0.4	2.7	4.4	2.3	0.2
Shipbuilding and marine engineering	0.9	1.0	0.2	2.1	2.8	2.1	1.4	2.1	0.6	1.9	2.1	0.4	4.4	6.3	5.1	3.6	5.5	1.7
Metal manufacture	1.1	1.2	2.1	1.7	0.2	6.8	7.4	5.6	1.9	2.3	2.6	4.5	4.1	0.5	19.3	28.9	24.2	7.9
Leather and clothing	1.3	2.7	1.2	1.2	1.0	3.3	1.6	1.3	0.2	4.1	8.4	3.8	3.9	3.3	12.3	7.0	5.9	1.0
Textiles	3.7	0.6	1.2	0.8	2.5	2.8	1.1	0.5	0	17.6	2.9	5.7	4.3	14.3	20.7	9.6	4.5	0.2

CONSTRUCTION	1.0	3.9	6.5	4.4	2.9	3.9	5.3	3.5	0.6	1.0	4.1	6.8	4.9	3.2	4.4	6.6	4.8	0.9
SERVICES of which	1.1	1.3	1.7	1.4	0.7	1.7	3.9	1.9	0.4	0.1	0.2	0.3	0.2	0.1	0.3	0.6	0.3	0.1
Financial, business, professional and miscell.	0.2	0.5	0.4	0.5	0.2	0.3	1.2	0.9	0.1	0.1	0.1	0.1	0.2	0.1	0.1	0.3	0.3	0.0
Transport, communications and distributive trade	0.6	0.7	0.9	0.3	0.4	1.2	2.3	0.8	0.3	0.3	0.3	0.4	0.4	0.2	0.6	1.2	0.4	0.2
Public administration, defence and utilities	0.3	0.2	0.4	0	0.1	0.2	0.4	0.2	0	0.7	0.2	0.4	0	0.1	0.2	0.4	0.2	0.0

Note *1983 January–March only.
SOURCE REMIT, 1979, No. 4, table 3; 1981, No. 8, table 3; 1983, No. 15, table 4.

TABLE 6.4   *Net Migration from the Northern Region, 1966–81*

1966–71*	5142
1974–7*	3333
1978	7000
1979	5000
1980	9000
1981	8000

Note   * Annual average.

SOURCE   EUROSTAT; OPCS; various issues, *Monitors*.

caused by the sharp crude-oil price increases of 1973/4 and 1979 (see Frank, 1980, pp. 20–102). There has been, however, no simple, mechanistic relationship between these long-period movements in the capitalist world-economy and accelerating de-industrialisation within the north-east; rather, their effects have been mediated via the policies of the UK state (with changes within it at the level of parliamentary and party politics between Conservative and Labour governments playing a not unimportant role) with the state deeply implicated in a variety of ways in this decline, and by social and political structures within the north-east itself, as well as by those within the wider UK social formation.

In particular, two themes will be explored in relation to this recent decline. The first is that of nationalised industry policies and the effects in and on the north-east of operating these in response to politically determined 'national' objectives; in particular, policies within the coal, steel and shipbuilding industries will be examined, the effects in terms of job loss being graphically revealed in Tables 6.2 and 6.3. The second theme is that of disinvestment by private capital from the north-east as, in the conditions of intensified international competition and of a sharp fall in fixed capital investment in manufacturing which accompanied global recession in the 1970s, the region ceased to appear an attractive location to manufacturing capital in the way that it had done in the 1960s, because of the impacts (though not necessarily always intended ones) of implementing a variety of state policies. This declining attraction of the region in the 1970s and consequent further industrial decline did not so much reflect any absolute deterioration in the conditions it offered to capital for profitable production but rather a relative deterioration because of a combination of the effects of changes in national UK policies and the policies of other nation states to attract manufacturing investment. For in these circumstances the types of 'new' manufacturing activities and particular stages in overall corporate production chains that had been established in the region in the 1960s proved particularly vulnerable to closure, while the north-east was no longer attractive to manufacturing capitals as a location for the current 'round of investment' (Massey, 1979). Thus, the north-east's declining attraction to manufacturing capital cannot be divorced from the effects of the UK state's macroeconomic monetary and fiscal policies; for example, via the regional effects of sterling exchange-rate policies and of the abolition of controls on capital exports by the Conservative government after the 1979 election, which led not only to a surge in portfolio investment in net terms to over £4 billion in 1981, but also an 'unprecedented deficit on direct investment in 1981' of over £4 billion (*Barclays Review*, 1982, centrespread), greatly exceeding the annual deficits in net direct investment over the preceding decade. The surge in redundancies in the north-east in 1980–1 and the fact that, relatively, these were more severely felt there than nationally and in other regions such as the South-East (Table 6.5) bears ample testimony to these national policy effects, as well as to the types of manufacturing operations that had previously been established in the region. At the same time the deindustrialisation of the north-east (and regions like it) is intimately linked to the selective industrialisation of parts of Mediterranean Europe and the Third World, and of the extension of capitalist relations of production into some of the countries of the COMECON bloc via international subcontracting; in summary to the emergence of the new international division of labour in manufacturing (Frobel *et al.*, 1980), as multinational capital scours the globe in search of locations that will offer surplus profits.

2. Nationalised Industry Policies and De-industrialisation

Implementation of nationalised industry policies has resulted in a severe decline in industrial capacity and employment opportunities

TABLE 6.5 *Confirmed Redundancies per 1000 Employees, South–East and Northern Regions, 1977–82*

	1977		1978		1979		1980		1981		1982	
	N	SE	N	SE	N	SE	N	SE	N	SE	N	SE
ALL INDUSTRIES of which	15.0	3.4	15.0	3.5	12.0	3.6	27.4	9.4	35.5	14.7	29.5	11.5
INDEX OF PRODUCTION of which	28.6	7.9	30.2	8.4	25.3	9.2	58.6	24.6	76.6	38.9	68.4	25.2
Manufacturing	25.7	8.1	32.1	8.9	28.1	10.0	70.3	28.8	85.2	45.4	73.7	28.4
Services	2.7	1.2	1.9	1.3	0.9	1.0	2.6	2.7	5.9	4.7	3.0	6.0

SOURCE Department of Employment.

for those members of the working class resident in the north-east. Over the last three decades it has been the major proximate cause of regional de-industrialisation and employment decline. To put this claim into perspective, consider the following data for the Northern Region: between 1952 and 1981 total employees in employment in the region fell from 1 204 000 to 1 079 000, those in mining and quarrying and manufacturing from 588 700 to less than 350 000 (Fothergill and Gudgin, 1978, pp. 43–8); considering *only* the parts of the same period during which the industries have been nationalised, employment decline in coal-mining (since 1951), iron and steel (since 1967) and shipbuilding (since 1977) accounted for no less than 80 per cent of the total net employment decline in mining and manufacture – and to this decline of 200 000 jobs as a result of nationalised industry policies can be added another 20 000 in rail transport. To appreciate why this has happened requires a brief consideration of the general rationale for nationalisations and the imperatives that have subsequently guided nationalised industry policies, prior to examining specific industries in more detail.

In this context, as in many others, it is important to draw a distinction around 1979 for the election of the Thatcher government marks an important watershed. Over the preceding three decades an important area of consensus had gradually emerged within the UK state between Conservative and Labour governments as to the way in which and criteria by which the nationalised industries were actually to be operated. This measure of agreement emerged despite important ideological differences that were especially sharp in the 1940s and early 1950s, with Conservatives committed to the market as the principal economic steering mechanism and Labour committed to taking the 'commanding heights' of the economy into public ownership. It developed because the various industries that were partially or wholly nationalised were central to the performance of the national economy, but could hardly be described as its 'commanding heights'. They were, on the occasion of their various nationalisations, technically backward, with a long history of inadequate investment. Manufacturing capital in the UK was not opposed to the state assuming direct responsibility for them, particularly as generally they held out little promise of profit; indeed, the only cases where nationalisation was seriously opposed by the capitalist interests involved and reversed by Conservative governments (iron and steel and road transport) were those where there did seem to be potential for profit (Hudson, 1981a; McEachern, 1980).

In these circumstances such industries presented a paradox to manufacturing capital in the UK: it required their outputs to be provided cheaply and efficiently to help guarantee its own competitive position yet individual capitalist enterprises were not prepared to invest in them, given the rates of return such investments would yield. Nationalisation offered a means of resolving this paradox: the broad class of manufacturing capital in the UK was willing to let the state take over and guarantee the production of key services and inputs of energy and materials that were vital to it being able to continue to produce profitably while the former owners of these industries were happy to be rid of them, in view of the generosity of the compensation offered which allowed them to switch their capital into more profitable activities and locations (in itself an important factor in the industrial decline of regions such as the north-east). Equally the UK state had an interest in underpinning the competitive position of manufacturing capital located within its national space as this had a direct bearing on national output and growth rates, taxation yields, the balance-of-payments position and so on, which both influenced its room for manœuvre in economic policy formation and the resources available to it (though there tended to be differences at the party political level between Conservative and Labour governments in their stated reasons for seeking higher national output and growth, governments of both persuasions were united in this pursuit). Furthermore, the organised labour movement in the UK had a long-standing commitment to the extension of public ownership via nationalisation as a way of furthering its own interests though, decisively, it did not encompass a challenge to its class position as wage labour.

Thus it appeared that, in these particular cases of nationalisation, the interests of capital, labour and the state coincided but, equally, drawing the boundary between private and public sectors in the 'mixed economy' in the way that such instances of nationalisation implied had quite precise implications as to how the industries must subsequently be managed – implications that came to be accepted by Conservative and Labour governments alike and, indeed, by fractions of the workforces and trade unions within them. For since the objectives set for them were defined in terms of underpinning the competitiveness of private manufacturing capital and the national economy, they had to be operated on the same sorts of 'efficiency' criteria as those used by private capital itself – this being made explicit with the introduction of rate of return on investment criteria in 1961 (HMSO, 1961, Cmnd 1337) – criteria that have subsequently remained and been strengthened. If the pursuit of 'efficiency' had undesirable consequences for particular regions or localities within them, then this was something that those affected had to suffer and accept, part of the price to be paid in the necessary pursuit of 'the national interest'.

Since 1979, however, the political environment in which the nationalised industries operate has changed decisively, leading to even more serious consequences for those regions in which their activities are concentrated. For the election of the Thatcher government produced a much closer and more visible identification of the state with the class interests of capital than had been seen for many years and led it to pursue its triple goals of a more restrictive monetary policy, cutting public expenditure and rolling back the boundaries of the state and encouraging privatisation, and smashing the power of trades unions. A central element in this has been the launching of a fierce assault on the nationalised industries, resulting in a de-nationalisation programme comparable in scale only to the original post-war nationalisations.

This has been especially so in the case of the British Steel Corporation, which has been used as an example to private capital of the government's determination to cut back the scope of the public sector and of the sort of savage restructuring that it needs to engage in to increase labour productivity, international competitiveness and profitability. The effect of this hardened attitude towards the nationalised industries has been further to accelerate industrial decline and employment loss in regions such as the north-east in which the industrial basis had already been seriously eroded.

It is against the background of these general remarks that the formation and implementation of nationalised industry policies and their effects on the north-east will now be considered.

(i) *National Coal Board Policies*   The period from nationalisation until 1958 was one of comparative stability in coal-mining in
the north-east, with output rising gently and capacity and employment falling slightly, primarily because of continuing heavy national dependence upon coal as a primary fuel source. Increasingly
from that date, output, capacity and employment in coal-mining
(and related activities such as rail and water transport) all fell
considerably, though the pace of pit closures and job losses fluc-
tuated considerably (see Krieger, 1979). This secular decline reflected a decision at national level by the UK state to switch to a
multi-fuel economy in an attempt to cut unit energy costs, made
possible by the immediate availability on the international market
of large amounts of cheap oil and the longer-term possibilities
offered by nuclear power.

Consequently, total coal output was cut and production concentrated on larger, more mechanised collieries with lower unit costs
of winning coal. Output, capacity and employment were thus cut
on the north-east coalfield (Table 6.6), while within the region
there was a distinctive locational patterning to closures, with
production being concentrated on the larger east-coast collieries
(see Hudson, 1984; Regional Policy Research Unit, 1979, part 4).

This run-down of the industry within the region largely went
uncontested by the regional branch of the National Union of
Mineworkers, which confined itself to negotiating over the pace
and timing of closures rather than opposing them. Nevertheless,
the continuing run-down of the coal industry nationally and,
particularly but not only after the Conservative victory in the 1970
general election, specific attacks upon the coal industry as well as
more general ones against the trade union movement, led to major
national strikes in 1972 and 1974, the latter toppling the Heath
administration (see Hall, 1981, pp. 166–221). The endorsement in
1974 by the newly elected Labour government, as part of a tripartite steering committee with the NCB and NUM, of the *Plan for
Coal* (National Coal Board, 1974) seemed to recognise that the
assumption of the preceding years of unlimited cheap oil for ever
was no longer tenable and that coal must occupy a more central
place within a national energy strategy. This view was reiterated,
with some modification, in a later 1977 report from the tripartite
group, *Coal for the Future* (Hall, 1981, p. 224).

While this apparently indicated a new climate of opinion as to

TABLE 6.6 *Number of Collieries, Manpower and Saleable Output in the North-East Coalfield, 1947–82*

	Number of collieries			Employment (thousands)			Output (thousand tons)		
	Total	Durham	Northumberland	Total	Durham	Northumberland	Total	Durham	Northumberland
1947	201	134	67	148.7	108.3	40.4	34.8	24.1	10.7
1959	163	113	50	130.7	93.0	37.7	35.1	23.3	11.8
1974	39	27	12	38.3	27.2	11.1	13.5	8.6	4.9
1982	20	14	6	26.3	19.1	7.3	12.4	8.5	3.9

Notes 1947 and 1959 refer to the relevant calendar year, Jan.–Dec. 1974 and 1982 refer to the twelve months ending in March of those years.

SOURCE National Coal Board, 1983, *North East Coal Digest, 1982–3.*

the role of the coal industry within a national energy policy, the implications for the north-east were continuing colliery closures and job losses. For the emphasis remained heavily on producing coal 'competitively' within the context of a multi-fuel economy, with nuclear energy continuing to feature prominently, more so after the 1979 election. The national coal output target for deep-mined coal of 150 million tonnes set in 1974 (and reduced to 120 million in 1977) was thus to be attained by running down production in high-cost collieries, most of those in the north-east being placed in this category, and concentrating investment into existing or new low-unit cost production collieries (such as Selby). The emphasis upon producing competitively and upon rate-of-return criteria in determining the location of new investment was strengthened as a result of public expenditure constraints first imposed in 1975/6, but was further reinforced after the 1979 election. As a result of such policy emphases there has been some expansion of open-cast mining in the north-east, but a continuing run-down of deep-mining: between 1974 and 1982 seventeen collieries were closed, employment was cut by over 9000 (this coming on top of the reduction of over 90 000 in the preceding fifteen years), while labour productivity was increased sharply as new machinery was introduced and work practices reorganised in the remaining pits so that output fell by only 300 000 tonnes (Table 6.6).

Nevertheless, by 1981/2 all but three of the NCB's collieries in the north-east were classified as loss-making by the Monopolies Commission (Table 6.7) – and one of these three has subsequently closed – so that pressures from government to close them intensified in an attempt to force the NCB into profitability. Such pressures were at one level resisted, not least in 1981 when the threat of strike action by the traditionally moderate Durham branch of the NUM led to the NCB apparently abandoning plans to close five collieries, and subsequently by sporadic opposition at colliery level to the closure of individual pits. Nevertheless, within weeks of the 1981 closure plans being withdrawn by the NCB, one of the five listed collieries had closed and others have since closed – often not only without serious opposition but with the tacit encouragement of miners eager either to obtain what appear to them as individuals to be generous redundancy payments or to be transferred to other pits where productivity bonuses are higher

TABLE 6.7 *Profit and Losses by Individual Colliery in the North-East, 1981–82*

	Loss per tonne (£)		Profit per tonne (£)
Sacriston	26.4	Ellington	5.6
Horden	24.4	Whittle	4.3
Herrington	21.2	Boldon	2.0
Bearpark	19.7		
Lynemouth	17.1		
Marley Hill	15.2		
East Hetton	15.2		
Brenkley	13.9		
Hawthorn Complex	12.4		
South Hetton	12.3		
Ashington	12.0		
Shilbottle	8.8		
Bates	8.6		
Easington	6.0		
Vane Tempest	5.8		
Seaham	3.7		
Westoe	2.3		
Dawdon	1.0		
Wearmouth	0.7		

Note Boldon, East Hetton and Marley Hill are now closed; the closure of Lynemouth is imminent.

SOURCE *Newcastle Journal*, 24 June 1983 (in turn, Monopolies Commission).

(see Section 6.4). There is no doubt that a large question-mark hangs over the future of most, if not all, collieries in the north-east, a threat personified in the appointment of Ian McGregor as NCB Chairman following his performance as BSC's Chairman in savagely reducing the scope of its activities and given real substance by the existence of plans to cut output of deep-mined coal by 1988 while opening new low-cost collieries and with the closure of between seventy and eighty loss-making pits and a reduction of employment nationally by 70 000 in a further attempt to compel the NCB to operate at a profit (*Newcastle Journal*, 7 July 1983).

(ii) *British Steel Corporation Policies* Following its formation in 1967, BSC embarked on a series of corporate planning exercises, with the intention of restoring profitability. These resulted in substantial capacity cuts and a reduction of employment of 10 600 by December 1972 in the Northern Region, most of which were concentrated in the north-east on Teesside (Northern Region Strategy Team, 1976, p. 19). Nevertheless, by 1971 the Corporation realised that implementing these plans would not produce a profitable, internationally competitive and technically sophisticated nationalised industry and, in a further attempt to attain these aims, in 1973 it produced a *Ten-Year Development Strategy* (HMSO, 1973, Cmnd 5226). This centred on a massive programme of fixed capital investment (£3000 million at 1972 prices), capacity expansion (from 27 to 33–35 million tonnes per annum by the early 1980s) and sharp increases in labour productivity (with employment cut from 230 000 to 180 000). The strategy was rapidly rendered obsolete, however, by the combination of deepening global recession and the accelerating decline of the UK manufacturing sector. Rather than expand as the Plan assumed, BSC's annual output declined, from about 25 million tonnes in the early 1970s to less than 20 million in 1975 and to much lower levels after 1979 – around 8 million in 1981.

These reductions in output reflected not simply the collapse of BSC's market but also direct political pressures to restructure in search of the elusive, perhaps illusory, goal of profitability. These arose initially from the IMF's insistence that public expenditure be cut as a condition of granting credit to the UK, but increasingly were associated with the state's move towards monetarist economic policies, particularly after the 1979 election, when BSC was singled out for rationalisation in an uprecedented way by the Thatcher government. The fact that in the steel industry the workforce is especially fragmented by inter-union, inter-regional and inter-plant rivalries was undoubtedly a crucial factor in its being chosen by the government as the premier example on which to practice its economic doctrines (see Hudson, 1984; Morgan, 1983; Sadler, 1982, 1984).

The consequences of these successive waves of cut-backs, in terms of abandoned investment plans, capacity closures and employment losses within the north-east and the Northern Region have been severe (as indeed they have been elsewhere: see

Morgan, 1983; Ward and Rowthorne, 1979). Even before the 1973 plan had formally been abandoned, employment in iron and steel production in the region had declined by over 13 000 (almost 25 per cent) since nationalisation (Table 6.2). Indeed, despite considerable new fixed capital investment at the Redcar/south Teesside complex, the employment created there failed even to match losses in the rest of Teesside, to say nothing of those elsewhere (Hudson 1984). As a consequence of jettisoning the 1973 strategy, the scale of development at the south Teesside complex was drastically curtailed: only one blast furnace was completed and plans for new steel-making capacity abandoned (Bryer et al., 1982, p. 211). Furthermore, that there is only one blast furnace in the complex, coupled with the fact that the government has given no assurances as to the continuation of steel-making in the five coastal complexes beyond 1985, must cast a considerable shadow of doubt over the future of the entire south Teesside complex (for a contrary view see Cambridge Economic Policy Group 1980, p. 8).

A second major consequence of the retrenchment policy is that much of the capacity that did exist in 1978 has been scrapped and in those plants that remain there have been substantial job losses and the restructuring of work practices to raise labour productivity – in both cases producing considerable employment reductions in Consett, on Teesside and at Workington. Between 1978 and 1981 BSC had cut or had announced plans to cut employment in the Northern Region by well over 20 000, with these losses very highly concentrated in a few localities (see Hudson, 1984). While to some extent these plant closures and job losses have been contested, principally at Consett, these protests have not been successful (see Hudson and Sadler, 1983, 1984, also Section 4).

(iii) *British Shipbuilders' Policies* The nationalisation of the shipbuilding industry followed a decade and a half of increasingly direct state intervention in it, largely predicated on the assumption that the industry should be internationally competitive and that its problems related to its internal organisation, structure and the strength of trades unions within it in resisting reorganisation of the labour process. Thus the Shipbuilding Industry Board (SIB), established in the wake of the influential Geddes Report (HMSO, 1966, Cmnd 2937), concentrated on promoting mergers and amalgamations within the industry and reorienting production to what were perceived to be commodities with growing markets (such as supertankers). The basis for this form of intervention dissipated in the 1970s as the market for new ships (especially supertankers) collapsed. The shipbuilding companies were saddled with fixed price contracts, entered into prior to 1973 as a way of securing orders in a competitive international market, at a time of rapidly escalating inflation, together with the costs of funding the long-overdue but, by international standards, limited fixed capital investments that had been made associated with the SIB's restructuring initiatives.

Thus on vesting day in 1977 British Shipbuilders (BS) inherited an industry with a chronic profitability crisis and serious overcapacity relative to the share of the international market that it could command: in this connection the attitude of the UK state was crucial. For it essentially continued to accept the erroneous assumption built into the Geddes Report that the international market for ships was fairly and freely competitive and refused to encourage domestic ordering by UK shipping capital or impose levels of tariff protection comparable to those imposed by other industrial states in the face of the fierce challenge of much lower-cost producers in the newly industrialising countries, notably South Korea (see Balassa, 1981; Edwards, 1979, pp. 72–5; Thomas, 1983). In these circumstances, in 1978, nine months after nationalisation, BS drew up plans to cut employment nationally by 12 000 to 75 400, a reduction of 13.7 per cent which it hoped to achieve largely via encouraging early retirement. The combination of deepening recession and the outcome of the 1979 election further confirmed this position and hardened government attitudes so that by the end of that year cuts had taken place on a far larger scale than had been envisaged in the 1978, with employment reduced by 27.7 per cent. BS, like other nationalised industries charged to return to profitability, was forced into proposals for further substantial capacity closures and job losses, the reorganisation of production in those yards that remained open in order to increase labour productivity and its own reorganisation in the 1980 Corporate Plan into commercially rather than geographically based divisions (British Shipbuilders, 1977/8–1981/2, *Annual Reports*): thus by March 1983 employment in BS had been cut to 65 400, with further cuts of 9000 being pursued (*Financial Times*, 19 Mar 1983). The pressures on BS to act in this way, especially in the Merchant Shipbuilding division, have been further intensified

TABLE 6.8 *Capacity Closures by British Shipbuilders in the North-East, 1977–83*

Location	Company	Type of facility
TEESSIDE		
Hartlepool	Clark Hawtorn	Engineering works
Haverton Hill	Smiths Dock	Shipbuilding yard
TYNESIDE		
Hebburn	Swan Hunters	Shipbuilding yard coverted to training facility
South Shields	Swan Hunters	Closure of building berths at former Redheads yard
South Shields	Tyne Ship-repair	Closure of former Redheads repair yard
Walker	Swan Hunters	Shipbuilding yard on to care-and-maintenance basis
WEARSIDE		
	Austin & Pickersgill	South Dock shipbuilding yard closed
	Sunderland Shipbuilders	North Sands shipbuilding yard closed

SOURCE   British Shipbuilders, 1977/8–1981/2, *Annual Reports*.

as such financial aid as it has been given by government to combat South Korean dumping prices has been made conditional upon restructuring.

Such policies have had severe impacts in north-east England: of the 34 shipbuilding, ship-repair and allied engineering companies taken over by BS, (27 on vesting day and another 7 subsequently) 8 are located in the north-east, concentrated within the region around the Tees, Tyne and Wear estuaries. The period since 1977 has seen severe capacity reductions and plant and yard closures (Table 6.8). The severity of these reductions within the north-east reflect its product specialisation in merchant shipbuilding, repair and engineering, all heavy loss-making divisions within BS rather than the more buoyant (not least, following the military expedition to the Falkland Islands) and profitable warships division, since of the north-east yards only Swan Hunters has any degree of speciali-sation in building warships.

Accompanying these closures and the reorganisation of working practices in those plants and yards remaining open, there have been substantial cuts in employment. By 1979 the BS workforce in the north-east had been cut since nationalisation by almost 20 per cent to 29 000 (North Tyneside Trades Council, 1979). Since then there have been further substantial reductions: by March 1983 employment had been reduced to about 21 000, 19 450 in the Tyne and Wear yards (Save Our Shipyards Campaign, 1983) and less than 2000 in those on Teesside. Since then BS has continued to seek further redundancies in the region, with considerable success. Furthermore, BS has succeeded in divesting itself of inland Wol-singham Steelworks in County Durham, plans for closure having been superseded by an apparently successful privatisation of the plant via a buy-out but at the cost of all but 100 of the jobs there (*Northern Echo*, 30 June 1983). These last two points will be returned to in Section 6.4.

3. Industrial Decline, the Flight of Private Capital and the Failure of the State's Modernisation Policies

The economic, political and social threats that might arise from mass unemployment following the collapse of all or part of the region's narrow industrial base became abundantly clear in the 1930s both to the state and to that fraction of the capitalist class with interests in it, and led to the advocacy of modernisation policies, of industrial diversification, as the mechanism to contain them (see Carney and Hudson, 1978). Over the course of subse-quent years, the Labour Party, trade unions and the labour move-ment came to accept this view so that capital, labour and the state shared a common view as to the legitimacy, even inevitability, of trying to solve the regional problem in this way, centred around a territorially based alliance of differing class interests. The role of the Labour Party within this was crucial, given its political hege-mony within the region for this led it to promulgate and defend policies which were based upon the fundamental premise that the only hope of solving problems of employment for working-class people in the north-east lay in pursuing policies which favoured the interests of some capitals, that in the final analysis there was an identity between their interests and those of labour.

For the twenty years or so from the late 1930s the trajectory of the regional economy and, in particular, labour market conditions, were such as to lead both the state and capitals located in the region to oppose any significant moves towards industrial diversification while the restoration of more-or-less 'full employment' (albeit achieved in significant part by net interregional migration) and rising real incomes dampened working-class demands for new, alternative employment. The Second World War, the Korean War and post-war reconstruction in a climate of mild international competition all led to a sharp recovery in effective demand for the commodities produced by the region's 'traditional' industries and led employers, both private capitalists but especially the NCB, vigorously and successfully to oppose the introduction of any new male-employing manufacturing industry (see Regional Policy Research Unit, 1979, Part 4; Hudson, 1983b; 1984). While there was a limited degree of diversification associated with the war-time dispersal of Royal Ordnance Factories and implementation of the Labour government's regional policy between 1945 and 1948 (see Regional Policy Research Unit, 1979, Part 2) this was mainly concerned with exploiting reserves of (married) female labour, drawing such women into wage-labour often for the first time rather than competing for male labour with already-established employers, and as a result was concentrated sectorally and spatially within the north-east (see North Tyneside Community Development Project, 1978: Hudson, 1976; 1980a, b).

After 1958 this situation began to alter, however, because of decisions by the UK state as to the future role of coal as a primary energy source (Section 2.i) and because of the fundamental change in the position of shipbuilding in the north-east in the international division of labour, its competitiveness and market share collapsing as other producers brought more modern production techniques on-stream (see Cousins and Brown, 1970). The accelerating break-up of workforces in these industries, especially coal-mining, led to the re-creation of extensive male and female labour reserves in the region at a time of tight labour market conditions in the growth regions of the UK economy as well as those in other major capitalist states (for further details, see

Hudson, 1981b; 1982a; 1983c). For many capitals, these labour reserves alone provided compelling reasons to locate part of their 'current round of investment' (Massey, 1979) in the north-east, providing flexibility on the market and opportunities to recruit a variety of types of labour-power. In particular, the region offered relatively large quantities of labour-power that was both pliant, either non-unionised or recruited into unions which promised trouble-free production in exchange for closed-shop arrangements so as to boost their memberships, and cheap – particularly during that period (1967–76) when the state directly subsidised the price of labour-power via the Regional Employment Premium (see McCallum, 1979).

In addition, however, the region offered a particularly attractive environment to capital in the 1960s for two other reasons, both linked in various ways to the responses of the working class and the state to employment decline and rising unemployment. For the concentration of job losses in coal-mining and shipbuilding from the late 1950s led not only to an overall rise in regional unemployment, but to a locational concentration within the region so that in particular localities unemployment rose sharply from the very low levels of previous years – for example to over 10 per cent in South Shields in December 1958 – reviving the spectre of the 1930s. Subsequently, job losses in these two industries were compounded by the more generalised effects of the trough of a national 'stop–go' cycle, largely induced by state macroeconomic demand management policies. This combination of national and regionally and industrially specific forces led to a sharp rise in unemployment in the north-east in December 1962, which continued into 1963 (Table 6.1, p. 172). This further heightened already growing pressures from the Labour Party and trades unions within the region for stronger measures to combat unemployment and these coincided with the re-election wishes of the Conservative government, leading to the appointment of Hailsham as Minister for the north-east and adoption of the Hailsham programme (HMSO, 1963, Cmnd 2206; Regional Policy Research Unit, 1979, Part 3), the implementation of which via increased public expenditure led to the creation of new general conditions of production and environments designed to attract fresh manufacturing investment in new industries into selected locations within the region (see Hudson, 1976; 1982a; Robinson, 1978; 1983).

The third element involved in transforming the north-east into an attractive environment for private capital was the enhanced central government financial incentives made available, especially after 1966, to capitals locating or already located there (or in similar regions) as part of a centrally-co-ordinated regional industrial policy (see Rhodes, Moore and Tyler, 1977). This made the region in general an attractive destination for investment in branches characterised by a high and rising organic and technical composition of capital and while it led to some inward movement of new plants, its principle effect was to facilitate the restructuring of existing capacity, especially in the chemicals branch (see Hudson, 1981b, 1983a; Taylor, 1981). Indeed, the Northern Region Strategy Team (1975, table 3) calculated that the net employment effect of regional policy on chemicals employment in the region over the period 1963 to 1973 was a loss of 25 700 jobs. Furthermore, such financial grants in combination with other state policy initiatives, such as the activities of the Industrial Reorganisation Corporation, were important in the attempts to restructuring other existing branches of production, such as power engineering (see North East Trades Union Studies Information Unit, 1976).

As a result of the combined and interacting effects of these three factors, together with changes internal to the organisation of production within companies, by the end of the 1960s there had been some diversification of manufacturing employment in the region, though with very little net growth and an overall substantial reduction in industrial employment because the losses in coal-mining (Table 6.2, p. 174). Furthermore, this diversification was accompanied by significant qualitative changes in the types of jobs available and in the gender composition of the wage-labour force, for almost half of the net increase in manufacturing employment was for women (see Hudson, 1983b, for details), symptomatic of the search for unskilled and supposedly non-militant labour power (Lipietz, 1980a) and having considerable implications for the configuration of the working-class and balance of class forces within the region, for working-class lifestyles (see Hudson, 1980a), as well as for the overall movement of the accumulation process in those capitals exploiting such sources of labour-power. While in one sense, then, the 1960s produced diversification in the range of industries operating within the region, in another sense they produced a tendency to homogenisation in terms of labour-processes and types of work. For what the north-east in this period provided was an environment that was particularly attractive to capitals in those branches which, because of a growing tendency to centralisation and concentration, allied to technical progress and changes in labour-processes associated with Taylorist and Fordist techniques of scientific management (Aglietta, 1979, pp. 111–22; Braverman, 1974), could literally profit from it by locating in branch plants there those parts of their overall production processes which required de-skilled labour-power. Thus the north-east became, for a time, simply one link in chains of corporate production and restructuring that were and are, increasingly, globally rather than nationally based. There is abundant evidence that changes in the north-east were and are related to these changes in the spatial division of labour: by 1971 40 per cent of all manufacturing plants in the Northern Region were branch or subsidiary operations (North East Trades Union Studies Information Unit, 1977) while employment in foreign-owned branch manufacturing plants in the region rose from 8500 in 1963 to 24 400 in 1971 (Northern Region Strategy Team, 1976) and 45 000 in 1978 (Hudson, 1983d). These changes in the north-east were in fact part of much wider processes whereby the 'traditional' pattern of regional specialisation in particular types of product within the UK was changing to a new spatial division of labour in which regions, for a time, characteristically fulfil a specific role in the overall process of production within a wider range of branches, with assembly and semi-skilled component manufacturing operations typically being assigned to region such as the north-east (see Hudson, 1983b; Lipietz, 1980a; Massey, 1978; Perrons, 1980). Thus the characterisation of the region as a 'global outpost' (Austrin and Beynon, 1979) is a particularly appropriate one, the more so once one recognises that this particular type of industrial development itself was a very transient one, reflecting further rapid change in the region's position within the international division of labour and its consequent continuing de-industrialisation: rather than being an 'outpost', it is simply becoming redundant to the requirements of an increasing number of capitals (see Anderson *et al.*, 1983).

For in the 1970s there was a further significant erosion in industrial capacity and employment in the region as a result of private capital's investment and disinvestment decisions, as well as those of the nationalised industries. There were several dimensions to this process of decline. One concerned oil and chemical production. In the earlier part of the 1970s there was continuing heavy fixed capital investment particularly focused on Teesside and the ongoing restructuring of ICI's production complex there and on the development of Seal Sands, and reflected in the Northern Region's rising share of national fixed capital formation in manufacturing (Hudson, 1983b, table 5). This investment was substantially underwritten by the UK state's industrial and regional policies and was associated with a drive to increase competitiveness and retain or increase world market shares for existing products, via increasing productivity through the use of automation in production, and the development of new products: as a result employment fell (see Hudson, 1981b). Furthermore, from the latter part of the 1970s, the competitive position of ICI's Teesside complex, especially the petro-chemical operations at Wilton, was seriously eroded as a result of the UK government's exchange-rate policies and high energy costs, and is further threatened by Shell and Esso's new production complexes at Mossmorran obtaining access to cheaper ethane feedstocks from the North Sea oilfields which would allow them to cut production costs for ethylene to 50 per cent of those of ICI at Wilton (see Etherington, 1983, pp. 133–7, Hudson, 1981b) and the opening of new production complexes in the Middle East (Merrett, 1981). In response to these changed conditions, ICI have reduced capacity and employment at Wilton (see also Table 6.2) and, indeed, has threatened to close its entire Wilton complex with a further loss of 9000 jobs (*Financial Times*, 29 June 1982), while on the Seal Sands site Rohm & Haas closed their plant in June 1981 only a decade after opening it (see Hudson, 1981b).

Other branches which used state financial aid in the 1960s and early 1970s to restructure existing plants within the north-east suffered a similar fate to that of chemicals, with the degree and pace of restructuring revealed as inadequate in the context of that of foreign competitors and the macroeconomic and trade policies of the UK state. This has been particularly so in mechanical engineering, with substantial employment decline as a result (Tables 6.2 and 6.3 – pp. 174, 176).

Furthermore, the 'new' industries, which first invested in the region in the period from immediately before to after the Second World War, but more particularly in the 1960s were increasingly affected by the recession – initially the earlier generation of plants but more and more those of the 1960s 'growth industries', vividly demonstrating that the modern, diversified sector of the region's economy was extremely fragile in the changed world market conditions of the 1970s and 1980s, not least because the UK state had met a substantial part of the fixed capital investment costs of the companies involved, facilitating their accelerated switching of investment between locations and the 'hypermobility of capital' (Damette, 1980). Branch plants set up to produce specific commodities were thus either operated at reduced levels of capacity utilisation in response to falling demand or were closed completely, their 'natural' life cycle truncated as capitals sought to restore profitability by cutting capacity or switching it to locations with cheaper production costs, such as Mediterranean Europe (see Hudson and Lewis, 1983; 1984) or parts of the Third World (see Frobel *et al.*, 1980). In other cases, such plants had been established or expanded to produce commodities that were technically obsolete, at the end of their product life cycle, but for which a specific, temporary demand then existed; once this ceased to exist they were closed. From the perspective of the capitals involved these switches in investment represent a rational response to crisis; from the point of view of manufacturing employment in the north-east their net result has been an accelerated decline since 1975 (Tables 6.2 and 6.3): thus in 1975/6 redundancies and employment decline were particularly associated with the clothing, textile and electrical engineering branches, those most susceptible to relocation to cheap labour locations (see Frobel *et al.*, 1980), later becoming felt over more and more branches leading to a second, much greater and more generalised wave of redundancies and job losses in the period 1980–2, which not only severely affected these branches, but was felt throughout the entire spectrum of 'new' and 'old' industries as the effects of changes in national state policies became translated, not only into accelerated decline in nationalised industries, but also into private capital disinvesting more rapidly from the region (Table 6.9).

The accelerated pace of industrial decline within the north-east in the early 1980s cannot, then, be separated from the results of the 1979 election. For the pre-1979 Labour governments had continued to reorient the goals of regional policy towards those of industrial restructuring *per se* (Cameron, 1979; Geddes, 1979) and

TABLE 6.9 *Redundancies in the Northern Region: the 'Thatcher Effect'*

	Average redundancies per annum		Redundancies as % of all manufacturing	
	1975–9	1980–3	1975–9	1980–3
Mining and quarrying	602	1 969	n.a.	n.a.
Metal manufacture	1 260	6 667	8.6	24.9
Shipbuilding	1 400*	1 908	11.2	7.1
All other manufacturing	11 420	20 092	79.2	68.0

Note *The figure conflates the pre-nationalisation 1975–7 rate of less than 800 with the post-nationalisation 1978–9 rate of 2450.

SOURCE Own calculations from data in Table 6.3.

had been forced by pressure from the IMF to curtail public expenditure increases, thereby restricting public service sector employment growth after 1975 as a counter to the loss of industrial jobs (see Hudson, 1980b) and to adopt an increasingly monetarist stance to economic management. The post-1979 Conservative government reinforced these tendencies to such an extent as to produce a qualitative change in views as to economic policy objectives in the decisive quarters of the central state organisations. The whole tenor of economic policy swung violently to allowing free, unfettered play to the forces of international competition as the mechanism to restructure the UK economy and produce a smaller, but more competitive manufacturing sector, seemingly oblivious to the fact that the UK alone of the major capitalist industrial states was behaving as if the economic clock had been turned back a century or more. Political objectives swung diametrically away from even any pretence at full employment as increasing unemployment became used as a weapon to smash trades union power and coerce workers into accepting savage restructuring and cuts in real wages as the only way of preserving some jobs. Much greater emphasis was placed on the reduction of inflation, guaranteeing 'sound money' via tighter control of the money supply, cutting public expenditure (including that on formal regional policy) and the scope of the public sector

(Section 6.2), and on the level of the sterling exchange rate, boosted in the late 1970s with the advent of the petro-pound. Thus, far from being regarded as something to be reversed, the industrial devastation of the north-east (and elsewhere) was seen as necessary, even desirable, in the interests of long-term national economic recovery.

4. Labour and the State: Responses to De-industrialisation within the North-East

A crucial issue is that of trades union, Labour Party and, more generally, working-class involvement in and responses to the quickening pace of de-industrialisation and job loss. Within the region a belief has evolved over a long period within the trades unions and the Labour Party that even if the interests of capital and labour may not be compatible, then plant closures and job losses are in some sense natural and inevitable, both in the private and public sectors; recently, the view has even re-emerged that real wage cuts must again be accepted as the price of some job preservation (see the foreword to this chapter; also Carney and Hudson, 1978). Thus massive run-down of the region's coal-mining industry in the 1960s was carried out against a background of the regional branch of the NUM negotiating with the NCB over the pace of closure, rather than questioning the need for closures and opposing them. By the later part of the 1970s, as the pace of de-industrialisation quickened and unemployment expanded, opposition to plant closures began to emerge. While there was the occasional exception, notably the threat to strike throughout the region to prevent pit closures in 1981, this opposition was generally confined to workers in the particular factory or pit under threat.

Moreover, the manner in which such anti-closure campaigns was fought has served to divide the working class within plants, between plants and between regions. Within threatened plants the effectiveness of opposition to closure plans has been weakened as workforces within them have been divided in various ways: for example, as a result of long-established inter-union rivalries (for example, at Consett: see Hudson and Sadler, 1983, 1984) and over the issue of redundancy payments, older workers in particular having often been more than willing to accept them (as recent events at Swan Hunters shipyard on Tyneside exemplify, with 900 workers volunteering for 510 redundancies: Section 6.2). A further way in which divisions within workforces have arisen and hindered attempts to contest closure plans is illustrated by reactions to the recent proposal to close Lynemouth Colliery in Northumberland: schisms appeared between those opposed to closure and those in favour of it because it would involve a transfer of some miners to the adjacent Ellington colliery one mile away, which would not only bring transfer compensation of £1550 but higher wages through productivity bonuses (*Newcastle Journal*, 19 July 1983). Whether such intra-plant and pit disputes are deliberately engineered by management is of less significance than the fact that their objective impact is to weaken and divide opposition to closure plans.

Furthermore, the campaigns for the retention of threatened factories or pits have mainly centred on arguments as to their actual or potential commercial viability, with at best some subsidiary consideration of the social costs of closure: for example, this characterised the arguments put forward against the closure of British Rail's Shildon works, BSC's Consett works (Joint Trades Unions Committee for Consett Steelworks, 1980), BS's Wolsingham plant and Vickers Scotswood works (Save Scotswood Campaign Committee, 1979). This had the effect of setting them in competition with other plants within the north-east and other regions: only rarely, as in the current campaign to save Fishburn Coke Works in County Durham, are the implications of closure of one plant in terms of threatening the closure of *other* plants emphasised (*Newcastle Journal*, 27 July 1983). This generation of inter-plant rivalry was one reason for the isolation in terms of region and class of the attempt to save Consett steelworks: for example, Consett was isolated from support on South Teesside by the initial implied link between Consett's closure and Teesside's development and from plants in other region's by BSC's management skilfully playing on chauvinistic regional divisions between workers in the steel industry (see Hudson and Sadler, 1983, 1984). More recently the deliberate creation of competition between plants in different regions was revealed in the announcement that three BS yards, each desperate to maintain their workload – Laird's on Merseyside, Swan Hunters on Tyneside and Vosper

Thorneycroft at Southampton – were to be invited to tender competitively for orders for two frigates (*Newcastle Journal*, 20 July 1983). But such inter-plant competition is perhaps most savage and divisive when part of a formerly nationalised industry is privatised and set in competition against the remaining plants in the nationalised industry: thus the proposal following its closure by BS by former workers at the Redheads ship-repair yard to buy it and reopen it in competition with BS's remaining ship-repair facilities has led to an alliance between BS management and shop-stewards and caused bitter divisions between shipbuilding workers in BS and their former colleagues at the Redheads yard (*Newcastle Journal*, 12, 14 and 25 July 1983).

One result, sometimes deliberate, sometimes inadvertent, of this burgeoning inter-plant competition in a desperate fight for survival, orders and jobs, has been to persuade or coerce workers into accepting new forms of working practices so as to enhance labour productivity, increasingly and visibly the measure against which plants are evaluated in decisions as to which will remain open, which close. Recent examples of this within the North East is the attempt by the NCB to introduce new shift systems at the loss-making Westoe colliery (Table 6.7) for 'efficiency reasons' (*Newcastle Journal*, 13 July 1982) and the introduction of a new shift system by Dunlop at their tyre plant in Washington New Town aimed at achieving an increase in labour productivity of over 20 per cent (*Newcastle Journal*, 1 July 1981).

The most extreme example, however, of proposals to reorganise work practices relates to BSC's Hartlepool plate and pipe mills. In January 1983 it was announced that there were to be a further 635 redundancies there, reducing the employment to 700, but BSC suggested a scheme to keep the redundant men on 'job standby', re-employing them temporarily as and when demand rose: this was condemned by local trades union leaders as 'a return to serfdom' and 'just like the Thirties, with men waiting at the factory gates to find out whether there's any work' (*Northern Echo*, 15 January 1983). Nevertheless, faced with further job losses in a town where male unemployment already exceeded 30 per cent, steelworkers whose jobs were threatened were later to attempt to put the proposals back on the agenda. At a deeper level the effects of inter-plant competition is to transform what is, structurally, a class struggle between capital and labour into one between different fractions of the working class delineated on a territorial basis.

Attempts at preventing plant closure and job losses have, however, generally either been unsuccessful or have not been contested: consequently, industrial employment has fallen and both male and female registered unemployment risen (Table 6.1). These increases also reflect falling labour demand in the South East and West Midlands and so reduced net out-migration and a growing labour supply within the north-east (Department of Employment, 1978). Even so, increases in registered unemployment understate the extent of the problem for, in addition to these, there are considerable numbers of young people kept off the unemployment register by various temporary job-creation or -preservation schemes. In the financial year 1982/3 46 000 young people in the Northern Region were engaged in some form of training and/or work-experience programme (Manpower Services Commission Northern Region, 1983; see also Manpower Services Commission, 1979); while the recent redefinition of unemployment demonstrated the way in which the real magnitude of the problem could be disguised by political expedient. Even so, the registered unemployment statistics demonstrate the extent to which, reflecting the sectoral incidence of unemployment, areas such as Consett, Hartlepool and Sunderland within the region have experienced disproportionate shares of the overall regional increase (Figure 6.2).

In contrast to the late 1950s and early 1960s, when much smaller increases in and much lower rates of unemployment produced vigorous political pressures from within the north-east for effective state intervention, the much greater increases and higher levels of the late 1970s and 1980s have been meekly accepted as inevitable and unavoidable; the extent to which the Conservative government's refusal to act so as to tackle unemployment is regarded as a legitimate one – or at least an unalterable one – is a measure of the extent to which its view of the world currently stands in a position of hegemony within contemporary political debates in the UK. Nevertheless, while at this level the state has been able to abandon any concern for the levels of unemployment and plight of unemployed people in the north-east (see Hudson, 1982b), within the region there have been more localised political pressures and initiatives from parts of the state within the region. For example, there have been sporadic calls for a Northern Development Agency, particularly from within the Labour Party, in response to the establishment of the Scottish and Welsh Development Agencies as

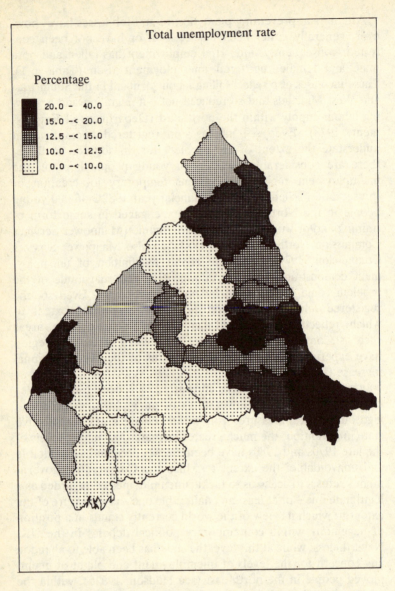

Total unemployment rate

Percentage

	20.0 – 40.0
	15.0 –< 20.0
	12.5 –< 15.0
	10.0 –< 12.5
	0.0 –< 10.0

FIGURE 6.2 *Unemployment Rates in the Northern Region – May 1984 (by Travel-to-Work Areas)*

SOURCE   Department of Employment;

part of the state's response to the political threats posed by nationalism (see Nairn, 1977). Indeed, this call for an NDA to allow the north-east to compete more fairly with Scotland and Wales for such new investment as is being made is symptomatic of a desperate interregional and international competition for new jobs, one in which the north-east is increasingly unsuccessful – between 1976 and 1978 only 52 new manufacturing plants were attracted into the Northern Region from other locations (13 from abroad and 16 from the south-east), providing 3300 new jobs as compared with the net loss of 61 000 manufacturing jobs over the same period (Tyne and Wear County Council, 1983). Such competition over the location of new employment both reflects existing divisions and further divides the working class on a territorial basis. A good – or bad – example of this recently arose over the decision of the frozen-food firm Findus to close a factory at Cleethorpes while expanding one in Newcastle. Responding to comments by representatives of the Cleethorpes' workforce as to the consequences for their area of this decision, Mr Garrett, Labour MP for Wallsend in whose constituency the Newcastle plant is located, commented that 'Newcastle's good news – and Humberside's gloom – is a fact of life in "this harsh commercial world. Every company has to make the most of all the opportunities that are available. Findus is established in my constituency and it has established a good reputation with union agreements and wage rates that compare with anywhere else. The company obviously saw better prospects, better industrial relations and better commercial possibilities. That is what influenced them."' (*Newcastle Journal*, 23 June 1983.) Garrett's reaction neatly encapsulates the sense in which there is a general acceptance of the appropriateness and inevitability of private capital's rationality in determining investment and disinvestment decisions and at the same time of the way in which particular localities must engage in a bitter struggle to sell themselves to capital as the most desirable location for its purposes, the more so in a time of deep recession and comparatively little new 'mobile' investment.

In the absence of a positive response from central government to proposals for an NDA and intense competition for such 'mobile investment' as there is, there has been an increasing local-authority involvement in economic development and employment programmes, sometimes in collaboration with *ad hoc* job creation agencies such as BSC Industry (as at Consett and Hartlepool).

These initiatives have centred on policies to encourage small-firm formation and growth, both in manufacturing and, reflecting a belated recognition of the decline in manufacturing employment, services (Northern Region Strategy Team, 1977). Related to this and promoting further intra-regional divisions and competition for employment, as well as carrying a more generalised price in the ideological battle as to an appropriate government stance regarding economic policy (see Anderson, 1983), there has been intense competition between local authorities in the region to be granted Enterprise Zone status for parts of their areas (Gateshead, Hartlepool, Middlesbrough and Newcastle being successful in this so far) as a further inducement to capital to locate there.

Nevertheless, the implementation of small-firm policies has had at best a marginal impact in creating new jobs (Storey, 1982), not least because of the conflict between them and central government fiscal and macroeconomic policies: Cochrane (1983) succinctly summarises the situation as one of 'draining the ocean with a teaspoon'. The real significance of such policies is that, as with those towards Enterprise Zones, they perform an important ideological role, their existence simultaneously allowing central government to lay off at least some of the blame for high unemployment on to the failures of local authority initiatives while the local authorities and councillors in the north-east can at least legitimise their own positions by claiming that they are attempting to do something to alleviate the position in circumstances not of their own choosing.

5. Concluding Comments: Breaking the Mould?

At a very abstract level Habermas (1976) suggests that the inevitable discrepancies between the stated intentions and actual outcomes of the actions of capitalist states, in specific circumstances, could spill over into the wider socio-political sphere and lead to a crisis of legitimation for the state. Carney (1980) more specifically argues that the failures of the state's attempt to solve regional problems can pose a challenge to its authority and provide opportunities for the emergence of new nationalist and regionalist movements which can, for a time, disrupt conventional forms of democratic political activity, citing several examples where this has been the case: Belgium (see also Mandel, 1963); Lorraine and Nord–Pas-de-Calais (see also Hudson and Sadler, 1984); Scotland (see also Nairn, 1977). In all these cases, even when the forms of protest spilled over into direct action and violence, the threats were contained within the confines of the relevant nation state and the social relations of capitalism. In north-east England, where the actions and policies of the UK state, both directly and indirectly, have been the chief proximate cause of the de-industrialisation of the region, of shrinking employment opportunities and rising unemployment, this has not been so (and the one attempt to mimic such forms of organisation and protest failed miserably; see Hudson and Sadler, 1983). Rather, in general there has been a largely passive acceptance by the working class within the region that economic decline, job losses and mounting unemployment are an inevitable part of the natural order, an acceptance made easier by memories of the 1930s and the cushion to consumption levels and living conditions, meagre though it is, currently provided through the Welfare State. To understand this it is necessary to consider the history of labourism and character and role of the Labour Party in the region; for historically it has been the prime representative of working-class aims and aspirations and for several decades effectively maintained political hegemony within the north-east. At the same time it has tended to adhere to a view that, in the final analysis, the interests of capital and labour are complementary and that the capital–labour relationship is a justifiable one – thus the emergence of a consensus around the politics of modernisation in the 1960s as the only route to full employment and social progress within the region. The Labour movement held a key role in both establishing the legitimacy of the resultant regional modernisation programme and implementing it. When this was at first accompanied and then followed by sharply rising regional unemployment the limits of this position were sharply revealed. Yet to transcend them would require extending the extent of state action both quantitatively and qualitatively, and ultimately challenging the legitimacy of capitalist social relations. Rather than moving to overcome these limits the current response within the Labour Party is one of internal division and fragmentation: it is no coincidence that the Social Democratic Party initially attracted such a disproportionate share of its support from erstwhile Labour MPs in the north-east, for its general ideological stance is to assert the complementary character of the interests of capital and labour. In the longer term, however, this party political realignment may offer precisely the opportunities needed to reorient the Labour Party in the region towards policies which address the real problems of the working class and transcend those limits which at the moment prevent these being placed at the forefront of an agenda for solving the regional problem.

Note

1. Unfortunately, central government's regional statistics refer not to the 'north-east', but to the 'Northern Region', which includes Cumbria as well as Cleveland, Durham, Northumberland and Tyne–Wear. As the main concentrations of industrial activity are (or were) in the north-east, the Northern Region data do give a reasonable indication of de-industrialisation trends there, and in any case can often be complemented with other data specifically referring to the north-east.

Acknowledgements

This chapter draws on the results of research projects funded by the Centre for Environmental Studies, Manpower Services Commission and Social Science Research Councils. I would also like to acknowledge valuable discussions on various points in the chapter with Huw Beynon, Peter Friis, Jim Lewis, Viggo Plum, Henrik Toft Jensen and David Sadler.

Bibliography

In addition to the references cited below, newspaper sources such as the *Financial Times, Newcastle Journal* and *Northern Echo* have been used; references to particular editions are given in the text.

Aglietta, M. (1979) *A Theory of Capitalist Regulation* (London: New Left Books).

Anderson, J. (1983) 'Geography as Ideology and the Politics of Crisis: The Enterprise Zone Experiment', in Anderson, J., Duncan, S. and Hudson, R. (eds) *Redundant Spaces in Cities and Regions?* (London: Academic Press) pp. 313–50.

Anderson, J., Duncan, S. and Hudson, R. (1983) (eds) *Redundant Spaces in Cities and Regions?* (London: Academic Press).

Austrin, T. and Beynon, H. (1979) 'Global Outpost: The Working Class Experience of Big Business in the North East of England, 1964–79' mimeo. (University of Durham: Department of Sociology).

Balassa, B. (1981) *The Newly Industrialising Countries in the World Economy* (London: Pergamon).

Barclays Review (1982) 'The Changing Structure of UK Balance of Payments, 1970–81', centrespread (London: Barclays Bank).

Blackaby, F. (ed.) (1979) *De-industrialisation* (London: Heinemann).

Braverman, H. (1974) *Labor and Monopoly Capital* (New York: Monthly Review Press).

British Shipbuilders (1977/8–1981/2) *Annual Reports* (Newcastle upon Tyne).

Bryer, R. A., Brignell, T. J. and Maunders, A. R. (1982) *Accounting for British Steel* (Aldershot: Gower).

Bulmer, M. (1978) 'Employment and Unemployment in Mining', in Bulmer, M. (ed.) *Mining and Social Change* (London: Croom Helm) pp. 150–65.

Cambridge Economic Policy Group (1980) *Economic Review* **6**, **2** (Farnborough: Gower).

Cameron, G. C. (1979) 'The National Industrial Strategy and Regional Policy', in Machenuan, D. and Parr, J. (eds) *Regional Policy: Past Experience and New Directions* (Oxford: Martin Robertson) pp. 297–322.

Carney, J. (1980) 'Regions in Crisis: Accumulation, Regional Problems and Crisis Formation', in Carney, J., Hudson, R. and Lewis, J. (eds) *Regions in Crisis* (London: Croom Helm) pp. 22–59.

Carney, J. and Hudson, R. (1978) 'Capital, Politics and Ideology: The North East of England, 1870–1946' *Antipode*, **10**, **2**, pp. 64–78.

Carney, J., Hudson, R., Ive, G. and Lewis, J. (1976) 'Regional Underdevelopment in Late Capitalism: A Study of North-East England', in Masser, I. (ed.) *London Papers in Regional Science*, **6** (London: Pion) pp. 11–29.

Carney, J., and Hudson, R. and Lewis, J. (1977) 'Coal Combines and Inter-regional Uneven Development', in Massey, D. and Batey, P. (eds) *London Papers in Regional Science*, **7** (London: Pion) pp. 52–67.

Coates, D. (1980) *Labour in Power?* (London: Longman).

Cochrane, A. (1983) 'Local Economic Policies: Trying to Drain an Ocean with a Teaspoon', in Anderson, J., Duncan, S. and Hudson, R. (eds) *Redundant Spaces in Cities and Regions?* (London: Academic Press) pp. 285–311.

Cousins, J. and Brown, R. (1970) 'Shipbuilding', in Dewdney, J. C. (ed.). *Durham City and County with Teeside* (Durham: British Association for the Advancement of Science).

Damette, F. (1980) 'The Regional Framework of Monopoly Exploitation', in Carney, J., Hudson, R. and Lewis, J. (eds) *Regions in Crisis* (London: Croom Helm) pp. 76–92.

Department of Employment (1978) *Employment Gazette* **86**, **9**, pp. 1040–3.

Edwards, A. (1979) *The Newly Industrializing Countries and their Impact on Western Manufacturing* (London: Economist Intelligence Unit Special Report no. 73) vol. 1.

Etherington, D. (1983) 'Local Authority Policies, Industrial Restructuring and the Unemployment Crisis: An Evaluation of the Formation and Impacts of Local Economic Initiatives in Cleveland 1963–82', unpublished MA thesis, University of Durham.

Fothergill, S. and Gudgin, G. (1978) 'Regional Employment Statistics on a Comparable Basis', *Occasional Paper no. 5* (London: Centre for Environmental Studies).

Frank, A. G. (1980) *Crisis in the World Economy* (London: Heinemann).

Frobel, F., Heinrichs, J. and Kreye, O. (1980) *The New International Division of Labour* (Cambridge: Cambridge University Press).

Geddes, M. (1979) 'Regional Policy and Crisis and the Cuts', Paper presented to a meeting of the Conference of Socialist Economists' Regionalism Group (London).

Habermas, J. (1976) *Legitimation Crisis* (London: Heinemann).

Hall, T. (1981) *King Coal* (Harmondsworth: Pelican).

HMSO (1961) *The Financial and Economic Obligations of the Nationalized Industries*, Cmnd 1337 (London).

HMSO (1963) *The North-East: A Programme for Regional Development and Growth*, Cmnd 2206 (London).

HMSO (1966) *Report of the Shipbuilding Inquiry Committee*, Cmnd 2937 (London).

HMSO (1973) *British Steel Corporation: Ten-Year Development Strategy*, Cmnd 5226 (London).

HMSO (1978) *British Steel Corporation: the Road to Viability*, Cmnd 7149 (London).

Hudson, R. (1976) *New Towns in North-East England*. Final Report, no. HR 1734, to the Social Science Research Council (London).

Hudson, R. (1980a) 'Women and Work: A Study of Washington New Town', *Occasional Publication no. 16* (University of Durham: Department of Geography).

Hudson. R. (1980b) 'Regional Development Policies and Female Employment', *Area*, **12**, **3**, pp. 229–34.

Hudson, R. (1981a) 'State Policies and Changing Transport Networks', in Burnett, A. and Taylor, P. J. (eds) *Political Studies from Spatial Perspectives* (Chichester: Wiley) pp. 467–88.

Hudson, R. (1981b) *North-East England* (Roskilde Universitats Centre, Institute for Geographi) Samfunds-analyze og datologi, Kompendium no. 25.

Hudson, R. (1982a) 'Accumulation, Spatial Policy and the Production of Regional Labour Reserves', *Environment and Planning, A*, **14**, pp. 665–80.

Hudson, R. (1982b) 'Unemployment in the North: The Human Costs of Industrial Decline', *Town and Country Planning*, **51**, **1**, pp. 8–10.

Hudson, R. (1983a) 'Capital Accumulation and Chemicals Production in Western Europe in the Post-war Period', *Environment and Planning, A*, **15**, pp. 105–22.

Hudson, R. (1983b) 'Capital Accumulation and Regional Problems: A

Study of North-East England, 1945–80', in Hamilton, F. E. I. and Linge, G. (eds) *Regional Industrial Systems* (Chichester: Wiley) pp. 75–101.

Hudson, R. (1983c) 'Regional Labour Reserves and Industrialisation in the EEC', *Area*, **15**, 3, pp. 223–9.

Hudson, R. (1983d) 'Comments on "Shifts in the Geography of Employment": papers by Peter Lloyd and Doreen Massey', paper presented to a meeting of the Royal Geographical Society, 9 May 1983 (London).

Hudson, R. (1984) 'The Paradoxes of State Intervention: The Impact of Nationalized Industry Policies and Regional Policy on Employment in the Northern Region in the Post-war Period', in Chapman, R. (ed.) *Public Policy Studies: The North-East of England* Edinburgh: Edinburgh University Press).

Hudson, R. and Lewis, J. (eds) (1985) *Uneven Development In Southern Europe* (London: Methuen).

Hudson, R. and Lewis, J. (1984) 'Capital Movements and Industrialisation in Southern Europe', in Williams, A. (ed.) *Southern Europe Transformed?* (London: Harper & Row) forthcoming.

Hudson, R. and Sadler, D. (1983) 'Anatomy of a Disaster: The Closure of Consett Steelworks', *Northern Economic Review*, **6**, pp. 2–17.

Hudson, R. and Sadler, D. (1983) 'Region, Class and the Politics of Steel Closures in the European Community', *Society and Space* **1**, pp. 405–428.

Joint Trades Unions Committee for Consett Steelworks (1980) *No Case for Closure* (Consett).

Krieger, J. (1979) 'British Colliery Closure Programmes in the North-East: From Paradox to Contradiction', in Cullen, I. (ed.) *London Papers in Regional Science*, **9**, (London: Pion).

Lipietz, A. (1980a) 'Inter-regional Polarization and the Tertiarisation of Society', *Papers of the Regional Science Association*, **44**, pp. 3–18.

Lipietz, A. (1980b) 'The Structuration of Spaces, the Problem of Land, and Spatial Policy', in Carney, J., Hudson, R. and Lewis, J. (eds) *Regions in Crisis* (London: Croom Helm) pp. 60–75.

McCallum, J. D. (1979) 'The Development of British Regional Policy', in MacClennan, D. and Parr, J. (eds) *Regional Policy: Past Experience and New Directions* (Oxford: Martin Robertson) pp. 3–42.

McCord, N. (1979) *North-East England: The Region's Development 1760–1960* (London: Batsford).

McEachern, D. (1980) *A Class Against Itself* (Cambridge: Cambridge University Press).

Mandel, E. (1963) 'The Dialectic of Region and Class in Belgium', *New Left Review*, **20**, pp. 5–31.

Mandel, E. (1975) *Late Capitalism* (London: New Left Books).

Mandel, E. (1978) *The Second Slump* (London: New Left Books).

Manpower Research Group (1981) *Review of the Economy and Employment* (University of Warwick).

Manpower Services Commission (1979) *Annual Report 1978–9* (London: MSC).

Manpower Services Commission, Northern Region (1983) *Remit*, **15**.

Massey, D. (1978) 'Regionalism: A Review', *Capital and Class*, **6**, pp. 106–25.

Massey, D. (1979) 'In What Sense a Regional Problem?', *Regional Studies*, **13**, pp. 233–43.

Merrett, E. R. (1981) 'Petrochemicals in Japan and Western Europe', *Barclays Review* (Nov) pp. 83–7.

Morgan, K. (1983) 'Restructuring Steel: The Crises of Labour and Locality in Britain', *International Journal of Urban and Regional Research*, **7, 2**, pp. 175–201.

Nairn, T. (1977) *The Break-up of Britain* (London: New Left Books).

National Coal Board (1974) *Plan for Coal* (London: NCB).

North-East Trades Union Studies Information Unit (1976) *The Crisis Facing the UK Power Plant Manufacturing Industry* (Newcastle upon Tyne).

North-East Trades Union Studies Information Unit (1977) *Multinationals in Tyne and Wear,* vols 1 and 2 (Newcastle upon Tyne).

North Tyneside Community Development Project (1978) *North Shields – Women's Work* (London: Home Office).

North Tyneside Trades Council (1979) *Shipbuilding – The Cost of Redundancy* (Newcastle upon Tyne).

Northern Region Strategy Team (1975) 'Evaluation of the Impact of Regional Policy on Manufacturing Industry in the Northern Region', *Technical Report no. 2* (Newcastle upon Tyne: NRST).

Northern Region Strategy Team (1976) 'Trends and Prospects in the Iron and Steel Industry', *Working Paper* no. 3 (Newcastle upon Tyne: NRST).

Northern Region Strategy Team (1977) *Strategic Plan for the Northern Region,* vol. 2 (London: HMSO).

Perrons, D. (1980) 'The Role of Ireland in the New International Division of Labour: A Proposed Framework for Regional Analysis', *Regional Studies*, **15**, pp. 81–100.

Regional Policy Research Unit (1979) *State Regional Policies and Uneven Development: the Case of North East England* (London: Final Report no. RP 270 to the Centre for Environmental Studies).

Reid, W. (1970) 'Coal mining', in Dewdney, J. C. (ed.) *Durham City and County with Teeside* (Durham: British Association for the Advancement of Science) pp. 294–302.

Rhodes, B., Moore, J. and Tyler, P. (1977) 'The Impact of Regional Policy in the 1970's', *CES Review*, no. 1.

Robinson, J. F. F. (1978) 'Peterlee: A Study of New Town Development', unpublished Ph.D. thesis, Durham University.

Robinson, J. F. F. (1983) 'State Planning of Spatial Change: Compromise and Contradiction in Peterlee New Town', in Anderson, J., Duncan, S. and Hudson, R. (eds) *Redundant Spaces in Cities and Regions?* (London: Academic Press) pp. 263–84.

Sadler, D. (1982) 'The Closure of Consett Steelworks: Isolation and Division within Region and Class', mimeo. (University of Durham: Department of Geography).

Sadler, D. (1984) 'Works Closure at British Steel and the Nature of the State', *Political Geography Quarterly* **3**, **4**, pp. 297–311.

Save Our Shipyards Campaign (1983) *Information Pack:* c/o Tyne and Wear County Council, Newcastle upon Tyne.

Save Scotswood Campaign Committee (1979) *Economic Audit on Vickers Scotswood* (Newcastle upon Tyne).

Storey, D. (1982) *Entrepreneurship and the New Firm* (London: Croom Helm).

Taylor, G. (1981) 'The Restructuring of Capital in the Teeside Chemical and Steel Industries', paper presented to a meeting of the Conference of Socialist Economists Regionalization Group, Durham.

Thomas, D. (1983) 'Shipbuilding – Demand Linkage and Industrial Decline', in Williams, K., Williams, J. and Thomas, D. *Why Are the British Bad at Manufacturing?* (London: Routledge & Kegan Paul) pp. 179–216.

Thompson, K. (1975) 'The Post-War Development of Shipbuilding and Associated Industries in the Tyne Valley', unpublished B.A. dissertation University of Durham, Department of Geography.

Tyne and Wear County Council (1983) *Economic Development Bulletin*, no. 17 (Newcastle upon Tyne).

Ward, T. and Rowthorne, R. (1979) 'How to Run a Company and Run Down an Economy: The Effects of the Closing Down of Steel-making in Corby', *Cambridge Journal of Economics*, **3**.

7

The De-industrialisation of the City

STEVE FOTHERGILL, GRAHAM GUDGIN, MICHAEL KITSON AND SARAH MONK

1. Introduction

The industrial city in Britain is the product of nineteenth-century capitalism. Technical innovations in production and the accumulation of capital led to the development of large factories. At the same time it was advantageous for factories to be clustered near the focal points of the rudimentary transport network, such as ports, canals and railway terminals, and workers had little choice but to live close by. Few restrictions were placed on urban development. The result was that cities grew in an uncontrolled and cumulative manner following the cost-and-profit calculations of entrepreneurs. Britain was the first country to become fully urbanised: by the middle of the century over half the population lived in the new industrial cities.

In the late twentieth century all this has changed. The virtually universal availability of power, telecommunications and transport, with minimal geographical variations in cost, has released the magnetic grip of cities on industry. The advent of cheap road transport, in particular, has finally removed the locational advantage of cities. Indeed, there has been a complete turnaround in the fortunes of the industrial city: in the late twentieth century the city is the principal location of de-industrialisation.

Three aspects of de-industrialisation impinge on the city. The first is the shift in the balance of employment in Britain as a whole away from manufacturing towards services. This process dates back to at least the end of the Second World War. Its cause is the difference in the rate of growth of labour productivity between

214

manufacturing and services. The nature of many tasks in manufacturing production facilitates the introduction of machinery to replace labour; in services this is not possible to the same extent. For any given growth of output the rate of increase in manufacturing employment is therefore lower than the rate of increase in service employment. The effect is a shift in the distribution of the workforce from manufacturing to the service sector. This has occurred in years of both high and low employment, and is likely to continue. It does not necessarily pose a major economic problem. Indeed, if the rate of growth of the economy is fast enough then there may be an increase in manufacturing employment even if the overall structure of employment is moving towards services. This occurred in Britain until 1966: manufacturing employment was expanding, but service employment was expanding faster and services thus accounted for an increasing share of all jobs.

The second aspect of de-industrialisation affecting the city is the failure of the British economy to grow at a sufficient rate to provide full employment. Manufacturing and service employment are both below what they would be if all available labour were utilised. Since 1966, manufacturing employment nationally has fallen by around 3 million and the gap between the supply of labour and the supply of jobs has widened, especially since 1979. Unlike the structural shift from manufacturing to services this aspect of de-industrialisation creates severe problems, the most obvious of which is the high level of unemployment that now affects nearly all areas. The reasons for the failure to achieve adequate economic growth are numerous. They include the deflationary economic policies pursued by governments, the competitive weakness of much of British industry and the constraints imposed by the underlying imbalance in Britain's trade with the rest of the world. Cities suffer de-industrialisation because of these failures but the solutions lie with national economic policy, not spatial policy.

The third aspect of the de-industrialisation of cities is specifically spatial: accompanying the national contraction of manufacturing and the reduction in its share of total employment, there has been a large urban–rural contrast in the rate of change. Until the recession at the beginning of the 1980s, small towns and rural areas experienced a long period of sustained expansion in industrial production and employment. Even after the recession, with national manufacturing employment at less than 60 per cent of its level of twenty years earlier, the number of manufacturing jobs in many small towns and rural areas remains greater than in the 1960s. Britain's cities, in contrast, have lost manufacturing jobs faster than almost any other part of the country.

This chapter concerns only this third aspect of de-industrialisation. It examines how and why the loss of manufacturing jobs has proceeded faster and further in cities than in small towns and rural areas. The explanation put forward is that the relative decline of cities as centres of industrial production is an almost inevitable consequence of the process of economic change within an 'advanced' capitalist economy. Just as the unrestrained operation of the market economy led to the development of ever larger cities during the last century, in changed circumstances the market economy is eroding their industrial base. The next part of the chapter describes the urban–rural contrast in manufacturing employment change and considers the consequences for unemployment, population distribution and 'inner city' problems generally. This is followed by a discussion of the national economic trends which have concentrated industrial job loss in Britain's cities. The chapter then looks at how the policies pursued by the Conservative government since 1979 have affected the industrial city, and concludes by considering whether the increasing range of urban economic initiatives adds up to an effective strategy for urban industrial regeneration.

2. Urban Industrial Decline

Table 7.1 shows manufacturing employment change between 1960 and 1981 in six types of area in Great Britain. Each local-authority district (there are about 450) has been classified on the basis of settlement size and employment has been measured using statistics that have been adjusted to be fully comparable through time. The table reveals the considerable locational change that has occurred.

Two points are worth noting. The first is the number of jobs involved. At one end of the urban hierarchy, London lost over half its manufacturing employment – nearly 700 000 jobs – during this period. To put this into perspective, the number of manufacturing jobs lost in London is not far short of the present number of

TABLE 7.1 *Manufacturing Employment by Type of Area, 1960–81*

	Employment (thousands)		Change 1960–81	
	1960	1981	(thousands)	(%)
London	1338	650	−688	−51.4
Conurbations	2282	1295	−987	−43.2
Free-standing cities	1331	950	−381	−28.6
Large towns	921	756	−165	−17.9
Small towns	1631	1609	−22	−1.4
Rural areas	527	655	+128	−24.2
GREAT BRITAIN	8031	5916	+2115	−26.3

SOURCE Department of Employment.

Conurbations:	Manchester, Merseyside, Clydeside, West Yorkshire, Tyneside, West Midlands.
Free-standing cities:	other cities with more than 250 000 people.
Large towns:	towns or cities with 100 000 to 250 000 people.
Small towns:	districts including at least one town with 35 000 to 100 000 people, plus coalfield areas.
Rural areas:	districts in which all settlements have fewer than 35 000 people.

manufacturing jobs in the whole of the West Midlands regions, and is considerably more than the total in Scotland, Wales or the Northern region. The second point to note is the consistency of the urban–rural contrast. Across the whole urban hierarchy manufacturing employment change is related to settlement size. As a general rule the larger the settlement the greater the decline. The consistency in aggregate trends mirrors consistency at the local scale: all the conurbations lost more than one in three of their manufacturing jobs during this period, and fifteen out of seventeen free standing cities lost manufacturing jobs. Stability or growth in manufacturing employment has occurred in relatively remote towns and rural areas as well as in places close to cities, indicating that the urban–rural contrast is more than merely the 'overspill' of jobs from cities to their immediately surrounding hinterlands. The decentralisation has also been largely unplanned. Although for thirty years until the late 1970s public policy encouraged the movement of people and jobs to New and Expanding Towns away from cities, these centres of planned growth account for only a small proportion of the shift to towns and rural areas (Fothergill, Kitson and Monk 1983).

An urban–rural contrast can be observed in all parts of Britain. In every region small towns and rural areas have fared better than larger settlements by a sizeable margin, an indication of the pervasiveness of the forces generating this shift in location. The decline in the number of manufacturing jobs in cities and the relative growth elsewhere has also redistributed jobs between regions. Highly urban regions have declined; more rural regions have grown. It is no coincidence, for example, that East Anglia and the South-West have been the regions least affected by de-industrialisation. These are the most rural regions in Britain with comparatively little of their industry in cities. The North-West, at the bottom of the regional growth league, is possibly the most urban region, with a high proportion of its jobs in the Manchester and Merseyside conurbations.

It is difficult to assess exactly when the relative decline of urban industry began: appropriate statistics do not go back far enough. At least some manufacturing firms were moving out of London during the late nineteenth and early twentieth century, but the 1920s and 1930s still saw substantial industrial expansion in suburban areas. From the 1950s onwards it is easier to monitor the changing scale of the urban–rural contrast. Table 7.2 shows the average annual change in manufacturing employment in London and the conurbations during each of five periods since 1952. The first part of the table shows that during the 1950s their manufacturing employment increased a little. In the 1960s decline set in and accelerated. Between 1966 and 1973 London and the conurbations lost an average of 100 000 manufacturing jobs every year. In the mid-1970s the decline eased a little, but after 1978 the recession led to unprecedented job losses. The second part of Table 7.2 shows manufacturing employment change in London and the

TABLE 7.2 *Manufacturing Employment Change in London and the Conurbations, 1952–81*

	1952–60	1960–66	1966–73	1973–78	1978–81
ACTUAL CHANGE					
number per year	+20 000	–25 000	–108 000	–73 000	–154 000
% per year	+0.6	–0.7	–3.0	–2.6	–6.3
RELATIVE TO UK AVERAGE					
number per year	–24 000	–38 000	–63 000	–29 000	–28 000
% per year	–0.7	–1.0	–1.8	–1.0	–1.2

SOURCE Department of Employment.

conurbations relative to the national average. This is the difference between the employment change in these areas and the change which would have occurred if their employment had grown or declined at the national rate during each period. This provides a measure of the urban–rural contrast in each period because, by definition, the greater the relative decline of London and the conurbations the greater the relative growth of other areas. The picture is one of virtually uninterrupted decline in Britain's largest cities. In the 1950s the relative decline was more gentle than in the 1960s and early 1970s, and in the mid-1970s it eased again to nearer its 1950s rate, but it continued throughout the period up to 1981. These figures indicate that the shift of industrial employment away from cities is clearly a long-established trend, pre-dating the national economic difficulties which have dogged the British economy since the early 1970s.

The loss of manufacturing jobs in Britain's cities has consequences for employment in other sectors of the local economy and for the distribution of population. Some service employers in cities depend on manufacturing firms for their business or on the expenditure of wages earned in local industry. As manufacturing declines in the city, output and employment in local services therefore tend to decline. The loss of jobs in the city encourages the out-migration of population to small towns where there are more employment opportunities. As people leave the city this has a further depressing effect on local service employment, including public services such as health and education in which provision is related to local population levels. Because migration is the principal mechanism through which the labour market adjusts to the changing location of jobs, the increase in unemployment in cities has not been as large as the loss of jobs would warrant. London, for example, has maintained below-average unemployment, despite an above-average loss of jobs, by losing population to other areas: it now has two million fewer people than at its peak in the late 1930s. Thus as industrial employment leaves the city, the city itself moves into decline. Its population growth is halted, then reversed, and counter-urbanisation becomes the dominant trend.

A linear extrapolation suggests that by the early decades of the next century few manufacturing jobs will be left in Britain's largest cities. Following the manufacturing-led model of urban decline, discussed above, it would be tempting to suggest that cities might disappear entirely. A more likely outcome is that cities in future will be smaller and function primarily as service centres for their hinterlands rather than as centres of industrial production. Cities continue to offer locational advantages for some service industries, and in the economy as a whole service employment has proved more bouyant than employment in manufacturing. Eventually the high proportion of city employment in services is therefore likely to outweigh the continuing decline of a small residual manufacturing sector, and when this point is reached the cities' decline in employment and population may come to an end.

This is similar to what occurred in Britain's rural areas. Mechanisation led to a steady reduction in the agricultural workforce from its mid-nineteenth-century peak and to a loss of rural population. However, by about 1960 agriculture had shrunk to such a small proportion of employment in most rural areas that the number of jobs which continued to be lost in agriculture no longer outweighed the local growth in other sectors, notably manufacturing. Rural decline eased, and a new era of growth began. Exactly when cities might reach a similar turning-point is unclear, but it is unlikely to be soon because manufacturing still provides a large share of urban employment. Indeed, by the time a turning-point is reached the employment and population in Britain's cities may have fallen to such an extent that the urban structure of nineteenth-century Britain will have been substantially modified.

The industrial city, in particular, is likely to have lost its pre-eminence.

3. The Roots of Decline

Despite the large volume of theory on regional growth, urban spatial structure and industrial location, there is no generally accepted theory to account for the de-industrialisation of the city. In a survey of the literature on urban growth Richardson (1969) commented that what is available constitutes 'less a theory of urban growth than a prologue to the development of such a theory'.

There are two perspectives that might be adopted to try to explain the shift of industry from cities. One concentrates on the characteristics of cities themselves. It has been argued that certain features of city locations – inadequate premises, high rents or militant workers, for example – make them unsuitable locations for contemporary manufacturing industry. (See Scott (1982) for a review of these arguments.) The focus of such explanations is the city itself. A second perspective concerns the changing nature of the national economy. It has been argued, for example, that the decline of industry in cities is the result of the 'restructuring' and 'rationalisation' of industry in the face of the deepening crisis of the British economy (Community Development Project, 1977; Massey and Meegan, 1978). The logic of such arguments is that the interests of industrial capital and the maintainance of urban employment levels are irreconcilably opposed. The focus of this explanation is the economic system; characteristics of localities have little influence.

This dichotomy is misleading. The geography of employment growth and decline is in our view determined by the interaction of national economic trends and the characteristics of localities. Trends in the national economy confront firms with pressures they cannot easily resist – for example, to introduce new technology to keep costs down, or to close redundant capacity during a recession. Most firms face these pressures, though their nature and extent vary from industry to industry and from firm to firm. The extent to which each area is affected by these pressures depends on its mix of industries, and on the costs, opportunities and constraints it poses for firms. Taking this view of industrial location it is still necessary to identify the specific national trends and characteristics of cities which result in urban industrial decline. It is impossible to give full consideration to all the possibilities in this short chapter, but two theories that do not seem to offer a satisfactory explanation are worth mentioning.

One is the idea, derived from Keynesian economic theory, that the growth of industry in an area is determined by the growth of the market for its industries' products. Thus areas with a high proportion of their jobs in industries whose national or international market is contracting experience job losses, while an increase in employment normally results from a concentration of 'growth' industries. The mix of industries in each area and the national growth of those industries are the crucial influences, it is suggested. The relevance of this theory to the urban–rural contrast in manufacturing employment change in Britain has been exhaustively investigated (Fothergill and Gudgin, 1979; Moore, Rhodes and Tyler, 1980; Keeble, 1980; Danson, Lever and Malcolm, 1980). The unanimous conclusion is that it cannot account for any part of the urban–rural contrast.

The second theory, derived from neo-classical economics, is that cities are high-cost locations and that in a profit-maximising business environment production and employment are therefore diverted to towns and rural areas where costs are lower. The evidence relating to this theory is contradictory. For example, average manufacturing profitability in cities appears to be below average (Fothergill, Gudgin, Kitson and Monk, 1984), but not in all cities, notably London (Wellbelove, Woods and Zafiris, 1981). It is generally agreed that urban land costs are higher than in small towns and rural areas, but production costs in total appear to be no higher in cities (Fothergill, Gudgin, Kitson and Monk, 1984) or the inner city (Lever, 1981) while labour costs are above average in some cities and below average in others (Moore, Rhodes and Tyler, 1980). The conflicting nature of this evidence suggests that if cities are high-cost locations the disadvantage is unlikely to be large – otherwise these studies would have revealed more consistent differences – and that any resulting influence on the location of jobs is therefore likely to be modest.

We do not entirely rule out a role for cost differences in generating urban–rural differences in growth. However, if cost factors were the main or only determinant of locational choice the urban–rural contrast would probably be weaker and more patchy than it actually is. A more plausible explanation is that there are locational constraints which differentiate cities from other areas. Two constraints – the availability of land and labour – are the most likely candidates. Until the early 1970s surveys usually found that the availability of labour was a major factor in determining the location of new branch plants (e.g. Department of Trade and Industry, 1973). In an area of full employment firms were often short of labour in many areas, both urban and rural, but women's involvement in the labour market was relatively low in many coalfield and rural areas away from cities. Such untapped reserves of women workers almost certainly attracted some industrial jobs out of cities. However, during the last decade or so the availability of labour has been less of a problem in all areas, as unemployment has risen, and female 'activity rates' in most parts of the country have converged towards the national average.

It is therefore to land constraints that we turn for the main explanations for the urban–rural contrast in manufacturing employment trends. In essence, our view is that the continuing replacement of workers by machines leads to a loss of jobs in factories in all areas, while constraints on the supply of industrial land in cities mean that a disproportionately large share of new factory floorspace and new jobs are diverted to small towns and rural areas. Cities then lose out from the rising capital intensity of production; small towns and rural areas lose jobs for the same reason, but they receive most of the offsetting job gains. The full evidence supporting this explanation is published elsewhere (Fothergill, Kitson and Monk, 1984), but its main elements should now be explained.

4. National Trends: Local Constraints

Figure 7.1 shows the number of workers per thousand sq. metres of industrial floorspace in England and Wales between 1964 and 1982. Comparable figures cannot be calculated for Scotland and Northern Ireland because of the absence of floorspace statistics. Over this period the average employment density fell by nearly 3 per cent a year from 36.0 to 21.4 workers per thousand sq. metres. The decline accelerated during recessions and eased during upturns in the economy, but the long-term trend was unmistakably downwards. Adjustments to take account of changes in capacity

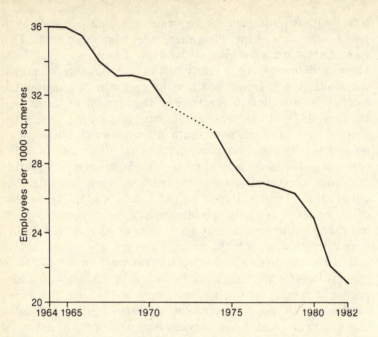

FIGURE 7.1   *Manufacturing Employees per 1000 sq. metres of Industrial Floorspace: England and Wales, 1964–82*

SOURCES   Department of Employment; Department of the Environment.

utilisation make little difference to this downward trend. The decline in employment density can be observed to varying degrees in every manufacturing industry and in all locations. However its significance for the location of jobs had largely been ignored. One implication is that in a factory where floorspace is fixed the reduction in density leads to a loss of jobs, irrespective of the commercial performance of the firm. Similarly, in a city in which the total stock of factory floorspace is fixed, manufacturing employment will tend to fall. Thus a town or city wishing to maintain a stable level of manufacturing employment must continually add to its stock of occupied floorspace merely to offset the loss of jobs arising from the fall in employment density on existing floorspace.

It is not the explicit intention of firms to reduce employment density. In a competitive economy what is important to firms is the efficient use of resources: how much output they can get from each worker and from each unit of floorspace. Employment density is a residual which emerges from attempts to maximise the productivity of labour and achieve the optimum use of space. To examine the underlying causes the decline in density can be disaggregated into these two components. By definition:

$$EF = \frac{Y/F}{Y/E},$$

where E = manufacturing employment
F = manufacturing floorspace
Y = manufacturing output.

Figure 7.2 shows how these components have changed since the mid-1960s. Output per unit of floorspace (Y/F) remained relatively

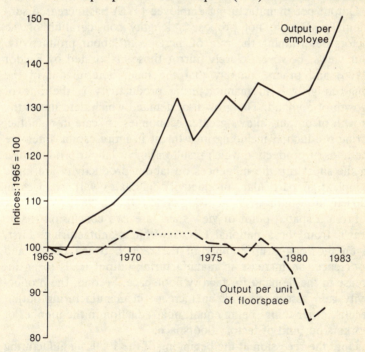

FIGURE 7.2 *Changes in Manufacturing Output per Employee and per Unit of Floorspace, England and Wales, 1965–83*

SOURCES Department of Employment; Department of the Environment; National Income and Expenditure Blue Book.

stable until about 1979, with small cyclical fluctuations resulting from changes in capacity utilisation. After 1979 there was a sharp decline, reflecting a reduction in manufacturing output which was not matched by a simultaneous reduction in the stock of manufacturing floorspace. The amount of floorspace actually in use probably did decline after 1979, but the stock of floorspace adjusts only slowly to lower levels of manufacturing output, as redundant factory buildings are demolished or changed to other uses. Assuming that the trend after 1979 is largely the result of an exceptionally severe recession, there is little evidence that the ratio between output and floorspace shows a long-term trend in either direction despite the introduction of new production methods. Technical change may thus change the physical requirements of individual industries, but in aggregate its effect on the productivity of factory floorspace appears to be broadly neutral.

Output per manufacturing employee (Y/E) has increased substantially. We do not propose a lengthy consideration of the factors determining the rate of increase in labour productivity. Our views, however, closely mirror those elaborated by Kaldor (1966) and others, namely that the main determinant of the long-run growth in manufacturing productivity is the rate of growth of demand. The growth of demand which determines the growth of output, allows greater economies of scale in manufacturing production including investment in more capital intensive methods of production which result in higher labour productivity. In the short run the influences on labour productivity are more complex: in particular, productivity fluctuates with changes in capacity utilisation over the trade cycle (Okun, 1962).

From a spatial point of view there are two conclusions to be drawn from these national trends within manufacturing. First, given the long-term stability of the ratio between output and floorspace, an increase in manufacturing output leads to an increase in the demand for factory floorspace. Second, the productivity gain associated with an increase in manufacturing output results, other things being equal, in a reduction in the number of workers per unit of factory floorspace.

Until the recession at the beginning of the 1980s manufacturing output increased, though slowly and unevenly. The resulting increase in the stock of factory floorspace is shown in Figure 7.3, again for England and Wales. There was an increase every year

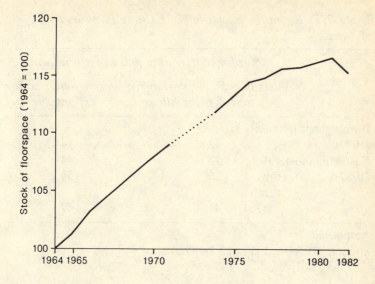

FIGURE 7.3 *The Stock of Industrial Floorspace in England and Wales, 1964–82*

SOURCE Department of the Environment.

from 1964 to 1981, though the rate of increase began to decline in the second half of the 1970s and the recession reduced the stock after 1981. Comparatively little of the stock is vacant, it should be noted. Statistics compiled by King & Co., a leading industrial estate agent, show that in April 1982 only just over 4 per cent was vacant and on the market, and prior to the recession the figure was between 1 and 2 per cent. The increase in demand for industrial land has been even greater than for floorspace. Modern industry prefers single-storey premises on spacious sites with room for car-parking, circulation of heavy lorries and, where appropriate, for outdoor storage and future expansion. This reduces the 'plot ratio' – the ratio between floorspace and land – in new developments to levels well below that in older industrial areas.

These national economic trends are important because areas vary in the extent to which they are able to accommodate physical increases in the stock of factory floorspace. In particular, cities are usually less able to accommodate increases than small towns and rural areas, so they receive few of the job gains but share in the job losses associated with the reduction in employment density.

Table 7.3   *Room for Expansion of Existing Factories by Type of Area*

| | *% of manufacturing jobs in factories with:* | |
	less than 50 per cent of site covered by buildings	*vacant land next to existing site*
Birmingham inner city (1979)	12*	14*
East Midlands: cities (1982)	28	44
towns	26	50
rural areas	41	57

* estimated

Source   JURUE, Industrial Premises Survey.

There are three ways in which the stock of industrial floorspace is increased: by extensions to existing factories, by building new factories and by changes of use (from warehousing for example). The last of these, changes of use, does not differentiate cities, towns and rural areas. Increases in floorspace arising from extensions and new buildings, however, occur at a slower rate in cities than elsewhere. Our research suggests this has a great deal to do with the availability of land for industry.

In cities, factories are more likely to be on highly developed sites, hemmed in by existing urban development, so that they are unable to extend their premises either on their existing sites or on immediately adjacent land. Table 7.3 illustrates this point using figures for factories with twenty-five or more employees. The figures are the result of two studies: a survey we conducted of industrial premises in the East Midlands and a survey by JURUE (1980) of the industrial building stock in inner Birmingham. It is difficult to know the precise extent to which factory sites in Birmingham and the East Midlands are typical of areas elsewhere, though the percentage change in manufacturing employment in urban and rural areas in the Midlands has been broadly similar to that in similar types of area in Britain as a whole. Table 7.3 shows that the proportion of employment in factories with room for expansion on site, and the proportion with vacant land next to

TABLE 7.4   *Available Industrial Land by Type of Area, 1982*

	Hectares	Hectares per thousand manufacturing employees
London	746	1.0
Conurbations	4 661	2.8
Free-standing cities	4 213	4.3
Large towns	4 418	6.3
Small towns	9 732	6.9
Rural areas	6 439	10.9
GREAT BRITAIN	30 208	4.9

The following counties are excluded: Derbyshire, Nottinghamshire, Hereford and Worcester, Essex, Oxfordshire, Berkshire, Surrey, Buckinghamshire (except Milton Keynes), Gloucestershire, Devon.

SOURCE   Local authorities.

their site, are both more than three times greater in the rural parts of the east Midlands than in inner Birmingham.

Table 7.4 presents figures on land for new factories. This is the land which local authorities consider to be 'available' for new industry, in both the short and long term, and it excludes land reserved for specific firms and land within the curtilage of existing factory sites. As with room for on-site expansion, there is a marked urban–rural contrast. In absolute terms and especially in relation to the size of the manufacturing sector in each type of area, there is less land for building new factories in cities. This is probably because most city land is already in use, because other uses compete with industry for the city land that becomes available, and because of restrictions (such as green belts) on peripheral urban development. The limited availability of industrial land in cities sets a ceiling on the amount of new factory building in these places and means that they are unable to offer firms the number and range of potential sites that are available elsewhere. Additional problems in cities include the higher price of land, the expense of reclaiming sites which have fallen derelict, and the scarcity of very large sites suitable for development as trading estates by the private sector.

On the whole, manufacturing industry is neither able nor willing to overcome the constraints on the supply of industrial land in cities. Firms without room for on-site expansion mostly cannot buy up the adjacent land they need, even at a high price. In many cases the land market simply does not operate. Surrounding land uses may be roads, railways, canals or rivers, public parks, schools, hospitals or churches, and these cannot be bought when needed. The highly dispersed ownership of private housing also makes it difficult for firms to assemble large plots in cities, and of course planning controls impose further restrictions. Office developments avoid these constraints by building upwards – an unattractive or impractical option for most manufacturing firms – and in any case manufacturing's land requirements are much greater. Office growth therefore remains in the city, but manufacturing growth is squeezed out.

Urban industrial decline is thus rooted in national trends within manufacturing, and in the nature of cities as densely developed environments where alternative uses compete for a limited supply of land. The increase in manufacturing output leads to an increase in the aggregate demand for factory floorspace; it also induces increases in productivity leading to a loss of jobs on existing floorspace. Given the physical constraints in cities, most of the new floorspace and the jobs that go with it are diverted to small towns and rural areas.

Urban industrial decline cannot therefore be blamed on deliberate decisions by companies to avoid or desert cities. Some firms no doubt do have preferences for rural locations, though others benefit from being in a city and continue to prefer urban locations. Instead, we are suggesting that the urban–rural contrast in manufacturing employment change has its origin in national economic trends affecting a wide range of companies and places. Locational preferences may be relevant to an understanding of change within an individual firm, but in aggregate such preferences probably make little difference to the overall shift in the location of manufacturing jobs.

5. The Impact of Thatcherism

The economic strategy of the Conservative government in 1979 differed from those of the previous Labour and Conservative governments during the post-war era. The commitment to full

TABLE 7.5 *Manufacturing Employment Change, 1960–78 and 1978–81, by Type of Area*

	1960–78 (as % 1960)	1978–81 (as % 1978)
London	–42.5	–15.5
Conurbations	–26.5	–22.7
Free-standing cities	–13.8	–17.2
Large towns	–2.2	–16.0
Small towns	+15.7	–15.2
Rural areas	+38.0	–10.0
GREAT BRITAIN	–11.5	–16.8

SOURCE   Department of Employment.

employment through public intervention was finally abandoned, and the new government sought a shift in the balance of industrial power away from organised labour. As a consequence, several trends in the national economy altered after 1979, the most significant change being the severe contraction of manufacturing production and employment during the following three years. Since national economic trends are so important in generating urban decline, the impact of 'Thatcherism' on the city needs to be considered.

The contrast in manufacturing employment trends before and after 1978 are shown in Table 7.5. Before 1978 there was a large urban–rural contrast, and small towns and rural areas experienced absolute growth despite the national decline. After 1978 all areas suffered large job losses, but the pattern of change was more complex. Conurbations and other cities continued to fare worse than towns and rural areas, but London's manufacturing employment fell by a little less than the national average – a reversal of a trend dating back at least to the 1950s. London also lost a smaller proportion of its manufacturing jobs than the conurbations, again the opposite of the trend prior to the recession.

Physical constraints in cities influence where expansion is located in times of economic growth. Falling manufacturing output, such as occurred between 1979 and 1981, reduces the need for increases in factory floorspace because many firms need to cut their productive capacity. In a severe recession, towns and rural areas all therefore suffer from the contraction in employment; physical constraints are less important in allocating jobs between location. Some investment in new factories and factory extensions continues, even in recession, and this continues to favour small towns and rural areas. However, the magnitude of job loss in different localities mostly reflects other factors, though these are only partly understood.

One reason why London has suffered less than the national average and less than the conurbations is that a relatively small share of its manufacturing jobs is in steel, motor-vehicles and textiles, three industries that were hit exceptionally hard by the recession. Using a simple technique known as 'shift-share analysis' we have estimated that London's mix of industries meant that its manufacturing employment could have been expected to fall by 3 per cent less than the national average between 1978 and 1981. In fact, London's manufacturing employment did not hold up as well as this, indicating that the weak employment performance of London firms which marked the period up to 1978 also continued during the recession. The conurbations, on the other hand, were burdened by a mix of industries that led to above-average job losses during the recession. This accounts for a large part of the divergence between trends in London and the conurbations after 1978. The concentration in London of headquarters plants with an above-average proportion of jobs in research and development, marketing and administration is another factor which probably helped London avoid the worst of the recession. Branch plants undertaking routine production, many of them in the assisted areas, appear to have been the most prone to closure and redundancies.

The post-1979 recession had further implications for urban industry. Previously the growth of labour productivity was associated with the growth of output. In the initial stage of the recession, falling output led to falling productivity, but thereafter there was a substantial increase in productivity even though output remained depressed. This increase reflected the closure of less efficient factories and changes in labour practices facilitated by the weakening of trade-union power in a period of rising unemployment. Increasing labour productivity reduces employment densities, as we noted, reducing still further the potential employment capacity of urban factories.

The boost to productivity during the recession and the resulting fall in employment density may be once-and-for-all occurrences. The low level of manufacturing investment, compared to the 1970s, suggests that the introduction of new machinery and techniques will not be sufficient to create a sustained acceleration in the growth of labour productivity. Much therefore depends on the Conservative government's success in continuing to force changes in labour practices – in obtaining the same output with fewer workers and the same machines. The extent to which this may occur is uncertain. A sustained increase in labour productivity would, however, reduce employment densities still further, leading to fewer jobs in physically constrained urban factories.

If there is a major recovery in industrial production – engendered by new working practices or by traditional reflation – the consequences for manufacturing jobs in urban and rural areas are likely to differ, at least initially, from those during previous upturns. The severity of the post-1979 recession pushed output far below capacity. Many firms have spare capacity within their factories and for the first time in three decades the level of manufacturing production and employment in cities has probably been pushed well below the ceiling imposed by the stock of industrial land and premises. In the initial stage of a recovery, the expansion in output and employment would therefore be accommodated mostly within existing factories in all areas. There would be little tendency for urban and rural employment trends to diverge. As spare capacity was used up, more growth would be diverted into premises which are currently vacant, many as a result of closure during the recession. Since by historical standards the stock of vacant industrial premises is high in all areas, all areas might again benefit during this stage of a recovery.

But the long-term problem in cities would remain. Once the spare capacity in existing and vacant factories had been utilised, physical constraints in cities would reassert themselves. Small towns and rural areas would gain a disproportionately large share of new factory floorspace and new jobs, and the urban–rural contrast in manufacturing employment trends would widen. Moreover, some of the manufacturing jobs which have been lost in cities since 1979 would have disappeared from cities for ever: the reduction in employment density means that, even at full capacity, most factories will not employ as many workers as they did before the recession.

6. **Urban Policy**

The decline of the industrial city is widely acknowledged to be a political problem. Labour's 1977 White Paper on the inner cities placed the blame for deprivation and dereliction on the erosion of the cities' economic base; the subsequent Conservative government has not dissented from this view. Effective action to stem the drift of industry from cities is harder to find. Along with other areas, the Tyneside, Clydeside and Merseyside conurbations are designated as 'Special Development Areas' by the government's regional industrial policy. This entitles manufacturing firms to grants towards the cost of new capital investment, and the government builds advance factories in these places. These conurbations' assisted status pre-dates the concern over inner-city industrial problems: regional aid was first available in these areas during the 1930s. Also, in the cases of Tyneside and Clydeside, the area eligible for assistance includes not only the conurbation but also its hinterland, including in Tyneside's case almost the whole of north-east England. Regional policy thus impinges on urban areas, but it is not a specifically urban initiative.

In contrast, the government's Urban Programme is directed at inner cities, but not just at industry. Central government makes funds available to a hierarchy of urban local authorities, the most important of which are 'Partnership Authorities', to finance schemes designed to revive inner areas. The finance, which has never been generous, is spread across projects as diverse as aid to community groups and the preparation of industrial sites. Its potentially beneficial effect is, however, more than offset by the withdrawal of grants from the same authorities as part of the squeeze on local-government expenditure.

The establishment of inner-city 'Enterprise Zones' – areas where firms are exempt from paying rates and where planning controls are relaxed – has been the most notable Conservative initiative to promote urban industry. These have been criticised for a number of reasons: for example the zones are exceptionally small, and within cities they are liable to fill up with firms relocating from just outside the zones, with little net benefit to the city as a whole. Other Conservative initiatives include the setting up of urban development corporations in London's docklands and Liverpool along the lines of those operating in the New Towns, the provision of an 'Urban Development Grant' to encourage private sector property development, and a modest relaxation of planning controls on industry. There have also been numerous exhortations to the private sector to put its money into declining inner cities. In addition, an increasing number of local authorities are becoming involved in promoting urban industry. This is done mainly by providing land and small premises, and in a few authorities by direct financial assistance to firms, though the scale of local-authority intervention is severely limited by the funds available.

In all, these policies do not add up to very much in the light of the formidable national trends leading to the de-industrialisation of the city. In our view national economic recovery is an essential step towards stemming the loss of industrial jobs in urban areas, especially since the recession of the early 1980s has pushed manufacturing output so far below its potential in all areas. Cities would benefit directly from a recovery. Local firms could expand production and employment within their existing buildings, and further growth would be possible in factories which had space for expansion on site. Investment in new factories would increase, and cities could expect to gain some of these. Also the expansion of job opportunities in small towns and rural areas would enable those who wanted to move out of cities to do so, further reducing inner city unemployment. However, we do not think that the economic policies pursued by the Conservative government since 1979 are likely to create a sustained recovery of this sort; what is needed in particular is an increase in the level of demand through reflationary fiscal policy, and international co-ordination to prevent foreign-exchange crises which might scupper a recovery.

But even if such a recovery were to occur, the relative decline of the industrial city would not be at an end. As this chapter has explained, there are constraints on industrial growth in cities, and the gap between employment trends in cities and other areas could actually be expected to widen during sustained recovery as new factory floorspace was diverted to small towns and rural areas. In the long run, increases in labour productivity and the expansion of output are not compatible with the maintenance and expansion of industrial employment in cities.

To do anything about this aspect of urban de-industrialisation – the decline relative to other areas – requires spatial policies. The problem highlighted in this chapter is the physical constraint on industrial expansion in cities. Even in relatively depressed economic conditions, many individual firms and some industries have the potential for growth. However, many factories in cities do not have room for expansion on-site, and at the same time many firms in cities operate in old premises, often multi-storey and designed for products and processes that have long since been abandoned, which impose handicaps on operating efficiency. These obstacles can frustrate expansion. They also mean that in order to increase production and employment many city firms have to move to other areas.

The most useful step would be for urban authorities to get together with the major industrial employers in their areas to plan for their future land requirements, in particular land for expansion next to existing factories. In some instances employers may face no shortage of land. In others there may be straightforward steps – the redesignation of vacant land, for example, – which would permit local expansion that would otherwise be thwarted. To supplement such initiatives urban authorities should ensure that within their areas there is a sufficient quantity and range of sites available for local relocations and for incoming factories. Some authorities already do this as a normal part of their activities; a surprising number do not.

This approach to urban industrial decline will not, of course, bring an end to the urban–rural contrast in manufacturing employment change; to some extent the physical constraints on industry in cities cannot be removed even by energetic planning. But these policies could make a valuable contribution at the local level.

Bibliography

CDP (1977) *The Costs of Industrial Change*, An Inter-project Report (London: Community Development Project).

Danson, M. W., Lever, W. F. and Malcolm, J. (1980) 'The Inner City Employment Problem in Great Britain, 1952–76: A shift Share Approach', *Urban Studies*, **17**, pp. 193–210.

Department of Trade and Industry (1973) Memorandum on the Inquiry into Location Attitudes and Experience, *Minutes of Evidence*, Trade and Industry Subcommittee of the House of Commons Expenditure Committee, Session 1972–3, pp. 525–668 (London: HMSO).

Fothergill, S. and Gudgin, G. (1979) 'Regional Employment Change: A

Subregional Explanation', *Progress in Planning*, vol. 12, pp. 155–219.

Fothergill, S., Gudgin, G., Kitson, M. and Monk, S. (1984) 'Differences in the Profitability of the U.K. Manufacturing Sector Between Conurbations and Other Areas', *Scottish Journal of Political Economy*, **31**, pp. 72–91.

Fothergill, S., Kitson, M. and Monk, S. (1983) 'The Impact of the New and Expanded Town Programmes on Industrial Location in Britain 1960–78', *Regional Studies*, **17**, pp. 251–60.

Fothergill, S., Kitson, M. and Monk, S. (1984) *Urban Industrial Decline: The Causes of the Urban–Rural Contrast in Manufacturing Employment Change* (London: HMSO).

JURUE (1980) *Industrial Renewal in the Inner City: An Assessment of Potential and Problems*, DOE Inner Cities Research Programme Report no. 2.

Kaldor, N. (1966) *Causes of the Slow Rate of Economic Growth of the United Kingdom* (Cambridge: Cambridge University Press).

Keeble, D. (1980) 'Industrial Decline, Regional Policy and the Urban–Rural Manufacturing Shift in the United Kingdom', *Environment and Planning A*, **12**, pp. 945–62.

Lever, W. F. (1981) *Operating Costs as an Explanation of Employment Change in the Clydeside Region*, Paper presented at the 'Industry and the Inner City' Conference, University of Newcastle upon Tyne (May 1981).

Massey, D. and Meegan, R. (1978) 'Industrial Restructuring versus the Cities', *Urban Studies*, **15**, pp. 273–88.

Moore, B. C., Rhodes, J. and Tyler, P. (1980) *New Developments in the Evaluation of Regional Policy*, Paper presented at an SSRC Urban and Regional Economics Conference, University of Birmingham (May 1980).

Okun, A. M. (1962) 'Potential GNP: Its measurement and Significance', reprinted in Okun, A., *The Political Economy of Prosperity* (Washington, D.C.: Brookings Institution, 1970) pp. 132–45.

Richardson, H. W. (1969) *Regional Economics: Location Theory, Urban Structure and Regional Change* (London: Weidenfeld & Nicolson).

Scott, A. (1982) 'Locational Patterns and Dynamics of Industrial Activity in the Urban Metropolis', *Urban Studies*, **19**, pp. 111–42.

Wellbelove, D., Woods, A. and Zafiris, N. (1981) 'Survival and Success of the Inner City Economy: The Case of Islington', *Urban Studies*, **18**, pp. 301–13.

8
Thatcherism and Britain's Industrial Landscape

RON MARTIN

1. Introduction

The modern British economy is the product of a long history of developmental and structural changes, but this evolution has been far from smooth and incremental. The greatest changes have occurred during and in the wake of major 'crises' that have periodically disrupted the old economic order and fostered the rise of a new. These crises are decisive in the sense that they mark the transition from one socioeconomic structure of accumulation to another and, as an integral part of this process, from one spatial surface of economic differentiation to another, as new geographies of employment, production and profit become imbricated upon the pre-existing forms. There have been two such historical turning-points this century. The inter-war decades of the 1920s and 1930s, punctuated by the slump of 1929–32 which produced record levels of mass unemployment, not only changed the structure of British industry, involving the contraction of the nineteenth-century heavy engineering, metals and textiles sectors and the growth of new light engineering and consumer goods industries, but in so doing promoted a major realignment of the space economy, the all-too-familiar decline of peripheral industrial Britain and the rise of a prosperous south-east and midlands. Equally significant, however, these economic and social upheavals of the period laid the foundation for a war-time and post-war co-operation between trade-unions, employers and the state that helped to underpin the full-employment growth achieved with the aid of Keynesian methods of macroeconomic stabilisation during the 'golden decades' of the 1950s and 1960s.

The second crucial turning-point began in the early 1970s. Manufacturing employment had reached its historical peak in 1966, and was already on its downward secular path. After 1973 the reversal of Britain's post-war expansionary long wave became increasingly evident as the growth of output and productivity suffered a sharp slow-down, job loss from manufacturing continued apace, and a steadily worsening problem of 'stagflation' – the combination of rising inflation and worsening unemployment – progressively undermined government attempts to restore full-employment growth through Keynesian policies of deficit spending. By 1976 the case for Keynesian state activism had become difficult to sustain and, under pressure from the IMF, the Labour government of the day was forced to concede:

> We used to think that you could spend your way out of a recession, and increase employment by cutting taxes and boosting Government spending. I tell you in all candour that that option no longer exists, and that insofar as it ever did exist, it only worked by injecting a bigger dose of inflation into the economy, followed by a higher level of unemployment at the next step. Higher inflation followed by higher unemployment. . . . That is the history of the last twenty years. (James Callaghan, 1976.)

This disavowal of traditional demand management, and the subsequent adoption of tougher controls on public expenditure, has since been widely interpreted as signalling the first shift towards a more monetarist-inspired policy stance, the beginnings of a quiet counter-revolution that was to erupt into full ascendancy under the Conservative government at the end of the decade.

Indeed, the landslide election of the Conservative government in May 1979, under the leadership of Mrs Thatcher, might have been little more than a psephological curiosity had it not marked the final abandonment of the Keynesian consensus and its overthrow by an all-embracing 'ideological monetarism', a new orthodoxy of 'Thatcherism' committed not only to the control of the money supply, but also to the principles of the free-market order, to a belief in the self-regenerative powers of the 'enterprise' economy, and to the 'rolling back' of the frontiers of state spending and intervention. The state was no longer to pursue the 'illusory and false goal' of minimising the level of unemployment: 'full employment is not in the gift of Government. It should not be promised and it cannot be provided.' (Joseph, 1978, p. 32.) Instead the Conservative government was to pursue new policies of monetary and fiscal restriction, together with measures aimed at 'liberalising' and 'reprivatising' the economy so as to allow the release of competitive market forces. These policies, it was argued, were necessary to break the inflationary spiral and help remove the barriers to profitable private production. They would also help to promote the long-overdue restructuring of British industry that was required in order to halt the country's industrial decline.

This 'sea-change' in political philosophy and economic policy coincided with the onset of the most severe recession for fifty years. In the rapid downswing between mid-1979 and mid-1981 manufacturing employment in Britain declined by 14 per cent (from 7.1 million to 6.1 million), manufacturing output by 20 per cent and fixed investment in manufacturing by 23 per cent. Total employment fell by 1.25 million over the period, and unemployment more than doubled to reach 2.3 million or just under 10 per cent of the working population. The geography of the slump was far more widespread than had been the case in 1929–32, impinging not only on the traditionally depressed industrial regions like Wales and the North, but also on the previously relatively prosperous manufacturing heartland of the country, covering the North-West, the West Midlands and Yorkshire–Humberside (Figure 8.1; Martin, 1986). Since mid-1981 industrial output and productivity have recovered and inflation has fallen to single figures. Total employment, however, continued to decline until early 1983, and although it has risen since then it still remains well below its pre-recession levels. Manufacturing employment continued to fall well into 1984 before it 'bottomed-out': some small increases have subsequently been recorded, but as yet there is no evidence of any substantial recovery of employment in this sector. Thus in a space of just five years, from mid-1979 to mid-1984, Britain's manufacturing employment base contracted by 1.7 million or 24 per cent, a reduction equivalent to more than half of the total decline that has occurred since 1966.

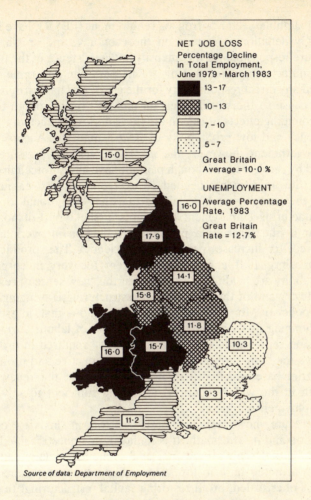

NET JOB LOSS
Percentage Decline
in Total Employment,
June 1979 - March 1983

13 - 17
10 - 13
7 - 10
5 - 7
Great Britain
Average = 10·0 %

UNEMPLOYMENT
16·0 Average Percentage
Rate, 1983

Great Britain
Rate = 12·7%

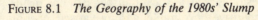

Source of data: Department of Employment

FIGURE 8.1 *The Geography of the 1980s' Slump*

SOURCE   Department of Employment, *Employment Gazette*

Even in the face of this collapse, and the continuing rise in unemployment to well over 3 million, the Thatcher government has refused to adjust its monetarist policies to permit any reflationary expansion of the economy. Yet there is copious evidence to indicate that the government's own policies, by raising taxes and interest rates, over-valuing the exchange rate, and reducing the nominal public sector borrowing requirement (PBSR), have had a strongly deflationary impact on the economy, and are in large measure responsible for the intensity and persistence of the trough in manufacturing activity. But, for its part, the government has denied any direct responsibility for the crisis, and has attributed its basic cause to the world recession and its extreme depth to the compounding effects of the underlying inferior productivity, poor efficiency and low profitability of British industry. According to the government, however, the market forces and pressures released by the recession, though painful, have at last forced firms to make the adjustments needed to overcome these weaknesses. Thus the government has claimed that the 'exceptional' drop in manufacturing employment represents a 'shake-out' of hoarded labour in the sense of a permanent reduction in overmanning required to increase productive efficiency. The productivity 'boom' since 1981 and the more recent recovery in corporate profitability are held to be indicative of this 'new sense of realism' in industry and of the benefits that restructuring is bringing. The clear policy of Mrs Thatcher's government shows that, in its view, the slimming down of capital and shake-out of labour during the recession represented the 'short-term costs' required in order to achieve the 'long-term gains' of a more productive and profitable industrial base which will in its turn stimulate the renewal of growth in the wider economy on a scale sufficient to solve the unemployment problem.

There are, however, some serious errors in this view of the recession and its aftermath. It is founded on a questionable interpretation of Britain's industrial and economic malaise, and on an unwarranted faith in the supposed spontaneous regenerative powers of crisis-led, profit-restoring capital restructuring. In addition, it presumes that a 'recapitalised' Britain, in the sense of a more competitive, profitable and privatised economy, will be capable of reabsorbing the resources 'freed' by the restructuring and rationalisation process. The fact of the matter is that the slump has been so deep and as much structural as cyclical in nature that large sections of the capital and labour displaced are unlikely to be easily re-employed. The problems of adjustment and reabsorption seem all the more difficult because, unlike the 1920s and 1930s, the contraction of manufacturing has been generalised across almost all industrial sectors and, by being embedded in an underlying process of de-industrialisation, largely permanent in its effect. Moreover, like the massive job losses that took place between 1979 and 1984, the prospects for economic recovery and the reabsorption of labour are far from equal across the different regions of the nation, and appear most favourable in those areas *least* afflicted by the decline. The geography of restructuring and 'recovery' is likely to be the more uneven the more market forces are relied upon to 'regenerate' the economy. The basic theme of the remainder of this chapter is that of all forms of state policy, the free-market conservatism of the Thatcher government is the most likely to exacerbate these widening disparities in Britain's industrial landscape. We begin by examining the government's explanation of Britain's ailing industrial performance.

2. De-industrialisation: The New Conservative View

It would be incorrect to suggest that the Thatcher government has articulated a fully coherent and rigorous explanation of the decline of British manufacturing. Rather, the government's views derive from an ensemble of ideas drawn from the tenets of monetarism, the doctrine of economic libertarianism, and the economics of the New Right, an ensemble considered by the government's own leading ideologues as sufficiently distinctive to constitute the 'New Conservatism' (Thatcher, Howe and Joseph, 1978; Lawson, 1980, 1982). Following Milton Friedman, the pre-eminent monetarist, and Friedrich von Hayek, the leading exponent of the 'Austrian school' of economic libertarianism, the 'New Conservatives' insist that a free-enterprise exchange economy provides the only kind of social organisation which guarantees and preserves individual liberty. Only the free market, it is alleged, can throw up the appropriate, relevant 'signals' – prices, personal preferences, costs – to guide the socio-economy towards the most effective and efficient allocation of resources. The corollary of this appeal to the 'moral and material benefits of the market order' (Joseph, 1976a), to the virtues of 'enlightened self interest' and subjective individualism, is that state production, intervention and subvention in the economy discourages efficiency, distorts the allocation of resources, and stifles productive private enterprise. Thus the government should reduce the spending, welfare and regulatory functions of the state to the minimum required to manage the money supply, promote free competition and ensure the security of property and contract through the rule of law (Thatcher, 1978). The central maxim is that of 'free economy and strong State' (see Gamble, 1979).

A further strand of the New Conservatism comes from the assemblage of ideas associated with the economics of the New Right, with its anti-state, anti-egalitarian, and anti-union emphasis, and its concern with supply-side and structural inflexibilities (especially in the labour market). An important base camp for this branch of economic thinking that has consistently supported the Thatcher government, and attained its own apotheosis thereby, is the Institute of Economic Affairs. This body has become a key proselytiser of neo-market policies and ideology (Keegan, 1984), a platform from which economic evangelicals of neo-Conservative persuasion have urged campaigns against the 'Keynesian consensus' on a variety of fronts – public spending, the role of unions, industrial subsidies and regional policy, to name but a few. Not surprisingly, the pro-capital, anti-union orientation of the New Conservatism and its inspirational sources has struck a welcome chord among the chief representative organs of industrial capital itself, including the financial City, the Institute of Directors and, on most issues, the Confederation of British Industry.

Drawing on this political and philosophical foundation, New Conservatives and Thatcherites argue that the malaise of the British economy in general, and the industrial sector specifically, can be attributed to the interrelated impact of three basic problems: (i) high and persistent inflation; (ii) the expansion of the public sector; and (iii) the excessive power and demands of organised waged labour.[1] These factors are regarded to have been cumulative and self-reinforcing, producing over the past two decades an economic environment in which private sector activity has been depressed, profitability has been squeezed, investment and productivity growth have been undermined, and competitiveness and export performance reduced.

Of these three problems, the post-war growth of the state sector is claimed to be the main reason for economic decline. The increasing scale of the welfare system, of public services, and of deficit financing in an attempt to minimise the level of unemployment, are all considered responsible for having put upward pressure on government expenditure. This rise in public spending has been financed by increased taxation of the private sector, by borrowing, and by increasing the money supply. The latter in particular is inflationary, and as a result also erodes private profitability and investment. Thus, it is argued, the burden of rising government expenditure has been borne by the private enterprise sector of the economy. To compound matters, the expansion of the public sector is seen as an *inherent* obstacle to capitalist growth because it competes directly with the private sector for workers and capital funds. This view is graphically portrayed by Sir Keith Joseph, who claims that 'the state sector or wealth-eating sector . . . spread like bindweed at the expense of the non-state [private] sector, the wealth-creating sector, strangling and threatening to destroy what it grew upon.' (Joseph, 1976b p. 22.)

There is no doubt that this belief that the public sector has 'crowded out' the private has been much influenced by the work of Bacon and Eltis (1978), who argued that British industrial decline could be blamed on successive post-war governments for allowing the growth of a large 'non-market', 'non-productive' state sector which has squeezed 'market', productive activities of resources. In consequence, they maintain, a shrinking productive base has had to supply the output for an expanding army of dependent, non-productive consumers in the public sector and among the (resultant) unemployed. References to the extra goods that have to be produced by manufacturing, or else imported, 'for the consumption of the vastly larger number of teachers, social workers and civil servants', and to the fact that, for example, 'Oxfordshire County Council now employs more workers in Oxfordshire than British Leyland' (Bacon and Eltis, 1978, pp. 24–5) have been 'music to the ears of Conservative supporters anxious to find a cloak of intellectual respectability for their new found fundamentalism' (Grant, 1982, pp. 10–11).

Moreover, this 'crowding out' thesis has been used by some New Conservatives and the New Right as the basis of a wider contention that *social democracy itself* has become incompatible with capitalist growth. The argument is as follows. Partly because of the war-time legacy and partly to maintain legitimacy, post-war governments have had to respond to escalating demands from working people for social welfare provision, better education, trade-union rights and so on. The expansion of state activity in these spheres created still further opportunities for the generation of such demands, which the state, because of the competitive vote-seeking process, has been compelled to meet. The result is an irresistible rise in public spending on social welfare and social infrastructure. In contrast, there is no such pressure to raise taxes. The combined result of an expanding social Welfare State and a responsive democracy, therefore, is that public expenditure out-strips governmental revenues, leading to budget deficits, inflation and excessive use of taxation and borrowing in an attempt to close this structural gap. The basic problem is that democracy, viewed as a system of political competition, itself imparts a systematic up-ward bias to expectations, and leads society to demand too much from government at too little cost (Brittan, 1977; Littlechild, 1978; Rowley, 1979). Through the inevitable financial and physical 'crowding out' that follows, higher public spending and output leads to an offsetting fall in private output and investment. In this way Britain's industrial stagnation is blamed on the 'social drag' inherent in the post-war growth of the Keynesian social democratic state (see Mouffe, 1981).[2]

Furthermore, the argument continues, the expansion of social welfare and the pursuance of economic policies to promote full employment have enabled unions, in both the private and public sectors, to grow in strength and militancy. And in an attempt to minimise the potentially disruptive impact of the growth in union power, successive governments have been forced to make various concessions to organised labour in order to gain its support and co-operation. This, however, has merely consolidated the bar-gaining position of the unions and reinforced their ability to contest managerial authority at the workplace. On the one hand, the unions are accused of having abused their monopoly power to push up real wages much faster than productivity growth, thereby 'pricing their members out of work' (Joseph, 1979a). Thus Minford (1982), for example, asserts that since the 1960s British unions have 'destroyed' more than 1 million jobs in this way. On the other hand, the unions are charged with having delib-erately resisted and thwarted the introduction of new, efficiency-improving technologies and work practices of a kind and on a scale that would have increased productivity sufficiently to redress the squeeze on profits caused by escalating real wages. On both counts, then, because of their excessive wage demands and productivity-retarding attitudes, the unions are judged by the New Conservatives to have had serious dysfunctional effects on profitability.

It cannot be denied that these arguments contain some elements of truth and raise some important issues; for example, concerning the division of economic activity between the private and public sectors, about the distinction between 'productive' and 'non-productive' activities, the financing of the public sector, the role of the capitalist state and about the balance of power between capital and labour. But the claim that Britain's industrial stagnation can be traced primarily to an over-large and profligate state sector and to over-powerful and anti-enterprise trades unions is too totalising, too one-sided and is not consistent with all the facts. It is an explanation which puts almost exclusive emphasis on the negative effects of public spending, social democracy and unionised labour on the capitalist economy, and under-values their beneficial role. This is not to suggest that these counteracting positive influences are necessarily always stronger than the negative effects, but that both should be considered together.

It is in its treatment of the public sector as being parasitic on the private that the radical Right is most vulnerable. Public spending and social welfare have important positive effects on productivity and economic growth: expenditure on health and education helps to create a healthy and well-trained workforce; spending on infrastructure and utilities helps to facilitate and stimulate private sector production. To regard public sector activity as 'unproductive' is a misleading simplification, for as Gough has argued, the bulk of state expenditure is in fact in the 'indirectly productive' area:

> The single most important conclusion that emerges is that an increasing proportion of the total are productive expenditures, producing inputs for the capitalist sector. The share of social services, infrastructure and accumulation expenditures is growing, while that of unproductive . . . expenditure is declining. It is wrong, therefore, to regard the growth of the state as an unproductive 'burden' upon the capitalist sector; more and more it is a necessary precondition for private capital accumulation. (Gough, 1975, p. 80.)

Thus, given that a large portion of state activity is functional for profitable private production, the expansion of the public sector does not necessarily deprive or squeeze the private sector of labour or capital resources in the simple 'zero-sum' fashion assumed by the radical Right.

In fact, the Bacon and Eltis argument that public employment growth has been directly at the expense of the private market sector fails to demonstrate that the private sector has wanted the manpower absorbed into the public sector. Much of the growth in public employment in the 1960s and 1970s took the form of part-time females previously not in the labour force, during a period when the private sector was shedding employees, mainly full-time males (Wilkinson and Jackson, 1981). At the same time there was a growing pool of unemployed labour which would have welcomed work in the private sector if there had been any jobs available. Similarly, the monetarist argument that the excessive growth of the public sector, through its impact on the public sector borrowing requirement (PSBR) and on the money supply, has pre-empted the private sector of financial resources, is also open to question. By international standards the growth of public expenditure in Britain has not been exceptional or abnormal. While total government spending rose from 33 per cent of GDP in 1960 to 44 per cent in 1979, this 11 percentage point increase was one of the lowest in the EEC, and identical to that in Japan. Moreover, throughout the past twenty-five years the public expenditure/GDP ratio in Britain has not been much different from that in most West European countries, and directly comparable, for example, to the ratio in West Germany (Heald, 1983, pp. 22–32). Up to the early 1970s the growth in public spending did not generate any substantial rise in government borrowing: taxation rose in parallel. But here too, the increase in the taxation/GDP ratio has been no greater than elsewhere in Western Europe. Although the nominal PSBR did rise sharply after 1972, the significance of this has been the subject of divergent assessments (see Heald, 1983, pp. 41–9). In particular, if the nominal PSBR is expressed as a percentage of GDP, so that the effect of inflation is removed, then the rise in the borrowing requirement in the 1970s is considerably moderated and, moreover, is replaced by a rapid fall after 1976 back down to levels not dissimilar to those in the mid-1960s. Furthermore, contrary to the New Conservative view, the rise in the PSBR during the 1970s can be explained as a conjunctural phenomenon, *following from* the stagnation of the economy during this period, not precipitating it. Even if we were to concede that the rise in public spending and borrowing is part of the crisis, this hardly amounts to the public sector squeezing private industry. It would seem, then, that the Thatcher government's claim that 'public expenditures lies at the heart of Britain's present economic difficulties (HM Government, 1979) is a bald statement for which the evidence is far from unequivocal.

This still leaves the second main argument used by the New Conservatives and the New Right, that the excessive real-wage push by organised labour has eroded corporate profitability and undermined productive performance. It cannot be disputed that the membership, strength and militancy of the British trades union movement have increased markedly during the post-war period, and especially since the late 1960s (Hodgson, 1981), or that labour has succeeded in extracting a progressively larger share of net output. Within manufacturing the real product wage (which approximates the share of wages in net value added) grew steadily throughout the 1950s and 1960s and then more rapidly during the 1970s (Figure 8.2). And as the wage share has risen so the profit share has fallen, from 26 per cent of net output in 1955–62 to 19 per cent in 1965–71, and 12 per cent over 1976–81 (*British Business*, 1984); and this in turn has been a major factor in the decline of the net profit rate, which fell from 19 per cent in 1965–71 to 12 per cent in 1965–71, and 6 per cent by 1976–81. Trade union resistance to a fall in the real wage has been considerable, and whether because of direct working-class pressure, accommodative government policies or favourable labour market conditions, or some combination of all three, real wages have risen faster than the growth in productivity and cut into profits.

It does not simply follow, however, that union real-wage push has caused industrial decline. The secular fall in the profit rate is not peculiar to Britain, but to a greater or lesser extent is evident in other industrial countries (see Figure 8.3) where it is difficult to link it with strong and militant unions. What is significant is that profitability in British industry has generally been low by international standards. This reflects not so much high real wages – in fact wage costs in Britain's manufacturing sector are lower than in most of her competitors – as a problem of low levels and rates of growth

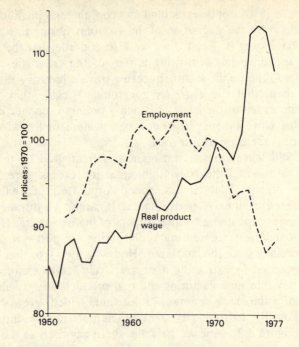

FIGURE 8.2   *Wages and Employment in UK Manufacturing, 1950–77*

SOURCE   *Midland Bank Review*

of labour productivity. For the radical Right this problem is also attributed to the unions, to their intransigence and inflexibility over new work practices, manning levels and the introduction of new technology. It is true that in many enterprises and certain segments of capital low productivity performance can be traced to worker resistance or outmoded production methods; and, unlike their foreign counterparts, British unions can and do bargain over changes to the labour-process, especially if these changes threaten established skill divisions, levels of work intensity, etc. (Kilpatrick and Lawson, 1980). However, as Williams, Williams and Thomas (1983) show, to single out union disruption as the main factor behind low productivity is inadequate; and even if a link from union attitudes to inefficient work practices and low productivity can be clearly established for particular firms, this does *not* mean that every instance of low labour productivity, or the problem in

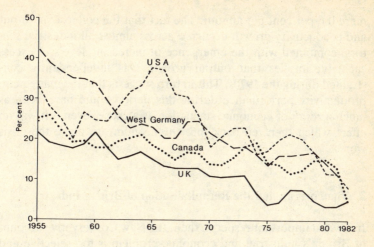

FIGURE 8.3 *Profitability in Manufacturing: Some International Comparisons, 1955–82*

SOURCE *British Business*. Pre-tax net rates of return to fixed capital at current replacement cost.

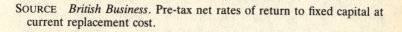

general, can be automatically assumed to be caused in this way. Deficiencies in output per worker derive from a host of interacting factors – poor management, product design, the age and quality of capital, the quality of the workforce, corporate organisation and strategy – which may not only intersect with union and worker attitudes, but also shape those attitudes.

Nor should the influence of economic conditions be ignored. There is strong evidence to suggest that productivity advance in British manufacturing has been held back by the relatively slow growth in output demand (see Wragg and Robertson, 1978; Wenban-Smith, 1981). During the 1950s and 1960s manufacturing output in Britain grew at about 3 per cent per annum, half the rate in other EEC countries. In parallel the rate of productivity growth in British manufacturing (around 4 per cent per annum) was considerably lower than in other industrial nations. After 1973 output growth slowed down everywhere, but particularly in Britain where manufacturing output actually declined by 0.7 per cent per annum. And while productivity growth also slowed down in most industrial economies after 1973, in Britain it slumped to a mere 0.6 per cent per annum. The fact that the collapse in output and productivity growth occurred across almost all industrial sectors, combined with the emergence of increasing levels of excess capacity, implies that output growth was independently constrained during the 1970s. This in turn suggests that the inadequate productivity performance during this period could have been as much a *result* of economic stagnation as a cause, even if it was an effect which then fed back into the economy to make the crisis worse.

3. **Thatcherism and the Recapitalisation of British Industry**

In several important respects, then, the New Conservative account of Britain's industrial and economic problem is too selective and too simplistic. The focus on state expenditure and regulation and on union power and inflexibility as the primary culprits owes more to ideology and political premiss than to economic reality. It is not just that the radical Right's reborn faith in the ineluctable efficacy of the invisible hand of the free market gives political prerogative to private enterprise and the need to support the maximum scope for the activities of capital; it is that also, in consequence of this prerogative, problems of economic and industrial stagnation are automatically attributed not to failings *of* the market system, but to the interference *to* the market by collective institutions, especially the state and organised labour. The prescribed policy is therefore to free the market by curtailing the scope and activities of the state and the operation of the unions. Faith in the efficacy of the invisible hand thus determines simultaneously the diagnosis of the problem and the policy prescription for its solution.

An explicit interventionist policy for industrial revival is obviously ruled out under this neo-market philosophy. Rather the aim has been to restore profitable private enterprise by promoting, even forcing through, a wider 'recapitalisation' or 'restructuring' of Britain in an economic, social and ideological sense (Miller, 1978; Best and Humphries, 1981; Arnott and Krieger, 1982). The prosecution of policies to control money supply growth and to reduce public spending on the one hand, and of measures to deregulate business and regulate unions on the other, is intended to squeeze inflation out of the system, to inculcate the necessity of financial propriety ('living within our means') and, by releasing the 'natural' processes of competition, to provide the necessary discipline on firms and workers to adjust more readily to the signals of the market-place.[3]

A number of specific, interrelated areas of intended policy impact on industry can be identified (see also Leys, 1985).

(i) *The Improvement of Industrial Efficiency and Cost-competitiveness*

The policy of reducing inflation by restricting the growth of the money supply (the 'Medium-Term Financial Strategy') and reducing the real growth of the PSBR is also designed to induce greater competitiveness and produce efficiency in industry by holding down the cost of inputs and, by dampening the wage inflation process, especially labour costs. The constraint on borrowing is also intended to stimulate cost-saving and efficiency-raising restructuring within firms by preventing them from 'riding the crisis' by piling up debts. One of the objectives of the programme of 'monetary discipline', therefore, has been to encourage a 'leaner and fitter' industrial base by promoting, or at least certainly not moderating, the shake-out of excess labour and capital.

(ii) *The Renewal of Corporate Profitability*

The substantial and sustained revival of industrial profitability is a central component of the 'recapitalisation' objectives of the New Conservatism. By acting to bring inflation, real wage growth and public spending under control, the aim is to assist the restoration of real profitability in the UK company sector, to reverse the expansion of labour's share in value added and thereby re-establish the key dynamic of capital accumulation.

(iii) *The Reconstitution of Productive Investment*

As part of its drive to restructure the economy the Thatcher government has sought to promote the shift of resources from traditional industries and processes into new high-technology sectors, production methods and products. Policies that support and maintain senescent industries and firms are deemed to thwart the movement along the path of economic evolution and have in consequence come under attack. Although the government has expanded the package of aid and relief directed at accelerating investment in innovative and science-based 'sunrise' industries, the scale of assistance is still small by international standards (see Chapter 10). This so-called 'constructive intervention' is justified in economic terms – as an important source of new jobs, productivity growth and exports – but there are also strong ideological overtones: the small, innovative firm sector is, in Mrs Thatcher's view, the heart of the free enterprise spirit.

(iv) *The Privatisation of Public Sector Industry*

In line with its desire to reduce the size of the public sector and to revitalise private capitalistic production, the Thatcher government has developed an almost passionate aversion to the nationalised industries, which it argues 'are immunised from the process of spontaneous change which competition and fear of bankruptcy imposes on the private sector' (Joseph, quoted in Riddell, 1983, p. 170). By 1984–5 almost £6 billion of public industry assets had been sold off, mostly the more profitable parts. If the government's overall privatisation plans are all carried through, a further £8.5 billion of assets will have been sold off by 1988, so that over two Conservative administrations the Treasury will have been the beneficiary of around £15 billion raised in this form. Apart from the contribution that this de-nationalisation programme is intended to make to the Thatcher government's goal of reducing the economic role of the state, it is also defended on the grounds that it extends economic freedom, increases competition and weakens the wage-bargaining position and 'unique disruptive capability' of the public sector unions.

(v) *Restoring the Power of Capital over Organised Labour*

Given its belief that the power of organised labour has become too excessive, the Conservative government has introduced legislation to curb and regulate the activities of the unions. It has taken steps to restrict the lawful definition of industrial disputes, to reduce the coverage of employment protection and unfair dismissal provisions by exempting the small-firm sector and to regulate the operation of 'closed shops' and the internal voting procedures of the unions. Also, the Wages Councils, which set minimum wages for some 2.75 million workers in the low-wage sectors of the economy, have come under critical scrutiny and are to be attenuated in their scope and operation. The intention behind these and other legislative and exhortative measures is to fragment, decentralise and deinstitutionalise large parts of the labour market (see Riddell, 1983, pp. 186–91). While the legislation is allegedly directed at 'improving the flexibility of the labour market' and at 'democratising the unions' it is clear that the basic aim is to weaken the position of organised labour and help to shift the balance of power back in favour of employers: 'to enable managers to manage'. The resumption of managerial authority and control over the work process is regarded as vital if industry is to reorganise and restructure so as to increase efficiency and reverse the fall in the profit share.

These various objectives and policies do not of themselves constitute a planned or carefully co-ordinated programme for reviving British industry – far from it. Together with the squeeze on the money supply and on public spending they are intended to re-create the climate for 'free-market enterprise'. While it is acknowledged that tight monetary and fiscal policies will have a depressive impact on output, this, it is claimed, should only be a temporary side-effect (the main impact being on inflation), the duration and degree of any such impact on output being determined by how quickly firms and workers themselves adjust to the new economic reality. And in any case, the argument continues, the effects of the squeeze will fall where they are most needed, on the least efficient firms, workers and regions.

Indeed, much of the Thatcher government's diagnosis of industrial decline, and its 'recapitalisation' philosophy, has been carried over directly into its interpretation of Britain's regional problem. Thus the existence and persistence of markedly higher unemployment in the country's depressed industrial areas is considered to be the result of institutional rigidities in those regions. Workers and their unions in areas of traditional and stagnating industry have demanded real wages in excess of those warranted by their (lower) productivity and by local labour demand–supply conditions, thus creating unemployment and deterring new investment. Furthermore, workers in the depressed regions are accused of being particularly resistant to changes to improve productive efficiency, and of being insufficiently mobile occupationally and geographically. The spatial correlation of high levels of unionisation and high rates of unemployment in depressed areas is interpreted as empirical confirmation of this argument (see Minford, 1983, pp. 120–1). According to the radical Right, therefore, the higher unemployment in the country's depressed manufacturing regions is largely due to the social and institutional 'jamming' of the labour markets in these areas.

The New Conservative policy prescription for the regional problem is thus clear. First,

> regional differences [in employment] will not be reduced simply by redistributing money from taxpayers: there needs also to be local enterprise and plenty of co-operation in making business competitive and profitable. Nothing will do more for the prosperity of a region than a reputation for effective work, high productivity and co-operation between workforce and management. (Hansard, 1979.)

Second, the erosion of employment in the problem regions should be corrected

> through lower wages and unit costs than comparable work commands elsewhere. Wage flexibility, combined with a reputation for good work and a constructive attitude to productivity and industrial relations would increase the attractiveness to industry of areas of high unemployment. . . . The Government believe that wage bargaining must become more responsive to the circumstances of the individual enterprise, including its location. Their policies of privatisation, together with a reduction in the power of trade unions to set against their own members' interests, should help to achieve this. (HM Government, 1983, paras 9 and 10.)

Wages are already lower in the depressed industrial areas of the country than in the south, but evidently, in the government's view, they are not low enough.

The industrial problems of many of the urban centres in the regions are also considered to have been made worse by the spending and taxation policies of local-government authorities. This, in essence, is the application of the 'crowding out' thesis to the local state. According to the Thatcherites, local-authority spending on services and utilities has risen excessively, resulting in unreasonable levels of local taxation (rate burden) on the community, and on business particularly. This, it is contended, has threatened local and national economic activity in three ways: by frustrating the government's goal of reducing the PSBR and the overall level of taxation, and thereby contributing to inflation; by raising industrial costs with consequential effects on competitiveness, profits and employment; and by fuelling public sector wage demands, and hence real-wage pressures in general. The first and second of these effects are debatable: if local-government expenditure increases, but is financed by an equivalent increase in local taxes, then the PSBR remains unchanged; and as yet the argument that non-domestic rates have squeezed industry is unproven. Nevertheless, local-government spending has been subjected to a highly centralised and authoritarian system of controls and penalties, whereby the government imposes arbitrary expenditure targets on the local authorities and 'rate-caps' those that attempt to exceed their specified limits. This weakening of the role and autonomy of local government is justified in terms of the usual monetarist, neo-market arguments. However, it has also enabled the Thatcher government to single out those Labour-controlled authorities that have opposed its policies. Significantly, most of these authorities are in areas which have suffered acute problems of de-industrialisation and which need higher levels of spending on social and economic programmes.[4]

A central maxim underpinning these 'recapitalisation' aims is that the pressure of economic austerity and recession purges the economy of its inefficiencies and speeds up the process of 'creative destruction', whereby older, less efficient and backward firms are weeded out and 'release' their resources to other more cost-effective and advanced firms (see Stapleton, 1981). To survive the struggle, all workers and firms in a given region have to do is to keep wages and productivity in line with their competitors in other areas; all local authorities in the region have to do is to keep their spending and taxation levels in line with more thrifty local authorities elsewhere. The government does not, of course, possess any powers or policy machinery, nor are there any automatic mechanisms, to ensure that it is only inefficient firms that are slimmed down or eliminated, or that the resources 'released' are necessarily fully reabsorbed in other sectors of economic activity. Nor is it likely that the process of 'creative destruction' will be geographically neutral in its impact. *There is no logical necessity why the spatial configurations of the costs and the gains of rationalisation and recapitalisation should be well synchronised.* Not only are the locational requirements of new profitable production likely to differ from those of existing production, but also there is no region-specific process linking the disinvestment and reinvestment of capital. If left to market forces, industrial restructuring carries no obligations of regional equity.

4. Restructuring versus the Regions

Whether measured in terms of the contraction in output, investment or employment (Table 8.1) it is clear that since 1979 British industry has undergone the most intensive phase of retrenchment and rationalisation of its post-war history. While there would undoubtedly have been a major recession without the Thatcher government, it has been estimated that almost half the jobs lost can be attributed to the 'Thatcher effect'. The imposition of monetary and fiscal restraint in the context of underlying recession was inevitably strongly deflationary – equivalent to a reduction of 6 per cent in GDP over 1979–82 (Riddell, 1983, pp. 90–1). The result was to hinder rather than promote the improvement of competitiveness and to put an additional squeeze on output and profit margins. The scale of the slump surprised even the government, but was quickly reinterpreted as a virtue by its New Right supporters:

> *the destruction of unadaptable industry in a deep recession can be a major benefit, if not an essential pre-requisite for change . . . the deeper the recession, the better the long run health of the economy . . . a long recession has proved more effective than a short sharp one*, since when firms could rely on an early reversal of previous credit squeezes, they avoided the painful rationalisation process. (Stapleton, 1981, pp. 8–9; original emphasis.)

TABLE 8.1 *Slim-down and Shake-out in British Manufacturing*

	Estimated excess capacity %	Fixed capital expenditure £ mill 1980 prices	Output 1975 = 100	Company liquidations (England and Wales)	'Confirmed' redundancies (000s)	Employment (mid-year) (000s)
1978	16.9	7 220	109.6	5 086	119.3	7 147
1979	20.4	7 496	109.4	4 537	140.8	7 113
1980	29.8	6 471	100.0	6 890	402.0	6 804
1981	30.1	4 852	93.9	8 596	398.0	6 100
1982	30.3	4 685	94.5	12 067	281.4	5 788
1983	n.a.	4 619	96.9	13 406	221.7	5 502
1984	n.a.	5 327	100.2	13 721	150.6	5 415

SOURCES Department of Employment; Taylor, 1982, 1984; *British Business* (Various issues).

The reality of 'slim-down' and 'shake-out' has consisted mainly in the reduction of labour costs by cutting jobs and closing down productive capacity.

For many firms, extensive cost-cutting has not been possible or has proved insufficient to prevent bankruptcy, with the result that the numbers of company liquidations in manufacturing has reached an all-time high (Table 8.1). Many of these have been small and medium-sized firms, typically single-plant concerns, in which there is limited scope for selective scrapping and workforce reduction without jeopardising the entire business. Large, especially multi-product multi-plant, firms have been better placed to undertake and survive defensive retrenchment and rationalisation. The immediate focus in such companies has usually been on those labour-intensive areas of production where manpower could be reduced in large numbers so as to provide a quick cost-cutting response. In this way, many of Britain's biggest manufacturing companies have 'shaken out' labour on a colossal scale during the early 1980s, by as much as 50 per cent in major firms like GKN, British Leyland, Dunlop, Courtaulds, TI, Talbot, and BSR (see Table 8.2). While in some cases this contraction in employment has been associated with *in situ* rationalisation alone, in many others selective plant closure (not necessarily those making the smallest profits) has formed an important component of corporate restructuring strategy. This form of 'slim-down', particularly, has concentrated mass redundancies in specific communities and, especially where it has involved the loss of a principal employer in the locality, has caused acute problems of local labour market adjustment.

No part of Britain has escaped this collapse of industry since 1979: all of the regions have suffered a fall in manufacturing output and a substantial decline in manufacturing employment (see Tables 8.3 and 8.4). However, in proportionate terms, the regional territoriality of retrenchment has been distinctly uneven as between the south and east of Britain on the one hand and the rest of the economy on the other. Thus the fall in output over 1979–83 in the manufacturing sector in the South-East. East Anglia, and South-West regions was less than half that nationally, and less than a third of the decline in the three worst-hit areas of Wales the West Midlands and the North-West. Similarly, the decline in manufacturing employment in the industrial north and west has been twice that of the south and east. The brunt of the contraction of British

TABLE 8.2   *Labour Shedding by Major British Companies*

	Employment		Reduction in employment 1977–83 %
	1977	1983	
British Steel	209 000	81 100	−61
British Leyland	171 943	81 261	−53
British Shipbuilders	87 569	62 583	−28
ICI	95 000	61 800	−35
Courtaulds	112 009	56 336	−50
Lucas	68 778	49 042	−29
GKN	73 196	33 600	−54
TI	61 777	25 100	−59
Dunlop	48 000	22 000	−54
Vauxhall	30 180	20 527	−32
Massey Ferguson	21 486	13 066	−39
Talbot	22 800	7 109	−69
GEC	156 000	136 944	−12
Cadbury–Schweppes	29 096	22 897[a]	−21
BSR International	15 950	5 130[a]	−68
Rolls-Royce	57 164	50 000[a]	−12

Note   [a] 1982 figure.

SOURCE   *Financial Times* (1984).

industry has clearly been borne by workers not only in the traditionally depressed regions but also by those in the country's core manufacturing areas. Comparison of the regional anatomy of job loss over 1979–84 with that over the previous five-year period 1974–9 (Table 8.4) indicates that although the problem of de-industrialisation has now spread to all regions of Britain, the gap between the relatively more buoyant south and east and the industrial heartland (West Midlands, Yorkshire–Humberside and the Nort-West) had widened considerably.

This differential regional impact of labour shedding by manufacturing is only partly explained by geographical variations in industrial specialisation (Martin, 1982; Townsend, 1982), for the worst-hit regions have suffered higher rates of employment loss across most of their industries. Moreover, not only has the *rate* of

TABLE 8.3   *The Unequal Geography of Output Decline in Manufacturing during the Recession*

	Percentage change in output 1979–83	Contribution of manufacturing to total output (per cent)		
		1974	1979	1983
South-East	−6.1	23.6	23.9	22.0
East Anglia	−3.0	25.2	27.2	25.2
South-West	−4.5	26.3	24.6	22.9
West Midlands	−23.3	43.5	40.2	34.1
East Midlands	−12.4	36.0	34.3	30.4
Yorkshire–Humberside	−18.3	34.7	32.1	27.3
North-West	−19.3	36.1	35.6	30.0
North	−15.7	35.5	32.1	28.6
Wales	−20.0	31.2	26.2	21.1
Scotland	−14.0	29.6	27.8	24.1
Great Britain	−13.3	30.9	28.2	24.0

Note   Output measured as gross domestic product (GDP), net of stock appreciation, at 1980 prices.

SOURCE   *Economic Trends.*

labour shake-out differed across regional Britain, equally important so has the *manner* in which the employment loss has occurred. The greater the rate of employment decline the higher has been the proportion of compulsory redundancies in the total discharge of labour (Martin, 1984). Firms in the industrial north and west have not only cut back on labour more intensively than firms and plants elsewhere, but in doing so have resorted far more to large-scale redundancies (Table 8.4). While redundancy payments have become a major cost item to firms undertaking cost-saving rationalisation and reorganisation, this has become increasingly accepted as a justifiable, necessary expenditure no different from spending on new capital. But in making their own calculations such firms have had scant regard for the wider social costs of their actions. A large proportion of firms' redundancy payments are recoverable through rebates from central government. At the same time, because of the increased unemployment generated, the

TABLE 8.4 *The Unequal Geography of Labour Shake-out in Manufacturing during the Recession*

	Percentage change in employment 1974–79	1979–84	Confirmed redundancies average rate per 1000 employees 1979–82	as a proportion of total discharges 1980–2
South-East	−7.0	−17.5	28.1	)
East Anglia	+1.0	−14.5	31.0	) 14.8
South-West	−2.5	−16.7	42.1	26.5
West Midlands	−8.8	−28.5	47.5	28.6
East Midlands	−1.6	−19.7	42.8	21.5
Yorkshire–Humberside	−7.6	−28.0	61.5	29.7
North-West	−11.3	−29.0	65.2	34.2
North	−12.4	−29.8	64.3	36.0
Wales	−6.3	−33.0	84.3	46.0
Scotland	−10.8	−27.7	69.2	34.1
Great Britain	−8.1	−23.6	49.1	25.9

Note Employment change measured from mid-year to mid-year.

SOURCES Department of Employment and Manpower Services Commission.

government loses tax and National Insurance revenue, while being forced to pay out additional social security and welfare benefits: each unemployed person now costs the Exchequer at least £5000 per annum. There are significant local cost implications as well: on top of the immediate increase in local unemployment following mass redundancies there are various knock-on effects on other local firms and services, on local income and on the operation of the local labour market. And for the local authority there is a loss of rate revenue from factory closures, and increased costs of rent and rate rebates for the extra unemployed. If the total social and economic effects of the recent phase of retrenchment and rationalisation were to be calculated in this way the overall costs of promoting 'private efficiency' would be enormous, far exceeding the direct costs to the corporate sector (Harte and Owen, 1985).

And in any case it is certain that many of the job losses and plant closures that have taken place over the early 1980s were not necessary in a narrow economic efficiency sense, but have occurred because of the continued impact of recession and the government's austerity policies on firms which happened to experience short-term financial and liquidity difficulties. For, as Tomlinson (1983, p. 44) argues, in the short term 'deflation is likely to weed out firms with short-run cash flow problems, high current investment levels and other short-run problems as much as those companies inefficient in some long-run sense'. On this issue one may suggest that the government's rhetoric of 'slim-down' and 'shake-out' misunderstands the nature of the capitalist competitive process: deflation and monetary squeeze may generate a process of survival of the large and of the lucky as much as the survival of the fittest.

But the government's rhetoric is misplaced for another and in many ways more fundamental reason: within the big-firm sector, where the bulk of job-shedding within manufacturing has occurred, the rationalisation and retrenchment of jobs and plant in the UK has been accompanied by an expansion of productive capacity overseas. Against a background of falling domestic investment, many of Britain's leading multinational companies have streamlined or closed down factories in the UK while simultaneously acquiring or building new ones abroad. This outflow of capital and 'switching of production' was undoubtedly encouraged by the Thatcher government's abolition of exchange controls soon after it came into office in 1979. At the time it was argued by the government that the abolition of exchange controls would not in itself lead to an appreciable increase in overseas investment. First, it was argued that most direct investment was carried out by multinationals which already had the capacity either to reinvest profits generated overseas or else to raise loans abroad. Second, it was argued that portfolio investment overseas would level off quickly after the initial rush prompted by the ending of the burden of the dollar premium, since Britain would continue to be an attractive home for funds due to the rapid rise in British domestic share prices.

Both arguments proved to be false. Direct investment overseas almost doubled between 1979 and 1981 (from £2.7 billion to £5.1 billion), while portfolio overseas investment soared from around £1 billion to £4.1 billion. Over the same period domestic investment in manufacturing fell from £7.5 billion to £4.8 billion, and total home investment by almost £3 billion or 10 per cent. During this same three-year interval overseas production by British companies increased while home production slumped. The top fifty British manufacturing companies increased their overseas production between 1979 and 1982 from 36 per cent to 44 per cent of their global output. At the same time they cut their UK workforce by almost 400 000 while increasing their employment abroad by some 40 000. For these companies, which dominate British manufacturing, 'slim-down' and 'shake-out' in the recession have been an integral part of a wider global restructuring strategy of overseas expansion as a means of restoring profitability and protecting dividends for shareholders:

> As the recession has cut a swathe through domestic earnings, the comparative success of overseas subsidiaries often has kept companies in profit overall and obviated the need for embarrassing dividend omissions. (*Financial Times*, 18 May 1982.)

This trend towards increased internationalisation of British industrial capital at the expense of UK output, jobs and exports is well illustrated by IMI, formerly the metals division of ICI and a traditional bell-weather of British manufacturing. Between 1979 and 1983 IMI cut its workforce by almost one-third and its direct exports dropped by 10 per cent, whereas overseas production almost doubled, aided by new acquisitions and investments in the US. According to the managing director of IMI, the pressure has been on to have more productive activity outside the UK: 'In this country we can depend neither upon an economy likely to show continued growth nor a stable political environment conducive to business development.' He argues that many of Britain's large companies have improved their profits during the recession by shifting production outside the UK, and concedes that this 'may be good for the health of an IMI, but whether it is good for the UK is another matter' (*Financial Times*, 1984, pp. 10–11).

The localised rationalisation and disinvestment impact of this thrust towards the increasing internationalisation of British capital has been a major factor shaping the unequal geography of job loss during the recession. This point is well illustrated by the West Midlands and the North-West, both of which lost more than 280 000

Table 8.5   *Employment Change in Some Major West Midlands Companies, 1978–82*

	% Employment change domestic	% Employment change overseas	UK absolute employment change
GEC	−7	+66	−11 000
GKN	−46	+2	−31 600
Cadbury	−21	−14	−6 088
Dunlop	−48	−35	−23 000
Lucas	−29	+16	−20 231
TI	−56	−43	−33 750
IMI	−32	−9	−8 716
Delta	−40	0	−9 375
Glynwed	−22	+61	−3 159
BSR	−72	+593	−13 079

Source   Adapted from Gaffikin and Nickson (1984).

manufacturing jobs, almost 30 per cent of their total, between 1979 and 1984. Manufacturing employment in the West Midlands has traditionally displayed a higher than average concentration in a small number of large companies (Gaffikin and Nickson, 1984). In 1978 the top ten companies in the area, all transnational in their operations, employed a total British workforce of more than 513 000, of which 135 000 (26 per cent of the British total) was in the West Midlands. This was equivalent to 14 per cent of the total manufacturing employment in the region. By 1982 as a result of extensive retrenchment and restructuring these companies had reduced their British workforce by 30 per cent (Table 8.5) involving a loss of over 150 000 jobs, of which more than 50 000 were lost through redundancies in the West Midlands alone. Thus these top ten companies in the West Midlands cut their labour force there by some 38 per cent, accounting for 18 per cent of the region's total fall in manufacturing employment over the period. Meanwhile, the combined overseas workforce in these same companies actually increased slightly in spite of world recession. Moreover, whereas the total value of home production (including exports) by these firms increased by less than 2 per cent per annum over the period, the value of their overseas production increased by 12 per cent per annum (Gaffikin and Nickson, 1984).

TABLE 8.6 *Employment Change in Some Major North-West Companies, 1975–83*

	% Employment change		UK absolute
	domestic	overseas	employment change
Courtaulds	−49	−13	−61 039
Ford	−3	−3	−800
BIC Cables	−19	+30	−7 120
Metal Box International	−16	−13	−5 934
Computers	−30	+53	−7 007
Rank, Hovis, MacDougall	−24	+1	−13 567
Pilkington	−21	+29	−6 501
Tootal	−45	+28	−8 818
ICI	−43	−8	−57 300
Plessey	−40	−13	−22 154
Renold	−46	−28	−5 157
Unilever	−20	−5	−18 142
Turner & Newall	−21	+12	−4 269
British Leyland	−51	+34	−83 754
Imperial Group	−5	+463	−4 728

SOURCE Adapted from Lloyd and Shutt (1985).

Similarly, local employment decline in the Nort-West region has been intensified by this process of corporate internationalisation and switching of production overseas. Around one-third of the manufacturing shop-floor labour force in the Nort-West is employed by just 31 British companies. Between 1975 and 1982 these companies reduced their combined workforce in the UK by 422 000, and in the North-West region alone by 87 000. Over the same period these firms expanded their overseas workforce by around 163 000. In some of the companies this transfer of employment abroad has been very substantial indeed (see Table 8.6). Even in those companies which have rationalised production and shed labour overseas as well as in the UK, the focus of 'slim-down' and 'shake-out' has frequently been directed at British-based plants, so that the net effect has still been a shift in the balance of production and employment towards overseas locations.

Examples like these call into question the whole concept of British de-industrialisation. The rationalisation of Britain's industrial base, welcomed and urged by the Thatcher government, has not been characterised by any simple process of efficiency-raising 'slim-down'. It has also involved a more complex process of industrial restructuring associated with the decentralisation of productive capacity abroad.[5] The UK is not an isolated island of backward inefficient industry; British manufacturing capital has been inextricably bound up with the international restructuring process. The commitment of successive post-war governments, both Labour and Conservative, to the revitalisation of Britain's international role has favoured international fractions of capital while penalising domestic industry (see Chapter 2). The Thatcher government, with its strong-free market and free-trade ethos, has accentuated this asymmetry still further: the recent growth of foreign assets is viewed as an indicator of economic recovery and strength, as an important generator of increased profits. The negative impact on British employment and visible exports seems to have received far less emphasis. The basic point is that, both directly and indirectly, the Thatcher government's policies have promoted and accelerated the 'internationalisation' of Britain's ailing industrial regions. Both the recent wave of rationalisation, and its specific regional impact, must be interpreted in a global context, against a background of a new phase of transnational capital restructuring. In regions such as the West Midlands, the Nort-West and the North many externally controlled and locally owned leading companies have increased the international configuration of their operations at the expense of locally based production and jobs. While this form of restructuring may well have increased corporate profitability and shareholders' dividends, the costs borne by such regions have been substantial. And at the same time this restructuring process has left the home market exposed to foreign penetration, with further possible adverse implications for the industrial base and jobs in these regions. This internationalisation of British capital is perhaps one of the most disturbing aspects of the regional consequences of the acceleration of de-industrialisation that has occurred under the economic policies of the New Conservatives.

5. The Dismantling of Regional Industrial Aid

One direct manifestation of this differential regional impact of 'restructuring for profit' has been the widening of regional and local unemployment disparities. Regional percentage-point unemployment differentials are now wider than at any other time since the inter-war period. It is precisely such geographical disparities in unemployment and employment opportunities that regional industrial policy is supposed to alleviate. While the rapid shrinkage of industrial waged employment over the past few years has exacerbated the 'regional problem', it has simultaneously militated against the traditional regional policy mechanism of diverting manufacturing investment and jobs from prosperous core regions (the south and the midlands of Britain) to the depressed industrial periphery. It is no secret that the Thatcher government would like to abolish regional industrial policy altogether (Hansard, 1984, col. 67). It has refrained from doing so presumably because of the implications for receiving assistance from the European Regional Development Fund, and for political vote-seeking reasons. But it has taken steps to cut aid to the depressed industrial regions back to the minimum it thinks consistent with these considerations.

Over the past decade or so the whole post-war consensus on regional industrial policy has come under harsh and repeated criticism. First, the rising level of unemployment in the prosperous core regions of the South-East and particularly the West Midlands has been blamed on regional policies which constrained the economic vitality of these regions in order to steer activity to the Assisted Areas. Although this opinion has found its strongest support among the New Right exponents of free-market economics, it has also circulated among some of the strongest advocates of state intervention in industrial development. It is a valid criticism that as the pace of overall economic growth and accumulation has slowed, Keynesian-inspired regional policies have served less to foster industrial regeneration of the Assisted Areas and more to set different regions and localities in competition with one another over attracting whatever new jobs and investment are available. Second, there has been mounting concern about the poor value for money provided by the Regional Development Grant (RDG) scheme, arising from payments of grants to capital-intensive industries which have generated few if any new jobs (low employment-to-assistance ratios), and in respect of projects which would have located in the Assisted Areas anyway (large 'deadweight' effects). For example, of the £4.4 billion spent on RDGs since 1972–3 nearly one-quarter (£1.03 billion) has gone to one sector, the chemical industry, in which the job-creation impact has been minimal (some have argued negative) and the deadweight problem substantial. These problems, in combination with the progressive relaxation of industrial development controls in the South-East and midlands regions in the 1970s, suggest that during that decade regional industrial aid became less a means of promoting new employment in the Assisted Areas and more a subsidy to industrial capital to help it restructure and reorganise in order to stave off the growing squeeze on profits (Pickvance, 1981). Nor is it surprising, in view of these trends, that the cost of each new job created by regional policy over the past couple of decades has been so high, around £35 000 (1982 prices) on average (Committee of Public Accounts, 1984, p. 22).

It is this set of interrelated issues that the Thatcher government has seized upon in its desire to reduce regional industrial aid. Outwardly this political imperative has been presented in terms of the savings needed to help reduce overall public expenditure and the necessity for greater cost-effectiveness, but as we have seen (Section 8.3) the government's free-market philosophy and its social-cum-institutional explanation of the regional unemployment problem are firmly embedded in its attitude to regional policy. Since coming into office the Thatcher government has implemented two major reviews of regional industrial assistance, each designed to reduce state intervention and expenditure in this field. The first review, introduced by Sir Keith Joseph in 1979, imposed a phased rolling back of the map of regional aid from its original coverage of 44 per cent of the working population to a reduced coverage of 27.5 per cent, the intention being to limit aid to only 'those parts of the country with the most intractable problems of unemployment' (Hansard, 1979). Large tracts of the Development and Intermediate Areas (DAs and IAs) lost their assisted status altogether, and a number of Special Development Areas (SDAs) and DAs were downgraded (see Figure 8.4, p. 273). In addition to this 'steamlining' of the map the rate of RDG in the DAs was reduced (from 20 to 15 per cent) and the more restricted RDG in the IAs completely abolished. By means of these changes the government had hoped to cut projected expenditure on regional industrial assistance by more than one-third by 1982–3. As it turned out, however, real spending on regional industrial aid actually continued to increase up to 1981–2, and only then was it put into sharp reverse under growing pressure from the Treasury, with a cut in real expenditure of more than £200 million by 1983–4. When the Conservatives came to power in 1979 annual spending on regional aid stood at £842 million (1980 prices); by 1983–4 this had been reduced to £560 million, a cut in real terms of exactly one-third (Table 8.7).

The second review, signalled by the 1983 White Paper on Regional Industrial Development (HM Government, 1983), and introduced in late 1984, was clearly directed at continuing this commitment to financial discipline. Further changes to the map and related reductions in the rate of grant, together with the introduction for the first time, of a cost-per-job limit, and the abolition of grants towards modernisation and replacement investment, are designed to reduce projected nominal spending by a further 40 per cent by 1987–8 (from £700 million down to £400 million). While the total proportion of the working pupulation covered by some form of industrial assistance has been increased back up to 35 per cent, this largely reflects the granting of IA status to parts of the West Midlands. For more than forty years the leading 'workshop' region of Britain, this area has now joined the list of localities deemed as requiring industrial aid. The designation of the West Midlands, justified in view of its very rapid de-industrialisation since the late 1970s, was in large part politically motivated, following considerable lobbying from the regional branch of the CBI and from Members of Parliament representing parts of the area. Nevertheless, although the Assisted Areas have been extended, the cost has been a wholesale downgrading of the regional policy map. The upper SDA tier has been abolished, and the areas formerly so designated downgraded to DAs, thereby receiving a reduced rate of grant. Likewise, many of the former DAs have been demoted to IAs, thus losing their entitlement to RDG altogether, and being eligible for regional selective financial assistance (RSA) only. The net result is that the proportion of the working population now eligible for automatic regional development grants has been reduced by 30 per cent. In this sense, therefore, the assisted area map has been 'rolled back' yet further (Figure 8.4; Martin, 1985).

The desire for greater cost-effectiveness or better value for

TABLE 8.7 *Expenditure on Regional Industrial Assistance 1977–8 to 1984–5*

£ million	Financial Year							
	1977–8	78–9	79–80	80–1	81–2	82–3	83–4	84–5
(a) *Outturn prices:*								
Regional Development Grants	393	417	441	491	617	540	440	—
Regional Selective Assistance	44	104	78	74	76	90	82	—
Land and buildings	52	85	110	141	161	137	105	—
Total	489	606	629	706	854	767	627	590*
(b) *At 1980 prices*								
Total	752	842	749	706	776	685	560	

Notes The figures for Regional Development Grants allow for the deferment of payments between June 1979 and November 1982.

Constant price series calculated using the implicit deflator for gross fixed capital formation.

* Official target.

SOURCES Department of Trade and Industry, *The Government's Expenditure Plans* (1984, 1985).

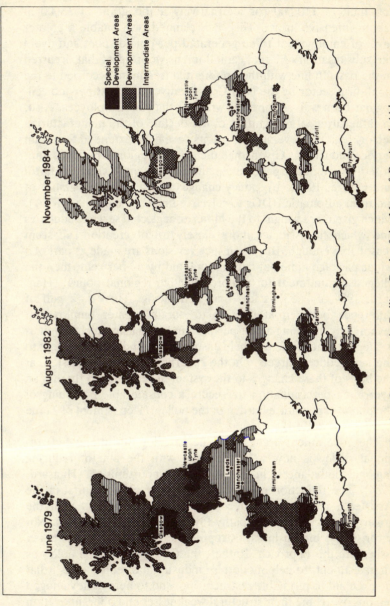

FIGURE 8.4 *The Thatcher Government's Rolling Back of the Map of Regional Aid*

SOURCE Department of Trade and Industry.

money from regional aid is to be achieved by imposing a cost-per-job limit of £10 000 (or alternatively a job grant of £3000 in labour-intensive firms). This, it is claimed, will enable a greater level of employment to be generated per pound spent and avoid the subsidisation of large, capital-intensive projects that occurred in the past. In line with the preferential treatment accorded to the small-firm sector by the New Conservatives, the cost-per-job ceiling has been waived for firms with less than 200 employees. Also, in rather ironical recognition of the decline of the manufacturing sector, regional development grants have been extended to certain service industries. Given that the aim of regional policy is supposedly to reduce spatial inequalities in unemployment (Martin and Hodge, 1983a, b), policy changes which shift the balance of aid from automatic RDGs to selective financial assistance (RSA), which give more weight to the hitherto-neglected service industries and which tie assitance more closely to job-creation, all seem reasonable enough. But when such revisions are made as part of a wider package aimed at cutting total aid by 40 per cent, then the alleged commitment to 'a more effective regional policy' (Hansard, 1984, col. 53) is less than convincing. There is a gulf of difference between attempting to obtain greater employment leverage by imposing a cost-per-job limit, and using such a limit as a safeguard mechanism to help ensure that spending can be kept to the new reduced targets. On the government's own admission, at the basis of these changes to the system of regional aid there is an overriding determination to 'secure a considerable lightening of the public expenditure burden of the policy' (Department of Trade and Industry, 1984).

The government argues that the case for (an attenuated) regional policy is now a 'social' one, with the aim of reducing regional imbalances in employment opportunities (Hansard, 1984). The reduction of large automatic grants to capital in the Assisted Areas is also, of course, entirely consistent with the government's general antipathy towards industrial subsidies. Not surprisingly, big business, as represented by the CBI, has taken issue with this approach. Rather, the CBI sees regional policy as an investment 'to help modernise industry and reduce costs'; that is, as an aid to profitable restructuring, and to help disadvantaged regions overcome their structural weaknesses and poor innovation record, and thereby 'compete with the rest of the economy'

(*Financial Times*, 2 Feb. 1985). To argue the case for regional policy on purely 'social' grounds is misplaced. If a weak regional policy is pursued against a background of continued conditions of economic austerity and deflation its 'social' role is likely to be limited to spreading mass unemployment more 'fairly' around the country while providing little boost to overall economic activity or to local economic regeneration. This could lead to a continued outflow of skilled workers from the depressed areas and the erosion of the (taxable) resource base of the local public sector in such localities. The 'social' objective of reducing regional imbalances an employment would thus become yet more difficult and costly to achieve. Interestingly, if Assisted Area designation still followed the unemployment-rate criteria used prior to the review in 1979, by 1984 the Assisted Area map would have extended to account for all but 0.2 per cent of the British working population. Only 4 out of 380 travel-to-work areas would be without Assisted Area status. No doubt the public expenditure implications of this observation has figured prominently in the government's determination to roll back the map of regional aid.

But the run-down of regional policy is only one part of the dilution of industrial aid in general. In real terms government spending on industrial support declined by over 40 per cent between 1980–1 and 1983–4, just as state subsidies and protectionism increased among many of Britain's industrial rivals. Spending on public corporations was more than halved over this period, and because of the particular geographical distribution of these industries this is bound to have had a differential regional impact. Admittedly support for so-called 'constructive intervention' – aid for scientific and technological development and small firms, especially in 'sunrise' or 'leading-edge' sectors – has doubled since 1980–1, but the scale of this aid is minimal (£370 million in 1984–5) and still represents only 18 per cent of the aid budget of the Department of Trade and Industry.

Partly in response to the regional policy vacuum, partly in desperation, and partly in direct opposition to the economic policies of the government, since 1979 scores of local authorities have increased or developed their own economic initiatives to fight the impact and implications of industrial decline in their areas.[6] Local authorities of all political persuasions have become involved in some form of economic regeneration and job-creation schemes, but it has been the Labour-controlled large urban and metropolitan authorities that have taken the lead by setting up their own enterprise boards and economic development companies. It is no coincidence that some of the most interventionist forms of economic initiative are to be found in these authorities. But this is not to say that the policies and programmes being pursued by Labour-controlled authorities and their off-shoot industrial development bodies form a coherent or unified political-economic movement: the differences between them are as striking as their similarities. Thus the Greater London Enterprise Board (GLEB), for example, puts much greater emphasis on the need to 'restructure for labour', on promoting new forms of ownership and work organisation, especially co-operatives and municipal enterprises, and on mobilising and channelling new technologies towards 'socially useful production'. The acccent is on the quality of employment, not just the quantity of jobs maintained or created. The West Midlands Enterprise Board (WMEB), on the other hand, focuses its resources on purchasing equity stakes in the medium and large-firm sector where investments can have the greatest impact on preserving jobs in the county. And unlike GLEB, the WEB evaluates investments according to strict criteria of long-term commercial viability. At the same time, however, the large numbers of redundant skilled engineers in the area has provided a strong potential for small worker co-operatives in the West Midlands.

Each of these local initiatives, involving not just Greater London and West Midlands, but also several other major urban–industrial areas such as West Yorkshire, Cleveland, Lancashire, Merseyside, Tyne & Wear and Derbyshire Councils, has responded in its own particular way to the precise character of its industrial problems. But all are based on one or more of the following assumptions:

(i)   There should be a greater planning of production and investment involving firms, the local authority and workers;

(ii) Local authorities should not compete with one another for capital investments, but should evolve a development policy which is appropriate to their locality;

(iii) Firms need to be more accountable to the local area in terms of their employment and investment strategies;

(iv) There is a need to provide long-term capital, rather than short-term subsidies, in order to assist firms' financial restructuring and capital formation;

(v) Much greater use should be made of institutional finance for productive investment in industry.

Most of these local enterprise boards and economic development companies now have substantial capital funding, and many have utilised their own funds as a lever for mobilising private sector finance for industrial investment.

The radical nature of these local-authority economic initiatives, and particularly those of the large metropolitan authorities, has been strongly contested by the Thatcher government. Although local authorities are allowed to fund economic development programmes by raising the product of a 2 pence rate annually, and can harness private sector funds, if in so doing they exceed their overall spending targets imposed by central government they become liable to the government's system of financial penalities referred to earlier (Section 8.3). In addition, the government's decision to abolish the Metropolitan Councils in 1986 clearly has implications for the future of local economic initiatives in these areas. The growth of local authority involvement in economic development has unfortunately become caught up in the general conflict over local spending that now exists between the central and local state: the government believes that the increasing activity by local authorities in the economic development realm will hinder its own macroeconomic policies, yet the growth of local authority economic initiatives is in large part due to the frustration of local authorities with the impact of those policies. The reality is that for local economic regeneration one must look ultimately to the implementation of favourable, expansionary macroeconomic measures, because only central government has the resources and the power to significantly influence demand and investment. On the other hand, for effective local economic recovery to take place, central government should recognise the worth of local-authority-based initiatives – especially on the supply side – in contributing to national economic regeneration. The Conservative government is unwilling to concede any such recognition.

6. The Uneven Geography of 'Recovery'

The economic and social costs of the New Conservatism have been enormous. The promise has been that these have been necessary and inevitable in order to create the basis for economic recovery. Already several benefits are being claimed for the restructuring and 'recapitalisation' of the past five years: a major breakthrough in industrial efficiency, as evidenced by a marked rise in productivity; a recovery in corporate profitability; a greater realism in worker attitudes and expectations; a boom in small-firm growth; and an expansion of total employment.

There has been a sharp increase in productivity, a rise of 5 per cent per annum between 1980 and 1984, but whether this is an indication that a 'productivity miracle' in the making is not yet clear. Productivity normally behaves highly cyclically, at first falling as companies cut back output faster than employment, and then rising as labour is shed faster than output falls. That is, the worse the slump the greater the shake-out of labour and the more pronounced the rise in productivity (Figure 8.5). Certainly between 1979 and 1982 labour productivity moved almost exactly as one would predict in the light of previous recessions. Allowing for the reduced level of utilisation of resources the bulk of the rapid growth in productivity from late 1980 to late 1982 appears to have been due to the closure of inefficient plants and dishoarding of labour rather than to widespread changes in work practices. Since 1982 the slow upturn in manufacturing output has contributed to the further growth in productivity, but the latter has still reflected the continued fall in manufacturing employment. By 1984 labour productivity was 15 per cent above its 1979 level; but output in manufacturing was 9 per cent below its 1979 level and employment some 24 per cent lower.

What is probably happening is that productivity growth is returning to its pre-1973 trend (Buiter and Miller, 1983). Clearly, unless output growth increases, the rise in productivity will only be sustained by further labour shedding and/or an acceleration in the introduction of new work practices. The threat of closure, the government's anti-union posture and mass unemployment itself have undoubtedly undermined the power of organised labour. A number of firms have pushed through new systems of work organisation aimed at greater flexibility and intensity of worker effort (e.g. Rolls-Royce in 1982). Multi-skilling, flexible job assignments

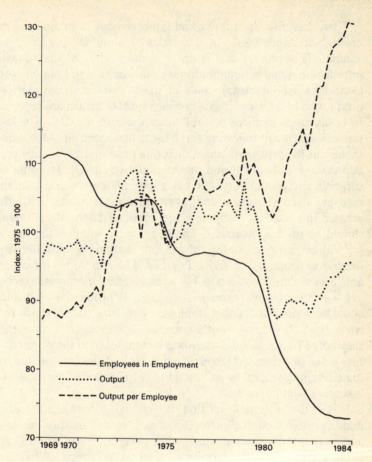

FIGURE 8.5 *Employment, Output and Productivity in UK Manufacturing, 1969–84*

SOURCE Department of Employment; *Employment Gazette* (various).

and the use of contract labour have been introduced as part of the drive to raise efficiency, and are likely to be increasingly on the corporate restructuring agenda. The weakening of the ability of the unions to resist new technology and work systems may be a necessary condition for securing additional productivity gains, but it is unlikely to be sufficient. While recession, government legislation and mass unemployment may have enabled 'managers to manage again', there is no guarantee that they will manage well.

There has also been a marked improvement in manufacturing profitability since 1982, of the order of about 20 per cent per annum. This reflects the jump in productivity associated with retrenchment and rationalisation, the slower growth in input costs (especially labour costs), and, in many instances, the shift of production to overseas plants in which rates of return are reported to be as much as three or four times those in the UK. The fact remains that even following the most pronounced slim-down and shake-out for fifty years, manufacturing profitability remains very depressed by historical and international standards. It would be surprising if profitability did not show an improvement in the recovery from recession, and, as in the case of productivity, the greater the scale of scrapping and rationalisation, the stronger should be the improvement. The key issue is whether the rise so far will be sustained sufficiently to halt the long-term underlying decline in profit rate described earlier. The conditions for profitable accumulation could possibly be established if economic recovery was strong and permanent enough, if productivity advance could be maintained, and if employers were able to hold down real wage rises. It is quite another matter, however, to assume that they could be sustained if there was a resurgence in the power and resistance of organised labour. In this context the continuation of high unemployment as a 'disciplinary mechanism' is likely to assume a vital importance.

It is at the regional level that the imbalance between the costs and uncertain 'benefits' of recession and 'recapitalisation' is most acute. The north–south dualism in the pace of decline seems likely to be replicated in the pattern of relative 'recovery'. While the major companies in the depressed peripheral and industrial regions of the north and west may now be leaner and fitter, the industrial and employment base of these regions is in consequence smaller and the potential for reindustrialisation weaker than in the southern half of the country. There are in fact several reasons for believing that the economic crisis in the depressed and peripheral regions will linger on even if there is a sustained improvement in the national economy. First, the decline in manufacturing jobs and the de-skilling of many of those remaining can be expected to continue throughout the 1980s. Most major British manufacturers are predicting further significant changes in their labour requirements, involving a modest increase in highly qualified technicians, a

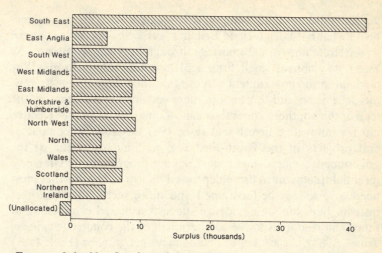

FIGURE 8.6 *Net Surplus of Business Starts over Stops, by Region,
1980–83*

SOURCE   *British Business.*

relatively small workforce of unskilled or semi-skilled personnel,
and few if any conventionally skilled workers. Part-time employment is also likely to continue to displace full-time employment,
and the direction and thrust of technological change seems certain
to cause additional job loss in the traditional sectors of manufacturing. All of these trends may be expected to impinge unfavour-
ably on the already hard-hit peripheral and depressed regions
because of their particular industrial structures and because of
their disadvantaged role in the division of labour within many of
the country's major multinational companies.

Second, it is these very same regions that have low net rates of
new firm formation (see Figure 8.6), and an under-representation
of innovative and technologically advanced industry. As is well
known the spatial distribution of the so-called 'sunrise' industries
is already distinctly skewed towards the more prosperous south
and east of Britain (see Chapter 10). Not only do the peripheral
and depressed industrial regions appear to have a low potential for
new-firm formation and science-based activity, they lack the cumulative concentration of qualified manpower, research and development functions, conducive market conditions, and financial

and infrastructural advantages, that seems to increasingly characterise what has been termed Britain's 'sun belt', that area south of
an arc stretching from Cambridge through Berkshire to Bristol. As
was noted above, small firms and new technology form a key
element in the government's 'recapitalisation' objectives. Its various schemes of aid to promote these sectors are accentuating the
lead of this southern zone: thus almost one-quarter of the selective
aid for innovative investment since 1981 has gone to companies
and projects in the South-East region. Similarly, none of the
government's employment and training programmes confer preferential treatment to those depressed industrial regions that most
need a reskilled, better-trained and more technical workforce:
instead, here too, the evidence suggests a biased channelling of
funds and resources to the southern half of the country (*Financial
Times*, 1983). According to one eminent geographer (Hall, 1981)
there is little hope of the new high-technology sectors developing in the old industrial areas; instead the free-market spatial
locus of the coming economic upturn based around the microelectronics revolution of the 'fifth Kondratieff cycle' will be in
the south of England. In Hall's view the government should not
attempt to divert this trend and seek to revive the ailing economies
of the depressed industrial regions and decaying inner cities, but
rather focus its efforts on preparing for the migration of surplus
labour to the new growth centres in the south wherein lie the main
hopes for future employment prospects. In other words the government should assess the 'economic trend' and plan to meet it rather
than question the trend or try to redirect it to other areas of
Britain. In essence this is a plea for a return to the discredited
labour transference ideas ('moving workers to the work') that
were tried in the economic crisis of the late 1920s and 1930s.

Third, most of the regions worst-hit by industrial decline have
also experienced the highest rate of cyclical decline in service
employment, so that this sector has provided even less of what
compensation if once did for the job loss in manufacturing. Moreover, in as much that the decline in manufacturing embodies a
structural shift towards a service-based economy, this trend too
appears to be benefiting the south and east rather than the industrial regions. The availability at the local level of a comprehensive
pool of producer and business services, the fastest-growing
branches of the service sector, is a vital factor for the present and

TABLE 8.8 *Regional Job Growth, March 1983–June 1985*

	Total	Male	Female		Manufacturing
			Part-time	Full-time	
South East	208	1	157	49	43
East Anglia	43	2	19	22	3
South-West	76	15	62	−2	1
West Midlands	22	−6	28	−1	−23
East Midlands	30	−14	34	9	1
Yorkshire–Humber	−16	−34	29	−11	−20
North-West	30	−31	70	−8	−41
North	−21	−39	19	−1	−18
Wales	10	−16	21	6	−9
Scotland	37	−27	58	5	−20
Great Britain	418	−148	497	69	−169

Change in employees in employment (000s)

Note Employment totals may not equal sums of male and female components because of rounding errors.

SOURCE *Employment Gazette* (Historical Supplement, April 1985, and October 1985), Department of Employment

future economic performance of the depressed areas. Yet business and producer services are already more concentrated and expanding faster in the southern half of Britain than elsewhere; and the emerging tendency towards the globalisation of the leading producer services is likely to militate further against the growth of such activities in the peripheral regions (see Chapter 9).

Finally, the government has recently made much of the fact that although unemployment is proving resistant to decline, there is considerable job growth occurring. It is true that between early 1983 and mid-1985 employment in Britain grew by 418 000 (2 per cent). However, this was made up of a rise in female employment of 566 000 and a fall in male jobs of 148 000. Moreover, 88 per cent of the increase in female employment was in part-time work (Table 8.8). This general pattern is found across almost all of the regions. But, in addition, it is clear that, thus far, the rise in employment has been overwhelmingly a feature of the south and east of the country: more than 80 per cent of new job growth has been in the four regions of the South-East, East Anglia,

South-West and East Midlands (whciht together account for 52 per cent of total employment). On the evidence to date, therefore, the geography of this increasingly publicised 'recovery' in employment is distinctly uneven: not only has the industrial north and west of Britain suffered the largest proportionate decline in employment over 1979–83, but these same regions are now failing to share on equal terms in any new job growth that occurs. In fact these depressed areas are still losing male jobs, whereas male employment in the South-East, East Anglia and South-West regions has actually increased slightly.

If the combined economic impact of recession and Thatcherism has been regionally divisive, so too are the signs of 'recovery'. The cyclical recovery since 1982, induced as much by credit-financed consumer spending as by a fundamental revival of investment, has as yet done little to raise employment hopes in the ailing industrial areas, and holds out few prospects of a major revival of manufacturing jobs. The depressed regions of Britain, including now the country's manufacturing heartland, would seem to occupy a distinctly unfavourable position with regard to the possible sources of industrial and economic regeneration based on market forces. The Thatcher government's aims to effect a restructuring of Britain, being identified not so much with a significant expansion of manufacturing and employment, but with a smaller, more technologically advanced, competitive, and increasingly internationalised industrial sector, have inherently favoured the southern half of the nation. The economic gap between north and south that was already growing during the second half of the 1970s, has widened considerably since 1979 (Table 8.9). Under the New Conservatism the restructuring of regional Britain has served merely to extend and intensify the spatial economic disparities that for more than fifty years previous successive governments have sought, albeit with only partial success, to reduce. In fact, spatial inequalities are an integral feature of the Thatcher government's drive to secure a new structure of accumulation, a recapitalised Britain. The 'new consensus' contains – indeed depends upon – a new set of asymmetrical coalitions and agreements: high-technology industry, workers in growth sectors and residents in the southern (and rural) regions of the country are the main beneficiaries; while other groups, such as the unions, low-income and unskilled workers, urban residents and workers in older, more traditional industries

TABLE 8.9 *Regional Gross Domestic Product Per Head, as a Percentage of the UK Average*

	1974	1979	1981	1983
South-East	113.1	115.3	115.9	121.5
East Anglia	92.8	94.8	97.0	97.1
South-West	93.3	93.6	95.3	95.8
West Midlands	100.5	95.8	90.4	88.1
East Midlands	95.9	95.5	95.5	94.8
Yorkshire–Humberside	94.8	93.4	92.4	91.4
North-West	96.6	96.6	95.1	94.1
North	91.1	92.0	94.5	89.6
Wales	86.5	86.5	84.6	83.8
Scotland	96.1	95.4	98.4	96.4

Note UK base figure excludes North Sea activities

SOURCE *Economic Trends* and Department of Employment

and regions, are required to bear the main sacrifices and constraints (see Connolly, 1981). For the New Conservatives it is rational for all parties and sections to consent to this revised economic and social terrain because, it is contended, 'there is no alternative' scenario which can cope with the problems of industrial stagnation, unemployment, inflation and poor worker motivation that plague the British economy. A commitment to Thatcherism, in other words, is a commitment to the intensification of selective economic austerity.

Notes

1. This is a distillation of the varying lists of factors invoked by different followers of the New Conservatism and the radical Right as 'explanations' of Britain's economic decline. A typical list is that drawn up by Sir Keith Joseph (1979b):

   I reckon there are six, six poisons which wreck a Country's prosperity and full employment: excessive government spending, high direct taxation, egalitarianism, excessive nationalisation, a politicised trade union movement associated with Luddism, and an anti-enterprise culture. Six of them. Now most of our rivals have one of these poisons, some have two; we're the only country in the world that has all six. And sometimes I think that the miracle is that with all of these six poisons in our system we still do as relatively well as we do.

2. This disaffection with the Keynesian social democratic state by the radical Right clearly bears some striking parallels with the Marxist critique of the late capitalist (Welfare) State as found, for example, in O'Connor (1973), Gough (1979) and Offe (1984). Like the radical Right, these Marxist writers all point to the basic lack of correspondence in advanced capitalist societies between their political and economic structures, a lack of fit that is the result of an overload of demands that the state cannot absorb without creating inflation and jeopardising the profitability of capitalist enterprise. For the Marxist the interventionist state of recent decades is now faced today with a growing fundamental conflict between the twin imperatives of accumulation and legitimation. Although the radical Right and the Marxist left thus share a common concern, their terminologies and values obviously differ markedly. While the radical Right distrusts the Welfare State as a vehicle for collectivism, Marxists view the capitalist state as an obstacle to socialism. For the radical Right a free-market exchange economy promotes economic efficiency and enhances individual freedom; for Marxists the institution of free-market competition divides society into antagonistic classes and generates conflict and inequality. According to Hodgson (1984) both schools ignore certain insights of the other: there is just as little recognition of the importance of social class and distributional conflict in the literature of the free-market economics as of the usefulness of markets in Marxist literature.

3. As such the 'monetarism' of the Thatcher government is more than just a new set of economic nostrums. It is intended to be a remodernising, anti-state doctrine, a new operational framework to deal with the problems of governing the UK. It seeks to reverse the drift towards 'corporatism', and to manage the economy on the basis of policies less open to interference from awkward domestic influences such as unions. Despite its anti-interventionist anti-state rhetoric, the political economy of Thatcherism rests firmly on the reassertion of central autonomy and control not only in the vital field of macroeconomic management, but also increasingly in the microeconomic realm of the labour market, industrial relations, employment conditions and so on (Leys, 1985).

4. For anyone interested in British territorial politics the Thatcher government's approach to the role and financing of local government marks an important phase in the development of centre–local relationships. The post-war dual polity, resting on the relative autonomy of both central and local government, has proved to be at variance with the aims, methods and success of Thatcherite economic manage-

ment. In consequence local autonomy has been significantly curtailed, and the old territorial code replaced by a new system of more extensive and effective central control over local authorities.

5. For more detailed discussions of this trend towards greater internationalisation of British capital see *Labour Research* (1983 a, b). This dimension of de-industrialisation is not confined to traditional sectors of manufacturing. The electrical and electronics sector, the type of industry that the government has highlighted as providing the basis for the future of the British economy, lost 42 000 British-based jobs between 1978 and 1982, while expanding its overseas workforce by 33 000 during the same period.

6. The development of economic initiatives by local government over the past few years is only one aspect of the burgeoning 'localism' movement that is under way. The private sector has also become involved in promoting local economic regeneration. As part of a growing so-called sense of 'corporate social responsibility', several of the country's largest industrial companies (many of which have been shedding large numbers of employees) now provide support, in cash or in kind, for community redevelopment programmes in areas of high unemployment. Also most of these companies have been involved in the establishment of local enterprise agencies and trusts, of which there are now about 200 scattered across Britain. Typically these local enterprise agencies, run with the assistance of local firms and often in partnership with local authorities, are aimed at fostering new small-business activity, the bulk of which to date has been in the service sectors.

Bibliography

Arnott, T. and Krieger, J. (1982) 'Thatcher and Reagan: State Theory and the Hyper-Capitalist Regime', *New Political Science*, **8**.

Bacon, R. W. and Eltis, W. A. (1978) *Britain's Economic Problem: Too Few Producers*, (London: Macmillan) (2nd ed).

Best, M. and Humphries, J. (1981) 'Thatcherism', *Democracy*, **1**, **3**, pp. 37–51.

British Business (1984) 'International Comparisons of Profitability, 1955–82', *British Business*, 28 Sep, pp. 166–7.

Brittan, S. (1977) *The Economic Consequences of Democracy* (London: Temple Smith).

Buiter, W. H. and Miller, M. H. (1983) 'The Macro-economic Consequences of a Change in Regime: The UK under Mrs Thatcher', *Discussion Paper 179* (London School of Economics and Political Science: Centre for Labour Economics).

Callaghan, James (1976) *Report of the Annual Conference of the Labour Party*, (London: Labour Party).

Conolly, W. (1981) 'The Politics of Re-industrialisation', *Democracy*, **1**, 3, pp. 9–21.

Committee of Public Accounts (1984) *Regional Industrial Incentives*, House of Commons Report 378, Session 1983–84 (London: HMSO).

Department of Trade and Industry (1984) Regional Industrial Policy, *Press Notice 681* (Nov) (London: DTI).

Financial Times (1982) 'Overseas Subsidiaries can keep UK Parents in Profit', 18 May.

Financial Times (1983) 'Rich Areas Favoured by Share-out of MSC Funds', 21 Apr.

Financial Times (1984) *Wrestling with Recovery* (London: The Financial Times Ltd).

Financial Times (1985) 'Main Aim of Regional Policy Should be to Increase Competitiveness', 2 Feb.

Gaffikin, F. and Nickson, A. (1984) *Jobs Crisis and the Multi-Nationals: The Case of the West Midlands* (Birmingham: Birmingham Trade Union Resource Centre).

Gamble, A. (1979) 'The Free Economy and the Strong State', *The Socialist Register* (London: Merlin Press) pp. 1–25.

Gough, I. (1975) 'State Expenditure in Advanced Capitalism', *New Left Review*, **92**, pp. 53–92.

Gough, I. (1979) *The Political Economy of the Welfare State* (London: Macmillan).

Grant, W. (1982) *The Political Economy of Industrial Policy* (London: Butterworth).

Hall, P. (1981) 'The Geography of the Fifth Kondratieff Cycle', *New Society*, 26 Mar, pp 535–7.

Hansard (1979) 'Statement on Regional Industrial Policy by Sir Keith Joseph', *House of Commons Parliamentary Debates – Session 1979-80, Official Reports*, **970**, cols 1302–20.

Hansard (1984) 'Co-operative Development Agency and Industrial Development Bill, Considered', *House of Commons Parliamentary Debates – Session 1983–4, Official Reports* 61, cols 21–103.

Harte, G. F. and Owen, D. L. (1985) 'Fighting De-industrialisation: The Role of Local Authority Social Audits', Department of Accounting and Business Method (University of Edinburgh), mimeo, 35 pp.

Heald, D. (1983) *Public Expenditure: Its Defence and Reform* (Oxford: Martin Robertson).

HM Government (1979) *The Government's Expenditure Plans 1980/81*, Cmnd 7746, (London: HMSO).

HM Government (1983) *Regional Industrial Development*, Cmnd 9111, (London: HMSO).

Hodgson, G. (1981) *Labour at the Crossroads* (Oxford: Martin Robertson).

Hodgson, G. (1984) *The Democratic Economy: A New Look at Planning, Markets and Power* (London: Penguin Books).

Joseph, Sir Keith (1976a) 'Moral and Material Benefits of the Market Order', in Joseph, Sir Keith, *Stranded on the Middle Ground: Reflec-*

tions on Circumstances and Policies,(London: Centre for Policy Studies), pp. 57–66.

Joseph, Sir Keith (1976b) 'The Quest for Common Ground', in Joseph, Sir Keith, *Stranded on the Middle Ground: Reflections on Circumstances and Policies* (London: Centre for Policy Studies) pp. 19–34.

Joseph, Sir Keith (1978) 'Conditions for Fuller Employment', in Thatcher, M., Howe G., and Joseph, Sir K., *The Right Angle: Three Studies in Conservatism* (London: Bow Group).

Joseph, Sir Keith (1979a) *Solving the Union Problem is the Key to Britain's Recovery* (London: Centre for Policy Studies).

Joseph, Sir Keith (1979b) 'Transcript of *The Charlton Interview*', 30 July (London: BBC Television).

Keegan, W. (1984) *Mrs Thatcher's Economic Experiment* (London: Allen Lane).

Kilpatrick, A. and Lawson, T. (1980) 'On the Nature of Industrial Decline in the U.K.', *Cambridge Journal of Economics*, **4**, **1**, pp. 85–100.

Labour Research (1983a) 'Multinationals: Better at Exporting Jobs than Goods, **72**, **4** (London, Labour Research Department).

Labour Research (1983b) 'Unemployment, Multinationals and Manufacturing Employment', **72**, **5** (London, Labour Research Department).

Lawson, Nigel (1980) *The New Conservatism* (London: Centre for Policy Studies).

Lawson, Nigel (1982) *What's Right with Britain* (London: Centre for Policy Studies).

Leys, C. (1985) Thatcherism and British Manufacturing, *New Left Review*, **151**, pp. 5–25.

Littlechild, S. C. (1978) *The Fallacy of the Mixed Economy*, Hobart Paper 80 (London: Institute of Economic Affairs).

Lloyd, P. and Shutt, J. (1985) 'Recession and Restructuring in the North West Region, 1975–82: The Implications of Recent Events', in Massey, D. and Meegan, R. (eds) *Politics and Method: Contrasting Studies in Industrial Geography* (London: Methuen) pp. 16–60.

Martin, R. L. (1982) 'Job Loss and the Regional Incidence of Redundancy in the Current Recession', *Cambridge Journal of Economics*, **6**, pp. 375–95.

Martin, R. L. (1984) 'Redundancies, Labour Turnover and Employment Contraction in the Recession: A Regional Analysis', *Regional Studies*, **18**, **6**, pp. 445–58.

Martin, R. L. (1985) 'Monetarism Masquerading as Regional Policy? The Government's New System of Regional Aid', *Regional Studies*, **19**, **4**, pp. 379–388.

Martin, R. L. (1986) 'Industrial Restructuring, Labour Shake-out and the Geography of Recession', ch. 1 in Danson, M. (ed.) *Recession and Redundancy: Restructuring the Regions?* (Norwich: Geobooks) pp. 1–22.

Martin, R. L. and Hodge, J. S. C. (1983a) 'The Reconstruction of British

Regional Policy, 1: The Crisis of Conventional Practice', *Government and Policy*, **1**, pp. 133–52.

Martin, R. L. and Hodge, J. S. C. (1983b) 'The Reconstruction of British Regional Policy, 2: Towards a New Agenda', *Government and Policy*, **1**, pp. 317–40.

Miller, S. M. (1978) 'The Recapitalisation of Capitalism', *International Journal of Urban and Regional Research*, **2**, pp. 202–12.

Minford, P. (1982) 'Trade Unions Destroy a Million Jobs', *Journal of Economic Affairs*, **2**, **1**, pp. 73–9.

Minford, P. (1983) *Unemployment: Cause and Cure* (Oxford: Martin Robertson).

Mouffe, C. (1981) 'Democracy and the New Right', *Politics and Power*, **4**, pp. 221–35.

O'Connor, J. (1973) *The Fiscal Crisis of the State* (New York: St Martin's Press).

Offe, C. (1984) *Contradictions of the Welfare State* (London: Hutchinson).

Pickvance, C. G. (1981) 'Policies as Chameleons: An Interpretation of Regional and Office Policy in Britain', in Dear, M. and Scott, A. J. (eds) *Urbanisation and Urban Planning in Capitalist Society* (London: Methuen) pp. 231–65.

Riddell, P. (1983) *The Thatcher Government* (Oxford: Martin Robertson).

Rowley, C. K. (1979) 'Liberalism and Collective Choice', *National Westminster Bank Quarterly Review* (May) pp. 11–22.

Stapleton, R. G. (1981) 'Why Recession Benefits Britain', *Journal of Economic Affairs*, **1**, **2**, pp. 7–11.

Taylor, J. (1982) 'Productive Potential in the UK Manufacturing Sector: How Much is Being Used?', *Working Paper* (University of Lancaster: Department of Economics).

Taylor, J. (1983) 'Unused Productive Capacity in the UK, 1950–1982', *Working Paper* (University of Lancaster: Department of Economics).

Thatcher, Margaret (1978) 'The Ideals of An Open Society', in Thatcher, M., Howe, G., and Joseph, Sir K., *The Right Angle: Three Studies in Conservatism* (London: Bow Group).

Thatcher, Margaret; Howe, Geoffrey; and Joseph, Sir Keith (1978) *The Right Angle: Three Studies in Conservatism* (London: Bow Group).

Tomlinson, J. (1983) 'Does Mass Unemployment Matter?', *National Westminster Bank Quarterley Review* (Feb) pp. 35–45.

Townsend, A. R. (1982) *The Impact of Recession* (London: Croom Helm).

Wenban-Smith, G. (1981) 'A Study of the Movements of Productivity in Individual Industries in the UK', *National Institute Economic Review*, **97**, pp. 57–61.

Wilkinson, G. and Jackson, P. M. (1981) *Public Sector Employment in the U.K.* (University of Leicester: Public Sector Economics Research Centre).

Williams, K., Williams, J. and Thomas, D. (1983) *Why Are the British Bad at Manufacturing?* (London: Routledge & Kegan Paul).

Wragg, R. and Robertson, J. (1978) 'Britain's Industrial Performance Since the War', *Department of Employment Gazette*, **86**, pp. 512–19.

9
Producer Services and the Post-industrial Space Economy

PETER DANIELS

1. Introduction

The shift from an industrial to a post-industrial or post-affluent (Gappert, 1982) economic system is now well under way in Britain. While there remains a great deal to evaluate in detail, it is generally recognised that advanced economic systems, such as that of Britain, are undergoing some fundamental changes. Relative to the evolution of agricultural to manufacturing-based economies over the last 200 years the recent changes are rapid; they have only been manifest during the last 20–25 years. But the events are perhaps best characterised as a transition which has not been readily recognised by academic, central government and other observers whose perception of an economic system founded upon manufacturing industry has exerted an inertia which is out of proportion to its contemporary significance.

The change was spotted early by Clark (1940), who drew attention to the significance of the tertiary or service sector, but the 'belief is still widespread that society can survive . . . without much servicing outside what can be performed through do-it-yourself methods' (Gottman, 1983, p. 62). As manufacturing industry has become more efficient, capital intensive, productive and, in consequence, less labour intensive its share of national employment has declined dramatically; between 1974 and 1984 some 2.3 million jobs in manufacturing were lost while service industries expanded by some 1.1 million. Between 1976 and 1981 the contribution of manufacturing industries to gross domestic product (GDP) decreased from 28.2 per cent to 24.2 per cent (Central Statistical Office, 1983) while the growth rate in manufacturing industry in the UK as a whole was much lower than in non-manufacturing industry. The difference in average growth rates between these two sectors, if reflected across the Economic Planning Regions, clearly disadvantages those regions with a large manufacturing sector and favours regions at the other end of the scale with more favourable industrial structures. Of course some of the employment contraction in the manufacturing sector has been a by-product of the nation's macroeconomic condition during recent years, but this only partially disguises an underlying trend, as elsewhere (Greenfield, 1966; Stanback, 1979; Polese, 1982), which involves a gradual change of emphasis from goods producing to information handling activities which are predominantly concentrated amongst service rather than manufacturing industries. Some care must be taken, however, in equating this with a decline in manufacturing; it has been suggested by Gershuny (1978), for example, that some services are being substituted with domestic facilities provided by durable goods such as freezers, washing machines or video recorders. This creates a demand for goods-related services (repair, maintenance, installation) provided by the manufacturers or their agents.

The contraction of the manufacturing sector has been described as de-industrialisation (Blackaby, 1978; Thirlwall, 1982). This concept fits in with the classical theories of the economic development process whereby national economies evolve through a sequence beginning with the dominance of agriculture, followed by manufacturing and, ultimately, services (Clark, 1940; Rostow, 1960; Fuchs, 1968). But there is some disagreement about how best to define de-industrialisation (see, for example, Thirlwall, 1982); it is most important here, however, to stress that it seems inappropriate to equate it solely with an absolute loss of jobs by manufacturing industries. Rather it represents a wider process of job loss from all industries, *including services*. Some of the latter are also losing more jobs than they create because the service which they provide is outmoded or has been replaced by modern technology.

Industrial restructuration may be the more accurate way to characterise a process in which selected industries, and their associated occupations, have steadily moved towards a more pivotal position in overall economic structure. Consequently, they now exert a significant influence on the economic potential of regions and cities, many of which are endeavouring to adjust to the post-industrial transition, within the British space economy. The task is not straightforward because, although there has been a steady expansion of service industries insufficient jobs have been created to replace those shed by manufacturing industries; industrial restructuration is not necessarily a panacea for dealing with major socio-economic problems such as unemployment or the deep-seated difficulties confronting the inner cities. Indeed, this may to some degree explain the low esteem ascribed to service industries (see Bacon and Eltis, 1976, for example), but this should not be allowed to overshadow their current and future importance in the space economy where knowledge and information availability is just as important as a raw material in the production process as the more conventional physical inputs. Yet in the absence of any detailed knowledge of the location behaviour of services or their interplay with other components of the business and social environment it is unlikely that more effective ways can be found to maximise their contribution to the structural change and adjustment within the space economy which seems an inevitable corollary of advanced economic development incorporating a significant, and growing, services sector.

This chapter cannot provide detailed answers to these issues since much research remains to be undertaken. Attention is therefore confined to an elaboration, using limited recent evidence, of an important division within service industries between producer and consumer activities, the broad regional patterns revealed by the former, some preliminary evidence about their location and related behaviour from some recent studies, and an attempt to assess their significance in the space economy and whether it will be useful to try to influence their growth and locational preferences.

2. Some Basic Empirical Evidence

The transition to a service-based economy has been equated with absolute employment expansion but relative, and, in some cases, absolute decline of individual service activities, either as a result of market forces such as in the case of transport and communication or consequent upon public expenditure policies and their consequences for employment in public administration and defence. Some 45 000 jobs in transport and communication were lost between 1978 and 1981 (just over 3 per cent of the 1981 total) and 38 000 by the latter (Department of Employment, 1983a). This compares with an increase during the same period of 128 000 jobs in insurance, banking and finance (equivalent to 9.8 per cent of the 1981 total) and 169 000 in miscellaneous services which includes a number of publicly-provided services such as education and medical services which have increased their employment demand rapidly during the 1970s (equivalent to 6.7 per cent of the 1981 total). The contribution of miscellaneous services (together with professional and scientific services) to GDP has therefore improved from 21.2 per cent in 1976 to 22.8 per cent in 1981 and in insurance, banking and finance from 8.1 per cent to 9.1 per cent. The absolute change in the GDP of this sector (117.6 per cent) was also larger than for any other group. The contribution to GDP by the other service industries has remained the same or even declined and the change in the value of GDP has been much the same or lower than the GB average.

Service industry expansion has therefore been selective and has mainly taken place in those services which 'business firms, non-profit institutions, and governments provide and usually sell to the producer rather than to the consumer' (Greenfield, 1966, p. 1). Collectively, these are classified as producer (or intermediate) services and, in theory at least, are distinguishable from consumer or private services which are largely provided in response to final demand. Hence, insurance, banking and finance, together with transport and communication, can be used as surrogates for producer services in analyses of, for example, regional economic structure and change (Keeble, Owens and Thompson, 1981). But such a definition is too narrow since it neglects the wider incidence of producer service functions within the service industries as a whole. Also it is now possible to make use of the finer detail now available as classes, groups and activities within the revised Standard Industrial Classification (SIC) introduced in 1980 (replacing the previously-used 1968 SIC). An attempt is therefore made here to measure the size and distribution of producer activities within the service sector, both at the aggregate national level and in relation to the Standard Regions for which the most recent data are available.

Inevitably, perhaps, it is easier to articulate the concept of a producer/consumer dichotomy within service industries than it is to translate it into its empirical and ultimately, spatial, attributes. As Greenfield (1966) observed it is difficult to find suitable measures for dividing activities into their producer and consumer components, a difficulty which arises largely from the fact that relatively few services can be readily assigned to one or the other. Census and other returns containing employment or output information do not distinguish between the proportion of workers engaged in, or output attributable to, producer functions. One solution is to introduce another category of services which can be described as 'mixed' (see Marquand, 1980) since they are neither mainly producer- nor mainly consumer-oriented. Rather than assign activities in this way, however, it may be more constructive to attempt to estimate the proportion of total employment in each service group and activity of the 1980 SIC which is devoted to producer functions. The guidelines for undertaking such an exercise are very limited, however, and the resulting estimates (Table 9.1) are first approximations based on earlier work by Marquand (1979) and more particularly by Greenfield (1966). The latter used detailed breakdowns of revenue for a small number of industries together with an analysis of inter-industry input–output tables to derive ratios for the proportion of total employment in service industry allocated to producer/non-producer functions. This task is formidable and even more difficult when trying to identify producer services within public administration. The finer detail provided by the classes and groups listed in Table 9.1 is helpful, but still far from satisfactory.

On the basis of his analysis, Greenfield estimated that 12.5 per cent of total US employment in 1950 was in producer services, rising to 13.2 per cent in 1960. The estimates in Table 9.1 suggest that the growth trend indicated in Greenfield's data has been continuing so that by 1981 it is estimated that almost 22 per cent of employment in Britain was producer-oriented; or one in three jobs within the service sector. Slightly less than half of the producer service employment is attached to transport and communication and insurance, banking and finance although the latter has three times as many producer jobs as expected from its overall share of service sector employment. Some 25 per cent of producer service employment is attached to distribution and related activities and to other services (including the public sector). Thus, producer service

TABLE 9.1 *Estimated Distribution of Producer and Consumer Employment within the Service Sector, by Industry, Great Britain, 1981*

SIC (1980) Division and Class	in employment[1]	Total employees (000) producer	consumer	% producer
Wholesale distribution	840	840	*	100.0
Dealing in scrap and waste metals	23	23	*	100.0
Commission agents	13	13	*	100.0
Retail distribution	2 060	*	2 060	*
Hotels and catering	938	234.5	703.5	25.0
Repair of consumer goods and vehicles	238	59.5	178.5	25.0
DISTRIBUTION, HOTELS AND CATERING REPAIRS	4 112	1 170	2 942	28.5
Railways	174	87	87	50.0
Other inland transport	404	208	196	51.5
Sea transport	66	50	16	75.0
Air transport	70	35	35	50.0
Supporting services to transport	100	100	*	100.0
Miscellaneous transport services and storage	168	151	17	90.0
Postal services and telecommunications	424	212	212	50.0
TRANSPORT AND COMMUNICATION	1 406	843	563	60.0
Banking and finance	478	239	239	50.0

Insurance, except compulsory social security	225	169	56	75.0
Business services	831	831	*	100.0
Renting of movables	91	91	*	100.0
Owning and dealing in real estate	98	98	*	100.0
BANKING, FINANCE, INSURANCE, BUSINESS SERVICES AND LEASING	1 723	1 428	295	82.9
Public administration, national defence and compulsory social security	1 505	752.5	752.5	50.0
Sanitary services	372	37	335	10.0
Education	1 422	142	1 288	10.0
Research and development	121	121	*	100.0
Medical services	1 285	*	1 285	*
Other services provided to the general public	552	*	552	*
Recreational and other cultural services	430	86	344	20.0
Personal services	180	*	180	*
OTHER SERVICES	5 867	1 138.5	4 736.5	19.4
ALL SERVICES	13 108	4 579.5	8 536.5	34.9
ALL INDUSTRIES AND SERVICES	21 148	–	–	21.7

Note [1] Employees in employment, Sep 1981 (000s).
*Zero (0), to negligible
SOURCE Estimates derived from base data in Department of Employment (1983) *Employment Gazette*, Occasional Supplement no. 1 (May) table 4.

employment is not insignificant in these two sectors where it represents 28.5 per cent and 19.4 per cent respectively of total employment. With almost 4.6 million workers in producer service employment it is clearly not an insignificant component of national employment.

3. The Demand for Producer Services

The growth in demand for producer services can be traced to several, and sometimes interrelated, factors. Assuming that business enterprises are anxious to sustain any given level of output at an acceptable cost it may be necessary to establish whether any of the inputs can be obtained at lower cost from outside the firm. This is especially relevant for the assembly of specialised inputs which may only be required very infrequently, but are important when the demand does arise. In these circumstances it will very likely not be cost-effective to maintain in-house labour to occasionally provide the input when, because several firms may require the same input at different times, an external organisation can be engaged full-time in providing it. This will lower the unit cost for the external organisation of providing the input as well as to the user. It is also likely that it can also be supplied more efficiently and exactly at the time required. Greenfield (1966, p. 38) equates this with the principle of comparative advantage in that 'a firm will purchase services from other firms which may have absolute and/or relative advantage over itself in the performance of a specified function'. A good example is the recent expansion of computer services which assist other companies with the task of choosing suitable computers, provide assistance with the installation and use of computer facilities, and devise procedures and programs which best fit the requirements of each client. Computer service bureaux have also developed to provide clients with time-sharing and batch facilities centred on a major installation operated by the computer service organisation.

The importance of comparative advantage will probably increase as enterprises are required to use recent advances in production, telecommunications and information technololgy to remain competitive (see, for example, Otway and Peltu, 1983; Hills, 1982). This will lead to changes in organisational structure and decision-making (Crozier, 1983; Simon, 1977) as well as allowing improvements in the quality or quantity of output, but the product or service must still be directed at the most appropriate segments of the market, and knowledge of this kind is obtainable through marketing and advertising research. Larger business enterprises will be able to operate departments concerned with these functions, but even they may still need to use specialised agencies to undertake studies outside the range of their own resources and expertise or because they value an independent assessment of product image or of their marketing strategy and prospects. Smaller firms will clearly have to 'buy in' this kind of specialist advice, especially if they plan to diversify or to expand market coverage. Finally, externally-purchased services provided by management consultants or financial analysts are required to give firms a detached perspective on their operations, management procedures or the prospects for growth, survival or diversification. In their efforts to streamline costs or to impose as much simplicity as possible on their internal organisation or the range of staff which they retain, for example, business enterprises have provided an ideal environment for stimulating the development of existing, new and as yet unrealised producer service functions.

4. The Spatial Distribution of Producer Services

Assuming that the demand and ultimately the growth of producer services is going to continue it is necessary to consider whether this will have any consequences for the British space economy. As technical and business services become more specialised, business enterprises are going to increasingly rely on imported inputs and it then follows that the supply of such services could have a significant influence on the relative development of the interacting components of the space economy; the urban places, regions, economic activities and the flows of goods, people and information which join them together. The rules applicable to the operation, structure and distribution of economic activities in a system founded upon a post-industrial economy could well be different to those associated with the industrial phase because of the growing importance of intangible rather than tangible inputs and the rather different locational behaviour exhibited by the producer services which supply many of these new types of input.

Some clues to the locational behaviour of producer services are provided in Table 9.2 where the net changes in employees in employment in the ten Economic Planning Regions between 1978 and 1981 are expressed as a proportion of the total change for manufacturing, services and all industries and services. Some 46 per cent of the net increase of 0.2 million employed in service industries was located in the South-East. Only two regions, the North and Yorkshire–Humberside, recorded a reduction in the numbers employed in services. Some disaggregation of this information, but using the industry groups defined in the 1968 SIC and defining insurance, banking, finance and business services and professional and scientific services as the principal producer activities, is possible. It is apparent that insurance, banking, finance and business services have increased their labour forces in every region with the South-East again associated with a large proportion (49 per cent) of the net increase of 128 000. The only other services to achieve absolute increases in almost every region are miscellaneous services, which include some producer employment such as that in research and development. The emphasis on expansion in the south-east is, however, rather less pronounced (35.5 per cent of the total increase of 169 000). Employment in professional and scientific services actually contracted or remained stable in all but two regions, the South-East and Scotland, so that the net change is only marginal (2000). All the other service industries show reductions in the numbers employed, but the changes in absolute terms are much smaller than those in the manufacturing sector where substantial reductions have taken place in every SIC category; mechanical engineering and vehicles losing some 300 000 jobs between them in three years. Nevertheless, industries with a large producer-service component have therefore been prominent in the limited employment expansion which has taken place between 1978 and 1981 and spatial bias is a common feature.

More detailed confirmation is provided by disaggregating the estimates for producer-service employment given in Table 9.1 into their regional components, by industry class, in 1981 (Table 9.3). This is not, of course, the most satisfactory scale at which to examine the data, but at the time of writing, apart from marginally more disaggregated information for the South-East region, this is the only level for which recent and comparatively detailed employment information is available. Data problems are a recurring lament among those interested in the recent, let alone the histori-

TABLE 9.2 *Change in Employees in Employment in Services, by Region, Great Britain, 1978–81*[1]

Region	Service industry orders (SIC 1968) (000)[2]							Manu-facturing	All industries and services	Per cent change
	XXII	XXIII	XXIV	XXV	XXVI	XXVII	Services			
South-East	−8	1	55	11	60	−20	99	−220	−144	2.0
East Anglia	3	2	5	−1	8	−1	16	−18	−7	4.0
South-West	*	−7	8	1	18	−5	16	−56	−41	1.6
West Midlands	−5	−1	13	−17	16	7	14	−216	−217	1.3
East Midlands	3	3	6	−2	17	−13	13	−84	−77	1.7
Yorkshire and Humberside	−6	−2	9	−6	4	−2	−2	−139	−158	−0.2
North-West	−17	*	13	*	26	−5	16	−182	−186	1.1
North	−4	−4	5	−4	3	−3	−6	−80	−115	−0.9
Wales	−3	−3	6	*	7	−4	3	−77	−84	0.5
Scotland	−6	5	8	20	10	7	44	−119	−97	3.6
Great Britain	−43	−5	128	2	169	−38	214	−1 193	−1 126	1.6

Notes [1] June 1978 to September 1981
[2] XXII (Transport and communication); XXIII (Distributive trades); XXIV (Insurance, banking, finance and business services); XXV (Professional and scientific services); XXVI (Miscellaneous services); XXVII (Public administration and defence)
* zero (0), to negligible

cal, development of the service sector and its components. Until the 1981 Census of Population economic activity statistics are published it will be difficult to examine at group and activity level the location trends of producer-service employment during the period since the last Population Census (1971). The cross-sectional information given in Table 9.3 does, however, suggest some significant inequalities in the regional distribution of producer-service employment when measured against all service employment and total employment in each region.

Convergence indices have been used to show that producer-service employment has yet to achieve a regional distribution which mirrors the distribution of total employment (Table 9.3). With less than 34 per cent of national employment but over 42 per cent of national producer-service employment, all the service industry classes in the South-East have indices greater than 100, i.e. that region's share of employment in each class is higher than the region's share of total employment. But the degree of regional surplus varies and is largest for insurance, banking, finance and business services, in which almost 83 per cent of employment has been estimated as producer-related (see Table 9.1). This is also the class revealing the greatest range for the convergence index which reaches as low as 62 per cent in three regions: the North, the West and East Midlands. Outside the south-east, only the south-west region has a score for the index which exceeds 90 per cent. The ranges revealed by the other service industry classes, in which producer-related employment, although presently is less prominent, are narrower and a number of regions outside the South-East also have index values greater than 100. Producer employment in Other Services is notable in this regard; the prominence of public sector employment and policies for the dispersal of civil servants from the South-East to other regions (Civil Service Department, 1973) have probably contributed to the high convergence indices for Wales and for Scotland. In general, however, it is possible to conclude that every region outside the South-East has less producer-service employment than would be expected from its share of all employment in manufacturing and services.

It must be stressed that the spatial distribution conveyed in Table 9.3 may understate the difference between the South-East and the rest of the country. An assumption has been made that the proportion of producer employment in each industry class and

TABLE 9.3 Convergence Indices for Producer-Service Employment, by Industry Class and Region, Great Britain, 1981

Region	Convergence index (SIC 1968)[1]				Share (%)	
	Distribution, hotels and catering	Transport and communication	Banking, finance, insurance, business services	Other services	Total employment	Producer services
South-East	106.8	128.9	146.0	111.5	33.9	42.2
East Anglia	106.3	103.1	81.2	103.1	3.2	3.1
South-West	115.3	81.9	90.2	100.0	7.2	7.1
West Midlands	97.1	73.9	62.3	85.5	9.4	7.7
East Midlands	97.1	73.9	62.3	85.5	6.9	5.5
Yorkshire and Humberside	103.8	88.3	69.8	76.7	8.6	7.2
North-West	96.6	96.6	81.2	88.9	11.7	10.5
North	79.2	83.0	62.2	92.5	5.3	4.1
Wales	81.8	84.0	68.2	122.7	4.4	3.9
Scotland	90.3	97.8	84.9	110.8	9.3	8.8
Great Britain (000)	1 167	844	1 439	1 145	21 148 (100)	4 595 (100)

Note [1] Region's share of producer-service employment as a proportion of region's share of total employment.

SOURCE Calculated from the estimates in Table 9.1 using Department of Employment Census of Employment data.

activity is constant irrespective of the regional location. In practice the ratio of producer to non-producer employment in the South-East may be higher because, for example, of an expressed preference by organisations to locate headquarters in that region (Evans, 1973; Marquand, 1979; Dicken and Lloyd, 1981), or for research and development establishments to be located there (Buswell and Lewis, 1970; Howells, 1984). According to the Census of Employment (Department of Employment, 1983b) almost 66 per cent of employment in advertising in 1981 was located in the South-East; 53 per cent of business service employment, including 71 per cent of the 45 000 jobs in central offices not allocable elsewhere (mainly national or regional head offices), and 57 per cent of the 53 000 workers employed in computer services. With reference to the latter, a recent study (Department of Industry, 1983) has shown that 69 per cent of the head offices of more than 1000 computer-service companies are located in the South-East. Some 34 per cent of the branch offices of these companies are also located there, but over 70 per cent of all the branches are controlled by computer-service head offices in that region.

Evidence of this kind confirms the earlier indications of a highly uneven distribution of producer-service employment within the British space economy. The number of producer-service jobs per 10 000 resident population of each region is negatively correlated with regional unemployment rate ($r = -0.586$, not significant at 0.05 level), but positively correlated with regional share of GDP ($r = 0.933$), commercial office floorspace as a proportion of all floorspace in each region ($r = 0.942$), and the proportion of total employment in service industries (0.770). It would seem, therefore, that the level of producer-service activity is not unconnected with the relative economic performance of regions. It is also connected with the prominence of urban areas as the base from which a large majority of producer services operate.

5. Urban Concentration

Data for Greater London can be used as a guide to the situation prevailing in other regions with major urban areas such as Leeds, Manchester and Edinburgh (Table 9.4) (see also Daniels, Edwards and Burn, 1981; Daniels, 1983a). While just less than half of all

TABLE 9.4 *Estimated Share of Producer-Service Employment in Greater London Relative to the South-East and Great Britain, by Industry Class, 1981*

	Producer-service employment (000)				
SIC Division (1980)	Greater London	South-East	%	Great Britain	%
Distribution, hotels and catering, repairs	218	423	51.7	1 167	18.7
Transport and communication	222	369	60.2	844	26.3
Banking, finance, insurance, business services and leasing	467	713	65.5	1 439	32.4
Other services	208	433	47.9	1 145	18.1
All service employment	2 646	5 000	52.9	13 090	20.2
All industries and services	3 513	7 168	49.0	21 148	16.6

SOURCE Department of Employment (1983) *Employment Gazette*, Occasional Supplement no. 1 (May) estimated from data in Table 9.4.

employees in employment in the South-East in 1981 were located in Greater London and almost 53 per cent of those engaged in service industries, more than 60 per cent of producer-service employment in transport and communication and 65 per cent in insurance and banking was located in Greater London with many of the latter in the central area. Therefore, while Greater London accounts for 20 per cent of all service jobs in Great Britain it is the base for more than 32 per cent of the producer-service employment in banking and finance. Assuming that a similar situation prevails in the other parts of the country, then the association between urban agglomeration and the incidence of producer services is probably significant for the supply of such services and their potential contribution to economic growth.

The allocation of these urbanisation/agglomeration economies must, however, be seen within the context of concentrated decentralisation because much of the growth in services as a whole in the

South-East has taken place outside Greater London, especially in the Outer Metropolitan Area. In absolute terms only insurance, banking, finance and business services and miscellaneous services (SIC 1968) increased their employment in Greater London between 1978 and 1981, but in both cases the absolute increase at locations elsewhere in the South-East was larger. The absolute numbers in all the other service categories decreased in Greater London only to be counterbalanced by large positive changes in the remainder of the South-East. Producer-service employment has participated in these locational trends, but on a more limited scale than those service industries which are more dependent on the spatial distribution of consumers.

A measure of the significance of this change is that if present trends continue there will, by the early 1990s, be more commercial office floorspace in the rest of the South-East (i.e. outside central London) than in central London itself (Warman, 1983; see also Greater London Council, 1983). In 1974 the latter had almost 26 per cent of the nation's office space and the rest of the South-East 14.5 per cent. Central London's share had fallen to less than 24 per cent by 1982 and the rest of the South-East had risen to more than 17 per cent. Some of the demand has come from corporate headquarters in that the outer South-East's share of the top 1000 companies increased from 7 to 15 per cent during the same period. Ominously for the provincial regions, their combined share decreased from 40 to 31 per cent. The implication is that the expansion in the rest of the South-East has been at the expense of provincial cities rather than of central London which has retained its absolute level of activity.

Using employment data for metropolitan economic labour areas (MELAs) between 1971 and 1977, Marquand (1979, 1983) suggests that there are hierarchical factors which encourage the concentration of producer services in the larger cities and a tendency for under-provision to occur in smaller urban areas, especially in the regions outside the South-East, East Anglia, the South-West and Scotland. It is also the case that areas with a high level of dependence on manufacturing industry have a low level of producer-service activity.

6. The Significance of Spatial Inequalities

As producer services are in some respects the embodiment of the structural changes currently taking place in advanced economies it seems essential to know more about their role in economic development and whether, as Marquand (1983) asks, it matters if they are unevenly distributed. In so far as many organisations are able to internalise their intermediate inputs (see, for example, Daniels, 1984), the location and availability of possible exogenous sources may not be a significant consideration. But many firms must, if only for reasons arising from their limited size or an infrequent requirement for a particular kind of specialist input, seek to fulfil their objectives from external sources. Many small manufacturing firms are in this category and if they are to retain their comparative advantage they will require knowledge of and an easily accessible supply of producer services. Unless these are available locally (i.e. within the same urban area or region), the cost of obtaining them (travel time to meetings, telecommunications charges), the likelihood of delays caused by the inability of client and supplier to meet as often as required, may be a sufficient deterrent to limit utilisation or, more seriously, to prevent use altogether and so cause firms to grow less slowly than might otherwise be the case or even to cease production because of an inability to compete with firms in those cities and regions with easier access to a comprehensive pool of producer services. Goddard (1978) has stressed that the availability at the local level of the kind of information and advice provided by producer activities such as business services is a vital factor for the present and future economic performance of peripheral areas; yet until comparatively recently relatively little has been known about the actual characteristics of the interdependence between manufacturing activity and the demand for business services in particular (Marshall, 1982, 1983).

The conventional view of the supply of producer services in a city or region is that they arise directly from the demand generated by manufacturing firms. When this demand declines, for reasons connected, for example, with changes in the organisation of manufacturing and therefore greater internalisation of service inputs (Burrows and Town, 1971; Crum and Gudgin, 1977), the supply of producer services will be adversely affected. In practice the relationship is less clearcut because, as Marshall (1982) has shown, the service sector is itself experiencing organisational changes which affect the local supply of producer services. Merger and acquisition among insurance companies, for example, has created larger, more centralised, organisations in which internal provision of accounting, marketing and some computer services via head office, has replaced the autonomy of smaller, often locally based financial and insurance companies which obtain producer services from local suppliers. The parallel among manufacturing companies is the reduced autonomy of branch plants which are less likely to use local producer services than local independent firms; Marshall (1982) found that manufacturing firms with less than 60 employees obtained more than 50 per cent of their service purchases from outside the firm and over 80 per cent of these purchases were made within the same planning region. Equivalent figures for large establishments (300+employees) were 31 per cent and 68 per cent respectively. Imported services are provided via headquarters which, if it does require to purchase some of these inputs, will obtain them from the location, invariably in London or the South-East, where it is situated. The presence of headquarters establishments in a city or region is therefore important because of the demand which they generate for locally supplied producer services (Burrows and Town, 1971; Daniels, 1984).

The significance of this has recently been demonstrated by Marshall (1983) in a study of manufacturing firms in Birmingham, Leeds and Manchester which included 63 branch plants. More than 90 per cent of the branch plants (19) with headquarters in London obtained services from within their own company compared with just over 70 per cent (22) of those headquartered in areas used for the study. Hence almost 30 per cent of the service inputs of branch plants with a local headquarters were obtained from the same area. Marshall (1982) also notes that the presence of a major producer service complex within a region ensures that a larger proportion of the demand emanating from local branches and headquarters remains within the region. The North-West (Manchester) and the West Midlands (Birmingham) fair rather better in this regard than Yorkshire–Humberside, which has a far less dominant regional capital (Leeds) and a wider dispersal of producer services among a number of smaller secondary centres. Indeed, Manchester is used as a source for business services by firms in Yorkshire–Humberside and in the West Midlands.

Interregional transfer of business services which is not oriented towards London and the South-East has also been noted in a study of manufacturing and service firms in a number of other British provincial cities (Daniels, 1984). Such links are largely confined to contiguous regions, however, and are best developed among insurance, banking and finance activities (Daniels, 1984). There are also hierarchical links in the destinations of interregional business-service output and by far the largest proportion of the sales income of some producer services clearly originates from cities or regions well outside the local market area, especially for smaller firms. The significance of this for regional economic adjustment towards a post-industrial structure is that, contrary to common belief, producer-service development in under-provided provincial areas can perform an export (basic) as well as import-substitution (non-basic) role.

The notion that producer services mainly exist only as a response to local manufacturing demand seems some way off the mark (see also Marshall, 1983). Of course the link is an important one (see Stanback, 1979, for example), but industrialisation and the subsequent diversification/adaptation of manufacturing would not have been possible without the 'enabling' role performed by transportation, or by business services such as the financial institutions, or by professionals such as accountants and surveyors. In such circumstances it seems axiomatic that the relationship should at worst be considered symbiotic, i.e. on an equal footing rather than 'manufacturing first, producer services (or services in general) second' (see also Daniels, 1983b).

7. External Influences on the Spatial Pattern of Producer Services

The location of producer services in the space economy and their potential contribution to restructuring regional economies is complicated by the pressures arising from the increasing globalisation of producer-service activities. Historically, most producer services have operated within the national context with the notable exception of the insurance broking and commodity trading functions of the City of London. But foreign direct investment by multinational business services has been increasing (Dunning and Norman, 1983) in an effort to capitalise more effectively upon the highly specialised technical knowledge, managerial skills or information which they have to offer. Instead of giving licences to local national companies, multinational business services are now discovering that their expertise is best provided, and protected, by retaining ownership and installing their own operational establishments at foreign locations. This procedure also offers the prospect of cost savings as a result of reduced executive travel and related overheads when providing a service from the 'home' country.

The locational choices for such international producer services invariably favour the major corporate complexes where they are able to capitalise upon good international communications both with the parent country and with other potential markets, obtain ready access to the diverse group of ancillary services integral to the corporate complex (Cohen, 1979; Corey, 1982), are readily accessible to existing or potential clients and are able to draw upon a labour pool in which the occupational skills are already likely to be available. Dunning and Norman (1983) traced some 261 US-based business services in the UK in 1976 and 82 per cent (213) operated from establishments in central London, a further 13 per cent from locations elsewhere in London, and only 5 per cent from places elsewhere in the country (mainly within the South-East region from towns such as Reading). Management consultancy and executive search, advertising, accountancy, insurance, banking, engineering design, legal practices and other producer services are all represented and clearly add to the attractiveness of London and the South-East as the key location for knowledge capital. This is reinforced by the location of regional headquarters of multinational manufacturing enterprises, 69 per cent (85) of which were located in London in Dunning and Norman's 1976 data. The result is a producer-service complex which must also act as a magnet for national producer (as well as non-producer) activities.

8. The Scope for Adjustment

The trend towards internalisation of producer-service provision as a consequence of the growth of large multi-site organisations, together with the national and international location behaviour of business and other services is clearly helping to exacerbate the distinction between the core and the periphery within the British economy. This must lead to some consideration of whether there is any real prospect for ameliorating the cumulative attraction of one major region of the country for producer services as a way of providing a more appropriate and firmer platform for making the adjustment to a post-industrial economic system. There are a large number of ways in which this might be achieved: by stimulating interregional movement of existing producer-service firms; as a result of the introduction of branches of national or regional producer services at provincial locations; by encouraging the development of new producer-service enterprises at provincial locations; or by *in situ* expansion of indigenous local, regional or national establishments.

Throughout the second half of the 1960s and during most of the 1970s official policies designed to encourage the interregional movement of office establishments, including producer services, were singularly unsuccessful although shorter distance movement to locations in suburban London or elsewhere within the South-East took place at a substantial scale (Daniels, 1978; Hall, 1972; Location of Offices Bureau, 1975). Insurance, banking and finance were prominent among relocating organisations, but only a few moved to provincial centres. Most of these moves also invariably involved lower-order functions rather than the information-using, knowledge-seeking, decision-making functions which might contribute to the development of provincial corporate complexes conducive to the growth of ancillary and dependent economic activities such as modern, high-technology manufacturing. Marshall (1983) found that only 2.4 per cent of the aggregate change in employment in business service establishments in Leeds, Manchester and Birmingham between 1976 and 1980 was connected with relocation of pre-existing establishments from other locations.

A more specific study of computer services (Department of Industry, 1983) confirms the extremely limited potential for interregional mobility. New branch formation has also been limited with computer services headquartered in the South-East showing a clear tendency to locate branches in Manchester and for computer services headquartered in the North-West to set up new branches in Leeds or Sheffield. Apart from considerable caution about opening branches (some computer services were already withdrawing or merging existing branches), in a number of cases strict criteria over and above the expectation of a suitable market were cited in order for a good case to be made for a new branch; the number of staff likely to be employed (5 to 12), an expected annual turnover of between £100 000 and £300 000, an ability to generate at least 15 per cent of total company business, or the anticipation of sufficient business for at least one year might together or individually be used. An added problem for branches is that they are often required to provide a wider range of services than the manpower or expertise available allows. As a result an activity may lack the quality sufficient to ensure its attractiveness to potential clients and so make the task of ongoing viability more difficult to achieve. The dilemma for provincial areas is that local manufacturing and other producer-service users may be adversely affected by their absence and because the existence of latent demand is difficult to measure with sufficient confidence to justify investment, computer service and similar high-order producer services are reluctant to set up branches, thus helping to sustain their comparative disadvantage relative to the South-East.

Much greater reliance must therefore be placed on the contribution of indigenous producer services or on the decisions by those firms operating at the national or regional scale to place branches in provincial locations (Douglas, 1981; Marshall, 1983; Daniels, 1983b). Almost 48 per cent of the employment growth recorded in Marshall's study arose from the birth of business services in the local economy and more than 40 per cent through the introduction of branches by firms with head offices elsewhere. It is important to stress, however, that most of the job increases arose from *in situ* expansion rather than the introduction of new establishments during the period between 1976 and 1980. Most of the indigenous firms had been at their present sites, for example, for an average of almost 28 years. In a study of business and professional service establishments in eight provincial cities (Daniels, 1983a) it emerged that indigenous establishments were significantly more likely to have increased their employment between 1975 and 1980 than non-indigenous establishments. The latter retained their 1975 employment levels or were more likely to have contracted.

This is an important distinction in so far as it underlines the limited dynamic of provincial producer-service growth (assuming that the results for business services are also applicable to producer functions in other types of services) and its vulnerability to the 'branch establishment syndrome' which has been such an important factor in the withdrawal of manufacturing employment from provincial regions. In the context of developing the basic function of provincial producer services this is relevant because of the distinction between indigenous business services which have strong links with local manufacturing and local private consumers and the less mixed, often externally controlled producer services which have the strongest links with markets extending much further afield (Marshall, 1983). The ratio of indigenous to non-indigenous producer-service establishments in a provincial region/city may therefore be a critical consideration; slow-growth centres tend to be dependent on decisions by externally controlled establishments and to have non-indigenous establishments out-numbering indigenous establishments by two to one.

One way of responding to these difficulties is to provide producer services with an incentive to expand or to start up in areas of under-provision. Government assistance to service industries (commercial, distributive or professional) is available under the Office and Service Industry Scheme (OSIS), which directs financial aid for job creation, ranging from £2500 per job in the Intermediate Areas to £8000 per job in the (former) Special Development Areas where unemployment and other problems are most serious. R & D laboratories, administrative offices and other self-sufficient parts of an organisation may also qualify for assistance. A contribution of up to £10 000 or a maximum of 25 per cent of the cost of consultants' fees for a feasibility study is also available, together with a fixed grant of £2000 for essential employees moving with their work.

All the indications are that this kind of pump-priming assistance is inadequate both with reference to the level of grant per job created and the absence of aid directed at improving the access of service firms, and especially producer activities, to the latest telecommunications and information technology. Such assistance may also lead to an increase in output without adding to the demand for labour; but if the volume of output is increased there is a real possibility of multiplier effects elsewhere in the local economy. It would also seem important to direct assistance towards retraining opportunities for local labour forces in the kinds of skills required by producer and other services in circumstances where expectations tend to relate to 'traditional' employment in blue-collar occupations.

The OSIS scheme also imposes criteria for eligibility which discourage the expansion and diversification of indigenous or *in situ* producer services. To be eligible for consideration firms must have a genuine choice of location for the establishment qualifying for assistance although certain 'firms providing specified producer services to others . . . may not need to have this choice to qualify for assistance' (Department of Industry, 1982); this overlooks the fact that many producer services move into provincial locations by setting up new branches rather than by relocating existing branch or headquarters establishments and their employees. It has been demonstrated earlier in this chapter that producer services do possess an export function (Daniels, 1984, Douglas, 1981), but the likelihood of exporting beyond the Assisted Areas will depend upon the location of a service centre within it since, with some exceptions, there is clear distance decay function for producer service exports beyond the planning region in which the source is located.

There is some information available about the distribution of OSIS support (Table 5). OSIS grants account for a relatively small proportion, less than 7 per cent, of all regional financial assistance given since 1972 (under Section 7 of the Industrial Development Act 1982 and its predecessor, the Industry Act 1972). It might be expected that the areas of greatest need would receive the largest proportion of OSIS assistance. Although in absolute terms the value of grants given to firms in Special Development Areas has been greater than in Development or Intermediate Areas, as a proportion of total aid within these areas OSIS accounts for the lowest proportion in the SDAs (5.8 per cent). The associated net employment effects (Table 9.5) have also been lower in absolute terms in the SDAs than in the Intermediate Areas and in proportional terms compared with both the Intermediate and Development Areas.

Interest in OSIS among service sector firms is also limited. This is indicated by some data for companies in the computer services industry (Department of Industry, 1983). A total of 20 offers to 18 companies have been made with additional employment of 805 jobs using financial assistance of just over £1.6 m. or £2000 per job. In view of the transitional costs faced by companies moving all

TABLE 9.5   *OSIS Assistance, by Type of Area, 1972–83*

Area	Type of grant	Number of grants	%[1]	Value (£m.)	%	Estimated new employment	%
Special Develop-	OSIS	180	6.9	23 402	5.8	8 795	5.2
ment Area	Total	2 618		402 778		167 944	
Development	OSIS	139	7.1	19 874	11.3	7 435	7.2
Area	Total	1 967		175 271		103 905	
Intermediate	OSIS	210	6.4	14 693	7.6	12 385	8.5
Area	Total	3 260		192 487		146 549	

Note   [1] OSIS as a proportion of total.

SOURCE   Department of Trade and Industry (1983) *Industrial Development Act 1982: Annual Report* (London: HMSO).

or part of their activities from other locations (Rhodes and Kan, 1971) and the uncertainties about the costs of retaining existing linkages, communication with head office or tapping new markets at the provincial location, the level of assistance given to computer service firms would not seem very significant. Indeed, the Department of Industry (1983) study showed that those firms aware of the assistance (less than 25 per cent of those interviewed) only considered it as a bonus and certainly less significant than market factors. Many firms had not considered the question of assistance and thought it unlikely that it would affect their locational decision-making.

All these difficulties primarily affect those producer services which are potentially mobile. By overlooking the needs of the *in situ* producer services or latent entrepreneurial skills in the Assisted Areas, government policy is limiting the opportunities for strengthening the foundations of areas suffering from under-provision. Of course, in many ways the risks of investing in new start-ups are much greater than those attached to supporting existing and often larger producer-service firms with proven records. The prospects for small businesses, which many producer services remain even when they become well-established, are undoubtedly uncertain; adequate finance to see them through the critical first twelve months is essential, but some evidence from the computer-services industry (Department of Industry, 1983) suggests that, because of the hardware required, between £10 000 and

£20 000 is the minimum required to start an operation. It might be less than this where a market is guaranteed, but for many producer services this is unlikely to be the case. Assistance of this kind is not currently available although there are many small business agencies in provincial cities. Since producer services thrive best in contact-intensive, diversified business environments, recent contractions of the areas where OSIS is available excludes the kinds of major urban locations where they might be encouraged. Perhaps OSIS should become more place-specific for services only, irrespective of whether urban areas are located within or outside the Assisted Areas.

9. Conclusion

An assessment of the role of producer services in the British space economy is encumbered by the paucity of constructive empirical information. It is therefore difficult to address the policy and other issues arising from the transition to a post-industrial economic system and some of the reasons for the present circumstances have been explored elsewhere (Daniels, 1983b). If the distribution of employment is used as a crude surrogate for the availability of producer services in the nation's regions and cities, it seems beyond question that significant spatial inequalities exist. By exploring locational patterns, at either the aggregate regional level or more recently with reference to selected service industry subsectors such as business services, geographers have been active since the mid-1970s in showing the origins of supply-side spatial inequalities. But there is far less certainty about possible spatial variations in the demand for producer services in relation, for example, to industry sector of origin, the volume and value of transactions, the types of service required or the response of business enterprises if their requirements for specialised intermediate inputs cannot be fulfilled. By pursuing these and related questions, such as the supply-demand equation, the consequences of spatial variations in producer service activity for the evolution of the space economy may become rather more transparent than at present.

There are, however, encouraging signs that research and policy directions within central government departments or local-government economic development agencies are beginning to change and to recognise, not before time, a service industry dimension in regional, industrial and employment affairs. Recently, for example, the Department of Industry, long the champion of the manufacturing sector, has become actively involved in both in-house and externally funded research in the general field of producer services. A project on regional development and product services and their development is currently in progress (in association with the Commission of the European Communities) along with two other studies, one on the location trends and influences in the insurance, banking and financial services sector (including the impact of new technology on location and organisation, and the other on the location of research and development units. A project on the location of international offices in Britain was also commissioned during 1982. This increased research interest incorporates regional and urban dimensions, is increasingly focused on sub-sectors within services (especially the producer-oriented categories) and is motivated mainly by a need to refine regional policy instruments. Indeed, the government's White Paper published in December 1983 proposed new regional aid policies in which, for the first time, emphasis will be shifted from manufacturing to service industries in the belief that computer services or insurance firms, for example, will be more likely to create jobs in problem areas of the country than capital-intensive manufacturing.

Given the place-specific, urban orientation evident in the location behaviour of producer services, it may be important for central government policies to be pinpointed at relatively precise locales within the Assisted Areas. In order to do so, however, more information than is currently available is needed about the behaviour of producer services in urban areas; in particular a better understanding of the way in which they act either as a catalyst, or a drag, upon evolution and change within urban economies. The studies reported by Marquand (1983) and Marshall (1982, 1983), for example, point the way and a possible, but by no means comprehensive, list of further questions arising from such work might include the following. First, is it possible to distinguish between the growth rates of producer services in urban areas with fast, intermediate and slow-growth characteristics? Fothergill and Gudgin (1982) have demonstrated that employment growth has been most rapid in intermediate-sized and small,

free-standing towns rather than in the major cities and conurbations. Second, to what extent have such differentials been associated with specialisation in particular types of producer-service
activity? Third, to what extent can the contribution of producer
services to urban economic development be attributed to contrasts
in birth-/death-rates, *in situ* growth, and inter-urban relocation?
Fourth, are there any connections between the expansion/contrac-
tion of producer services and the incidence of similar changes in
other local economic activities? Greenfield (1966) showed that
those regions exhibiting high rates of employment growth were
usually those with significant concentrations of producer services
and where overall growth rates were high producer service groups
also grew quite rapidly. Fifth, is there any relationship between
the expansion and range of producer services in urban areas and
the incidence of local or central government administrative functions? Finally, in what way, if any, does the absence of easily
obtainable producer services impede local and regional development and would an increase in the availability of such services
stimulate other kinds of economic development as well as creating
additional employment.

The task is formidable; rather belatedly it seems, a great deal of
'catching up', which could have been avoided if the significance of
producer services in space economies had been recognised at an
earlier stage, is now necessary. These efforts are taking place
against a background of high unemployment and rapid technological change which is revolutionising the information-handling and
communications capabilities of producer-service activities. Such
capabilities could have far-reaching consequences for conventional
ideas about the nature of work and the organisation of space
economies. Even though social inertia may restrain the adoption,
and therefore the impact, of information technology it seems likely
that producer services will be greatly affected. The problem may
not therefore be where should producer services be located in the
interests of avoiding unbalanced regional and urban development,
but what is the best way to deploy activities with the prospect of a
diminishing labour force, increasing specialisation, and a more
pivotal role in a society in which knowledge is capital.

Bibliography

Bacon, R. and Eltis, W. (1976) *Britain's Economic Problems: Too Few Producers* (London: Heinemann).
Blackaby, F. (ed.) (1978) *De-industrialization* (London: Heinemann).
Burrows, E. M. and Town, S. (1971) *Office Services in the East Midlands* (Nottingham: East Midland Economic Planning Council).
Buswell, R. and Lewis, E. W. (1970) 'The Geographical Distribution of Industrial Research Activity in the UK', *Regional Studies*, **4**, pp. 277–306.
Central Statistical Office (1983) *Regional Trends* (London: HMSO).
Civil Service Department (1973) *The Dispersal of Government Work from London* (London: HMSO).
Clark, C. (1940) *The Conditions of Economic Progress* (London: Macmillan).
Cohen, R. (1979) 'The Changing Transactions Economy and its Spatial Implications', *Ekistics*, **46,** pp. 7–15.
Corey, K. E. (1982) 'Transactional Forces and the Metropolis', *Ekistics*, **297**, pp. 416–23.
Crozier, C. (1983) 'Implications for the Organization', in Otway and Peltu, op. cit. pp. 86–101.
Crum, R. E. and Gudgin, G. (1977) 'Non-production Activities in UK Manufacturing Industry', *Regional Policy Series 3* (Brussels: Commission of the European Communities).
Daniels, P. W. (1978) 'Service Sector Office Employment and Regional Imbalance in Britain, 1966–71', *Tijdschrift voor Economische en Sociale Geografie*, **69**, pp. 286–95.
Daniels, P. W. (1983a) 'Business Service Offices in British Provincial Cities: Location and Control', *Environment and Planning, A*, **15**, pp. 1101–20.
Daniels, P. W. (1983b) 'Service Industries: Supporting Role or Centre Stage?', *Area*, **15**, pp. 301–9.
Daniels, P. W. (1984) 'Business Service Offices in Provincial Cities: Sources of Input and Destination of Output', *Tijdschrift voor Economische en Sociale Geografie*, **75**, pp. 123–39.
Daniels, P. W., Edwards, L. E. and Burn, S. (1981) 'Office Activities in Provincial Centres: A Preliminary Assessment', *Working Paper 3*, Dynamics of Office Activities in Provincial Cities Project, (University of Liverpool: Department of Geography).
Department of Employment (1983a) *Employment Gazette*, **91** (Feb) p. 65.
Department of Employment (1983b) *Employment Gazette*, Occasional Supplement no. 1 (May) pp. 2–9.
Department of Industry (1982) 'Office and Service Industries Scheme: Could Your Company Benefit?' (London: HMSO).
Department of Industry (1983) 'The Location, Mobility and Financing of the Computer Services Sector in the UK', (London: South-East Regional Office) (mimeo.).

Dicken, P. and Lloyd, P. (1981) *Modern Western Society* (London: Harper & Row).

Douglas, S. (1981) 'Business Service Provision in Newcastle upon Tyne', unpublished M.Phil. thesis, Department of Geography, Newcastle upon Tyne Polytechnic.

Dunning, J. and Norman, P. (1983) 'The Theory of the Multinational Enterprise: An Application to Office Location', *Environment and Planning, A*, **15**, pp. 675–92.

Evans, A. W. (1973) 'The Location of Headquarters of Industrial Companies', *Urban Studies*, **10**, pp. 387–95.

Fothergill, S. and Gudgin, G. (1982) *Unequal Growth: Urban and Regional Employment Change in the UK* (London: Heinemann).

Fuchs, V. R. (1968) *The Service Economy* (New York: Bureau of Economic Research).

Gappert, G. (1982) 'Future Urban America: Post-Affluent or Advanced Industrial Society?', in Gappert, G. and Knight, R. V. (eds) *Cities in the 21st Century* (Beverley Hills: Sage) pp. 9–34.

Gershuny, J. (1978) *After Industrial Society?* (London: Macmillan).

Goddard, J. B. (1978) 'The Location of Non-Manufacturing Occupations Within Manufacturing Industries', in F. E. I. Hamilton (ed.) *Contemporary Industrialization: Spatial Analysis and Regional Development* (London: Longman).

Gottman, J. (1983) *The Coming of the Transactional City* (College Park: University of Maryland Institute for Urban Studies).

Greater London Council (1983) 'Office Work and Information Technologies', *Strategy Document 10* (London: GLC Economic Policy Group).

Greenfield, H. I. (1966) *Manpower and the Growth of Producer Services* (New York: Columbia University Press).

Hall, R. K. (1972) 'The Movement of Offices from Central London', *Regional Studies*, **6**, pp. 385–92.

Hills, P. J. (ed.) (1982) *Trends in Information Transfer* (London: Pinter).

Howells, J. R. L. (1984) 'The Location of Research and Development: Some Observations and Evidence from Britain', *Regional Studies*, **18**, pp. 13–29.

Keeble, D. E., Owens, P. L. and Thompson, C. (1981) *Centrality, Peripherality and EEC Regional Development* (London: HMSO).

Location of Offices Bureau (1975) *Office Relocation: Facts and Figures* (London: Location of Offices Bureau).

Marquand, J. (1979) 'The Service Sector and Regional Policy in the United Kingdom', *Research Series 29* (London: Centre for Environmental Studies).

Marquand, J. (1980) 'The Role of the Service Sector in Regional Policy', *Regional Policy Series 3* (Brussels: Commission of the European Communities).

Marquand, J. (1983) 'The Changing Distribution of Service Employment', in J. B. Goddard an A. G. Champion (eds) *The Urban and Regional Transformation of Britain* (London: Methuen) pp. 99–134.

Marshall, J. N. (1982) 'Linkages Between Manufacturing Industry and

Business Services', *Environment and Planning, A*, **14**, pp. 1523–40.

Marshall, J. N. (1983) 'Business-service Activities in British Provincial Conurbations', *Environment and Planning, A*, **15**, pp. 1343–59.

Otway, H. J. and Peltu, M. (eds) (1983) *New Office Technology: Human and Organizational Aspects* (London: Pinter).

Polese, M. (1982) 'Regional Demand for Business Services and Inter-regional Service Flows in a Small Canadian Region', *Papers of the Regional Science Association*, **50**, pp. 151–63.

Rhodes, J. and Kan, A. (1971) *Office Dispersal and Regional Policy* (London: Cambridge University Press).

Rostow, W. W. (1960) *The Stages of Economic Growth*, (London: Cambridge University Press).

Simon, H. A. (1977) *The New Science of Management Decision-Making* (Englewood Cliffs, N.J.: Prentice-Hall).

Stanback, T. M. (1979) *Understanding the Service Economy: Employment, Productivity, Location* (Baltimore, Md: John Hopkins University Press).

Thirlwall, A. P. (1982) 'De-industrialization in the United Kingdom', *Lloyds Bank Review*, **144**, pp. 22–37.

Warman, C. (1983) 'Surging South-east', *The Times*, 8 Dec.

10

Re-industrialisation in Peripheral Britain: State Policy, the Space Economy and Industrial Innovation

KEVIN MORGAN

1. Introduction

Time was when the notion of 'Peripheral Britain' was largely synonymous with such major Development Area Regions (DARs) as west-central Scotland, South Wales and north-east England. Yet it is now a measure of the proliferation of industrial decline that, on the unemployment index at least, large swathes of the country could now be classified as such. It is precisely this pervasive absence of waged employment opportunities – as opposed to the stark contrast between interior and periphery in the 1930s – that has largely aborted the conventional rationale of regional policy. Ever since the historic 1944 commitment to a 'balanced distribution of industry', regional policy depended upon and contributed to interregional flows of (manufacturing) employment from 'core' to 'periphery'. Regional policy addressed itself not so much to the *generation* of employment within DARs, but to its *redistribution* from donor to recipient regions. In short, it was predicated on a historically specific period of capitalist growth (1945–73) in which donor regions, principally the South-East and West Midlands, would remain buoyant labour markets.

With the erosion of this historically specific conjuncture the donor–recipient rationale of regional policy has been severely compromised and is gradually being replaced by what might be called one of 'regional autarky' inasmuch as a major dimension of regional policy now consists of indigenous efforts to *generate* growth and enhance the competitive performance of firms already installed. Central to this indigenous effort is the attempt to promote advanced technology as a means of reindustrialisation in Britain generally and in the DARs in particular.[1] This is certainly a novel prescription but, as I hope to show in Section 10.5, some of the problems that have to be confronted in the traditional DARs are of a familiar, long-established character.

The problems of British uneven development (whether of unemployment, output and employment, growth or industrial innovation) are not simply to be understood in subnational terms. Indeed, on all these counts Britain as a whole constitutes something of a problem and the relative peripheralisation of its *national* (industrial) economy has had an immensely important effect on its capacity for ameliorating internal forms of uneven development. More than a decade ago the Institute of Economic Affairs bemoaned that 'Britain' is clearly confronted not by a regional but a national problem' (Hallett, 1973). So although 'Peripheral Britain' has traditionally referred to the DARs, there is a very real sense is which the national industrial economy can itself be said to fall under this rubric.

Nevertheless, mass unemployment and widespread industrial dereliction should not obscure what are officially canvassed as exemplars of reindustrialisation: the most celebrated being the burgeoning of 'high-tech' industry along the so-called 'Western Corridor' of the M4 (selectively embracing Berkshire, Wiltshire, Avon and Gwent) and in parts of central Scotland.[2] The 'Western Corridor' is the latter-day equivalent of Hayes and Southall, Longbridge and Solihull, the roses in the cross of the previous great depression in the 1930s. Of course, the contemporary islands of growth have been exaggerated, just as the feasibility of reproducing such growth in Consett or Birmingham has been. Besides, whatever the actual extent of 'high-tech' employment, what is already clear is that it performs a very important ideological function for the Thatcher government: namely, that other areas should reproduce the social, economic and environmental milieu of these 'islands' of growth (Neil, 1983).

In the following sections I want to focus on some of the issues which seem most important to industrial innovation in the British (space) economy. But first, it should be said that no strict meaning is attached to what I have called 'reindustrialisation'. Rather, I use it loosely to refer to the restructuring of existing, and the emergence of new, sectors and firms through adaptation to and exploitation of advanced technologies such as microelectronics. This usage clearly does not imply that the manufacturing sector – the focus of this chapter – will necessarily regain a significantly greater share of total employment in Britain. Indeed, even in sectors which have enjoyed rapid output growth (such as electronics) reindustrialisation is associated with net employment decline, so that it becomes possible to speak of growth without development or jobless growth. One of the major implications of this chapter is that an exclusive focus on the so-called 'sunrise' industries can only have profoundly uneven social and spatial consequences.

2. Industrial Innovation: Britain as a 'Regional' Problem

Even though the indices of Britain's relative peripheralisation as an industrial economy are familiar enough, the mechanisms responsible remain fiercely contested (Blackaby, 1979; Beckerman, 1979; Gamble, 1981). Notwithstanding this lack of consensus, sufficient evidence exists to suggest that a poor performance as regards industrial innovation lies at the centre of this relative decline. With notable exceptions (e.g. defence-related industries, chemicals, mining machinery) decline has been multi-sectoral in character, evidenced by the comparatively low unit value of a wide spectrum of British exports. To the extent that this trend continues, large sections of British industrial capital are threatened on two fronts: by being ousted from potential advanced technology, skill-intensive product markets by leading OECD capital on the one hand, while on the other, becoming increasingly exposed to price competition from NICs in less sophisticated markets (Pavitt, 1980). Although the EEC industrial bloc as a whole has suffered a deterioration in its technological comparative advantage *vis-à-vis* Japan and the US, Britain's position within the EEC appears to be worsening if advanced technology export performance is any guide: between 1963 and 1981 skill-intensive exports grew less rapidly than those of any other EEC country (Commission of the European Communities, 1983).

Two of the most widely acknowledged indices of industrial innovation are research and development (R & D) and patenting activities. With regard to the first, while British R & D expenditure as a proportion of GDP is comparable to other leading OECD countries this is deceptive: first, because this relates to a consistently lower GDP per capita and so, in absolute terms, the British R & D expenditure is about 50 per cent that of the German Federal Republic. Second, a higher proportion of British R & D is devoted to defence, greater than any other OECD country except the US. Indeed, of gross government R & D expenditure within industry in 1979–80, 81 per cent went into defence (largely towards the electronics and aerospace industries), while 'other industry, trade and employment' – which is mainly relevant to the engineering industries as a whole – received a derisory 4 per cent. State support for *civilian* R & D in Britain is miserably low as compared with other leading countries both absolutely and as a proportion of GDP, while industry-financed R & D in Britain has increased more slowly than in every other OECD country apart from the US and Switzerland (National Economic Development Council (NEDO), 1981; Select Committee on Science and Technology, 1983).

Patenting data – the other major index of innovation – reveal that the British share of patents granted in the US between 1964 and 1978 slumped from 30 per cent to 18 per cent: the most severe relative decline recorded. Although all sectors suffered, chemicals declined least while the steepest fall was registered by the electronics sector (Select Committee on Science and Technology, 1983). Declining indigenous innovative performance might have been offset via greater utilisation of overseas technology, but the limited number of foreign licences taken by Britain – traditionally judged as a sign of self-sufficiency – should more appropriately be regarded as evidence of a 'worrying complacency and parochialism among sections of British industry' (ACARD, 1980a).

What needs to be more *popularly* established is that scarce R & D resources are massively skewed to the military sector when the civilian sector has been both unable and unwilling to boost its own R & D commitments. Futhermore, this has been paralleled by a long-standing and pervasive orientation towards prestige technologies and 'big science' (e.g. high-energy physics and radio astronomy). Little wonder then that the British R & D effort has for long been out of joint with those (civilian) sectors and product groups most crucial in terms of international growth; all of which led ACARD to speak of a 'misapplication of British scientific and engineering expertise' and to call, instead, for greater emphasis on the 'sciences related to manufacture with special attention to the relationship between production processes and the design, quality and reliability of products' (ACARD, 1978).

Among the other determinants of Britain's relatively poor innovative performance the most apparent are:

(i) Comparatively low levels of domestic industrial investment and the absence of 'patient money': British industrial capital has suffered a greater squeeze on its profitability than its major competitors, with less internal funds to support innovation. Yet external funds, available in principle, have been denied in practice because these are too short-term in character, thereby exacerbating a tradition of quick returns on industrial investments. This lack of 'patient money' is testimony to the relatively unique disjunction between British finance and industrial capital, which in part reflects technical illiteracy in much of the City (ACARD, 1978; Fellowship of Engineering, 1983).

(ii) The management of innovation: international studies indicate that many British companies (especially in the core engineering industries) accord less prominence to innovation in their corporate strategies than elsewhere, tending to regard R & D as a luxury rather than as a key to future survival. This is partly a function of the profitability crisis and lack of 'patient money', but it also reflects poor technical competence: lower utilisation of engineering experience pervades much of British industry, particularly at company board level. A comparatively low level of investment has often been compounded by less than efficient use of new investment and this is in part an index of poor technical competence (Pavitt, 1980; NEDC, 1982a).

(iii) Allied to this 'semi-skilled' character of management is the low incidence of skilled personnel (especially in craft and technician grades) in the UK labour force: Britain has one of the worst educated and trained workforces in the EEC (Pavitt, 1980).

(iv) These problems are not simply 'technocratic' failings, since many – absence of 'patient money', poor educational and training provision, the imperial pretensions of the British state as regards its R & D support – betoken a *political* impasse. The impasse consists of the failure of both Labour and Conservative Parties in being able to mobilise a sufficiently stable coalition of interests, powerful enough to underwrite a developmental strategy for the *domestic* industrial economy. Instead, the 'stop–go' measures which the British state has taken to 'stabilise' the domestic economy; its marked bias towards Britain's internationalised overseas sector (the domestic corollary being an open or exposed national economy); past commitments to a prestige role for sterling; and now the primacy of anti-inflation policy, have been such that it often appears that the British state has been intent on *weakening* the domestic industrial economy (Murray, 1972).

Given past performance, ACARD thought it unlikely that British industrial capital would keep abreast of accelerating technological change on its own indigenous (and currently deployed) resources, so it concluded by calling for greater technology transfer from abroad (ACARD, 1980a). Surveying this past record the *Financial Times* argued that the poor innovative performance of British industry was: 'putting at risk the nation's survival as a trading nation, not to speak of hundreds of thousands of jobs – far more than will be lost if trade union resistance . . . succeeds in delaying the adoption of new technology' (8 January, 1980). The penalising costs of belated innovation are now escalating because of the quickening pace of technological change, and yet the international context in which British capitalism operates is far less propitious than was the case two decades ago when industrial capital failed to sufficiently embrace the 'white heat' of the technological revolution. Currently, Britain's situation should be viewed in terms of three superimposed levels: a severe supply-side weakness of domestic industrial capital; a wider process of 'jobless growth' (i.e. increases in output combined with falling employment) in manufacturing in the advanced capitalist countries; and the general international recession (Morgan and Sayer, 1983a).

The purpose of this section has been merely to indicate that whatever the shortcomings of Britain's peripheral regions as regards their relatively poor potential for industrial innovation, Britain itself constitutes a problem on this score. Moreover, it is the international, rather than the interregional, reference which dominates state policy, and the improvement of Britain's national position would appear to entail increased internal spatial inequality; so much is suggested by the recomposition of industrial aid now underway.

3. State Policy and the Space Economy: The Recomposition of Industrial Aid

Although the peripheralisation of Britain's industrial economy has long pre-dated the end (in 1973) of what *now* appears as a 'golden age' of growth, this past decade has produced a new industrial geography – largely of redundant labour and abandoned, or else under-utilised, fixed capital – to which many people, even now, remain unadjusted. What I am concerned with here is the recomposition which this has induced in state industrial aid and the apparent shift from spatially-specific to 'non-spatial' forms of aid. If early indications are any guide, state programmes for industrial innovation seem most calculated to underwrite re-industrialisation in places outside the formally designated areas of assistance: indeed, this was already apparent, though not proclaimed, under the last Labour government's industrial strategy (Cameron, 1979). In particular, I want to focus on (i) the reconstitution of regional policy and (ii) the emerging, and ostensibly 'non-spatial', forms of aid (e.g. for advanced technologies).

In much orthodox academic debate on the spatial role of the state – noticeable too among sections of the labour movement – it is common to identify spatial policy almost exclusively with regional policy, when this is simply the most *visible* of the state's formal, spatially-specific policies. Clearly, there are few state policies that have *no* spatial effect whatsoever, and the role of the state sector itself in accentuating the demise of those peripheral regions (once) based on coal, steel and shipbuilding has been well-established (Hudson, Chapter 7 of this book; see also Morgan and Sayer, 1983a). Yet, even though conventional regional policy is now largely marginal to the social needs of the working class in the areas of its remit – and its value declined by nearly 50 per cent in real terms between 1976 and 1983 – this has not prevented territorial demands (by both capital and labour) from such areas for the retention of regional policy. Nor has it prevented territorial coalitions outside its remit from demanding designated 'status' (e.g. Inner London Consultative Employment Group, 1983). The reconstitution of regional policy warrants consideration *not* because it represents a significant vehicle for reindustrialisation in itself, but because it can function as a surrogate for more fundamental alternatives. That is to say it can become a focus for territorial chauvinism within the labour movement and foreclose debate on the more meaningful questions of social control over the location and *nature* of investment and employment in capitalist society.

For a number of reasons regional policy has recently been radically recast, principally because its map excluded the victimised areas of the past decade (especially in the West Midlands), because it has had pitifully little purchase on employment and is therefore an expensive form of job-creation; and not least because the regional aid programme is being severely cut to as little as £400m. in 1987–8. This follows the 1979 'review' which imposed cuts of £233m., reduced coverage from 44 per cent of the working population in 1979 to around 28 per cent in 1983 and abolished the Industrial Development Certificate system, the traditional 'stick' for controlling development in central regions (see Chapter 8; Morgan, 1985).

The case of the West Midlands in instructive as regards the territorial conflicts inherent in the reconstitution of regional policy. Prior to 1983 it had been excluded from the *official* map of 'Peripheral Britain' because the Department of Industry judged that it had not suffered a 'semi-permanent structural change in employment', besides which designation would suggest that Britain had not a regional, but a national problem (Committee of Public Accounts, 1981). Although the slump in employment in the West Midlands has largely assumed the form of *in situ* job loss, it remains the case that regional policy is pervasively credited with its undoing (Joseph, 1981; Forth, 1983). It is no coincidence that among the most vociferous opponents of regional policy is the Birmingham Chamber of Industry and Commerce, who have demanded that: 'all Government aid based on geographic areas should be abolished . . . and the monies released be redirected to investment in selected industries regardless of location' (Birmingham Chamber of Industry and Commerce, 1983). Significantly, BCIC does not embrace the current neo-market repertoire;

instead it subscribes to the need for a national industrial strategy because 'it is not good enough to leave the future shape of industry to the short-term forces of the marketplace' (BCIC, 1983). Though less visible opponents of regional policy, the West Midlands TUC had nevertheless expressed its opposition to the region being cast as the 'rich parent' to regional policy (Regional Council of West-Midlands TUC, 1981). The 1983 'review' has inevitably led to some areas of the West Midlands being given regional aid status.[3] But the actual employment effect of such status will be small and seems totally out of proportion to the effort devoted to achieving it. As much as anything else, this is a comment on the *visibility* of regional policy as a form of spatial aid (Morgan, 1985).

Up until now one of the most conspicuous features of regional policy is that, with the exception of regional selective assistance, such aid has become progressively detached from any employment obligations. Its primary effect has been to boost capital investment – in no way equivalent to job-creation – through regional development grants. RDGs constitute the major component of regional aid and also dwarf the sectoral and general schemes of aid under the Industry Acts (Table 10.1). However, aid shown in Table 10.1 does not exhaust direct industrial aid, and Tables 10.2–10.4 summarise the total picture. From Table 10.2 it is clear that 'sectoral development and structural adjustment' (broken down in Table 10.4) is by far the most significant and, of this, some 94 per cent was absorbed by the NCB, BSC, BL, BS, Rolls-Royce and Concorde in 1982/3: in fact these corporations accounted for 42 per cent of *total* direct industrial aid. Although this is not classified as spatially-specific aid, it is in effect, and so it can be argued that aid to the NCB, BSC and BS reinforces regional aid to the formally assisted areas, just as BL represents aid to the West Midlands. Even so, much of this 'hidden' regional aid is designed to manage contraction and, as such, should be distinguished from aid for industrial innovation, research and development. Crude monetary comparisons can often obscure the different *functions* of such aid schemes, and their role in reproducing uneven development.

Early indications are that advanced technology aid schemes (e.g. for microelectronics, flexible manufacturing systems, computer-aided design and test, fibre optics, etc.) are biased in take-up towards the South-East largely because of its connections of

TABLE 10.1 *Regional Analysis of Payments under Parts I, II and II of the Industrial Development Act 1982 and Parts I and II of the Industry Act 1972, to 31 March 1983*
£ m:

Area	Regional development grants	Section 7		Industry schemes grants	General schemes		Totals	
		Grants	Loans/equity		Grants	Loans/equity	Grants	Loans/equity
Scotland	1 129.0	109.8	41.9	16.3	18.0	nil	1 273.1	41.9
Wales	697.6	53.5	21.4	4.8	13.3	nil	769.2	21.4
North-East	1 139.7	81.9	18.3	11.4	12.1	0.5	1 245.1	18.8
Yorkshire and Humberside	252.9	48.9	9.3	42.2	16.4	nil	360.4	9.3
East Midlands	32.5	9.6	1.0	32.6	11.7	nil	86.4	1.0
South-East	nil	nil	nil	41.0	26.6	0.4	67.6	9.4
South-West	65.2	12.5	5.0	16.0	6.6	nil	100.3	5.0
West Midlands	2.7	0.1	0.1	34.4	19.8	nil	57.0	0.1
North-West	679.0	119.1	26.7	32.0	17.8	nil	847.9	26.7
Northern Ireland	nil	nil	nil	1.2	nil	nil	1.2	nil
Other	nil	nil	nil	7.1	16.0	4.9	23.1	4.9
Total	3 998.6	435.4	123.7	239.0	158.3	5.8	4 831.3	129.5

SOURCE *Annual Report, Industrial Development Act* (1983) (London: HMSO)

TABLE 10.2   *UK Government Assistance to Industry – Summary*

£ m.	1976/77	77/78	78/79	79/80	80/81	81/82	82/83
Regional policy measures	954	763	928	878	1 132	1 288	1 313
Research, development and innovation	263	256	289	386	441	488	524
Small firms	–	–	–	–	–	–	12
Sectoral development and structural adjustment	915	764	1 759	1 847	2 342	2 406	2 433
Employment and training	92	187	191	178	562	627	601
Assistance to exports	235	134	236	357	493	629	557
Total	2 459	2 104	3 403	3 646	4 970	5 438	5 440

SOURCE   for Tables 10.2–10.4: NEDC (1983) 49.

advanced technology sectors, particularly the electronics industry (Department of Industry, 1981; Nicholson, 1981; Lloyd, 1983a).[4] Furthermore, the pattern of industrial assistance is now accelerating towards the 'encouragement of innovation and growth', while regional policy and aid for the management of contraction are being cut back (NEDC, 1983b). Rarely considered as a form of industrial support or spatially-specific aid is the equipment budget of the Ministry of Defence which, in 1983, stood at £7.2 *billion* and was largely devoted to aerospace and electronics equipment. With few exceptions, the spatial distribution of primary contractors is largely outside the formally assisted areas and concentrated in particular in the southern England (Counter Information Services, 1982). The implication is not that this MoD budget should be used as leverage for regional development, but that it ought to be more widely acknowledged how state spending has itself underwritten the concentration of advanced technology sectors in southern Britain. Enough has been said to indicate that the exclusive identification of spatial policy with regional policy is both a naïve

TABLE 10.3 *Department of Trade and Industry Assistance to Industry – Summary*

£ m.	1976/77	77/78	78/79	79/80	80/81	81/82	82/83
Regional policy measures	423	428	505	396	554	701	666
Research, development and innovation	115	129	146	212	219	237	272
Small firms	–	–	–	–	–	–	12
Sectoral development and structural adjustment	833	651	1 553	1 565	2 062	1 999	1 637
Assistance to exports	235	134	236	357	493	629	557
Total	1 606	1 342	2 440	2 530	3 328	3 566	3 144

and impoverished conception of the state's impact on the space economy.

Despite neo-market rhetoric it needs to be remembered that Department of Industry (DoI) aid has actually increased under the Thatcher government (from a total of £1055m. in 1979/80 to £1813 in 1982/3) although the only DoI sub-programme projected to grow up to 1985/6 is that of scientific and technological assistance. Yet even this latter category of aid was no part of the initial Thatcherist project: but it is now rationalised as *practically* essential because without aid for innovation and 'adjustment', British capital would be disadvantaged given the accretion of state aid elsewhere, and because Britain would be unable to attract foreign capital which was an 'important source of new technology' (NEDC, 1983b). Nevertheless, as I show later. Thatcherism accords primary importance not to industrial, but to monetarist policy to effect *its* version of reindustrialisation.

Even though the recent reconstitution of regional policy tied regional aid more directly to job-creation, the sombre prospects for employment in the national economy imply that its effect will remain marginal to social need, especially in view of the devaluation of regional aid. Furthermore, it will have little or no effect on

TABLE 10.4 *Sectoral Development and Structural Adjustment*

£ m.	1976/77	77/78	78/79	79/80	80/81	81/82	82/83
Selective assistance to industries and firms	36	34	80	78	78	92	108
Invested grants	26	7	3	1	–	–	–
Concorde development and production	48	48	42	23	36	35	18
Finance for Rolls-Royce and other aero-engine projects	73	7	62	98	117	195	105
Home shipbuilding lending (net interest cost on refinancing and interest support)	44	22	38	59	68	60	43
Assistance to shipbuilding (intervention fund and redundancy)	14	35	20	48	70	72	72
Assistance to steel industry (principally redundancy)	2	3	8	22	40	112	108
Equity/loan finance:							
British Steel Corporation	490	445	850	905	1 233	806	743
British Shipbuilders	–	–	–	181	110	107	70
BL Ltd	100	50	450	150	300	520	370
Sub-total (DTI)	833	651	1 533	1 565	2 062	1 999	1 637
Selective assistance to energy-related industries	9	20	17	22	30	24	33
Coal industry – social grants (including redundancy)	62	69	72	79	93	139	165
– operational grants	11	24	117	181	167	244	598
Total	915	764	1 759	1 847	2 432	2 406	2 433

the imbalanced or 'headless' occupational structure (i.e. the relative absence of control and conception functions) which characterised so much of past industrial development in Britain's peripheral regions. This 'headlessness' is most vividly associated with the electronics industry, which is ubiquitously seen as one of the principal bases of reindustrialisation generally and an 'escape-route' for the traditional peripheral regions in particular.

4. Reindustrialisation: The Electronics Industry in Britain

In view of its status as a 'heartland' technology and its relative resistance to recession, the electronics industry has become the foremost target of both national and regional development agencies.[5] Though not at all typical, the strategic significance of this industry is such that it merits particular consideration.

Its relative resistance to the slump in manufacturing output is illustrated in Table 10.5, which also shows that the character of its 'growth' needs qualification given the emergence of 'jobless growth'. The impact of recent changes in the electronics industry have been such that:

(i) The UK market for all electronics products is increasingly met by imports so that a trade surplus of some £150m. in 1975 was estimated to have become a deficit of over £1 billion in 1982. Although the UK remains relatively strong in software and in the protected defence sector, UK companies have retreated from the fastest-growing markets and the UK electronics industry is now in relative decline while the 'culture gap' between civil and military sectors, often within the same firm, is widening (NEDC, 1982b; 1983c).

(ii) The UK has become one of the most targeted locations for international capital because it provides a low-wage platform from which to penetrate the EEC, because of certain strengths (such as software) and because of its 'liberalising' state policy.

(iii) Between 1975 and 1984 total employment in the electronics sector declined by 19 per cent (from 414 000 to 334 000). This general profile of job-loss conceals a profound recomposition of labour between occupations: conventional craft grades

Table 10.5 *Jobless Growth in the Electronics Industry in Britain, 1975–81*

| | Output (1975=100) | | Employment (000s) | | | | |
	MLH 363–67 (Total Manuf.)		MLH 363 Telecoms	MLH 364 Components	MLH 365 Consumer	MLH 366 Computers	MLH 367 Capital goods
1975	100	100	87.0	137.8	56.9	43.9	87.9
1977	103.0	104.9	67.0	128.8	49.9	44.1	91.5
1979	104.2	130.9	64.4	130.1	47.1	47.0	94.9
1981	89.4	139.0	66.2	107.3	37.9	43.1	102.3

SOURCES *British Business* (23 July 1981); Department of Employment *Employment Gazette*.

have marginally declined, while 'multi-skilled' technicians, managers, scientists and engineers have markedly increased over the past decade. But the most dramatic occupational change has been the 'collapse of work' in the semi-skilled operator category, all of which suggests not a simple process of de-skilling, but a polarisation of the skill hierarchy so that company retraining programmes have little or no purchase over the emerging occupational chasm between operator and technician grades (Sayer and Morgan, 1986).

(iv) Since the operator grade is a well-known ghetto of female labour, a 'de-feminisation' of the electronics industry has been underway in Britain. Females accounted for over 80 per cent of total job-loss between 1974 and 1981 in this sector, and the 'collapse' of the operator grade, largely induced through the automation of assembly work, is the major reason for this gender-specific form of displacement (Engineering Industry Training Board (EITB)), 1982).

As yet it is not all clear what the precise spatial implications of these trends are; what *is* clear is that the South-East – which had 53 per cent of total British employment in the electronics industry in 1981, while no other region had more that 10 per cent – is poised to gain most from the growth of high-grade, non-production occupations, offset by the fact that the South-East also has the highest absolute number of operators. This absolute dominance of the South-East is shown in Table 10.6.

The simple, but fundamental, point to be made is that not all areas or regions are uniformly in a position to capitalise on new employment growth in the electronics industry, and the extent to which some are able to do so depends in no small way on their place or function in the hierarchy of the spatial division of labour in this industry. Broadly this spatial division is characterised by the fact that the South-East is the only region to have a deep complement of all functions in this hierarchy (most notably those of control and conception in the shape of corporate headquarters and R & D activities) while the remainder of the country is conspicuous for the predominance of truncated or 'headless' activities associated with production and modest R & D (Massey, 1983). It is this *qualitative* dimension of uneven development in the electronics industry – to some extent the spatial expression of the

TABLE 10.6 *The South-East Share of the Electronics Industry in Britain, 1981*

Employment, thousands
(% share in brackets)

	MLH 363 Telecoms	MLH 364 Components	MLH 365 Consumer	MLH 366 Computers	MLH 367 Capital goods	All
South-East	21 (34.4)	51 (45.9)	17 (64.0)	36 (59.0)	71 (64.5)	196 (53.2)
(Greater London)	15 (24.6)	21 (18.9)	10 (40.0)	13 (21.3)	20 (18.2)	79 (21.4)
(Rest of South-East)	6 (9.8)	30 (27.0)	6 (24.0)	23 (37.7)	51 (46.3)	11 (31.8)

SOURCE Department of Employment, *Employment Gazette.*

internal technical division of labour of the multinational company – which above all needs to be emphasised when considering the regional prospectus. For illustrative purposes it is useful to briefly distinguish three different regional profiles within the electronics industry: the 'Western Corridor', central Scotland and South Wales.

The 'Western Corridor', a classic example of non-metropolitan growth in general, is becoming the central nervous system of the electronics industry in Britain. Fashioned by a combination of indigenous growth and foreign inward investment, its apparent attractions are well enough known: they include a critical mass of highly skilled personnel; accessibility and, especially important for multinationals, proximity to Heathrow; a nest of government research establishments, access to which is important for defence contractors; a 'rural' work environment able to accommodate elite lifestyles; and a relative absence of trades-union traditions, so that non-union company policies reportedly coincide with non-union labour practices (*New Society*, 5 May 1983). The narrow definition of the electronics industry adopted here underestimates the strategic role of the 'Corridor''. For instance, the South-East accounts for some 70 per cent of Britain's computer-service companies, the majority of which are situated to the west of London, and while these may not be numerically important, their strategic significance stems from the fact that the 'critical future factor will be *personnel* and the Western Corridor has the image and facilities to farm this important growth group' (Davies and Smyth, 1983).

The distinctive array of corporate HQs, public and private R & D facilities and international marketing functions along the (English) M4 has enabled incoming capital to recruit, though not necessarily retain, key personnel quickly, while the elite occupational structure associated with these prestige activities spawn and sustain new firms more readily than in other areas. The vast corpus of recently established electronics firms appear to be locationally inert – immobility of professional staff being the most important reason – and, of those considering expansion to DARs, the 'major requirement was for a pool of low-cost labour' (Department of Industry (DoI)), 1982).

While the bulk of Britain's local and regional development agencies 'boast' of large pools of willing and flexible semi-skilled labour to solicit electronics branch plants, English authorities in the 'Corridor' play upon their 'pools' of sophisticated labour, in a rural–pastoral environment, so as to entice not branch plants, but R & D, marketing and proto-production activities, all of which are occupational growth areas (Davies and Smyth, 1983). Needless to say, this form of growth – underwritten by public investment in communications, R & D and military procurement – has created its own brand of problems, e.g. critical skill shortages, systematic poaching and, most importantly, a conspicuous mismatch between the labour demands of the electronics industry and the untapped supplies of semi-skilled labour (Berkshire County Council, 1982). However, it is the specificity of the 'Corridor' which needs to be more fully appreciated, not least because vulgar injunctions – like 'Britain needs more Berkshires' (*The Economist*, 30 Jan 1982) – to reproduce such growth belittle its relatively unique form, as well as its underlying conditions. At bottom, injunctions of this sort exaggerate the opportunities, but ignore the constraints, of the hierarchical spatial division of labour in the electronics industry – and the 'leading-edge' of this hierarchy is to be found not in the 'Corridor', but in the US and Japan.

Although the core functions of the electronics industry (in Britain) are largely concentrated in the South-East and the 'Western Corridor', this does not mean that all other areas simply perform routine assembly functions. Too often central Scotland is dismissed in precisely this way (*The Economist*, 30 Jan 1982). Currently, a total of some 38 000 are employed in the electronics industry in Scotland (broadly equivalent to combined Scottish employment in the coal, steel and shipbuilding industries) while central Scotland now represents the largest concentration of semi-conductor manufacturers in Western Europe. Unlike the 'Corridor', the 'Scottish' industry is largely based on non-Scottish capital: the indigenous sector accounted for only 10 per cent of employment in 1978 (Booz, Allen and Hamilton, 1979). Even though overseas multinationals do not perform their 'leading-edge' R & D work in Scotland, their operations involve far more than routine assembly. US firms, for instance, are frequently engaged in secondary R & D work to adapt products to the nuances of the European market. Such secondary work can be quite advanced by the standards of the British civil electronics industry, so much so that 'branch-plant' status is not necessarily an index of just routine assembly (Electronics Location File, 1983/1; Morgan and Sayer, 1983b).

Furthermore the attractions of central Scotland as a base for the electronics industry should not be reduced to its capital subsidies and its relatively low labour costs: increasingly important is the small but significant pool of key personnel (e.g. in such fields as Very Large-Scale Integration (VLSI), opto-electronics, artificial intelligence and software applications). Indeed, it seems that central Scotland commands an advantage over the 'Corridor' in the fact that, once recruited, such key personnel are more easily retained and labour turnover problems reduced. Nevertheless, it is the predominance of routine assembly functions in central Scotland that distinguishes it from the 'Corridor', while the overseas sector remains poorly integrated with multiplier effects which afford little secondary employment and, perhaps most important for long-term prospects, a significant indigenous sector has not developed (*Financial Times*, 8 Sep 1981). What is notable about some of the Scottish firms that have emerged is that, to keep abreast of international 'leading-edge' innovation, the likes of Rodime feel obliged to expand *outside* Britain soon after birth.

If the 'branch-plant' stereotype needs to be somewhat modified as regards central Scotland, its essentials are far more visible with respect to South Wales. Since total Welsh employment in the electronics industry in 1981 was only 14 000, South Wales occupies a marginal position in this industry in terms of both the level and the status of its employment. It has neither the limited R & D platform nor the small indigenous sector evident in central Scotland, and its attraction for the electronics industry lies largely in it being the subsidised end of the English 'Corridor'. The electronics enclave has even lower local multiplier effects than in Scotland, while the currently-installed overseas plants – which have proved more secure than their British counterparts – now appear to have reached the limits of their (employment) growth (Morgan and Sayer, 1983b). These illustrative examples merely confirm that 'high-tech' is not synonymous with a high-skill profile, that distinctions need to be made within 'the periphery' and that future employment growth is partly a function of the role which a region occupies in the hierarchy of the spatial division of labour.

Even though the electronics industry accounts for only 7 per cent and 6 per cent respectively of total manufacturing employment in Scotland and Wales, its ideological significance is more pervasive than its numerical importance might suggest. This is most apparent with respect to the 'new' management and labour practices which this industry has sought to introduce in these regions. Often, the main connection between the electronics industry and such traditional industries as coal and steel is that it is not ex-miners or ex-steelworkers who are sought, but their wives, daughters and sons, or those thought to have least to unlearn as regards 'traditional' work practices (i.e. unionism and demarcation consciousness). The electronics industry occupies a vanguard role in pioneering non-union environments. Although the 'Corridor' best exemplifies such an environment in Britain, more significant is the emergence of a conspicuous non-unionised workforce in parts of Scotland: in East Kilbride, for instance, 83 per cent of electronics firms are non-union. While such a phenomenon has yet to emerge on this scale in South Wales, there is much to suggest that unions are becoming more marginalised from the workforce (Morgan and Sayer, 1983b). The electronics industry is clearly inspiring an imitative effect since unionisation is increasingly portrayed as an 'artificial barrier' within advanced technology companies in general (*The Guardian*, 7 July 1982).

As for the general prospects of the electronics industry, two of the most fundamental questions relate to employment and control. First, while this 'growth' industry is poised for further output expansion, this currently promises little net employment growth: occupations above and including technicians seem certain to increase at the expense of semi-skilled labour, and such occupational growth will be focused towards southern Britain. Furthermore, to the extent that 'jobless growth' intensifies, this seems calculated to produce reindustrialisation *in*, rather than *of*, the space economy; that is, growth without development (Sayer, 1983; Morgan and Sayer, 1983a).

Second, as important as interregional differences remain, this should not obscure the relative deterioration of the British electronics industry as a whole. Having retreated from the fastest-growing (civilian) markets, the 'British' consumer sector is now 70 per cent foreign-controlled, not unlike the 'British' semiconductor industry, while the liberalisation of telecommunications has already induced North American companies into Britain. There is certainly a reindustrialisation occurring in the electronics industry in Britain, not a little of it driven by overseas agents. Far from being simply an index of the regional problem, external control applies to the national space economy too, and this external dependence is now being encouraged like never before.[6]

5. Industrial Innovation and the Development Area Regions: New Prescriptions for Old Problems

The diffusion of electronics-based technology clearly has a more pervasive significance than the electronics industry itself and for the DARs the threats appear to outweigh the opportunities as regards employment. Belatedly the official diagnosis of the traditional industrial regional problem seems to have shifted: for long this was attributed to 'over-dependence' on mature industries (coal, steel, etc.), now it is ascribed to 'low innovation potential' (Department of Industry, 1981). Industrial innovation embraces product and process innovation in existing and new applications and, also new-firm formation. As we should expect, both are unevenly distributed in the space economy. The first is said to be:

> associated with the imbalance in the regional distribution of professionally qualified scientists and engineers. The extent of product innovation in particular depends on the proximity of R & D facilities; the diffusion of process innovations is more even. In the less innovative areas, almost all innovation is undertaken by branch plants, but these have less R & D employment and are significantly less innovative than branch plants in the South East and inner South West. In the latter, smaller independent firms are often innovative too, whilst in the more peripheral areas these are slow to adopt innovation. (DoI, 1981; see also Oakey *et al.*, 1980; 1982.)

Unlike the former diagnosis this has the merit of acknowledging the qualitative dimension of uneven development referred to earlier, although, as we shall see, some of the new prescriptions are antithetical to current state policy.

With regard to the second (new-firm formation) it is hardly a novel insight that DARs have a poor indigenous potential for generating new firms, let alone the advanced-technology new firms currently canvassed as the 'vehicle for regeneration via innovation' (Rothwell, 1982). In such regions (central Scotland, northern England and South Wales) this derives largely from their former specialised role in the spatial division of labour: from a socio-economic structure profoundly unconducive to new-firm formation, or a class structure not simply economically ill-endowed to spawn entrepreneurial agents, but, culturally and politically, often hostile to (capitalist) entrepreneurship itself (Wales TUC, 1981). In this sense 'low innovation potential' has characterised these regions since their inter-war crises. What has now changed is the conjuncture which partly offset their low indigenous potential, namely, a 'golden age' of growth which enabled regional policy to redistribute employment in such a form as to promote sectoral – though not occupational – diversification. When the structural bases for such low indigenous potential are ignored, the problem becomes defined in terms of behavioural deficiencies – 'the Welsh are not a *race* of self-starters in business' (*Financial Times*, 4 Aug 1978) – the prescription for which is to engender a greater will to succeed: this behavioural interpretation of the regional problem is much favoured by the Thatcher government (Joseph, 1981).

Of current prescriptions for 'low innovation potential' in the DARs, the most common is for a regional innovation policy focused on raising their R & D base, promoting existing and new independent small firms and creating a more innovative supply-side infrastructure (Ewers and Wettmann, 1980). An often implicit assumption of the first is that R & D facilities or personnel are somehow infinitely expandable and, therefore, this is akin to a 'feeding-of-the-five-thousand' approach (Sayer, 1983). More significantly, it would have to offset the premium which both private capital and the public sector set on the current distribution of R & D: in 1980 the South-East had nearly 50 per cent of private (manufacturing) sector R & D establishments, but only 29.3 per cent of total manufacturing employment, and 54 per cent of government R & D establishments (Department of Industry (DoI)), 1981; Rothwell, 1982). Indeed, the Office and Service Industry Scheme (OSIS) already exists in part to decentralise R & D facilities, but with no apparent effect. Nor is conventional regional policy any guide since, in the past, it was able to 'bite' on (branch-plant) employment not least because this proved compatible with the spatial decentralisation of routine functions. Demand-derived schemes such as OSIS are unlikely to have much effect precisely because they run counter to the grain of corporate locational strategies for R & D facilities, and proponents of R & D decentralisation concede that it would be 'extremely difficult even for a strong interventionist government' (Ewers and Wettmann, 1980).

I have already indicated – with respect to the second element – that the potential for *new*-firm formation in the DARs is relatively low, while many of their *existing*, independent firms are locked into local–regional markets which are, to say the least, undemanding as regards their technological requirements. So much so that current nationwide schemes to promote the 'small-firm sector', while not spatially discriminating by design, are very much so in practice. The reasons for this are well-established: take-up broadly conforms to higher-status occupational strata, areas of small-plant bias and industries with lower barriers to entry, all of which combine to the advantage of regions that are already the more innovative (Storey, 1982).

Quite apart from the problems of new-firm formation in DARs is the *wisdom* of concentrating a disproportionate emphasis on small, relative to medium and large firms. The notion that the 'small-firm sector' is necessarily the most innovative rests on a highly selective vision and, though far from typical, exemplars are generally drawn from the electronics industry (e.g. Sinclair Research, see Figure 10.1).

Furthermore, their contribution to new employment has been much exaggerated: the probability of a wholly new manufacturing firm employing more than 100 in a decade is less than 1 per cent and it will tend to remain small, with an average of fifteen employees after a decade (Storey, 1982). Significantly, the Greater London Council has resolutely eschewed the '*grapeshot* of current small firms policy' and, instead, focuses on promoting particular products, skills and priority sectors, especially with respect to medium and large firms because their role in employment change is more important (GLC, 1983). What this suggests is not that indigenous small-firm support in DARs is without a rationale, but that this should not be at the expense of a strategy for the medium–large plants so prominent in their regional economies.

The third element, an innovative infrastructure, is a shorthand for the supply-side environment: among the more novel proposals here is for a network of regional technology transfer agencies, which would monitor and accelerate the diffusion of innovations, particularly on the product side, and especially for independent firms in the DARs, who are most disadvantaged (Oakey *et al.*, 1982). As important as such agencies are – and some already exist, such as the WDA's WINTECH – without a more significant

346

Where wealth accumulates and men decay...

Let's look at a possible future Britain.

A Britain where there are a few hundred thousand very rich people. But where the rest of them (or us) are unemployed, idle, and probably poor.

A Britain where wealth accumulates in a few hands, and men decay.

The Britain that is more than likely, unless we revise our uncritical approval of 'big' business, and our definitions of success in terms of people (not assets) employed.

It doesn't have to be like that. In Sinclair Research, we have a model for tomorrow's practical business company. Hugely successful: the world's leading home computer company. Innovative, with an electric town-car and flat-screen pocket TV on the stocks. Profitable – £14 million last year.

And tiny. Sinclair employs around 60 people direct, and has generated about 2,000 other jobs indirectly.

It may not sound a very comfortable alternative to British Leyland, British Steel, the National Coal Board, or British Shipbuilders. *But it made more profit than all of them put together!*

It's true that the same could be said of your corner shop. And it's true that we would need a good many Sinclairs to replace the jobs which, sooner or later, must almost certainly be abandoned in the traditional, loss-making, heavy industries.

But is that impossible? As a result of Sinclair's success, Britain has more home computers per capita than any other country in the world. We have a huge and growing army of people, old and young, who took to new technology when it was offered to them (not forced on them). From them could come not just the generals, but the rank and file who could ensure that Britain is one of the victors in the coming battle.

Sinclair Research is trying to show the way, and to provide some of the tools for the job.

Sinclair Research Ltd, Stanhope Road, Camberley, Surrey, GU15 3PS. Tel. 0276 685311.

FIGURE 10.1   *The (Selective) Face of the Future?*

SOURCE   *Sunday Times.*

delivery system of finance and skills, they are unlikely to have much purchase. Even assuming that new and enlarged sources of investment could actually be tapped in the DARs, no mean assumption since the shortage of 'patient money' is a national phenomenon, we return to the supply-side problem of social agents in the DARs. It was precisely this – the pervasive absence of social agents with the requisite management skills – which was a key impediment to the supply of *projects*, let alone finance, for workers' co-ops in Wales (Wales TUC, 1981).

This cursory assessment of the proposed regional innovation policy is pessimistic rather than dismissive. For its positive potential to be realised, a minimal requirement is that such local–regional initiatives be ratified by and allied to a national strategy and this was the major conclusion of a Department of Industry study (DoI, 1981). As it is, national innovation policies have little or no (conscious) spatial dimension and this is likely to accentuate contemporary forms of uneven development; so much so that the level and character of employment in the DARs depends, now as before, on the priorities set for the national space economy.

6. Reindustrialisation and the Neo-Market Repertoire

The neo-market repertoire of the Thatcher government is, above all else, a bold ideological project. Its agenda is to break out of the political impasse, noted earlier, so as to effect an economic regeneration based largely on *private* capital. Superficially, it may seem perverse to suggest that reindustrialisation forms part of this project when the contraction of the domestic manufacturing sector since 1979, which has been without parallel in the OECD, is far more attributable to a peculiarly harsh deflationary policy than to the effects of advanced technology.

Yet, a calculated rationale underlies the neo-market approach and it is this: the 'shake-out' of labour from the manufacturing sector, though largely a by-product of lowering inflation, was a desired object in the drive to improve productivity, chasten labour and enhance managerial authority. Furthermore, a severe monetarist context would compel capital to innovate or liquidate and, to the extent that companies failed to survive, their assets (suitably devalued) would be absorbed by the more efficient. And, due in part to the petro-currency status of sterling, a 'natural' shift of capital from manufacturing to the service sector would follow: consequently, de-industrialisation could be 'good for the UK' (Brittan, 1980). In the neo-market scenario then, reindustrialisation is not so much identified with a significant expansion of manufacturing employment, but with a smaller, more innovative, more competitive sector allied, it seems, to a greater overseas presence. In policy terms, the neo-market repertoire is somewhat erroneously cast as 'non-interventionist'. Admittedly, there is less recourse to *dirigiste* forms of intervention (though even this should not be underestimated, e.g. in BSC, BL, ICL and with the Alvey project for corporatist collaboration in advanced computer systems), but this is not equivalent to 'non-intervention' because monetary control is perceived as having far more profound effects than, say, the National Enterprise Board, with the added advantage that the illusion of 'limited government' is preserved.

A number of general points can be made regarding the current effects of this repertoire. First, the severe contraction of manufacturing activity should not obscure some significant forms of restructuring wrought by the Thatcher governments. Though still too early to assess the extent to which firms have won durable productivity gains, it is already clear that productivity advances have exceeded predictions in such sectors as vehicles, iron and steel, and engineering generally. In fact, BL's Austin Rover and Jaguar divisions have become (public-sector) exemplars of reindustrialisation for the Thatcher government, especially as regards productivity, investment in computer-aided design, test and production facilities, the reassertion of managerial control and the trading profit of Austin Rover. More generally, the first half of 1983 witnessed a 'profits surge' within both the oil and non-oil industrial sectors, even though the level of profitability remains low by historical and international standards (*Financial Times*, 29 Sep 1983).

Second, the major British manufacturing firms have further internationalised their activities since 1979: the leading fifty firms produced 44 per cent of their total output overseas in 1983 compared to around 36 per cent in 1979, and their foreign employment has expanded in contrast to the contraction of their domestic labour force. But this is simply part of a much greater external orientation of British capital because, in total, some £30 billion was despatched overseas between 1979 and 1983 (*Labour Research*, 1983; Smith, 1983).

Third, the Thatcher governments have placed a greater emphasis than hitherto on inward investment as a means of reindustrialisation, citing the gains of advanced technology and new
management practices in particular, while appearing less concerned about its displacement effects on domestic employment and
indigenous capabilities (Cooke *et al.*, 1984).

Finally, capital investment by manufacturing industry declined
by some 25 per cent in volume between 1979 and 1982.

The current plight of the British manufacturing sector is vividly
illustrated by its deteriorating trade performance: without oil, the
visible balance on the current account would now be recording a
massive deficit. Furthermore, although service sector investment
increased by 9 per cent between 1979 and 1982, it is not sufficiently
appreciated that this has actually contributed to the deteriorating
(non-oil) visible trade deficit. For instance, two-thirds of all computer installations are in the service sector and the most rapid
diffusion of computer technology has been in financial and business services. Yet, the service sector – particularly the financial
institutions division – has resorted largely to imported computer
technology. This reflects the renowned British propensity for
non-domestic manufactured goods, something which shows no
sign of abating because a conspicuous feature of the consumer
boom in autumn 1983 was that no less than 50 per cent of it was
met via higher import penetration. Indeed, NEDC sectoral assessments for the 1980s suggest that the consumer sectors in general
will have a difficult struggle to contain steadily increasing import
penetration and the loss of export share experienced by most of
these sectors in recent years. As for those sectors covering production engineering (tooling, machining, handling and assembly
equipment) and components (castings, electric motors, electronic
components, diesel engines), one of the major expected trends will
be a continuing shift towards international sourcing of *all* these
categories of equipment (NEDC, 1983a). This is hardly the stuff of
a sound domestic industrial revival.

Even from the outset the Conservative strategy recognised that
output and employment would both suffer given the centrality of
the struggle to reduce inflation but, as I have indicated, these were
seen as necessary costs. Nevertheless, these costs on the 'real
economy' have far exceeded anything envisaged in 1979 and this
macroeconomic environment has been less than hospitable to
industrial innovation: technology support schemes have in part

been vitiated by this lack of demand and some (e.g. the Small Engineering Firms Investment Scheme II) have proved difficult to allocate. But, quite apart from restrictive macroeconomic policies, a no less important determinant of sluggish adaptation to advanced technologies is the 'quality, skills and enterprise of management' in Britain (*Electronics Times*, 29 July 1982). In a sense, the political aspirations of the neo-market ideology are too advanced, or too unrealistic, to be realised by large sections of industrial capital, given the comparatively weak supply-side conditions referred to in Section 2. It is precisely this disjunction (between ideological aspirations and material capabilities) that underlies both the CBI's perennial requests for reflation and the more revealing demands for an industrial strategy and enhanced technological support (Select Committee on Science and Technology, 1983; NEDC, 1982b). However, a state-sponsored industrial strategy is not easily accommodated within the neo-market orthodoxy.

The NEDC strategy for the electronics industry serves as an illustrative example of this disjunction. NEDO's central recommendation was that government, industry and trade unions should collectively identify the actual and potential strengths of the UK electronics industry and these orientations should form part of a 'national planning process'. Despite the fact that the state-sector accounts for over 50 per cent of the UK electronics market, funds nearly 60 per cent of total electronics R & D and provides some 5 per cent of its gross investment, the Conservative government has eschewed the directive role envisaged by NEDO and yet criticises the major electronics firms for using defence contracts as a 'cushion rather than a springboard for risky international business outside the defence field' (*Financial Times*, 6 May 1982). The NEDC recommendations are anathema to the Conservative government because they entail a degree, and a form, of state intervention inconsistent with the axioms of the neo-market philosophy. Although this repertoire is not as pure as its rhetoric would suggest, the Thatcher governments have nevertheless steadfastly refused to accede to manufacturers' demands for either reflation or an industrial strategy. This might be ascribed as much to political blind faith on the part of the Conservatives, as to the continued political weakness of (domestic) industrial capital in Britain.

Even though manufacturing capital has certainly had its problems with the neo-market environment, labour has manifestly suffered the brunt of the monetarist experiment. Understandably, what is not proclaimed by the Thatcher government is that, without a strategy for growth, the combination of labour-saving innovation and increased productivity is a recipe for what the *Financial Times* called 'horrific unemployment'. If Britain had West German levels of productivity, at 1982 levels of British output, Britain's unemployment would be some 6 millions higher (*Financial Times*, 31 May 1982). So, while the slow *cyclical* recovery (since the trough of May 1981) has eased some of the pressures on the manufacturing sector, employment prospects are widely expected to deteriorate still further. Also, of all possible state strategies, the neo-market repertoire is most likely to enhance internal spatial inequalities. As was pointed out earlier, the non-metropolitan south occupies a particularly advantageous position as regards current bases of industrial growth. Its position is further bolstered by the fact that adult training programmes are increasingly oriented towards these current bases: such areas can expect to receive a greater share of training resources relative to existing depressed areas (Lloyd, 1983a).

Contemporary industrial reality hardly conforms to the scenario entertained by the Thatcher government in 1979. While it has certainly advanced its cause (most notably with regard to inflation, privatisation and the chastening of labour) the neo-market version of reindustrialisation has yet to emerge. Cyclical recovery, induced not by investment but by credit-financed consumer spending, should not conceal the fact that significant sections of manufacturing industry have been unable or unwilling to raise investment for advanced technologies, or that small and medium-sized firms, demonstrate a low interest in innovation (NEDC, 1983b). Notwithstanding apparent cases of industrial revival (e.g. BL cars and microcomputers) Britain now appears less an advanced workshop of the world than a consumption centre for luxury consumer goods and sophisticated engineering equipment produced elsewhere, while its indigenous product base is shrinking at an alarming rate: symbolically, perhaps, Britain became a *net importer* of manufactured goods in 1983 for the first time since the industrial revolution![7] Thatcherism seeks to realise the *levels* of industrial innovation attained in Japan without having comparable *means*:

namely, high and sustained levels of investment in (civilian) growth sectors, intensive training programmes, long-term corporate horizons backed by 'patient money' and a formidably interventionist state strategy designed to protect and develop the national industrial economy (Select Committee on Science and Technology, 1978). Nevertheless, to criticise current neo-market policy because it is insufficient as a *national* capitalist strategy is to partly misconstrue the Thatcher project, which associates itself not so much with a national, but with a *cosmopolitan* form of reindustrialisation. In other words, if domestic capital cannot compete in a neo-market environment then foreign capital is encouraged to play a more pervasive role within Britain even though the ultimate logic of increasing external dependence is that Britain moves closer to the status of a 'technological colony' (NEDC, 1983b). Confederation of British Industry demands for reflation and NEDC proposals for a national strategy suggest that neo-market policy is not an optimal course for domestic industrial capital. Still less is it a course for the recovery of employment.

Some of the current alternative attempts to 'restructure for labour' are referred to elsewhere (Chapter 8). But, as I indicated earlier, local and regional initiatives can have only a marginal effect if they are not allied to a supportive national effort in which far greater priority is accorded to innovation *and* employment. Of central importance is a recognition that the market has proved an inadequate mechanism through which to realise a technologically-advanced domestic economy in Britain, quite apart from the more general inadequacies of a mechanism which subordinates social need to private profit. This perspective underlies the three points with which I want to conclude.

First, internal spatial differences in innovative potential, though important, are now less significant than the fact that the *national* technological base needs to be substantially raised. There is no positive alternative to the organised adoption of advanced technologies and, while technological change is one potential form of job-loss, failure to adapt poses even greater, and more certain, threats to employment. Yet, the enthusiasm of labour can hardly be enlisted when it has little or no influence over the design and implementation of technology, nor any assurance that the threat to the level, character and location of employment will be in any way compensated. Without such influence it is impossible for popular social needs to be respected. This is now *formally* recognised within the labour movement whereas, during the flirtation with 'planning' in the 1960s, even such formal recognition was conspicuously absent (TUC–Labour Party Liaison Committee, 1982; Joint Trades Councils *et al.*, 1982).

Second, it is nonsense to suggest that there can be a 'non-interventionist' state stance when, for example, the public sector accounts for some 50 per cent of the British market for the domestic electronics industry and when the Ministry of Defence is the largest single source of technology in Britain. 'Non-intervention' is simply a political endorsement of the current deployment of resources. A state-sponsored redeployment is long overdue, so that the R & D base of the civilian economy receives the political commitment hitherto reserved for the military. In the context of such redeployment, a radical innovation strategy would depend on the public sector assuming a vanguard role in a number of ways:

(i) A public investment fund, combined with public control over 'domestic' financial institutions, would be vital if 'patient money' is to be raised and directed towards those technologies and markets of greatest growth potential (Table 10.7). The realisation of such objectives would require a planning framework to ensure that sectoral and spatial linkages are consciously organised as well as a greater role for public-sector enterprise to guarantee an indigenous presence in emerging sectors.

(ii) Public procurement possesses enormous leverage to induce and diffuse new products and processes, but it has never been sufficiently focused towards this end nor, because of idiosyncratic national specifications, has it realised anything like its full export potential (ACARD, 1980b).

(iii) Provision of skills has been woefully inadequate not just in peripheral regions, but throughout Britain: only a state-sponsored programme of training and re-training seems capable of redressing this key supply-side weakness.

Third, the manufacturing sector is unlikely to reabsorb labour on a scale necessary to significantly reduce unemployment. Consequently a radical innovation strategy would necessarily have to be orchestrated with a planned reflationary programme of reconstruction. Anything less offers little hope that labour – particularly in the more 'abandoned' areas – will extricate itself from the frightful

TABLE 10.7 *Potential Areas of UK Growth and of Stability or Decline*

Industry	Potential growth areas	Stable or declining areas
Agriculture		Agriculture, forestry, fishing
Mining and quarrying	Coal-mining Oil and gas extraction and distribution	non-metalliferous products
Food, drink and tobacco		Food and drink manufacture
Chemicals	Basic chemicals (including petrochemicals) Specialised organics Biotechnology Polymers and composites	
Metal manufacture	Specialised metallurgical processes and products	Iron and steel
Mechanical engineering	Waste-handling equipment Mining machinery Heating, ventilating, air-conditioning and refrigeration equipment Process plant	Machine tools Metalworking equipment Pumps and valves Diesel engines Construction equipment Mechanical handling equipment Printing machinery Packaging machinery Photographic equipment
Instrument engineering	Scientific instruments, control equipment	
Electrical engineering	Telecommunications Very large-scale integrated circuits Opto-electronics	Heavy electrical machinery Industrial electrical equipment Domestic electrical appliances Medical equipment

Engineering (general)	Information technology for home and office
	Navigation systems
	Medical electronics
	Equipment for:
	  Energy conservation
	  Waste water treatment
	  Air pollution abatement
	  Materials handling
	  Solid fuel technology.	

Shipbuilding		Shipbuilding
Vehicles		Motor-vehicles and components
Textiles		All textile products
Clothing and footwear		Clothing Footwear Building materials
Bricks, pottery, glass, cement	Pottery Glass	
Paper, printing		Paper and board Printing Tyres
Other manufacturing		
Construction	Energy saving buildings New building methods	Construction (general)
Gas, electricity and water	More efficient energy production systems	
Transport	Advanced passenger systems Advance transport control systems	
Services	Bank and financial services	Distribution Public services

SOURCE (NEDC) *Industrial Trends and Prospects*, NEDO (1981).

prospects of mass unemployment and growth without development.

Clearly much else is entailed (like trade management and socially-bargained measures to contain inflation), but, above all, such a prospectus needs to be popularly ratified in and beyond the labour movement, not least because it arrests the agenda-setting power of capital – and would therefore encounter formidable resistance – and seeks to establish criteria based on returns to the (social) community rather than to any single (private) investor.

Notes

1. See Maillat (1982), and Cooke *et al.* (1984).
2. In such counties as Berkshire this is not so much reindustrialisation, in the sense of an industrial transition, but more a first wave of industrial penetration of what has been appropriately called 'tamed rurality' (Massey, 1983).
3. Given its number of marginal constituencies and its accelerating economic decline, the West Midlands has been *politically* massaged by the Thatcher governments. Despite the Northern region having higher unemployment it was the West Midlands which was given an 'unofficial Minister' in April 1983, whose stated aim was to 'redress the balance in regional policy'.
4. Scotland is an exception to this as regards the Microelectronics Industry Support Programme; by March 1983 it had taken up the major allocation of MISP, because of its concentration of semiconductor firms.
5. The electronics industry is here defined in its *narrow* sense as MLH 363–7 of the SIC (1968). This section draws on a research project at Sussex University, under the direction of Andrew Sayer and supported by the ESRC.
6. While the question of spatial control should not be raised without the ultimately more important issue of *social* control, the former remains significant for labour because the probability of retaining labour skills is greater with indigenous control: union struggles to resist foreign takeover often testify to this.
7. This may seem added confirmation of a 'natural' trend to proponents of the 'post-industrial society', but these have yet to face the implications: while the manufacturing sector currently accounts for less than a quarter of UK employment, it represents some 75 per cent of UK visible trade exports. If the service sector had to replace this contribution the UK share of world service exports would have to increase from under 10 per cent to over 50 per cent, and this is an impossible task (see Select Committee on Science and Technology, 1983).

Acknowledgements

I would like to thank colleagues at the Science Policy Research Unit for their comments on a previous draft of this chapter. Especial thanks are due to Andrew Sayer for his 'sympathetic critique'.

Bibliography

Advisory Council for Applied Research and Development (ACARD) (1978) *Industrial Innovation* (London: HMSO).

ACARD (1980a) *Technological Change* (London: HMSO).

ACARD (1980b) *R and D for Public Purchasing* (London: HMSO).

Beckerman, W. (ed.) (1979) *Slow Growth in Britain* (Oxford: OUP).

Birmingham Chamber of Industry and Commerce (1983) *Reversing Structural Decline in the West Midlands* (Birmingham: BCIC).

Blackaby, F. (ed.) (1979) *De-industrialisation* (London: Heinemann).

Booz, Allen and Hamilton (1979) *The Electronics Industry in Scotland*.

Brittan, S. (1980) 'De-industrialization is Good for the UK', *Financial Times*, 3 July.

Cameron, G. (1979) 'The National Industrial Strategy and Regional Policy', in MacLennan, D. and Parr, J. (Eds) *Regional Policy* (Oxford: Martin Robertson).

Counter Information Services (1982) *The UK Arms Industry*, Anti-Report no. 31.

Commission of the European Communities (1983) *European Economy*, no. 16 (Brussels: Commission of the European Communities).

Committee of the Public Accounts (1981) *Measuring the Effectiveness of Regional Industrial Policy*, HC 206 (London: HMSO)

Cooke, P., Morgan, K. and Jackson, D. (1984) 'New Technology and Regional Development in Austerity Britain: The Case of the Semi-conductor Industry', *Regional Studies*, **18**, 4, pp. 277–89.

Davies, T. and Smyth, H. (1983) *The Western Corridor: The Shape of Future Growth* (Swindon and Bristol Futures Project) Report no. 1.

Department of Industry (1981) 'Regional Innovation Policies in the UK', unpublished.

Department of Industry (1982) 'The Location, Mobility and Finance of New High Technology Companies in the UK Electronics Industry', unpublished.

The Economist (1982) 'Britain's Sunrise Strip', 3 Jan.

Engineering Industry Training Board (1982) *Manpower and Training in the Electronics Industry*, RP/5/82.

Ewers, H. and Wettmann, R. (1980) 'Innovation-oriented Regional Policy', *Regional Studies*, **14**, 3, pp. 161–79.

Fellowship of Engineering (1983) *Modern Materials in Manufacturing Industry*.

Forth, E. (1983) *Regional Policy: A Fringe Benefit?* (*EDG*).

Gamble, A. (1981) *Britain in Decline* (London: Macmillan).

Greater London Council (1983) *Small Firms and the London Industrial Strategy* (London: GLC).

Hallet: G. *et al.* (1973) *Regional Policy Forever?* (London: Institute of Economic Affairs).

Inner London Consultative Employment Group (1983) *Inner London: The Facts and the Future*.

Joint Trades Councils *et al.* (1982) *Economic Planning through Industrial Democracy*.

Joseph, Sir Keith (1981) 'Regional Policy', *Hansard*, 8 July.

Labour Research (1983) 'Multinationals and Manufacturing Employment', May (London: Labour Research Department).

Lloyd, J. (1983a) 'Rich Areas Favoured by Share out of MSC Funds'. *Financial Times*, 21 Apr.

Lloyd, J. (1983b) 'Government Directs Aid Towards High Technology and Automation', *Financial Times*, 23 Sep.

Maillat, D. (ed.) (1982) *Technology: A Key Factor for Regional Development* (Saint Saphorin).

Morgan, K. (1985) 'Regional Regeneration in Britain: The "Territorial Imperative" and the Conservative State', *Political Studies*, **4**, pp. 560–77.

Morgan, K. and Sayer, A. (1983a) 'Regional Inequality and the State in Britain', in Anderson, J. *et al.* (eds) *Redundant Spaces in Cities and Regions* (London: Academic Press).

Morgan, K. and Sayer, A. (1983b) *The International Electronics Industry and Regional Development in Britain* (University of Sussex: School of Social Sciences).

Massey, D. (1983) 'The Shape of Things to Come', *Marxism Today*, Apr.

Murray, R. (1972) 'The Internationalisation of Capital and the British Economy' (University of Sussex: Institute of Development Studies).

National Economic Development Council (NEDC) (1982a) *Innovation in the UK* (London: NEDO).

NEDC (1982b) *Policy for the UK Electronics Industry* (London: NEDO).

NEDC (1983a) *Report on the Sector Assessments*. (London: NEDO).

NEDC (1983b) *Industrial Policy*, (London: NEDO).

NEDC (1983c) *Civil Exploitation of Defence Technology* (*Maddock Report*) (London: NEDO).

Neil, A. (1983) 'The Information Revolution', *The Listener*, 23 June.

Nicholson, C. (1982) 'The Spatial Impact of Microprocessor Technology – Evidence from the MAP Scheme'. Department of Industry, unpublished.

Oakey, R. *et al.* (1980) 'The Regional Distribution of Innovative Manufacturing Establishments in Britain', *Regional Studies*, **14**, 3, pp. 235–53.

Oakey, R. *et al.* (1982) 'Technological Change and Regional Development', *Environment and Planning, A*, **14**, **8**, pp. 1073–86.

Pavitt, K. (ed.) (1980) *Technical Innovation and British Economic Performance* (London: Macmillan).

Regional Council of West Midlands TUC (1981) *Our Future*.

Rothwell, R. (1982) 'The Role of Technology in Industrial Change: Implications for Regional Policy', *Regional Studies*, **16**, **5**, pp. 361–9.

Sayer, A. (1983) 'Technological Change and Regional Development', in Hamilton, F. and Linge, G. (eds) *Spatial Analysis, Industry and Industrial Environment*, III (Chichester: Wiley).

Sayer, A. and Morgan K. (1986) 'The Electronics Industry and Regional Development in Britain', in A. Amin and J. Goddard (eds) *Technological Change and Regional Development* (London: Allen & Unwin). pp. 157–187

Select Committee on Science and Technology (1978) *Innovation R & D in Japanese Science Based Industry*, HC 682–1 (London: HMSO).

Select Committee on Science and Technology (1983) *Engineering Research and Development*, HC 89–1 (London: HMSO).

Smith, M. (1983) 'Huge Flow of Funds from Britain', *The Guardian*, 22 Oct.

Storey, D. (1982) *Entrepreneurship and the New Firm* (London: Croom Helm).

TUC–Labour Party Liaison Committee (1982) *Economic Planning and Industrial Democracy*.

Wales TUC (1981) *Co-operation and Job Creation in Wales*.

Index